W9-CAY-764

Unauthorized

Unauthorized

Portraits of Latino Immigrants

Marisol Clark-Ibáñez and Richelle S. Swan

ROWMAN & LITTLEFIELD
Lanham • Boulder • New York • London

Published by Rowman & Littlefield
An imprint of The Rowman & Littlefield Publishing Group, Inc.
4501 Forbes Boulevard, Suite 200, Lanham, Maryland 20706
www.rowman.com

6 Tinworth Street, London SE11 5AL, United Kingdom

British Library Cataloguing in Publication Information Available

Library of Congress Cataloging-in-Publication Data

Names: Clark-Ibáñez, Marisol, author. | Swan, Richelle S., author.
Title: Unauthorized : portraits of Latino immigrants / Marisol Clark-Ibáñez and Richelle S. Swan.
Description: Lanham : Rowman & Littlefield, [2019] | Includes bibliographical references and index.
Identifiers: LCCN 2019000256 (print) | LCCN 2019017431 (ebook) | ISBN 9781442273832 (electronic) | ISBN 9781442273825 (cloth : alk. paper)
Subjects: LCSH: Latin Americans—United States. | Illegal aliens—United States.
Classification: LCC E184.S75 (ebook) | LCC E184.S75 C527 2019 (print) | DDC 305.868/073--dc23
LC record available at https://lccn.loc.gov/2019000256

Contents

Boxes and Tables

BOXES

TABLES

Acknowledgments

We are sociology professors at California State University San Marcos (CSUSM), which is a medium-sized, teaching-oriented, public state university. The joy of working at a CSU campus is the expectation that teaching and research inform each other. We are able to teach what we research and our students inspire what we study. We have both enjoyed supervising dozens of master's theses on issues related to inequality and the Latinx or immigrant communities of San Diego. We work with students and community members who must navigate their immigration status while working, going to school, being activists, and also just going about their daily lives.

Dr. Marisol Clark-Ibáñez is a Peruvian-Irish-American immigrant Latina who is proud to work alongside of and learn from her students and colleagues. She interweaves immigration themes across her courses in children's rights, education, and methods. She has been active on campus, in the community, and with educators in the region related to supporting undocumented students and their families. Dr. Clark-Ibáñez served as lead author for a monograph called *Undocumented Latino Youth: Navigating Their Worlds* (2015), training and writing with a team of undergraduates and community members to investigate the educational pipeline for Latinx undocumented students. She is the faculty director for the National Latino Research Center at CSUSM where, in partnership with research director Dr. Arcela Nuñez-Alvarez, she supports projects that include civic engagement, immigration, youth, and post-incarceration. With Carolina Valdivia, Dr. Clark-Ibáñez co-directs *UndocuResearch Project—A Study by, for, and with Undocumented Students*, which focuses on the post–election of Trump experiences of undocumented high school students and teachers who work with them. She is also on the board of directors for UURISE, Unitarian Universalist Refugee and Immigration Services and Education, a nonprofit legal center that focuses on immigration. She is grateful for the long friendship and collaborations with Dr. Swan, which began with coauthoring a book on teaching sociology using film, and now more recently they are working together on a research project about immigration courts and have coauthored an article on the impact of DACA.

In addition to these amazing collaborators, Dr. Clark-Ibáñez is grateful to her immediate family members who have supported her through this project. She grew up with Mercedes Ibáñez as a fierce poet mother whose immigrant journey and successes in a new country formed in her daughters solid roots of resistance and resiliency. Her sister Giselle Clark-Ibáñez and her partner Will Warren (parents to beautiful Nina Mercedes and Lucia Karina) are champions of human rights, radically political, and just fun to be around. Bill Clark, her dad, possesses pragmatism and a great sense of humor, which helped so much during hectic workweeks; he also hosted sleepovers with grandkids while she attended long night meetings. Finally, partner Dr. Luke Lara helped with this project at every level—editing, sounding board, fun breaks, date nights, and community work. Pablo Vicente and Cecilia Catalina are their children and entice Marisol into a sacred, blessed balance away from work that includes day trips, beach, art, song, and hanging out.

Dr. Richelle Swan primarily teaches undergraduate and graduate classes related to the sociology of law, community internships, and social justice. She serves as the CSUSM faculty liaison to JusticeCorps and enjoys supporting students as they develop a critical consciousness about justice issues both inside and outside of the classroom. Past scholarship that informs her contributions to this book includes examinations of civil gang injunctions' social control of communities of color; analyses of media, popular culture, and social constructions of crime, law, and targeted populations; and work on social movements and resistance in the context of Hurricane Katrina. She and her writing partner for this book have recently published an article examining the legal consciousness of undocumented students before and after the enactment of Deferred Action for Childhood Arrivals (DACA) and are continuing their examination of federal immigration courts in Southern California. She has happily worked with and learned from many graduate and undergraduate students who are pursuing community work and scholarship related to the impact of immigration on their lives.

As a person who can trace her birth family's immigrant roots back many generations to several countries in western and southern Europe (thanks to her mother's detailed genealogical research), Dr. Swan has deeply appreciated learning about the relatively recent immigrant experiences of her extended family and friends who have roots in a variety of countries, such as Mexico, Argentina, the Philippines, and Peru. She gives special thanks to her partner, Chendo, for his loving and supportive presence throughout the years of writing this book, and for sharing his thoughts and feelings about his immigration experience's indelible impact upon his life. She thanks Sara, Elisa, Carmela, and Jaime for serving as remarkable examples of resilient people who encountered daunting challenges on their path to establishing a life here in the United States. She also thanks Marisol for being such a generous colleague, collaborator, and friend, and her mother, Mercedes, for her longstanding encouragement and kindness. In addition, she is grateful to her dear friends, Maricela, Seba, Kim, Theresa, and Sonia, for the in-depth conversations related to many of the topics considered in this book over the years. Oftentimes these conversations took place in happy times accompanied by music, food, and celebration, and sometimes they were in more serious contexts with tears and difficult memories, yet, all have been equally appreciated. She also thanks her parents, Sharon and Rick, as well as Chandon, Jasmin, Gavin, and Olivia for all the fun breaks and family time that they have provided on weekends during this process. And last, but not least, she thanks Alicia, Brad, Bryce, and Avary for the laughter, love, and support they always send her way.

Our work and personal lives are intertwined with immigration and social justice. We live in a region where immigration is happening. Folks are coming and going through the border to visit family or the doctor. Youth are going to school and adults to work. We celebrate the milestones and grieve losses. Through all this, Customs and Border Protection (CBP) and Immigration and Customs Enforcement (ICE) are a strong presence. We are flanked on either side of our region by active checkpoints on the two major freeways. Local law enforcement sets up checkpoints that allegedly check for alcohol but are far away from social venues and deep in our Latinx communities. We support the work of grassroots organizations, such as *Alianza Comunitaria* (Community Alliance), which trains team members to be human rights observers and reports on verified checkpoints to their thousands of text message subscribers.

As professors, we teach students of diverse backgrounds and political ideologies. Both of us are committed to respectful, nourishing pedagogies that foster student growth. In class, we encourage students to consider multiple perspectives. We assign reflective writing assignments and facilitate active discussions. Most importantly, we stress the use of scholarly research, documentary film, and community voices to best understand the issues we grapple with in all of our classes.

We draw on our approach into this book for our singular mission: honoring and sharing the contemporary experiences of undocumented Latinx immigrants in the United States. Therefore, readers should not look to this book for a "balanced" perspective on undocumented immigration. We are fiercely progressive in our outlook on undocumented immigration. As full professors, talented teachers, and seasoned scholars, we are excited to share the evidence for a humanistic approach to understanding undocumented immigration.

We did not undertake this project alone. We acknowledge the stellar work of many sociology students who contributed to this book. We benefited from the graduate researchers who tracked down articles, news stories, and policy reports and provided personal narratives, including: Flor Saldaña, Lilian Briceño, Isaias Escamilla, Olivia Victory, Guillermo Salgado, Vanessa Martinez, Maria Jimenez, Denise Nealon, and Blanca Castro. Undergraduate assistants Brendon Tokoro and Ryan Bravo helped us find secondary sources as well.

We benefited from manuscript assistants Jose Ruiz Escutia, Blanca Carrasco, and Brady Smith, who helped organize the bibliography. Josefina Espino, Sarai Maldonado, and Dawn Lee served as image detectives and helped with the visual depictions of immigration in the book. Jose Luis Escutia allowed us to publish his beautiful original artwork in the book. Research assistants working on our immigration courtroom project—Jose Luis Escutia, Noemi Jara, Dawn Lee, Tanya Armenta, and Alyssa Victory—shared insights about the law that inspired several of the legal issues analyzed in the book. Professor Xuan Santos shared his immigration journey with us for inclusion in the book, as did numerous community members whom we thank for trusting us to illuminate their stories.

We really appreciate the support from Rowman & Littlefield. We especially want to thank Sarah Stanton for seeking us out to write a "readable book" about undocumented immigration; Rolf Janke for helping us finalize the manuscript; Alden Perkins for her professionalism, patience, and consideration as we completed the final edits; Courtney Packard for being so responsive and creative with cover art and graphics; typesetter Wanda Ditch; and Arc Indexing for their detailed work.

Finally, we are very lucky to work in a place that supports social justice and the rights of undocumented immigrant students and their families. Our work has benefited from deep friendships with professors Kristin Bates, Sharon Elise, Susan Miller, and Michelle Ramos Pellicia. Dr. Lorena Checa, Dr. Geoffrey Gilmore, Andres Favela, and Floyd Lai have been strong allies in our work with undocumented students and community members.

Our home department illustrates the type of work represented in this book. We thank our incredible colleagues for the inspiring work that they do. Two of them, Dr. Sharon Elise and Dr. Xuan Santos, authored a powerful statement that continues to shine on our department homepage and we share this excerpt:[1]

> Our society is rapidly moving backwards. We have seen presidential edicts for a "Muslim ban," and a "border wall," the rollback of access to healthcare and education, the refusal to stand against neo-Nazis and white supremacy, and most recently, the plan to repeal DACA.
>
> We are proud to serve a diverse student body and we are particularly proud of our students' success despite their struggles against so many forms of injustice—racism, sexism, and economic oppression. DACA students represent the perpetual striving to "make a way out of no way"—despite the slim promise of a future, they have committed themselves to work and school and they are succeeding. We have seen this year after year.
>
> We are dreamers, too. We dream of: Bridges not walls. Religious freedom, not intolerance and fear. Free education. Free healthcare. Affordable housing and childcare. Open borders. Right to a "living wage."
>
> The Statue of Liberty—"Mother of Exiles"—must be mighty angry to see how far astray we have moved. May her torch light our way to resistance, to secure social justice for all.

Indeed, our short- and long-term goal is justice. We are honored that you are joining us to learn about the stories and read about the research that support undocumented immigrants' right for dignity and equity across all American social institutions.

1

Introduction

In this book, we specifically address the myths related to undocumented immigration and respond with research findings and stories about undocumented Latinx immigrants of all ages, representing diverse countries of origin, and residing in an array of cities and states. We began our research for this book as the 2016 U.S. election cycle was ramping up; outrageous and false claims about undocumented immigration were common. Two years later, immediately following the 2018 midterm election season, the same vitriolic and unsubstantiated claims about immigrants are still in circulation. Although unauthorized immigration has been at the top of the U.S. news for the last few years, less attention is given to the scholars, activists, and policy experts who speak of humanity and facts.

Now, as we finish this manuscript about undocumented Latinx immigrants, the nation is once again focused on the U.S.-Mexico border where thousands are traveling in caravans from Central America in order to seek asylum from the United States. They are being met with a strong military presence, razor-sharp wires, tear gas, and threats that the government might separate children from their parent/s at the border again as they did earlier this year.[1] Yet, it is important to remember the Department of Homeland Security defines the border to be *within 100 air-miles* of any port of entry, water/beach border, or land border. This means that roughly two-thirds of the United States' population live in the border region.[2] We all have something at stake when we think about immigration. In this book, we propose that data and humanity must be at the forefront of all discussions, whether in our communities or on the news.

We wrote this book with diverse readers in mind. Are you undocumented and want to learn more about others' experiences across the country? Do you have an open mind and are curious about pressing social issues related to immigration? Do you watch the news and feel like something is missing but are not sure how to get

Figure 1.1. San Francisco's Balmy Alley mural reflects many of the fears and injustices related to immigration in the United States today.
Oren Rozen, Wikimedia Commons

more information? Do you need resources to better engage in respectful debate with your coworkers or family members? If so, this book will provide a helpful overview for you.

This book is also ideal for people who do not have the time or energy to immediately dive into the many scholarly resources on immigration written by our talented colleagues. We draw from multiple sources to provide a compelling overview of how undocumented immigrants experience some of our primary social institutions. Given that it is intended as an overview, we are not able to cover all topics related to undocumented communities, nor can we incorporate all of the incredible work that has been done related to each topic that we do cover. We also recognize that immigration policies, laws, and practices are ever-changing. Therefore, it is our hope that you will be motivated by what you read and continue your own investigation of the subjects that are important to you. Be sure to check out our detailed endnotes, as they will direct you toward some well-researched sources to put on your future reading list.

TAKING A CRITICAL HUMAN RIGHTS APPROACH

We approach the subject of undocumented or unauthorized Latinx immigration from a human rights perspective. This means we prioritize the inherent rights of all people to be treated with respect and dignity. This approach is in line with the United States' commitment to the Universal Declaration of Human Rights and basic principles of equity and justice.

The language we use in this book reflects this perspective, so we do not use the dehumanizing terms "illegal" or "aliens," unless in specific instances they may appear in a direct quote. Instead, we use the terms "undocumented" or "unauthorized immigrants/migrants/people." We use "undocumented" to refer to people who do not have papers documenting U.S. citizenship or residency (temporary or permanent). We use "unauthorized" to describe when people face legal obstacles as a result of their immigration status. In addition, we choose to use the gender-inclusive term Latinx/s in lieu of Latino/s or Latina/s except when we are quoting sources that use those terms or we are referring to people identified as boys/men or girls/women specifically.

In keeping with a human rights perspective, we approach the material in this book with the recognition that the lives of *all* undocumented people matter. The mainstream focus on undocumented youth leaves out adults, who are often ineligible for what little support there is for undocumented immigrants. When a "deservingness" narrative is developed in politics, media, and/or school settings with respect to immigration and immigration reform, it often privileges people who are considered high achieving, such as college students, and those who were brought to the United States as children. Although we certainly write about people from these subgroups as we examine the topic of immigration in the context of various social institutions, our scope has a broader focus. We are coming from the perspective that the experiences of *all* people who are undocumented are worthy of our focus. Immigration reform needs to include people who are left out of many proposed and enacted laws, such as adults who brought themselves here to survive and thrive economically, physically, and/or psychologically.

This book blends diverse forms of secondary sources with first-person testimonies and narratives from undocumented immigrants. This book is not a monograph or a research study. Our intent is to highlight information that counters mainstream caricatures of immigrants and immigration that are all too common today. The references and sources we use in this book follow these guiding principles. We challenge the stereotyping of immigrants and the exclusionary social and legal practices that target them. We integrate stories of the people affected by immigration laws and policies into our analyses of some of the most important issues of the day. Sometimes people shared stories directly with us or with our research assistants, in which case we have used pseudonyms when presenting their experiences. Other times, we found stories by way of news or social media. We agree with scholar Elvira Pulitano that the stories behind undocumented immigration "need to be heard if the United States intends to live up to its founding principles of dignity and respect for all people."[3] We believe that these stories are best understood when placed in the context of the latest findings on immigration from journalists, researchers, activists, and community members, which we have included as well. Using these multiple sources of information allows us to focus upon the marginalization the Latinx undocumented community faces, and consider how undocumented community members draw upon community cultural capital to resist criminalization and degradation.[4] In sum, our goal is to present an overview that paints a diverse portrait of unauthorized immigration that depicts challenges and opportunities in Latinx immigrant communities in the United States.

A QUICK LOOK AT THE NUMBERS

In the United States, one-fourth of immigrants are unauthorized.[5] The estimated eleven million unauthorized immigrants make up a total of 3.5 percent of the country's total population.[6] The majority of unauthorized immigrants in the United States have lived here for more than ten years (66 percent) and a minority have lived here for less than five years (14 percent).[7] The numbers of immigrants who are considered "lawful" immigrants include the eleven million people who are lawful permanent residents, the 1.7 million people who are temporary lawful residents, and the nineteen million people who are naturalized citizens.[8] The numbers of unauthorized immigrants in the United States have fallen to the lowest level since 2004; the peek was in 2012 with 12.6 million.[9]

According to a comprehensive analysis of the demographics of the undocumented population in 2014 by Pew Research Center authors Jeffrey S. Passel and D'Vera Cohn, most people (61 percent) live in twenty metro areas around the United States, five of which are in California:[10]

Table 1.1.   Twenty Metro Areas with Largest Population of Unauthorized Immigrants

1. New York–Newark–Jersey City (NY, NJ, PA)	1,115,000
2. Los Angeles–Long Beach–Anaheim (CA)	1,000,000
3. Houston–The Woodlands–Sugar Land (TX)	575,000
4. Dallas–Fort Worth–Arlington (TX)	475,000
5. Miami–Fort Lauderdale–West Palm Beach (FL)	450,000
6. Chicago–Naperville–Elgin (IL, IN, WI)	425,000
7. Washington–Arlington–Alexandria (DC, VA, MD, WV)	400,000
8. Atlanta–Sandy Springs–Roswell (GA)	250,000
9. Riverside–San Bernardino–Ontario (CA)	250,000
10. Phoenix–Mesa–Scottsdale (AZ)	250,000
11. San Francisco–Oakland–Hayward (CA)	240,000
12. Boston–Cambridge–Newton (MA, NH)	180,000
13. San Diego–Carlsbad (CA)	170,000
14. Las Vegas–Henderson–Paradise (NV)	170,000
15. Philadelphia–Camden–Wilmington (PA, NJ, DE, MD)	160,000
16. Seattle–Tacoma–Bellevue (WA)	150,000
17. Denver–Aurora–Lakewood (CO)	130,000
18. San Jose–Sunnyvale–Santa Clara (CA)	120,000
19. Orlando–Kissimmee–Sanford (FL)	110,000
20. Austin–Round Rock (TX)	100,000

In terms of the states' unauthorized immigrant populations, thirteen states had significant changes in their populations between 2009 and 2014.[11] Seven states had significant *decreases* in the number of unauthorized immigrants (California, Nevada, Nebraska, Illinois, Georgia, South Carolina, and Alabama). In all but one of these states (Alabama), this was due to a decline in unauthorized people of Mexican origin. Six states had significant *increases* in the number of unauthorized immigrants (Washington, Louisiana, Pennsylvania, New Jersey, Virginia, and Massachusetts). In five of them this was primarily due to an increase of people of non-Mexican origin, and in one, Louisiana, it was due to an increase of immigrants of Mexican origin.

The number of unauthorized immigrants from Mexico in the United States has decreased, which can be related to events besides a decrease in arrivals, such as people getting legal status, being deported, leaving the country voluntarily, or death.[12] There are significant increases in the numbers of undocumented people from a few other regions in the world who live in the United States. The number of undocumented people from Central America rose from 1.6 million in 2009 to 1.8 million in 2015, and the number of undocumented people from Asia rose from 1.3 million in 2009 to 1.5 million in 2015. There was a statistically significant *decline* of unauthorized immigrants from South America (from 725,000 people in 2009 to 625,000 people in 2015). The numbers of unauthorized immigrants from other regions in the world did not change in a significant way during the same time period: Europe/ Canada (550,000), the Latin American Caribbean region (425,000 people), Sub-Saharan Africa (250,000), and the Middle East (130,000).

We offer a special note about Temporary Protected Status (TPS) as it relates to Latinx undocumented immigration. In 1990, Congress created TPS to temporarily help countries cope with extraordinary natural disasters, armed conflict, and political crises.[13] TPS provides migrants from the designated countries deportation protection, temporary authorization to work in the United States, and allows for travel outside of the United States with permission (e.g., advanced parole).[14] Most individuals with TPS do not have a pathway to citizenship or residency. The Department of Homeland Security with the support of President Trump announced the end of TPS for Sudan, Nicaragua, Haiti, and El Salvador; however, a temporary injunction prevented its termination in those countries.[15]

As of August 1, 2018, ten countries have TPS status and include Latinx countries such as Nicaragua, El Salvador, and Honduras. TPS holders from El Salvador are the largest group: if protection were to end on September 9, 2019, as Trump had initially announced, it would mean two hundred thousand Salvadorans would lose their status.[16] The options for most are to legally fix their status (which few could do), return to their birth country (from which thousands are fleeing from in walking caravans), or stay in the United States and be considered undocumented. TPS holders have documentation in the form of protective status; however, they are not citizens or residents. The status of TPS is extremely tenuous.

WHY WE FOCUS ON LATINX
UNDOCUMENTED IMMIGRANTS

We focus this book on the contemporary experiences of Latinx undocumented immigrants primarily because of the estimated 11.3 million undocumented people in the United States, 67 percent or 7.5 million come from Mexico (53 percent of the total undocumented population), El Salvador (6 percent), Guatemala (5 percent), and Honduras (3 percent).[17] While Mexican immigrants have sharply decreased, a growing unauthorized immigrant population is from those originally from Central America.[18]

Within the Latinx population, there is variation among the states. In California, there are three million undocumented workers and 82 percent are originally from Mexico and Central America.[19] In Rhode Island, the majority of undocumented immigrants are from Guatemala, while El Salvador was the top population in Virginia, Maryland, and Massachusetts.[20] In this book, we will be featuring the diversity of undocumented Latinx immigrants across the United States.

Finally, undocumented Latinx populations' navigation through American social institutions are characterized by forms of inequality and injustices shaped by their specific life experiences. Each chapter in this book will share how undocumented Latinx immigrants are suffering hardships and also working towards a better life.

While our focus is on Latinx undocumented immigrants, there is diversity among the undocumented population. Sixteen percent of the undocumented population is from Asia and constitutes about 1.8 million immigrants; while 5 percent is from Europe and Canada, 3 percent is from Africa, and 3 percent is from the Caribbean.[21] We also acknowledge that Latinx populations had not been the fastest growing unauthorized immigration groups—Indian and Chinese immigrants were the fastest growing[22]—but recently have held their rate steady.[23] Research demonstrates that many non-Latinx migrants arrived in the United States with authorized permission, such as with visas to work, to study, or to visit—then they overstayed their authorization.[24]

Why Is There So Much Latinx Migration?

We also focus on Latinx migration because of the geographical, social, political, and economic history that has shaped migration from Mexico and Central America to the United States. Social and historical conditions have created a large Latinx undocumented population. Typically, we hear that the economic conditions on both sides of the border—the need for workers in the United States and the need for income in Mexico—have created a push-pull factor of immigration. The Bracero Temporary Worker program during World War II was an example of a formal work arrangement, but informal and long-term flows of migration have always occurred. Economists found that Mexican work migration in 1929 was higher in states like Kansas, Arizona, and New Mexico than it was in 1990.[25]

Figure 1.2. An array of signs at a rally challenges negative messages about immigration and migration.
Nitish Mena, Unsplash

The United States has long, deep, and intertwined ties with Mexico. For those interested in learning more about Mexico-U.S. relations, we suggest starting with *Occupy America: A History of Chicanos* by Rudy Acuña.[26] When the border was much more fluid (prior to the 1920s), communities and family networks were established and then grew. Militarizing the border has not stopped communities and families from living out the motto: "The border crossed us, we did not cross the border."

WHERE *IS* THAT "LINE"?

Something we often hear about undocumented immigrants is: "Why can't they get in line and do things the right way?" It is a fair and important question. Most undocumented immigrants would like to formalize their status to reduce the chances of deportation. However, most are not eligible for relief.

It is also important to remember that the law currently states that it is only a misdemeanor offense to enter the United States without inspection from an immigration officer. Immigration law is an administrative court—not a criminal court. However, under the Trump Administration, undocumented immigrants have become criminalized.[27]

There are three main ways to seek immigration status: employment, family reunification, or humanitarian protection. Most undocumented immigrants "do not have the necessary family or employment relationships and often cannot access humanitarian protection, such as refugee or asylum status," especially if they are from Mexico or Central America.[28]

Two-thirds of undocumented immigrants have entered the country with authorization, but overstayed their permission[29]—meaning, the *majority* of undocumented immigration did not cross the border "illegally." This speaks to undocumented immigrants who began the process with some type of status, such as visitor, work, or student visas, but for a variety of reasons stayed in the United States beyond their designated time. We will explore these circumstances in each chapter that follows.

Can a Person "Get in Line" by Being Sponsored by a Family Member?

The policy for family reunification process deserves important clarification. First, there is a "long line" for the petitions submitted. In 2015, there were 4.5 million waiting for a family-based permanent resident card (also known as the green card).[30] The American Immigration Council reports these astounding wait times:

> As of May 2016, for most countries, unmarried children of U.S. citizens must wait more than five years and siblings of U.S. citizens must wait more than 10 years. People from countries with high levels of immigration to the United States—Mexico, China, India, and the Philippines—generally have longer waiting times. For example, married children of U.S. citizens from Mexico must wait more than 20 years for a visa to become available, and Filipino siblings of U.S. citizens currently wait about 25 years.[31]

Previously, the fastest "line" to citizenship was an opportunity created through the Simpson-Mazzoli Act signed into law by President Ronald Reagan in 1986. Among other things, it gave amnesty and a pathway to citizenship to three million undocumented immigrants who had been in the country for at least five years.[32] Many activists and scholars believe that this is the most humane and fiscally responsible way to deal with undocumented immigration.

Second, all petitioners must be above the poverty line and have demonstrated the ability to support the family member they are bringing to the United States.[33] For this reason, contrary to popular belief, most "U.S.-born children do not 'anchor' parents by providing automatic pathways to citizenship."[34] While the U.S. Constitution's Fourteenth Amendment grants citizenship to all individuals born in the United States, a citizen child must wait until she or he is twenty-one years old to petition for parents. As discussed previously, the citizenship process—after petition begins—can take years, if not decades. The term "anchor baby" is offensive and should not be used because it has a negative connotation for American-born children of undocumented parents. Additionally, the notion that a child's citizenship can protect parents from being deported is false. Between 2015 and 2017, ICE deported 87,351 individuals who had at least one U.S. citizen child.[35]

Much of undocumented immigration is about family: about half of undocumented adults have U.S.-born children.[36] In terms of the undocumented Latinx population in general, about 81 percent live in households with citizens.[37] The families with mixed status—and those who come to the United States for a better life—also deserve to have basic rights for safety met. Creating a better, faster, and fairer line for undocumented immigrants would serve the immigrant populations and the nation at large. As we will see in the following chapters, undocumented immigrants offer numerous contributions to the United States.

SOCIAL INSTITUTIONS—FOR ALL OF US

We organized this book so that we could explore how undocumented immigrants engage in, negotiate with, and are challenged by American social institutions. Our diverse portraits of lived experiences of undocumented Latinxs living in the United States take us through the very same social institutions that we all share in the United States: media, economy, education, health, and the legal system.

When you consider the word "institution," you may think about a jail, church, school, or hospital. In other words, you may think of buildings or entities that you could touch or otherwise inhabit. This book is organized around the way sociologists think of social institutions, which is a bit more abstract. Social institutions are more about the systems that *govern* the jails, schools, etc. You cannot walk into a social institution, but you are a part of one and can feel its effects. If a store shuts down, the institution of economy continues.

Bear with us while we explain a bit further. A classic sociological way to understand social institutions is that they are loosely agreed upon ideas about how to behave and how things should go.[38] A social institution is a collective solution to a problem of social life. They are a system of norms, values, and behaviors with a specific purpose. They shape how we behave, set up expectations, and even inform our values. There are specific or manifest functions —intended goals—for why social institutions exist.

We list some traditional ideas below that should be familiar:

Institution: Education
Intended Function: Teaching skills for adult living and passing on culture
Institution: Health Care
Intended Function: Preventing and healing illness
Institution: Media
Intended Function: Communicating across distances
Institution: Economy
Intended Function: Producing and distributing goods and services
Institution: Legal System
Intended Function: Maintaining moral order and establishing punishment

However, every social institution has *unintended* or latent functions. When a critical lens is used to understand the roles of social institutions, we see that they actively work to reproduce societal inequalities rather than to ameliorate them. Whether you take a critical or general approach, there are undeniable inequalities experienced by undocumented immigrant families in all the major social institutions we describe. For example, while we all might agree that education is intended to teach young people the skills and knowledge needed for adult living, an unintended function is that mandatory public schooling also serves as a place for kids to be while parents work. However, that there are also significant inequalities in terms of types of schools, training of teachers, and quality of materials that students encounter. Therefore, a consequence of the educational system is that it creates and/or maintains inequality.

It is important to remember that social institutions shape us, yet we also create and shape them. There are a variety of forms of resistance and social action that are currently being used by undocumented people and their allies (covered in chapter 7), which are powerful responses to the injustices of the social institutions analyzed in this book.

CHAPTER OVERVIEW

Chapter 2—The Double-Edged Sword of the Media: The media are responsible for both fueling and challenging the many myths about undocumented immigration that we will consider throughout this book. We begin this chapter by examining the media framing of immigrants and immigration and the creation of moral panics around immigration. We look at the mixed messages of mainstream media coverage of the Latinx community in general and at media stereotypes of Latinx immigrants and immigration specifically. We follow with a look at stereotypes perpetuated by the mainstream news media and analyze how these are challenged by alternative media sources. We conclude with an examination of how people are using media forms such as comics, television shows, documentaries, feature films, and user-generated digital and social media to present humane depictions of the unauthorized immigrants and immigration.

Chapter 3—Shortchanged—Work and Labor: Long considered the "pull" to the United States, this chapter presents the social dimensions of work for undocumented immigrants in various industries such as agriculture, poultry factories, housecleaning, construction, slaughterhouses, day labor, landscaping, and fast food. We present a gendered discussion of labor and examine the precariousness of the informal economy to frame the lived experiences of those working "without papers." Myths that will be dismantled in this chapter include the idea that undocumented immigrants do not do their fair share, and that they are "taking" Americans' jobs. We consider the significant economic contributions of undocumented workers, the amount of taxes that they pay, and the unprecedented positive impact on local and state economies. In addition, we highlight undocumented migrant children and the major legal loopholes that subject them to dangerous work and exempt them from certain educational requirements. We end the chapter with a consideration of workplace raids and deportation, the stories of undocumented professionals, and a human-right-to-work framework.

Chapter 4—Educational Dreams and Barriers: Education is often the reason that families migrate to the United States, and it represents the hope for a better future. In this chapter, we consider the myth that undocumented students have broken the law and should not have the right to education by explaining that a decision by the U.S. Supreme Court (*Plyler v. Doe*) protects undocumented students' right to a public K-12 education. We show that although the leaking educational pipeline makes it difficult for undocumented students to graduate from high school, states are increasingly providing access to and financial support for college. Yet, access to education varies significantly from state to state. The chapter also includes a look at financial barriers and opportunities, the yet-unachieved federal DREAM Act, Deferred Action of Childhood Arrivals (DACA), the role of visas for undocumented workers, and stories of undocumented and formerly undocumented students to provide a rounded discussion of key educational issues. In addition, we present an overview of the work being done to increase educational access in the alternative educational institutions of Freedom University in Georgia (a state where undocumented students are barred from attending the main six public universities and denied in-state tuition to the other institutions of higher education) and the University of the People. We wrap up the chapter with an argument for why the United States should include the original Dreamers in future immigration reform.

Chapter 5—Freefall with No Safety Net: Health: We start this chapter by dispelling two myths: the health care provided to undocumented immigrants attracts them to the United States and unauthorized immigrants are "illegally" taking advantage of public medical care. We explain that health care is actually more accessible in immigrants' countries of origin, and unauthorized immigrants are not eligible for most medical and social services in the United States, yet they dramatically underuse the health services for which they are eligible. An examination of the only remaining federal health protection, limited emergency room access, and the differences between states' approaches to health care demonstrates why the majority of the undocumented population is truly freefalling without a health safety net. We delve into this reality by analyzing the major health concerns of the undocumented immigrant community: workplace accidents and abuse; immigration raids, detention, and deportation; mental health care; children's health; and labor trafficking. We also focus upon the often-overlooked health issue of dental care and feature community programs, such as *Boca Sana, Cuerpo Sano* (Healthy Mouth, Healthy Body), which train community leaders and provide dental care to immigrant communities. We conclude the chapter with a look at doctors who advocate for increased access to health care for undocumented immigrants.

Chapter 6—Legal Issues, Detention, and Deportation: We begin this chapter by challenging the myth that alleged unauthorized immigrants in the United States are subject to fair detention and deportation procedures and principles of decency enshrined in the law. Instead, we show that immigration law enforcement in the United States today challenges the principles often thought of as cornerstones of the country—fairness and equality. In order to understand the backdrop of the legal issues related to detention and deportation we consider the factors of crimmigration (the criminalization of migrants), free trade agreements, criminal immigrant stereotypes, and visas that address immigrant victimization (the U-Visa and T-Visa). We then provide an overview of the official roles and responsibilities of Customs and Border Protection (CBP) and Immigration and Customs Enforcement (ICE), as well as what happens when these agencies excessively use force. We outline the removal process and analyze current efforts to process alleged undocumented immigrants (even those intending to ask for asylum) through criminal courts in Operation Streamline. Then, we describe factors that are strongly linked: the desire of private correctional corporations to increase profits, the poor state of detention facilities, and the negative outcomes on immigrant detainees. The last section of the chapter focuses upon issues related to deportation, including informal methods of deportation, the deportation strategies of the Obama and Trump Administrations, legal representation (and the lack thereof) in deportation cases, hearings in detention centers, and veterans and deportation.

Chapter 7—Resistance and Social Change: We counter the myths that undocumented immigrants are scared to speak up against immigration policies and practices and only Latinx young adults who are undocumented are involved in today's immigrant rights movements. We look at individuals' and groups' involvement in social actions and consider how people use frame-shifting strategies to challenge inaccurate ideas about unauthorized immigration. We then focus upon the different methods of resistance used in immigrant social movements, such as marches, *testimonios* and truth-telling, civil disobedience and direct action, sit-ins, infiltrations of detention centers, hunger strikes, boycotts, art, self-deportation, and acts of sanctuary—as well as inspiring examples of the people who have used them.

Chapter 8—Conclusion: Our final chapter includes a set of our recommendations related to the topics of the media; work; education; health; law, detention and deportation; and resistance and social action. These recommendations act as a roadmap for how to improve the conditions and outcomes for undocumented immigrants. We connect what is occurring in the United States with the bigger context of global migration. And, finally, we circle back to what it means to believe in human rights and dignity for all in the current political climate.

2

The Double-Edged
Sword of the Media

Magdalena is a 28-year-old Latina who is undocumented. She was brought to this country in her early teen years and finished a college education. Every day on her way to work she listens to the news on the radio and throughout the years she has noticed how the words "illegal immigrants" or "illegal aliens" are used to signify that she, and others like her, are criminal. Magdalena feels a blend of emotions when listening to immigration news and hearing how the terms are used. She feels guilt for being undocumented. She knows it is not something she can control, but nonetheless, the feeling is there. She feels depressed because the term "illegal" means that her community is not welcomed in the country. Magdalena also feels anger, because her very own identity is deemed as criminal in media stories that are informing the nation.

Magdalena's identity as an unauthorized immigrant is one in which she always resists the label of a criminal. She says that she has always been a good citizen by paying her yearly taxes, working full time, and never being charged with a criminal act, and yet her identity is criminalized in media outlets that inform the masses. In instances when biased immigration news are delivered on the radio, TV, or computer, she reminds herself that she is not a criminal. She tells me it is an ongoing identity battle.

—Flor Saldaña

Myth: Media representations of Latinx communities reflect the wide range of experiences of unauthorized immigrants and the social and legal barriers they face.

Myth Busted: There is a long history of anti-immigrant media coverage that paints an incomplete picture of immigrant experiences. This tradition ignores the big picture: the policies, laws, and social practices that shape Latinx immigration in the United States. It also ignores the emotional lives of unauthorized immigrants themselves. Although this media tradition is still present today, it is being challenged by mainstream and alternative media sources dedicated to the complexities of authorized and unauthorized immigration.

The use of media is a double-edged sword that is wielded by a range of people for different reasons and outcomes; it can perpetuate and spread misconceptions or it can shed light on them and shift the popular dialogue. Scholar Angharad Valdivia sees the connection between the U.S. media and Latinxs as "a love-hate relationship" that involves treating some Latinx celebrities as hot property (e.g., Jennifer Lopez, Eva Longoria, and Salma Hayek), and treats Latinxs in general as "eternal foreigners having to continually assert their belonging and citizenship."[1] The predominant approach of the mainstream U.S. entertainment and news media on immigration has traditionally been to simplify and sensationalize the topic.

Magdalena's experiences of listening to biased immigration coverage described at the beginning of this chapter reflect the dehumanization and criminalization immigrant populations often experience at the hands of the media. In some cases, this is accomplished through language, image, or story choices that are negatively loaded; for example, referring to people as "illegal" or making a film in which the only immigrant character is someone who happens to rob, steal, and kill to "take advantage" of people in the United States. In other cases, the media assault on immigrant lives is even more direct and spreads anti-immigrant rumors, stereotypes, and/or threats of harm.

In contemporary times, there are also multiple forms of news, entertainment, and social media that provide accurate counter-representations. The creators of these media sources are using an assortment of formats to break down dominant and inaccurate messages about immigrants and immigration. In the midst of the many contrasting stories on unauthorized immigration being told, a person can feel a little lost trying to sort them all out. That is why it is helpful to consider how stories about immigration are framed.

MEDIA FRAMING OF IMMIGRATION AND IMMIGRANTS

Depictions of immigration and immigrants in news, entertainment, and social media often highlight the skewed perceptions of people in power. For example, the following two quotes from Donald Trump were burnt into the public consciousness during his campaign for the 2016 presidency due to their frequent repetition in the media:

> When Mexico sends its people, they're not sending their best. . . . They're sending people that have lots of problems, and they're bringing those problems with us. They're bringing drugs. They're bringing crime. They're rapists. And some, I assume, are good people. But I speak to border guards and they tell us what we're getting. And it only makes common sense. It only makes common sense. They're sending us not the right people. It's coming from more than Mexico. It's coming from all over South and Latin America, and it's coming probably—probably—from the Middle East. But we don't know. Because we have no protection and we

have no competence, we don't know what's happening. And it's got to stop and it's got to stop fast.

—Donald Trump, announcement of presidential campaign, June 2015[2]

One of my first acts will be to get all of the drug lords, all of the bad ones—we have some bad, bad people in this country that have to go out. We're going to get them out. We're going to secure the border. And once the border is secured, at a later date, we'll make a determination as to the rest. But we have some bad *hombres* here, and we're going to get them out.

—Donald Trump, third and final 2016 presidential debate[3]

The reason why inflammatory statements repeated on different forms of media matter is because people make sense of the world by means of our personal experiences (i.e., our *experienced reality*), and from information obtained from significant others: social institutions, such as schools, government agencies, religious groups and unions; and the mass media (i.e., our *symbolic reality*).[4] The mass media can be especially powerful influences in terms of symbolic reality because they offer easy access to information that most of us are not privy to firsthand, and they have the ability to selectively shape or *frame* images and stories.[5] The choices that journalists and reporters make when framing these images and stories are influenced by the desire to attract the biggest audience, and when they work for a for-profit news agency the pressure to do so is even greater than it is otherwise.[6]

Ultimately, the characterization of immigrants in the news media affects how the general public and public officials regard them, and shapes whether they will be treated humanely or targeted as outcasts.[7] Entertainment and social media are also very influential in today's world—a television show, film, or tweet can tell a story about immigration that observers may choose to believe, to disbelieve, and/or to actively support or challenge.

Creating a Moral Panic About Immigration

The America we know and love doesn't exist anymore. Massive demographic changes have been foisted on the American people, and they are changes that none of us ever voted for, and most of us don't like . . . this is related to both legal and illegal immigration. . . .

—Laura Ingraham on her Fox News show *The Ingraham Angle* (August 9, 2018)[8]

Much of the rhetoric about and public reaction to immigrants and immigration today constitute a *moral panic*.[9] A moral panic typically has a number of ingredients: the news and/or entertainment media spread exaggerated information about the prevalence and seriousness of an issue, interested community members and politicians pick up on the information, and attempts are made to fuel some sort of change or reform to the system. Regardless of whether any meaningful change is accomplished, the particular characterization of the problem tends to fade away, and comes back again later for another round of heightened concern.[10] The presentation of social issues in the mainstream media often unquestionably mirrors the existing power structure. For example, typical crime news stories disproportionately focus on the alleged wrongdoing of lower-income men of color and tend to exaggerate the likelihood of victimization of white, economically privileged members of society, elders, and children.[11]

Moral panics about immigration have occurred throughout U.S. history, and the one that began taking hold in the mid-2010s follows a well-established pattern. As we discuss at length in this chapter, the media often helps people with an anti-immigrant focus fuel panic about immigration, and unauthorized immigration in particular. This is done by demonizing a subgroup of people, usually low-income brown and black migrants, who come to the United States for safety and survival. In the process, little attention is given to the global economic systems and policies that have fueled this migration or the fact that many people are coming to the United States to apply for asylum. The moral panic results in a lack of humane narratives about immigrants themselves by disregarding the emotions and experiences of those central to the story.[12]

MIXED MESSAGES:
MAINSTREAM MEDIA COVERAGE OF LATINXS

Although Latinxs represent the second largest demographic in the United States, the coverage of Latinx issues is limited and focuses on sensationalized events such as Donald Trump's tirades against immigrants rather than providing in-depth analysis of immigration issues.[13] The National Hispanic Media Coalition (NHMC) and Latino Voices conducted a national survey that asked nine hundred non-Latinx participants questions about their media consumption and their opinions about Latinxs and immigrants. They also conducted an online experiment in which three thousand non-Latinxs were exposed to videos, articles, and audio sources related to Latinxs and immigrants. Their study discovered:

1. News and entertainment media have a strong influence on non-Latinx perceptions about Latinxs and immigrants.
2. Most people attribute a mix of positive and negative stereotypes to Latinxs and immigrants.
3. Media portrayals of Latinxs and immigrants can diminish or exacerbate stereotypically negative opinions about them.[14]

Common negative stereotypes attributed to Latinxs by respondents included being less educated than others, being welfare recipients, having too many children, refusing to learn English, and taking away employment opportunities from Americans.[15]

These stereotypes went hand-in-hand with the limited portrayals of Latinxs they noted seeing in the media: Latinxs as gang members or criminals, as landscapers and gardeners, and as housekeepers and maids.[16]

For people with little familiarity with Latinxs, media exposure to stereotypes was particularly influential in developing opinions and attitudes. When it came to the news, the type of news source consumed was associated with the non-Latinx respondents' perceptions of Latinxs. People who received their news from National Public Radio and MSNBC were far less likely than others to hold negative opinions about Latinxs, while people whose main source of news was Fox News were far more likely to buy into negative stereotypes. In terms of perceptions of Latinxs' legal statuses, between 48 and 62 percent of respondents believed that most Latinxs are "illegal" or undocumented immigrants. This was particularly apparent among respondents who were shown negative news stories about Latinxs from entertainment, TV news, radio, and print sources.[17] Even when people were exposed to positive media clips, if it was in the format of a positive clip from a TV show or a positive radio story, over 50 percent of participants still reported that to be Latinx is to be an "illegal immigrant." The authors concluded that this myth is such a strong one that it cannot easily be dispelled with one brief exposure to a positive story.

The conclusion of the authors is backed by a long history of documentation that shows myths about Latinxs are firmly woven into the historical fabric of media coverage in the United States. The stories about Latinxs that make it to network and cable news coverage are typically ones that focus upon social problems and that overemphasize coverage of undocumented immigrants.[18] As noted in Otto Santa Ana's book, *Juan in a Hundred: Representations of Latinxs on Network News*, very little news coverage of substance relevant to Latinx communities exists (only about one story in one hundred on major networks in 2004), and a basic ignorance of the differences between various Latinx populations from North America, South America, and Central America is apparent in the mainstream English-language media.[19] News stories that focus on Latinxs tend to be about emergencies, and rarely include the general coverage one would expect related to well-known community and national figures. Define American and the Norman Lear Center for the Study of Entertainment, Media & Society report that out of the 143 episodes of forty-seven television shows that they analyzed in 2017 and 2018, immigrants are underrepresented on the whole.[20] When they were included on television shows, they were overrepresented as criminals and incarcerated people. Women immigrants and black undocumented immigrants were underrepresented on television, and immigrants were portrayed as less educated on television than they are in real life.

The Latinx Disconnect in the Media

Frances Negrón-Muntaner and Chelsea Abbas found that there is a "Latino Disconnect" when it comes to the media in an age in which large media companies are merging together into mega-corporations such as Comcast-NBCUniversal.[21] The disconnect occurs in spite of the fact that there are more Latinxs both consuming and creating media than ever before. When companies merge there is not a corresponding increase in diverse programming, diverse leadership, or diverse employment in general.[22] The researchers did find one change after mergers occurred: an increase in the presence of Latinxs in stereotypical television roles as criminals/inmates, law enforcers, janitors, and maids. In terms of the news, over 64 percent of NBC news stories from 2012 to 2014 focused on Latinxs only in the context of "illegal immigration" and crime. The frequent characterization of Latinxs as threats has a particular power in this day and age when so many people depend on entertainment and news media for their information.

In spite of the fact that user-generated media content may hold some hope for challenging these stereotypes, some research indicates that user-generated material on YouTube overwhelmingly reinforces the same stereotypes of racial and ethnic minorities that are found in the mainstream media.[23] In the case of Latinxs, the stereotype of the sexualized woman was the most common, followed by that of the criminal or law breaker.[24]

MEDIA STEREOTYPES OF LATINX IMMIGRANTS AND IMMIGRATION FUELING FEAR

> If there has been one constant in both pre- and post-9/11 public discourse on national security, it has been the alleged threat to the nation posed by Mexican and other Latin American immigration.
>
> —Leo Chavez[25]

When Latinx immigrants are referred to in the media, it is often in negative terms as "invaders," "parasites," and "weeds."[26] Anthropologist Leo Chavez explains that popular discussions of immigration in the United States have long been characterized primarily in terms of "the Latino threat."[27] This threat is communicated through the use of several themes that are used so frequently through media stories that they eventually become believable to observers.

- Latinxs are a reproductive threat, altering the demographic makeup of the nation.
- Latinxs are unable or unwilling to learn English.
- Latinxs are unable or unwilling to integrate into the larger society; they live apart from the larger society, not integrating socially.
- Latinxs are unchanging and immutable; they are not subject to history and the transforming social forces around them; they reproduce their own cultural world.
- Latinxs, especially Latinxs of Mexican origin, are part of a conspiracy to reconquer the southwestern United States, returning the land to Mexico's control.[28]

As noted above, the threat of Latinx immigration has almost always been equated with Mexican immigration and immigrants specifically (until very recently when it has been expanded to Central American women and children).[29] In her essay examining the media's creation of a false immigration crisis, Sylvia Mendoza highlighted some fundamental questions about the unfair coverage of immigrants:

> Where is the fair coverage of immigrants? . . . When the camera swings on issues of illegal immigration, immigrants "taking" Americans' jobs, how government services are being funneled to illegal immigrants and costing taxpayers money, and terrorism threats, the B-roll pans on Latinxs, mostly Mexicans, although they are definitely not the only immigrants coming into the country.[30]

Inventing a Criminological Story

The implication that immigrants are especially likely to commit acts of crime does not have any factual backing. Scholars Rubén Rumbaut and Walter Ewing found by studying census data and other sources that incarceration rates among young men, both documented and undocumented, were the lowest among immigrants across the board.[31] Nevertheless, the unjustified association between Latinx immigrants and crime persists and is spread through multiple media forms. Visual depictions of the southern border of the United States often show startling pictures of law enforcement use of drones, guns, helicopters, and car chases in the news and entertainment media, which sends a message that the government is, and should be, protecting the country against dangerous border crossers.[32]

Promoting Hate Speech

The consideration of immigration in media often crosses the line from disagreements about policy to hostile and hateful characterizations of Latinx immigrants. For example, a recent study of readers' online comments on newspaper stories about immigration in border states demonstrated that they were often expressions of violence, racism, and xenophobia.

> Cockroaches, locusts, scumbags, rats, bums, buzzards, blood sucking leeches, vermin, slime, dogs, brown invaders, wetbacks. Drawn from online comment boards, these are among the terms used today to describe Latin American immigrants. These Latinxs, according to some of the more vicious commenters, should be hunted down like deer and shot on sight; left to die from choking on beans; eviscerated by piranhas; run over in the street like dogs and rounded up in cattle cars and roasted in oven chambers.[33]

The hate speech against Latinx immigrants on online newspaper forums is similarly present on talk radio. In fact, the National Hispanic Media Coalition conducted a study of talk radio coverage in which they found that the level and type of hate speech leveled at immigrants and their families in the United States was similar to that of the propaganda used in the Rwandan genocide to turn people against one another.[34] In one chilling example, they included transcripts of calls made during a 2011 Los Angeles radio show with hosts John and Ken on KFI AM (Clear Channel Radio). John and Ken were badmouthing immigrants and then encouraged listeners to target one specific immigrant activist, Jorge-Mario Cabrera, by giving them his cellphone number. He received over five hundred calls, many of which threatened his life and the life of others. Typical content of the calls included statements like, "You illegal immigrant piece of shit, motherfucker. We will do everything to fight you motherfuckers until you're all dead, you're all motherfucking dead."[35] When Spanish-language media outlets requested interviews with Ken and John, they stated that they would never talk to them because they would only speak to English-language reporters who have legal residents as their viewers, rather than "illegal aliens."[36]

Creating Threatening Imagery

In addition to written and spoken media forms, pictures and visuals are often used in news stories to communicate ideas about immigration. Kathy Bussert-Webb, a scholar of language education, studied news photos of a Latinx neighborhood in an unincorporated border area in Texas called "Esperanza" along with data from interviewees of local children, parents, and school staff.[37] She examined the messages conveyed about Esperanza by the photos and compared those messages to those of community members, a portion of whom were undocumented. She used a method related to poetics to summarize her findings. Bussert-Webb concluded, "The news photos portrayed Esperanza as a seedy site where criminals surged, yet community-based photos depicted a lively neighborhood where families converged." The children and parents in this neighborhood all had high aspirations for the children's educational achievement and future career paths, yet the negative portrayals of the neighborhood and the people in it put a damper on their ambitions.[38] This contrast between media coverage and the experiences of community residents is par for the course in much mainstream media. The internalization of negative messages collectively affects the morale and hope of a community marginalized in multiple ways.

The negative imagery that characterizes Latinxs as unwanted and badly intentioned migrants has been linked to public support for punitive legislation against undocumented immigrants. One example of this was the use of such imagery in the media to support the passage of Proposition 187 in California in 1994, which limited the access of undocumented immigrants to public services and institutions such as hospitals and schools (it was quickly stopped by the courts after it was passed by California voters). Sociolinguist Otto Santa Ana analyzed the metaphors used to describe immigration in the *Los Angeles Times* during the campaign for the proposition, and found that the primary one was "immigration as dangerous waters."[39] Immigrants were referred to as "a sea of brown faces," "a brown tide," and an "overwhelming flood" as well as in multiple other terms that invoked the image of a rough sea against which U.S. residents needed to brace themselves.[40] Ultimately, the message that was emphasized by the newspaper was that the "rising brown tide will wash away Anglo cultural dominance."[41]

In another example, news coverage of the Central American and Mexican immigrant communities in English-language media in Phoenix, Arizona, became more stigmatizing and negative during times in which punitive laws aimed at Latinx immigrants were proposed and passed than in times when they were not.[42] Sociologist Cecilia Menjívar studied this coverage and explained that loaded terminology like "criminal alien" and "illegals" was used more often in Phoenix's primary newspaper preceding the period when restrictive laws were passed than terms such as "undocumented" were.[43] In fact, the term "undocumented" was used much less in 2010 in the *Arizona Republic*'s immigration articles (in 11 percent of them) than it was in 2005 (in 36 percent of them), which mirrored the tough-on-immigrant trend that was going strong at the end of decade. These terminology choices, in conjunction with the media practice of shining light on public officials' and community members' characterizations of immigrants as uneducated, violent smugglers, and law breakers, helped cement the idea that Latinx immigrants were a social problem that must be dealt with punitively. Menjívar found that immigrant workers in Phoenix were disturbed by the negative media coverage and resisted it by emphasizing their role as law-abiding workers who contributed in various ways to U.S. society.

MOMENTS OF MAINSTREAM MEDIA RESISTANCE

There are moments in which we can witness mainstream media resistance to the marginalization of immigrants. An example of this was when the Associated Press agreed to quit using the term "illegal" to describe immigrants themselves, and to reserve it to describe actions if appropriate.[44] This change in coverage was inspired by immigrant and racial justice activists' campaigns, such as Drop the I-Word.[45] Their revised language policy resulted in a significant decrease in the use of the term in AP stories compared to the stories of other national news outlets, such as *USA Today* and the *Washington Post*.[46]

Another way that mainstream media resists the creation of moral panics about unauthorized migration is to produce detailed stories about *why* it occurs. Although television news and newspapers have been found to sometimes reference large-scale factors influencing immigration, such as the instability of Latin American countries' economies, they rarely discuss the United States' role in creating such instability or any possible actions to address macro-level factors.[47] Not surprisingly, journalists' recommendations to address immigration focused upon immigration reform or increased border patrol and law enforcement.

When media coverage of Latinx immigrants does counter the typical negative stereotypes, one common storyline is often used: news reporters share images and stories about "good" immigrant parents and children who are working toward the American Dream through hard work and merit.[48] Although the determination and efforts of immigrants are vital parts of the collective immigrant story, this type of reporting ultimately pits immigrants against each other in categories of worthy and not worthy. This is harmful because it hides the societal barriers that shape immigrants' ability to obtain a satisfying livelihood, financial stability, and safety and focuses only on individuals' actions. This type of incomplete storytelling about immigrants was apparent when the Development, Relief and Education for Alien Minors (DREAM) Act was being proposed and debated in the early 2010s. Newspaper coverage of that time emphasized stories about undocumented families who were in financial need, whose members were hardworking and/or excellent students, and were assimilating into American society.[49] The implication of such stories was that those who did not fit into the cookie-cutter mold of the "good" immigrant were undeserving of inclusion in immigration reform.

Humane Representations of Immigrants and Immigration

> This has just come out from the Associated Press. This is incredible. Trump administration officials have been sending babies and other young children (pauses, as choking up) to at least three (pauses, tearing up) . . . three tender age shelters in South Texas. Lawyers and medical providers . . . I think I am going to hand this off. Sorry, that does it for us tonight. We'll see you again tomorrow.
>
> —Rachel Maddow on her MSNBC show
> *The Rachel Maddow Show* (June 20, 2018)[50]

In spite of the many examples of inflammatory media coverage about undocumented Latinx immigration, people are using media forms to counter these misrepresentations. As the traditional news organizations slowly become more diverse, the news that is created and shared is also based on a greater diversity of experiences and sources.[51] Groups like the National Association for Hispanic Journalists and the National Latino Media Council are making waves by pushing for increasing Latinx representation in the news and entertainment media and stories that reflect the complexity of Latinx experiences. The tools that are now available to organizations producing online news, such as the use of web links to connect with additional content and embedded multimedia content, are being used to paint accurate pictures of the immigrant experience and the social factors shaping them.[52] Alternative news sources and forms also serve as counterbalances to stereotypical stories of lawbreaking immigrants.

In addition to humane coverage of immigrants in the news media, some films and television shows on mainstream English-language networks include complex characters that are undocumented. These portrayals challenge the status quo, similar to the tradition present in Spanish-language media.[53] Also, activists using traditional and social media tools are making significant headway in many campaigns in the immigrant rights struggle. Latinxs are an increasingly important consumer block, and are demonstrating a great deal of progress in terms of using the Internet and

Figure 2.1. Journalistic teams that aim for humanistic coverage of immigration stories challenge myths about immigration.
Jovaughn Stephens, Unsplash

digital tools to spread information.[54] The availability of programming such as National Public Radio's *Latino USA*, magazines like *Latina*, websites like the Immigrant Archive Project, Rewire.News, *Remezcla*—and all of their Twitter feeds—show that there are media spaces now where well-rounded coverage of immigration thrives. As discussed in Box 2.1, the expertise of nonprofit leaders in organizations like Define American are helping entertainment professionals develop humane representations of immigrants in their media products.

Comics

All sorts of media forms are being used to reject stereotypes and inform the audience—even comic books! Immigration rights activists have long used Superman as an example of the ultimate undocumented immigrant who crosses borders without papers.[55] In 2017, DC Comics Number 987 (written by Dan Jurgens) features Superman preventing Latinx immigrants from being killed by a white supremacist. In the issue the perpetrator is upset that he was laid off, blames his immigrant co-workers for taking his job, and attempts a mass shooting.[56] Superman acts as a shield and stops the shooting. He responds to the man's outcries of "They *stole* from me! *Ruined me!*" by stating, "The only person responsible for the blackness smoothing your soul—is YOU." Superman is shown leaving the scene by giving law enforcement officers instructions to make sure the workers are safe. Although Superman

BOX 2.1 DEFINE AMERICAN'S IMMIGRATION GUIDE FOR ENTERTAINMENT PROFESSIONALS

The nonprofit Define American has created a guide for entertainment professionals to help them create stories that reflect facts about immigration. The organization, founded by Jose Antonio Vargas, an immigration activist who came to the United States from the Philippines at the age of twelve and author of *Dear America: Notes of an Undocumented Citizen*, provides a glossary of general immigration and immigration law terms; a breakdown of the kind and quality of immigration representation in TV and film; tips for creating responsible media on immigrants; and an overview of DACA, the global economy, and the benefits that immigrants specifically bring to the U.S. economy! The guide links readers to news videos and to testimonies of young adults sharing their immigration stories.

In its guide, Define American shares the results of studies showing that the vast majority of immigrant characters on TV are heterosexual and male, and 50 percent of Latinx immigrants on television are represented engaging in criminal activity.

Define American concludes their report with resources and recommendations for entertainment professionals: "Reach out to immigrant organizations that will consult with them about scripts, storylines, and legal issues; support diversity in the workplace by including diverse writers as staff; encourage new storylines that avoid tired, harmful and fear-based stereotypes; create nuanced portrayals of immigrants that more authentically depict the immigrant experience; consider challenging stereotypes against immigrants through comedy; and add immigrant characters into everyday storylines."

Source: Define American. 2017. *Immigrants and Immigration: A Guide for Entertainment Professionals.* (https://defineamerican.com/ent/guide/).

ignored the important social factors that influence mass shooters in his response, he criticized the scapegoating of immigrants and relayed the message that social control agents need to be sensitive to the biases and hate aimed at immigrant workers.

In 2015, the writer of the Captain America comic started a new run of the series that focuses on a character, Sam Wilson (formerly the character Falcon), who shared the honor of being Captain America. The writer and the comic garnered a lot of attention because not only was the new Captain America black instead of white, but also because he defended the rights of undocumented immigrants against negative stereotyping and violence on the part of militias.[57] In one scene from this series, Captain America stands up against a group of militia members called the Sons of Serpents. The group is blocking undocumented immigrants from entering the country at the U.S.-Mexico border and the leader claims they all come with "trouble, disease, and crime."[58] The supremacists are shown capturing immigrants and sending them to be used in experiments. Captain America rescues Joaquin Torres, a Good Samaritan who leaves water in the desert for border crossers, from the clutches of the evil experimenters. Joaquin, a character who came with his mother and grandmother to the United States from Mexico when he was six, eventually becomes the new Falcon, and ally of Captain America. He engages in activities like protesting anti-immigration speakers at a college campus—something you don't see comic book characters doing every day.[59] Although many politically conservative comic book readers made it clear that they didn't like the idea that a superhero's sidekick, a "good" character in a comic, could be an undocumented person of Mexican origin, many others have considered it to be groundbreaking.

Television Shows

A new wave of television shows in the 2000s addresses immigrant experiences in complex ways. For example, *Master of None* and *Fresh Off the Boat* have drawn large numbers of viewers by examining the experiences of the children of immigrants (from India and Taiwan respectively) and those of their parents and grandparents. Writer Carolyn Framke notes that the shows that are successful in pushing back against conventional images of immigrants do the following:

1. They portray different immigration experiences through different generations.
2. They never reduce immigrants to one-note stereotypes.
3. Firsthand experiences are valued over secondhand assumptions.[60]

Some of the television shows that have highlighted the experiences of undocumented Latinxs in recent years on English-language television include *Ugly Betty, Jane the Virgin, The Good Wife,* and *One Day at a Time.*

Ugly Betty is a show that was adopted from the Colombian telenovela *Yo Soy Betty La Fea*, and the Mexican version of that show, *La Fea Más Bella*. During its time on the air (2006–2010), it was a primetime hit for a mainstream network, ABC, and featured a diverse cast of characters who directly addressed immigration laws and policies.[61] Betty Suarez, the main character played by America Ferrera, is a personal assistant at a fashion magazine in New York City. Her family is of Mexican descent and lives in Queens. Betty's father, Ignacio Suarez, played by Tony Plana, is revealed to be undocumented in the first season of the show. Subsequently, the show highlights the many financial and family dilemmas that arise as a result of his status—including his problems accessing health care and the need to hire an immigration lawyer.

In a stunning revelation, Ignacio reveals that he did not apply for citizenship because he killed someone who was abusing Betty's mother in Mexico and fled.

Ultimately, Ignacio is saved from being deported because a higher-up at Betty's workplace pulled strings to prevent it. Although there are elements of this storyline that can be seen as reinforcing stereotypes,[62] for example, the fact that Ignacio migrated to the United States after committing a crime, there are many other elements that counter stereotypes of immigrants as lazy and/or flawed. What is clear is that the show effectively shed light on the difficulties created by U.S. immigration policies. Producers Salma Hayek, Fernando Gaitán, and Silvio Horta, as well as the lead actors of *Ugly Betty*, have been vocal in support of humane immigration reform.[63] (Fun fact: Years after the end of *Ugly Betty*, America Ferrera was one of the speakers at the 2017 Women's March on Washington. She inspired others through a rousing speech in which she declared, "We will not go from being a nation of immigrants to a nation of ignorance."[64])

On *Jane the Virgin*, a hit television show on the CW network, Alba Villanueva, the grandmother of the main character, Jane, is an unauthorized immigrant from Venezuela. The character speaks in Spanish on the show and her lines are subtitled. In one of the show's episodes, Alba finds herself in the hospital with a coma. When hospital staff find out she does not have legal documentation nor health insurance, they tell her family that they will have to notify Immigrations and Customs Enforcement and deport her back to Venezuela.[65] At this point the producers of the show freeze the screen and show a typed message stating that medical repatriation is a real thing: "Yes, this really happens. Look it up #immigrationreform."[66] Although Alba is ultimately spared deportation after she awakens from her coma, her fear of being deported after forty years in the United States stays with her throughout future episodes of the show.[67] When she tries to talk to an immigration lawyer, she finds she might have difficulties applying for citizenship because her daughter who is sponsoring her has a criminal record. *Jane the Virgin*'s storyline points out how complicated the process is for people who are working towards legal residency. Nevertheless, on the show she is shown to eventually get a green card. Box 2.2 highlights the many ways that the actors and writers of *Jane the Virgin* support immigrant causes outside of the show as well.

BOX 2.2 *JANE THE VIRGIN* ACTORS AND WRITERS: SUPPORTING IMMIGRANT STORIES

Jane the Virgin actors and writers are among the leading Latinx advocates for richer portrayals of immigrant lives on television. Diane Guerrero, who plays Lina on the show, has used her celebrity status to tell the story of her family's experiences of being separated through deportation. Guerrero first shared her story with the *Los Angeles Times* in an editorial, explaining that when she was fourteen and living in Boston, her family members were deported back to Colombia. She was left living alone in the United States. Her book, *In the Country We Love: My Family Divided* (with coauthor Michelle Burford), presents a firsthand account of life in a mixed-status family. Fox Studios is using her story as the basis for a television show. Guerrero is a passionate advocate for just immigration reform, and she met twice with Barack Obama during his presidency to discuss the matter.

Gina Rodríguez, the star of *Jane the Virgin*, is producing two shows related to immigration for CBS. In the first, *Rafa the Great*, she is working with *Jane the Virgin* writer Rafael Agustin, an Ecuadorian immigrant, to create a family sitcom about his experiences after finding out he was undocumented during high school. The second show, *Have Mercy* (based on the German television show, *Dr. Illegal*), is a show about a Latinx immigrant who resorts to running an illegal medical clinic out of her home. This occurs after she migrates to Miami, Florida, and is no longer able to practice as a doctor.

In addition to her strong support of Latinx immigrants in the media, Rodríguez is also investing her money to help community members. For example, she convinced the network of her show, the CW, to use funds for Emmy season publicity to instead bankroll a four-year college education for a Latinx undocumented teen.

Sources:

Andreeva, Nellie. 2017. "Gina Rodriguez Producing Immigration Series Projects at CBS and the CW, 'LA Story' Reboot." *Deadline*, September 7. (https://deadline.com/2017/09/gina-rodriguez-immigration-projects-cbs-the-cw-la-story-reboot-1202162452/).

Bakare, Lanre. 2017. "'Daca Dramas': How Immigration Became US TV's New Obsession." *The Guardian*, September 13. (https://www.theguardian.com/tv-and-radio/tvandradioblog/2017/sep/13/daca-dramas-immigration-tv-us).

Corriston, Michele. 2016. "Actress Diana Guerrero on Her Parents' Deportation, Immigration Reform: 'I Definitely Fell Through the Cracks.'" SiriusXM, May 12. (http://blog.siriusxm.com/2016/05/12/jane-the-virgin-diane-guerrero-immigration-reform/).

Fernandez, Maria Elena. 2018. "Why You Could Be Seeing a Lot of Immigrant Stories This Fall." Vulture, January 23. (http://www.vulture.com/2018/01/immigrant-stories-could-be-fall-tvs-biggest-trend.html).

Khosla, Proma. 2018. "Meanwhile, Gina Rodriguez Used 'Jane the Virgin' Funds to Send an Immigrant Kid to College." Mashable, June 19. (https://mashable.com/2018/06/19/gina-rodriguez-jane-the-virgin-undocumented-college-student/#3yfDOj5GLqq6).

In another high profile example, on the television show *The Good Wife* (2009–2016), America Ferrera plays Natalie Flores, a former nanny of a state attorney candidate. Natalie is undocumented and on Season 2 of the show, one of the main characters, Eli Gold, the campaign manager of her state attorney candidate's opponent, is determined to use her status to help his candidate's political campaign. Yet, Eli ends up being so taken with her intelligence and ambition that he changes his mind. He instead works to prevent Natalie's father from being deported. In the course of the episodes dealing with Natalie's situation, the show addresses how comprehensive immigration reform would benefit many people who could develop their talents more fully than they could otherwise.[68] Later in Season 5, Natalie is again on the show seeking legal representation from the main character's law firm for her friend who was about to be deported unless he testified against a drug cartel leader (he was mistaken for someone with the same name). The storyline involved a number of complicated twists and turns, and highlighted the connections between the criminal justice and immigration systems in the United States.[69]

One Day at a Time, a series on Netflix, is a remake of the popular sitcom with the same name from the late 1970s and early 1980s, but set in Echo Park, Los Angeles with a Latinx cast. Justina Machado plays a veteran and the head of a Cuban-American family, Penelope. She and her mother, Lydia, played by legendary Puerto Rican actress Rita Moreno, guide her two children through life's ups and downs. In the first season, daughter Elena (Isabella Gomez) deals with the pain her best friend Carmen experiences after her parents get deported and she must move to another state. In the second season, son Alex (Marcel Ruiz) has to process what it means to have slurs like "Go Back to Mexico" yelled at him.[70] Lydia is also experiencing emotional upheaval as the result of the changes to federal immigration policy because she is not a U.S. citizen. The viewers see her struggle with the fear of deportation. Lydia's discussions with her landlord Schneider (Todd Grinnell), a Canadian from a wealthy background who is also not a U.S. citizen, help viewers understand the role that ethnicity, social class, and institutional racism play in the world of immigration law. Actress Justina Machado, whose parents are from Puerto Rico, has stated that she is proud of the realistic approach the show takes in light of the current political climate in the United States: "I don't even know what it feels like to be scared to be deported. But I do know what it feels like to be a Latina . . . and I love that this Cuban-American family is dealing with [Trump's presidency] the way this Cuban-American family would deal with it."[71]

Many other television shows have attempted to portray a rounded discussion of immigration issues in recent years, including *Scandal, Being Mary Jane, Last Man Standing, Newsroom, Superstore, The Affair,* and *Orange Is the New Black.* In spite of the uptick in shows countering stereotypes about undocumented immigrants, they still tend to give an unrealistic portrayal of what happens to folks caught at the crosshairs of the social control complex. Most of the time characters obtain citizenship status and/or are saved from deportation at the last minute, which increasingly does not happen in real life.[72]

Documentaries and Feature Films

The use of film to highlight issues of undocumented immigration is a powerful method to address stereotypes and preconceived notions of viewers. Films have long examined issues of immigration; unauthorized Latinx immigration in particular was aptly addressed in movies such as Gregory Nava's *El Norte* (a 1983 film about a brother and sister migrating without papers from Guatemala to the United States) and *My Family/Mi Familia* (a 1995 film about three generations of a family in L.A. who emigrated from Mexico). In the twenty-first century there have been a number of feature films that address the complexities of the topic. There has even been a short film in the form of a commercial for the *Jarritos* food brand (directed by Mexican actor Diego Luna) documenting the contributions of immigrants to the country![73]

Documentaries, films that document the lives of real people and events, are some of the most effective means of dispelling myths. In 2013, Jose Antonio Vargas, a journalist who was brought to the United States from the Philippines at age twelve, created a documentary, *Documented*, which addressed his life after revealing his legal status in the *New York Times Magazine*.[74] He explained that the simplistic view of undocumented immigration is troubling: "What I have found most tragic is how many people across the country use the term 'illegal' and Mexican interchangeably. Now I knew it was bad. I didn't know how bad it was until I really started traveling."[75] His documentary, which considers undocumented immigration among all groups of people, shatters stereotypes about who undocumented immigrants are and what they have achieved in spite of enormous obstacles.

Other recent documentaries take a similar angle. For example, in the 2010 documentary, *The Other Side of Immigration*, filmmaker Roy Germano, who was at the time a PhD student in political science, interviewed seven hundred people in small towns in Mexico in order to discover why so many people migrate to the United States and how it affects the folks that remain there. The documentary explores the social, economic, and political pressures that drive people to come to the United States, with or without legal authorization. A major idea in the documentary is that the immigration laws of another country matter very little when trying to simply survive. Germano explains:

> I suspect that most Americans would not think twice about migrating illegally to Canada if the U.S. economy was in ruins, or if we didn't have things like unemployment compensation or food stamps, and there were plenty of high-wage jobs to be done in Canada. By encouraging viewers to put themselves in the shoes of those doing the immigrating, I hope the film leaves Americans feeling uncomfortable with an immigration policy whose primary mission is to restrict entry.[76]

The documentary *Who is Dayani Cristal?*, directed by Marc Silver, takes a close look at the lives that are risked and sometimes lost as people migrate to the United States across the unforgiving desert.[77] The film begins in 2010 with an announcement in the background that parts of Arizona's draconian immigration bill SB 1070 were put on hold. It quickly cuts to footage of the Arizona Coroner's Office in Tucson where investigators are attempting to figure out the identity of a deceased body. The person has two large tattoos on his back, "Dayani" and "Cristal." In the rest of the documentary, the examiners and investigators are shown doing the gruesome work of trying to identify this body and the bodies of others who died in the Sonoran desert while migrating to the United States. This footage is interspersed with footage of well-known Mexican actor Gael García Bernal tracing the steps that Central American migrants often make by joining them on their journey to the U.S.-Mexico border. The film shows the harsh realities of immigration and makes it clear that the risks that people take are based upon the need to survive and to support themselves and their loved ones. The laws and policies that drive people to brave such harsh conditions to migrate are also prominent in the background of this film.

Don't Tell Anyone (*No Le Digas a Nadie*) tells the story of immigrant rights activist Angy Rivera, and her experiences living in the United States after migrating with her family from Colombia at three years of age.[78] In her 2015 documentary, filmmaker Mikaela Shwer addresses the many stressors that undocumented immigrants face and how legal status affects all aspects of life, including relationships and education. It shows how undocumented youth have to grow up fast and deal with a tremendous amount of stress. In an interview in *Latina* magazine about the film, Rivera noted that in her perspective the film has two main messages: (1) "Our fight for immigrant rights is way more beyond having immigration papers" and (2) that undocumented immigrants are shown as "people—people deserving of love, of support and also as survivors of assault—also surviving and being strong and powerful people."[79] Rivera experienced sexual abuse at the hands of her stepfather, and the film shows that she was able to apply for and obtain a U-Visa, a visa created in 2000 under the Victims of Trafficking and Violence Protection Act for victims of crime who have suffered serious mental or physical harm.[80] *Don't Tell Anyone* allows the viewers to focus on the story of Rivera and her mother and puts immigrant women's experiences in the spotlight.

Robert Reyes used an online format to distribute his short 2016 documentary, *Barbarians*, about two men who are attempting to cross back to the United States after being deported to Mexico. The documentary was inspired by Reyes' 2015 film, *Purgatorio*, which also examines the harsh realities and economic forces driving immigration.[81] *Barbarians*, which was made available on *The Atlantic* website,[82] begins with a powerful statement about how people say the United States is at war with the invaders who are crossing the border to come into the country daily. The narrator points out that building a wall is put forward as the only way to save us.

The documentary focuses on the experiences of twenty-five-year-old Victor and forty-six-year-old Alberto, who became friends after they were deported. They have no money and are hungry living on the streets. They discuss their families, the fact they haven't been able to talk with them for months due to their situations, and the beauty and poverty of the towns that they are from in Mexico. Both men are planning to get back across the border without the help of *coyotes* or drug smugglers. They go to the existing border wall where helicopters circle around them as they speak about the need to find work in order to survive. The viewers see Alberto scale the wall and stay on top for a minute or two. He comes back down and the film ends as Reyes notes:

> I realize that no matter how many times they cross the wall, they will not be the real invaders. The real invader does not need to cross the desert. It does not come from a strange land or speak a different language. It is not hungry or desperate to feed its family. The real invader is already here—with us. Sitting at our dinner table, an angry and paranoid creature born from our fears and nightmares.[83]

In addition to documentaries, there have also been traditional films released in the past decade that provide nuanced depictions of immigration and immigrants. *Under the Same Moon* (Spanish title: *La Misma Luna)* is a movie that focuses on the issues that arise when parents and children are separated due to migration. In the 2007 film, Rosario, the mother of a nine-year-old boy named Carlitos, migrates to Los Angeles to find work and leaves her son in Mexico with relatives. Rosario calls Carlitos every Sunday morning from a payphone to see how he is doing and he tells her he misses her dearly. Due to a chain of circumstances, Carlitos becomes the acquaintance of two *coyotes* who smuggle children over the border and decides he wants to cross over to the United States to see his mother again. The movie follows his journey and although a fictional account, it provides a sense of what unaccompanied migrant children experience and the challenges undocumented immigrants of all ages experience.

The movie *A Better Life* (2011) focuses on the story of a father and son who are undocumented and live in Los Angeles, California. The father, Carlos, is a gardener, and the son, Luis, is a high school student. Carlos is given the opportunity to buy out the owner of the business, his boss, but he is reluctant to because of financial reasons. After getting a loan from his sister to buy his boss's truck and tools, he runs into one complication after another. The film shows the intricate ways that people look out for their families in their home country by sending money back and putting them first. It also depicts the heart-wrenching tragedies that occur as families are torn apart by deportation orders in spite of doing their best to make a better life. The lead actor of the film, Demián Bichir, was nominated for an Academy Award for best actor for the film, and was the first Latino nominated for that award since 1964.[84]

Spare Parts (2015) is a film based upon the true story of four Latinx students from Carl Hayden Community High School in Phoenix, Arizona, three of whom are undocumented immigrants from Mexico, who entered a national underwater robotics competition against students from elite universities. This film was the second to cover this set of events and followed the 2014 documentary *Underwater Dreams*, directed by Mary Mazzio. It differed from the documentary, which included an in-depth consideration of immigration politics as well as the biographies of the young male team members and the founding female member who did not stay on the team. In *Spare Parts*, the viewer sees how the working-class boys creatively made the most of their limited resources and used spare parts to create their underwater robot that they affectionately named Stinky. With the help of their teachers, the team ultimately won first prize at the NASA-funded robotics competition. They won in spite of stiff competition from college teams from prestigious universities like MIT. Although the film does not address the larger forces that resulted in the youth's undocumented statuses in any depth, it does demonstrate that undocumented youth hold a great deal of promise and that investment in their success benefits society as a whole.[85]

User-Generated Digital and Social Media

Individuals and groups that use social media and their own user-generated digital media forms (e.g., digital audio-visual recordings, desktop publishing, computer-generated animation, image manipulation) are at the forefront of the cutting-edge media related to immigrants and immigrant rights today. We discuss social movements and resistance at length later in this book, so for now we will turn your attention to a few of the concrete ways that user-generated media are making an impact on the public's understanding of undocumented immigration. Whether these methods are focused on entertainment or activism, they allow immigrant communities and their allies to assert their presence and resist the normalization of negative stereotypes.

Armando Ibañez, an undocumented filmmaker and activist, created a YouTube web series called *UndocuTales* to provide a realistic look at the lives of immigrants.[86] Like Ibañez, the main character of the series, Fernando, is undocumented and came from Mexico to live in Los Angeles, California. The web series focuses on the ups and downs of Fernando's daily life as a queer man negotiating his sexuality and dealing with his legal status. Ibañez created the series to increase the accurate representations of LGBTQ Latinx people, to educate others, and to have others like him be able to say, "He doesn't have papers! That's me." He intends for the series to help unauthorized immigrants feel better and hopes it works to counter the anxiety and depression that is all too common in his community. He does this with one overarching goal in mind that he explains as, "I want to remind people how beautiful they are."[87]

Immigrant rights activists are using digital forms of media that focus upon what scholar Arely Zimmerman calls *transmedia testimonios*.[88] These *testimonios* allow activists to relay a message about their lives to the public through multiple media forms. For example, when youth activists were organizing around the DREAM Act, they "came out" and told the story about their undocumented statuses on digital videos and podcasts. These videos, inspired by coming-out videos by activists in the queer movement, were streamed on YouTube and linked to on Facebook.[89] By using these media forms, activists accomplished several important things: they helped build a collective identity as immigration activists with others sharing the same experiences, they organized actions to protest immigration policies and acts of enforcement, and they provided a counter story to the dominant negative story about undocumented immigrants.[90]

Media scholar and activist Sasha Costanza-Chock explains that transmedia organizing is characterized by vibrant and powerful efforts of youth activists:

> The history of the last decade of organizing by undocumented youth can be seen in the gorgeous graphics of Julio Salgado, in compelling, humorous, and emotional videos, in thoughtful blogs like *Undocumented and Unafraid* and Dreamactivist.net. In poetry, theater and films, such as *Mi Sueno, Papers, Define American,* and *The Dream Is Now,* and more.[91]

Individuals and groups have traditionally used digital media and social networking platforms such as Facebook, and its predecessor myspace, to get the word out about immigration-related causes. Groups like the Coalition for Human Immigrant Rights, United We Dream, Fair Immigration Reform Movement, the National Immigrant Youth Alliance, the National Day Labor Organizing Network, the National Council of *La Raza*, and Mijente currently all use Facebook as an organizing platform to send messages and post information about immigration related news and events. Presente.org used its Facebook page as one of several media strategies, including texting, to draw attention to their BastaDobbs.com ("Enough Dobbs!" campaign) and to recruit allies. The campaign focused upon ousting CNN network personality Lou Dobbs from his show due to his false statements about immigrants, his support for conspiracy theories and fear mongering, and his support of far right extremist groups' views.[92] Dobbs was released from his contract with CNN in November of 2009 and the campaign was thought to have been a central factor behind this event.[93] Undocumented students at UCLA used blogging as a powerful tool to organize a group known as Underground Undergrads. They took advantage of this low-cost communication tool, and with the help of staff and faculty at the UCLA Labor Center, created a strong network that led to the publication of a book about their efforts and the creation of a Dream Resource Center for undocumented students of all backgrounds.[94]

Twitter, the social networking tool that lets you reach your followers in relatively brief messages of 280 characters or less, has been used by immigration rights activists to good effect. Many hashtags such as #Not1More, #ShutDownICE, #Dreamers, and #keepfamiliestogether have caught on as scholars, community activists, and everyday people have spread the word about issues of immigration, law, deportations, and social organizing: In 2010, when Gaby Pacheco, Felipe Matos, Carlos Roa, and Juan Rodríguez spent four months walking from Miami, Florida, to Washington, DC, to deliver a series of messages to President Obama about immigration reform, they shared their journey with others via Twitter and Facebook. As Pacheco noted, their Trail of Dreams March and their social media presence was used "to show our love and all our passion and our desire to stay in the country."[95] The group of students shed light on the need to stop deportations, protect immigrant laborers, support the DREAM Act, and pass humane immigration reform.[96]

Figure 2.2.   User-generated social and digital media are allowing people to spread the word about the immigration rights movement in creative ways.
rawpixel, Unsplash

In another powerful example, in 2015 after one of Dora Sophia Ramirez's friends was faced with racist messages about immigration on Instagram, Ramirez worked with her and others to create the #WeAreSeeds campaign.[97] The campaign focused on resilience and the contributions of immigrant parents to the United States, and its name was inspired by a Mexican saying, "They tried to bury us, but they didn't know that we are seeds." They picked May 30th as the day for their campaign and their hashtag rapidly spread across the country.

As Sasha Costanza-Chock writes in *Out of the Shadows, Into the Streets: Transmedia Organizing and the Immigrant Rights Movement*, "the revolution will be tweeted—but tweets alone do not a revolution make."[98] In addition to widely publicized tweets, other social apps are useful for grassroots resistance and social change. In the aftermath of the Trump Administration's announcement of mass deportation plans in early 2017, social media apps were developed to help undocumented people deal with the attack on immigrants and their families. *Notifica* is an app that allows users to notify preexisting contacts with customized messages in the event that ICE detains them. The creator of *Notifica*, Adrian Reyna, stated that he wants to "do everything in my power to make sure that individuals aren't afraid and that they are able to live a life with the dignity and respect that they deserve."[99] Reyna, who is affiliated with United We Dream, worked with engineer Natalia Margolis at a digital agency called Huge to create the app. The app protects the messages that the user pre-loads with a

PIN in case something happens to the phone. There is an associated hotline as well for people who do not have a phone in reach when something occurs.[100]

Similarly, Cell 411 is designed for people to use in emergencies. It allows people to notify family and close friends when immigration officers come to question and/ or detain them.[101] The application has the ability for users to send their GPS coordinates to others so they can find them, as well as the ability to record and livestream videos that cannot be erased. Additionally, RedadAlertas is a web-based app that is in the works that will allow users to get secure notifications about ICE raids and checkpoints. The app idea was created by Celso Mireles, who was formerly undocumented, and it is being developed with the help of volunteers in accordance with social justice principles.[102]

Traditional media organizations have also used digital and user-generated social media tools to challenge the mainstream myths about immigration as well as to provide vivid footage about immigration enforcement. For example, when a woman living in Phoenix for over twenty years, Guadalupe Garcia de Rayos, was picked up by ICE and placed in a deportation van in February 2017, NBC news reporter Gadi Schwartz tweeted a picture of her son looking at her through the window of the van. Schwartz also explained that protestors in the area were trying to stop Garcia de Rayos' deportation by blocking the van.[103] The van had a poster on it that said "Keep Families Together" that was created by immigration advocates from the #Not1More anti-deportation campaign. In this case a representative of the mainstream media worked to reinforce a grassroots campaign's message. This type of reinforcement is increasingly common. In another example, *CBS This Morning* showed a video of undocumented children being held in a New York facility and interviewed the former employee who secretly taped it.[104]

Alternative news programs such as HBO's news program *Vice* and PBS's *Frontline* series create films and short documentaries with complex analyses about immigrants and the laws, policies, and social practices that affect them that are often streamed online. Cable news shows such as *The Rachel Maddow Show* regularly address the myths about undocumented immigration perpetuated by the Trump Administration and incorporate activists into their news coverage. For example, in one episode (April 17, 2017) Maddow's show featured the cofounder of United We Dream, Cristina Jimenez, who discussed the aftermath of Trump's deportation policies and shared a text message that could be used to join her group's campaign against deportation along with its Twitter hashtag #HereToStay. *LatinoUSA*, a radio show on National Public Radio, created a nearly hour-long podcast focusing on the Dream 9 and their experiences as leaders in a social movement for immigrant rights.[105]

ProPublica fueled concern about the family separation policy enacted by the Trump Administration after publishing an audio file of ten Central American migrant children loudly crying for their parents after being separated from them in mid-2018. The audio recording, made by an anonymous source inside of a U.S. Customs and Border Protection makeshift facility, included audio of a Border Patrol agent joking, "Well, we have an orchestra here. What's missing is a conductor."[106]

The audio recording was played for the U.S. Secretary of Homeland Security at a news briefing, and reporters asked her challenging questions about the family separation policy, which was officially rescinded by the Trump Administration two days later.[107]

In spite of a long tradition of denigration and disregard of unauthorized immigrants in the United States, all signs point to the fact that there is a developing trend of resistance underway. People are using new and traditional media forms in compelling ways that challenge stereotypical media portrayals of Latinxs and migrants. As we will see in the remaining chapters of this book, the use of different forms of communication is crucial to the illumination of everyday realities and the construction of new visions of a just world.

3

Shortchanged—Work and Labor

Arturo returns home from his landscaping job. His skin is burning and puffy mounds are swelling all over his body. His wife, alarmed, frantically pulls him to the kitchen table. She gives him cold water and demands to know what happened. She fears that it is a familiar story—and she is right. As his face begins to swell, Arturo tells her that he was cleaning a yard when his supervisor came to check on him. He pointed to some large bushes and told Arturo to take the blower and clean up fallen small branches that were just beyond the bushes. Arturo walked over to the bushes and put the blower on high, blasting what he thought would be small branches. Instead, he blew into a large beehive and the disturbed bees swarmed and stung him all over. His supervisor laughed uncontrollably, proud of the "prank" he pulled on Arturo. His wife is angry and urges Arturo to not return to the job. He insists that he must so that they can pay their rent and not risk the supervisor calling immigration on him. She pulls out towels, aspirin, and various salves that she brought from her hometown to begin treating the bee stings.[1]

The indignity, suffering, and fear that Arturo experienced at his job are not unique. Many unauthorized immigrants who work in the United States experience some form of human rights violation and affront to human decency at work. Some scholars describe the labor done by undocumented immigrants as the three Ds: demeaning, dirty, and dangerous.[2] More Latinx workers died in 2015 than in any year since 2007, according to the Payday Report; many of these deaths took place where there were high concentrations of undocumented workers.[3] In this chapter, we outline the contributions that undocumented immigrants make to our economy as well as the incredibly tough situations that many experience at work. We conclude with the consideration of a human rights framework that asserts the right for all to work in humane, safe conditions.

Myth: Undocumented immigrants don't do their fair share.
Myth Busted: Undocumented immigrants contribute more than they receive.

THE ECONOMIC CONTRIBUTIONS
OF UNAUTHORIZED IMMIGRANTS

The Institution on Taxation and Policy reported that undocumented immigrants contribute significantly to state and local taxes, collectively paying an estimated $11.74 billion a year.[4] In California, New York, and Texas, undocumented immigrants are paying the most (e.g., $3.1 billion, $1.1 billion, and $1.5 billion a year respectively in 2014).[5] If unauthorized immigrants were granted full citizenship, their state and local taxes would increase by over $2.18 billion a year, property taxes would increase by $362 million per year, and sales and excise taxes would increase by $702 million a year.[6] Every single state in the United States would benefit economically from giving citizenship status to undocumented immigrants.

Undocumented immigrants pay their "fair share" of taxes. Consider this: The top 1 percent of taxpayers pay an average nationwide effective tax rate of 5.4 percent on their income, whereas undocumented immigrants pay an average nationwide effective tax rate of 8 percent of their income in taxes.[7] Undocumented immigrants pay over $7 billion in sales taxes and $3.6 billion in property taxes. It is estimated that they pay $1.1 billion in personal income taxes.[8]

Big and small states benefit from undocumented immigrants' contributions. Of roughly 10.3 million immigrants, 2.9 million are undocumented or about 28 percent of all immigrants in California. The 2017 report, *Resilience in an Age of Inequality: Immigrant Contributions to California*, finds that immigrants comprise one-third of California's workers and that they contribute about one-third of the state's formidable GDP—some $715 billion each year, which is about the 2015 GDP for the entire state of Oklahoma. Yet, undocumented workers' households earn $16,100 per capita. (The per capita household income in California is $38,100.) Agriculture is the largest industry with undocumented immigrants. Farmworkers in California suffer more heat deaths and illness than workers in any other outdoor industry.[9] Also, in California, undocumented workers comprise a large share of the agriculture and construction industries, at 45 percent and 21 percent, respectively, and represent 10 percent of the state's total workforce.[10]

In Connecticut, a group called The New American Economy, which is a coalition of mayors and business leaders who support "sensible" immigration reform, found the nearly 130,000 undocumented Connecticut residents pay $397 million in annual federal, state, and local taxes, account for $3.1 billion in household income, and represent $2.7 billion in spending power.[11] In Connecticut, it is estimated that 13,028 are entrepreneurs. While Connecticut is one of the smaller states with undocumented immigrants, immigrants have a strong impact on the prosperity of the state.

A recent study of DACA recipients (undocumented people granted temporary work permits) and other undocumented young adults who were DACA-eligible by the Institute on Taxation and Economic Policy showed that state and local tax revenue increased about 1.7 billion dollars a year due to their contributions.[12] A total repeal of DACA would prevent 1.3 million undocumented people enrolled in DACA from contributing in the same way, and states and cities would lose approximately $700 million each year.[13]

The Surprising Role of the IRS

The Internal Revenue Service (IRS) has been a valuable source for economists and accountants to understand undocumented immigrants' fiscal contribution to the United States. The IRS does not discriminate on the basis of immigration status. About 50 percent of working undocumented immigrants pay income taxes through Individual Tax Identification Numbers (ITINs) and many who do not have ITINs still have payroll taxes taken out of their paychecks. In her investigative article, reporter Alexia Fernández Campbell described the "Earnings Suspense File," which is where uncollected taxes wait for workers to prove their employment and collect their benefits.[14] While efforts were made in 2014 to match unpaid benefits that have resided in the Earnings Suspense File since 1937, many believe that the 340 million unclaimed tax forms recorded were filed on behalf of employers for undocumented workers, who likely used false documents to obtain work and are unlikely to ever collect their benefits.[15] Stephan Gross, the chief actuary of the Social Security Administration explained: "Undocumented immigrants paid $13 billion into the retirement trust fund that year, and only got about $1 billion in benefits."[16] Fernández Campbell summarized that in 2010, about three million people paid over $870 million in income taxes using an ITIN, and ITIN filers pay $9 billion in payroll taxes annually.[17] Traditionally, a record of paying taxes through an ITIN can prove beneficial to an applicant's bid for citizenship.

A record of paying taxes and an ITIN has also helped some undocumented immigrants buy homes. The Pew Hispanic Center reported that 45 percent of undocumented immigrants living in the United States for over ten years own their own homes.[18] In Durham, North Carolina, the Latino Community Credit Union[19] and the Self-Help Credit Union[20] are local lenders that allow applicants to use their ITIN instead of Social Security numbers to obtain mortgages.[21] Citigroup, in partnership with Neighborhood Assistance Corporation of America, was the only national bank to offer this program.[22] ITIN loans in general outperformed standard loans through the Great Recession.[23] Unfortunately, state laws requiring Social Security numbers or proof of citizenship for driver's licenses limit the few financial lenders who are supporting undocumented families in this way.

As documented by economists, unauthorized immigrants pay taxes and this in turn helps local, state, and national economies. Until recently, there were incentives for undocumented immigrants to file tax returns. They helped demonstrate that people were contributing to the greater good in the United States and that they were responsible, which helped in citizenship cases and served as protective factors if ever faced with deportation orders. These incentives diminished with the election of Donald Trump as the forty-fifth president.[24] California Bay Area organizations that help low-income people prepare taxes for free immediately saw a drop in the number of appointments during the Trump Administration. Undocumented immigrants, once a significant proportion of their clientele, were feeling scared to file taxes.[25]

Francine Lipman, who teaches tax law at the University of Nevada, Las Vegas shared, "Sending in a tax return with your current address and information is very unnerving to a population that wants to comply with the law and is actually leaving significant refunds on the table by not filing tax returns."[26] Not only do undocumented immigrants lose out on showing their compliance with labor and tax laws, but the loss of tax revenue will likely be felt in future years.

Myth: Immigrants are "taking" Americans' jobs.
Myth Busted: There are different jobs for a diverse array of workers.

Figure 3.1. The cleaning and carework done by many undocumented workers fill an important demand.
rawpixel, Unsplash

THE SEGMENTED LABOR
MARKET AND THE MYTH OF JOB DISPLACEMENT

There have been public attempts to test the idea of undocumented immigrants' effect on the job market for citizens. Most economists explain that the myth of displacing jobs can be explained by the concept of a *segmented labor market*—there are all sorts of jobs for all sorts of workers and who are varyingly trained or prepared for these jobs.

Economist Kevin Shih explained immigration and the economy: Jobs are not a zero sum game—just because an immigrant has a job, it does not mean that a U.S.-born person loses a job.[27] First, since 2010, there has been a growth in jobs. Second, he shared the research of economists Giovanni Peri and Chad Sparber, who found that the influx of immigrants led U.S.-born workers to relative advantage (i.e., more communication-intensive jobs instead of labor-intensive jobs). Third, immigrants are not in every job sector, but rather are "highly overrepresented in either very low-skilled manual and labor-intensive jobs or very high-skilled science and engineering occupations."[28] Finally, he argued that beyond doing little-to-no harm, there is evidence that immigrants enhance the economy for everyone. Undocumented immigrants generate tax revenue that they may never use, and highly skilled immigrants increase innovation, and have been linked to modest gains in wages for highly skilled U.S.-born workers.

There are several well-publicized attempts at testing the "job threat" myth.[29] California senator Dianne Feinstein made available job openings for agricultural work to the many who were drawing unemployment from the government: none applied.[30] In South Carolina, Chalmers R. Carr III, the president of peach grower Titan Farms, told lawmakers at a 2013 hearing that he advertised two thousand job openings from 2010 through 2012. Carr said he was paying $9.39, which was $2 more than the state's minimum wage at the time. He ended up hiring 483 U.S. applicants, which was slightly less than a quarter of what he needed. On the first day 109 didn't show up for work. Carr testified that another 321 of the hires quit by the second day. Only thirty-one lasted for the entire peach season. In Sacramento, California, Brad Goehring, a fourth-generation farmer, advertised in local newspapers and accepted more than a dozen unemployed applicants from the state's job agency. Even when the average rate on his fields was $20 an hour, the U.S.-born workers quickly lost interest. He explained, "We've never had one come back after lunch."

International studies also find that immigrants do not displace citizen workers because of segmented labor markets—people with different qualifications take on different occupations within the same industry. Economists in the United Kingdom studied labor outputs from 1997 and 2007 and found that the UK economy benefited from immigrant labor, and one of the reasons for the increased productivity was that immigrants were found to work more hours.[31] However, this finding begs the question as to how well workers' rights were honored if they were working such long hours.

Labor Rights for Undocumented Workers

Undocumented workers have rights regardless of their immigration status. In California, the Industrial Welfare Commission Wage Order 5-2001 includes undocumented workers in all the codes created by the California Department of Industrial Relations, Division of Labor Standards Enforcement.[32] Some of these rights are relatively mundane, for example, for every four hours of work, every worker should have a ten-minute break or a meal period of thirty minutes if working more than five hours. Other examples are related to serious violations: any worker has the right to file a wage claim, to make a discrimination complaint, or to speak to the state labor commissioner office. Other laws are less known but equally important, such as if a worker reports for work as required by the employer, but the worker is not put to work, then the worker must be paid 50 percent of wages for that day. Also, an employer must pay an employee who is fired the same day or within seventy-two hours if the employee quits voluntarily. Finally, a crucial right for all workers is to file a workers' compensation claim and for the employer to provide the medical coverage for any injuries. However, the workers featured in this chapter are "shortchanged" and suffer enormously because of their precarious position as undocumented immigrants.

Agricultural Work: Backbreaking and Essential

According to the American Farm Bureau Federation, between 50 percent and 70 percent of all farmworkers in this country are unauthorized immigrants.[33] Agriculture is the occupation in the United States where undocumented immigrants are the majority.[34] Most farmworkers are no longer "migrant." The U.S. Department of Labor found that 78 percent of agricultural workers do not move with the seasons. And, there is a very small stream of newcomers from Mexico—just 2 percent—who enter the migrant seasonal workforce.[35] Researchers Ellen Kossek and Lisa Burke shared that "farmworkers are at the core of the $28 billion fruit and vegetable industry in the U.S., 85% of which is hand-harvested or cultivated."[36]

Food cultivation is no easy task; for example, the cultivation of strawberries is so brutal that it is twenty-five times more labor intensive than that of broccoli, and strawberries are referred to as *fruta del diablo* or "the Devil's fruit" as a result.[37] Strawberries are the most delicate of products, its pickers are among the lowest paid, and it is the crop most likely to be picked by undocumented workers.[38] Eric Schlosser included strawberries on his list of "black market" industries, along with marijuana production and pornography.[39]

Filmmakers of *The Unheard Story of America's Undocumented Workers* argued that agricultural workers in the Coachella Valley are "indispensable."[40] In 2015, California agriculture was a $47 billion industry. The average worker earned $21,000 a year for backbreaking, dangerous work. In the desert climate temperatures rise to 120 degrees in the summer, but in spite of the brutal heat, workers must cover themselves up completely due to the burn from pesticides. Agricultural labor rights legend César

Chavez worked extensively in the Coachella Valley. Hilario Torres, a union leader in Coachella Valley, explained that there is a long history of fighting for labor rights in immigrant communities. Yet there is also an intense fear in the community about immigration enforcement and concerns that beneficial educational programs for the children of agricultural workers may be ended. The hope of the next generation of agricultural worker families to break out of the low-income wage cycle depends on this support.

Undocumented immigrants are often vulnerable because employers can get away with not paying their wages if they are apprehended through workplace immigration raids and/or picked up by immigration enforcement in their communities or on their commute. While deportations were the highest during the Obama Administration (more so than all previous presidents combined), immigration raids have increased during the Trump Administration by 40 percent.[41]

Farmers, while often politically conservative, are advocating for immigration reform. They acutely feel the effects of workplace raids, a lack of workers, and fear in the community. In 2011, Alabama passed one of the harshest laws against undocumented immigrants. Although the law was deemed unconstitutional, the agricultural industry felt the reverberations:

> Tomato farms reported fewer than half their workers showed up the next week and chicken farmers said many of their employees flew the coop. The same for plant nurseries, building contractors, and more. Prices for tomatoes and other produce rose quickly up and down the East Coast.[42]

For those working in the fields, anthropologist Sarah Horton explained the problem of identity theft in the agricultural industry: "ghost" workers use someone else's Social Security card, sometimes provided by the labor recruiters or the farmers.[43] The people who provide their Social Security number to the employer to be used by undocumented workers get the bonus of getting Social Security benefits without having to work (they often pay for the employer to make this happen). This practice is used with both unauthorized workers and workers with legal status who use a different identity when working on Sundays—a day commonly known as "the day of the ghost."[44] This is how employers get around overtime and other labor violations.

The need for immigration reform to address such violations is apparent to not only the farmworkers themselves, but to their offspring, who have often worked hard to make the most of the opportunities that their families have provided. In Box 3.1, you can read the story of one such person who "shot for the stars" and made it there—but still remains very aware that the system is in need of serious change for it to be a just one.

Day Laborers: Vulnerable on the Streets

Home Depot is a place to buy supplies for construction and household repairs, and one can shop for labor in its parking lot. In Salt Lake City, Utah, reporter Lee

BOX 3.1 SHOOTING FOR THE STARS: ASTRONAUT JOSÉ MORENO HERNÁNDEZ

A little boy, after a long day working in the fields with his parents, looked up at the stars. He dreamt of one day being an astronaut and over the course of his life never gave up on his dream, despite enormous obstacles and repeated rejections. As one of the success stories of children of farmworkers, astronaut José Moreno Hernández has been vocal about needing to offer pathways to citizenship to undocumented immigrants.

Hernández was born in Stockton, California, to farmworking parents who followed the migrant seasons. As a child, he and his siblings joined his Mexican-born parents in the fields picking cucumbers, sugar beets, and tomatoes. His family would return to Michoacán, Mexico, between seasons, but permanently settled back in California after a second grade teacher insisted they stay for the sake of the children's education.

Hernández explained how space travel has impacted his view of the world and how he wishes leaders could share his perspective, recounting in a television interview: "I saw the world as one. There were no borders. You couldn't distinguish between the United States and Mexico." His autobiography, *Reaching for the Stars: The Inspiring Story of a Migrant Farmworker Turned Astronaut*, includes stories from his young childhood about learning English, and how he applied to the NASA Space Program eleven times before getting accepted. He also went on to become a mechanical engineer and even invented technology that is used to detect breast cancer.

Sources:

Clayton, Ashley. 2012. "From Migrant Farm Work to Shuttle Astronaut: Jose Hernandez Video." September 7. (http://www.space.com/17500-interview-with-former-astronaut-jose-hernandez-part-one-video.html).

Hernández, José. 2012. *Reaching for the Stars: The Inspiring Story of a Migrant Farmworker Turned Astronaut*. Center Street Publishers.

Watson, Julie. 2009. "U.S. Astronaut Says Legalize Undocumented Mexicans." Phys. Org, September 15. (https://phys.org/news/2009-09-astronaut-legalize-undocumented-mexicans.html).

Davidson covered the story about the day laborers in their town and the conflicts they encounter each day. The typical worker had a story like Gabriel, who waited each day at the edge of the parking lot hoping to get hired "landscaping, moving furniture, painting, installing drywall, demolishing concrete and, sometimes, snow shoveling."[45] He made $200 to $400 a week to support himself and multiple family members.[46] Several of the day laborers at the Home Depot site had been previously employed at the local meat processing plant, but because of immigration inquiries about working papers, they had to resort to unpredictable, temporary day work.

In the case of Salt Lake City, the security guards at Home Depot acted as de facto immigration enforcement agents, threatening and at times using physical force to harass the workers or prevent them from entering a contractor's truck. In an interview, a day laborer, Bulmio, explained that he was sixty-seven years old and justified his right to show up every day to the parking lot to look for employment, "We may not have papers, but there is still a human right to live. We are not trying to hurt anyone. We are just trying to work."[47] Day laborers in Salt Lake City frequently experienced wage theft because of their vulnerable status and had no recourse to recover wages. This finding was similar to that of the National Day Laborer Survey of 2,660 day laborers in twenty states that found the average pay for day laborers was $10 per hour, about half of the workers were denied water, food, and breaks on their jobs, and about half were victims of wage theft.[48]

In order to address some of the challenges day laborers face, some cities have created "safe zones" for them to safely solicit work. These centers offer bathrooms and refreshments. Often a city's labor rights center advocates for the workers when there has been an injustice reported.[49]

Aging White Americans and Undocumented Workers

A few decades ago, groups of formerly traveling Latinx migrant farmworkers began settling in a town of Washington County, Maine, called Milbridge, because it featured work in lobsters, sardines, seafood plants, blueberry picking, and wreath making.[50] The farmworkers had an impact on a white, aging population in a state with one of the lowest birth rates in the nation. The existing white population was growing older and their children were leaving the area for cities to work or to further their education. The influx of immigrants settling in the area reinvigorated population growth and the economy of Milbridge. It was found that "Latinos make up just over 1 percent of Maine's residents, and about 6 percent of Milbridge's residents are Latino."[51] However, the new families (and the browning) of Milbridge were not necessarily welcomed. For example, the town voted against building affordable apartments ten years ago, when more immigrants were coming to town. In order to combat the nativism that often reared its head among longtime residents, the community organization, *Mano en Mano* (Hand in Hand) was created. Advocates from the organization welcomed immigrants to the area, and helped them feel part of the community. They hosted migrant education and offered programs on parenting and affordable housing.

Pew Center researchers Jeffrey Passel and D'Vera Cohn concluded that "the number of working-age immigrants is projected to increase from 33.9 million in 2015 to 38.5 million by 2035, with new immigrant arrivals accounting for all of that gain."[52]

With this increase, immigrant labor will continue to be a boon to employers in the future. Charles Rudelitch, executive director of the Sunrise County Economic Council of Washington County, stated: "We're making the argument that over time, there will be a much bigger economy for all of us to have a share of if we welcome people who choose to move here."[53] Jennifer Crittenden, a scholar on aging at the University of Maine, views immigrant laborers ("new Mainers") as critical to the human capital needed to meet the care needs of older Mainers specifically and workforce shortages more broadly. It is clear that organizations like *Mano en Mano* have been crucial to building the cultural bridge between the established white community members and the newcomers who have so much to offer, along with supporting the rights and human dignity deserved by all.

Undocumented Women Workers

The intersection of being undocumented and being a woman at work is rife with alarming challenges. The Migration Policy Institute compiled a comprehensive report on immigrant women in the United States and included data on approximately five million undocumented women.[54] They found that a larger percentage of women were naturalized citizens compared to men: "49 percent (10.5 million) of all immigrant women were naturalized U.S. citizens, compared to 44 percent of all immigrant men."[55] They also found that:

> Women composed 46 percent of the 11.4 million unauthorized immigrants in the United States in the 2008–12 period. Four states and the District of Columbia have larger shares of unauthorized women than the U.S. average: Hawaii (55 percent), the District of Columbia (50 percent), California (47 percent), New York (47 percent), and Virginia (47 percent).[56]

In spite of their significant numbers, undocumented women's earnings are not equal to undocumented men's earnings, nor are their average earnings equal to women who are citizens. In Durham, North Carolina, Latinas who were undocumented worked just as much as Latinas who were citizens, but their work was characterized as unstable and they earned lower wages, which limited upward mobility.[57] Unjust immigration laws have "created a differentiated set of workers who face unique structural limitations."[58]

Sixty percent of undocumented women are employed off the books in domestic work— doing housecleaning, child care, and elder care. In New York, the women's immigration advocacy group, We Belong Together, reported that one-third of domestic workers in New York City had experienced some form of physical or verbal abuse, often because of their race or immigration status.[59] Pierrette Hondagneu-Sotelo's *Doméstica: Immigrant Workers Cleaning and Caring in the Shadows of Affluence*[60] and Mary Romero's *The Maid's Daughter—Living Inside and Outside of the American Dream*[61] are foundational works of scholarship that amplify the voices of Latinas working in the care industry. Of the major findings to emerge from these books—and those that build upon them—is that emotional labor (not just physi-cal labor) goes into caring for other humans or their homes. Therefore, the phrase often proclaimed by those who have cleaning or care help, "She is like family to me," denies the major power inequities at play.

In recent years, women working in janitorial positions have received attention in the state of California because of unionization campaigns. Women who work as janitors and security guards in San Diego, California, organized a rally bringing awareness to sexual harassment and sexual assault; their ultimate goal was to let other workers know of their rights.[62] Janitorial workers are members of the Service Employees International Union United Service Workers West and they shared pow-erful stories with the union. They explained that the night work they do increases isolation and increases the likelihood of harassment and/or violation by supervisors. Helen Chen, the coordinator for the Labor Occupational Health Program at Univer-sity of California, Berkeley, stated that between one-third to one-half of women are harassed at work, but many workers fear they will be fired or punished if they speak up.[63] Genoveva Aguilar, a union representative, noted that women underreported harassment for a number of reasons. However, the bottom line is that workers' top priority is keeping their job and that is what will shape their decisions to report or complain to the company or law enforcement.

A UC Berkeley Labor Center report detailed the experiences of workers in this industry.[64] They highlighted the significant differences in workers' rights and pay between contracted versus unionized property care workers; contracted workers typi-cally made less money and had fewer employer-provided health benefits. For victims of sexual harassment or violence, there was a lack of support, a fear of not being believed, distrust of government agencies, and lack of awareness of workers' rights. Outside cleaning contractors had less accountability, were employed by smaller com-panies, and had more layers that could prevent the rectification of abuses. There was very little training for supervisors, most companies lacked a sexual harassment policy, and when complaints were brought to the companies, there was scant enforcement.

Women represent 20 percent of the undocumented agricultural workers in Cali-fornia. They are among the most impoverished and vulnerable—and because of their gender, susceptible to harassment and sexual violence in the workplace on the part of colleagues and supervisors. *YES Magazine* reporters Trina Moyles and K. J. Dakin wrote a story featuring fifty-eight-year-old "Sofia" who has lived in the United States undocumented for over twenty-five years. She worked mostly in the agricultural in-dustry during this time and shared that when there is only one woman on an all-male crew, there are more chances for abuse than there are otherwise.[65] Chris Castillo, the director of Verity, an organization in Sonoma County that provides support for women in crisis due to domestic violence and sexual assault, echoed Sofia's concerns:

> In the vineyards, there can be lots of inappropriate sexual touching from bosses, or other farmworkers. Women are fearful to report it because of the risk of losing their jobs. So they tolerate it, but their stomachs are tied up in knots when they go to work.[66]

The women themselves unite to provide each other support, information, strategies, and many times, to seek justice for harassment and violations experienced in the agricultural fields. The program *Lideres Campesinas* (Rural Leaders) aids female migrant workers on their rights and helps them become more integrated with the existing Latinx communities. Luz, a farmworker who is part of *Lideres Campesinas*, balances several contracts across different companies during the peak season. She explains that some supervisors support her growth (e.g., teaching her how to trim vines, which is a male-dominated job) and some have concern for their workers (e.g., ensuring that they have shade and water). However, other supervisors neglect basic worker needs or, worse, actively violate their human rights as women and as workers. Workers should not have to rely on the whims of their supervisors' moods to be safe on the job.

The Southern Poverty Law Center interviewed 150 undocumented women in the food production industry, including farmworkers, to better understand the challenges they face.[67] The report, *Injustice on Our Plates*, depicts in detail women who were working in positions of double vulnerability due to their immigration statuses and their gender. In general, they found that "women typically earn minimum wage or less, get no sick or vacation days, and receive no health insurance."[68] All the women in their study reported having been cheated out of wages. For example, a woman in Florida reported that she picked tomatoes for two weeks and was then told there was no money to pay her. The Southern Law Poverty Center shared that it is difficult to follow up on cases because of employer tactics. For example:

> The workers were arrested for "trespassing," even though they were lawfully on the job during their work hours. These charges were dropped by the prosecutor within 24 hours, but by then the workers were already in immigration proceedings. "I'd rather not cause trouble," says Alicia, a 39-year-old Mexican. "It would be worse to lose everything."[69]

Emotionally draining, backbreaking, and often dangerous, the undocumented women's work is not valued by employers. The report concluded: "Regardless of what sector of the food industry these women worked in, they all reported feeling like they were seen by their employers as disposable workers with no lasting value, to be squeezed of every last drop of sweat and labor before being cast aside."[70]

Some employers simply cheat on hours or on the amount of work completed to underpay their employees, for example, by miscounting trays of peppers. While there were many instances of these types of oppressive and exploitative strategies, the following example details the callous nature and hopelessness after having completed honest work:

> Carina, a 24-year-old Mexican woman who began working the Florida fields a decade ago as a 14-year-old girl, says she was told by a crew leader that she would earn $6 for every box of green beans she picked. She worked seven days a week and kept track of the boxes she turned in. "At $6, it comes out to be $380 or $400," she says. "When you get your check, it's for $250." And we go and tell the crew leader. He says, 'I don't know.'"[71]

Ultimately, *Injustice on our Plates* brought to light the sexual violence experienced by undocumented immigrant workers. They were viewed as "perfect victims" by their abusers, who preyed on them because they often worked in isolation (usually in agriculture), felt scared to report to the police, and often did not have the language to communicate with English-speaking authorities. Additionally, there was a culture of disdain and disregard of reports of sexual advances and sexual violence by the employers, feelings of shame and self-blame on the part of the victims, and/or social isolation that resulted because the women workers often did not have family in the United States.

The Equal Employment and Opportunity Commission (EEOC) Office conducts outreach and even pursues cases, but often fails to achieve justice for the women victims in the criminal justice system. In one such case, an older farmworker from Mexico, Virginia Mejia, and others, sued the Rivera Farm, which grows grapes in California. They lost the case and Virginia was "blacklisted" from working in agriculture in that region. She explained women farmworkers' vulnerability:

> No one sees the people in the field. We're ignored. You have to let them humiliate you, harass the young girls just entering the field. Imagine, they have no protection. You allow it or they fire you.[72]

The EEOC knows of hundreds of cases where the women were exploited and suffering from abuse. Maria Ontiveros, a legal scholar, reviewed complaints made by female farmworkers and found that there were certain worksites that were known to the workers as being extraordinarily abusive:

> In Salinas, Calif., a worker told the EEOC that farmworkers there referred to one company's fields as the field de *calzon*, or "field of panties," because so many women had been raped by supervisors there. In Florida, women farmworkers dubbed fields "the green motel" for the same reason. In Iowa, women said they had encountered the problem so often that they believed it was a common practice in the United States to exchange sex for job security.[73]

As long as there is no legalization of immigration status, workers will be exploited. Therefore, one of the "take-aways" from this chapter is that unauthorized immigrants contribute greatly to local, state, and federal economies. As workers, their labor "counts" and should be legalized to safeguard them from systems of abuse and exploitation. We need to ask ourselves, what kind of country do we want to be a part of? One that honors a hard day's work or one that negates the efforts of workers contributing to our collective well-being?

Reporting Workplace Abuse

The Indiana Supreme Court recently ruled that undocumented workers are able to sue employers for injury.[74] A construction worker named Noe Escamilla fell and seriously injured his back while working on Wabash College's baseball stadium in icy conditions. The employer, Shiel Sexton Company, argued that because of his likelihood of deportation, the undocumented worker should not be granted future earnings as being lost. Initially, the local courts sided with the employer. Alexander Limontes, who worked on behalf of the appeal, argued that immigration issues should not be a part of the consideration, rather the decision should be based on (a) did the employee get injured? and (b) is the employer at fault? Escamilla's attorney, Timothy Devereaux, concluded that the Indiana Supreme Court reaffirmed the U.S. Constitution in their decision backing undocumented workers: "the courts are open to all . . . and [constitutional] rights belong to everyone." [75]

WORKING CHILDREN AND YOUTH

Everyone who comes here has a suitcase or a backpack full of dreams they left back home.

—an unaccompanied migrant youth living in Ohio[76]

In the last few years, headlines featured children and mothers fleeing their home countries in Central America and making the arduous trip to the U.S.-Mexico border, only to surrender to Customs and Border Patrol so that they could plead their case for refugee status and humanitarian treatment. However, another journey has been occurring for migrant youth that is centered on labor exploitation.

Laurel Morales reported on a case of ten young Central American teenagers in Ohio who were brought to the United States with a promise of work and the chance to attend school when they reached seventeen years old.[77] They were held prisoner in a dilapidated mobile home that crawled with cockroaches. Their working conditions were described as:

12 hours a day, six days a week of debeaking, vaccinating and cleaning up after chickens at an egg farm. . . . The other teenagers earned $500 a week, but the traffickers who lured them north kept all but $60. The trafficker, Arnoldo Castillo-Serrano of Guatemala, earned at least $225,000 off of the kids' labor. [78]

One of the youth recalled that he thought the traffickers were taking their wages as part of an arrangement with his family who had paid $15,000 for him to come to the United States. Although the unaccompanied youth migrating independently did not come from wealthy families, scholar Lauren Heidbrink found that families often gave traffickers the deeds to farms, homes, and other properties as collateral to fund one family member's migration.[79]

The traffickers held on to more than labor control—they ended up as official custodians of the youth. Morales explained:

When they first arrived in the U.S. the teenagers were picked up by the U.S. Border Patrol and put in federal custody. That's where [Arnoldo] Castillo-Serrano and his co-conspirators claimed them. They posed as friends of family. Federal officials at U.S. Health and Human Services handed the kids over to the trafficking gang.[80]

An Ohio immigration attorney who works with unaccompanied undocumented minors, Jessica Ramos, admonished the federal government: "The system was ripe for this to happen due to the surge and the way that the government reacted to it, the way that they relaxed their standards."[81] Sadly, many of the parents send their kids to the United States to escape the intense gang activity in their homelands. In the Ohio case, the youth helping to prosecute the traffickers are getting visas so that they can stay in the United States—if not to complete their own dreams, to support the dreams of their family members. In one case, Morales shared that one of the youth from Honduras, whose dream was to become a nurse, worked on a dairy farm and sent his income to his family so that his sister could become a nurse in their home country.

The Ohio trafficking case spurred many to critique the problems with immigration detention (i.e., too many people, too little resources) and the increase of unaccompanied migrant youth at the U.S.-Mexico border (in the three years from 2013 to 2016, at least ninety thousand migrant children from Central America came to the United States).[82] However, the egg farm and the poultry industry eschewed responsibility for the situation. Trullium Farms reported that they did not know their subcontractor was hiring undocumented minors. Brian DiFranco, an Ohio immigration attorney whose caseload was about one-third unaccompanied minors, stated: "Until employers increase wages or lawmakers accept the U.S. needs people willing to do hard work for little money, some will continue to take advantage of those less fortunate and abuse the system."[83] (See Box 3.2 for a closer look at the subject of trafficking and how it is linked to the lives of undocumented workers.)

Farmworker families working in the tomato and strawberry fields in East Tampa, Florida, faced similar fears.[84] Residents reported they do not want to go outside for fear of immigration enforcement that has been spotted with increased frequency. One farmworker noted that in spring and summer, they normally move to Georgia to pick peaches or to Michigan to pick peppers, but decided to stay put because of the anti-immigrant stance of the Trump Administration. After the 2016 presidential election, the waiting list to enroll in Head Start, subsidized preschool for migrant families, decreased by 43 percent.[85] To help with outreach, migrant student recruiters for the public schools, Irene Lara and Paulina Martinez, rode in a van and tried to locate families who were not sending their children to school to get them enrolled.[86]

Children and Agriculture: Major Loopholes Leading to Inequality

What happens when the law in the United States allows for minors to work? This is the case for United States' agricultural workers. Legal exemptions in agriculture allow children as young as ten years old to work in the fields with their parents,

BOX 3.2: A CLOSER LOOK AT TRAFFICKING

While many immigrants come to the United States seeking better wages than in their home countries, some individuals are trafficked because they are taken to the United States against their will or based on misleading circumstances. The majority of victims are undocumented adults.

In one of the largest studies about labor trafficking, San Diego researcher Sheldon Zhang and his colleagues found "30 percent of undocumented migrant laborers were victims of labor trafficking, 55 percent were victims of other labor abuses, and about half of these victimization experiences occurred within the past 12 months." The construction industry, followed by janitorial services and landscape businesses, had the highest reports of abuse and victims of trafficking. It is very hard to study this hidden population. The researchers gathered accounts from 826 trafficked immigrants. Their experiences were horrifying and defied the logic of an honest day's work. For example, a participant in the study explained that she was "forced to work 12 hours a day at a restaurant. Her employer would yell at her, throw saucepans at her, and hit her. When the respondent could no longer put up with the abuse and decided to quit, her employer refused to pay her for her last month's work." Another victim of labor trafficking who worked in a bakery shared that she "was not permitted by the employer to go anywhere or even take a break during the entire eight-hour shift. This 45-year-old woman was allowed to eat only standing up and quickly so she could resume working quickly."

Source:

Zhang, Sheldon X., Michael W. Spiller, Brian Karl Finch, and Yang Qin. 2014. "Estimating Labor Trafficking Among Unauthorized Migrant Workers in San Diego." *Annals of the American Academy of Political and Social Science* 653(1): 65–86.

compared to a minimum age of sixteen in most states for non-agricultural jobs. U.S. law explicitly states: "Children can do agricultural work that the U.S. Department of Labor deems 'particularly hazardous' for children at age 16 (and at any age on farms owned or operated by their parents). . . . In non-agricultural sectors, no one under age 18 can do such jobs."[87] In Alabama, school-aged migrant children are exempt from attending school.[88] In California, children and teenagers are brought into farmwork through family who are sharecroppers and they are crucial to the sharecropping unit.[89]

In a study of eighty-seven migrant farmworker youth, researchers in North Carolina found that they understood they had poor safety nets and voiced significant concerns about their often dangerous work conditions.[90] The youth explained that they often had wet shoes and clothing—conditions that increased the absorption of pesticides and nicotine and led to long-term health hazards. Additionally, a high percentage of youth reported sunburns, which also led to long-term problems.

Although the legal age to purchase cigarettes is eighteen years old in the United States, children are allowed to work in tobacco farms. Human Rights Watch interviewed 141 children and youth, ages seven to seventeen, who were involved in tobacco harvesting in the four states that comprised 90 percent of the industry: North Carolina, Virginia, Kentucky, and Tennessee.[91] The youth in this study were mainly U.S. citizens and their parents were often undocumented. Most began working the fields with their parents at thirteen years old with the intention of helping with the family income. Human Rights Watch noted,

> Child tobacco workers often labor 50 or 60 hours a week in extreme heat, use dangerous tools and machinery, lift heavy loads, and climb into the rafters of barns several stories tall, risking serious injuries and falls.[92]

The types of complaints shared by the children and young people were profound. Just a few of the conditions covered in the report were: a thirteen-year-old girl fainted and then went back to work; a sixteen-year-old boy was tired and exhausted returning home in the dark, only to get up again early in the morning, again in the dark; a fourteen-year-old girl wrapped herself in garbage bags to protect her clothes from getting wet, which intensified the toxins from tobacco—but then suffered from heat stroke; a sixteen-year-old boy had headaches that lasted several days and caused him to lose focus at school; a six-year-old girl vomited several times and then returned to work; a thirteen-year-old girl and her fourteen-year-old brother felt "woozy and tired" because of the pesticide being sprayed; a sixteen-year-old cut his leg with a hatchet; and, a fifteen-year-old girl hurt her back because of heavy lifting.[93] The report concluded that the youth were suffering from:

> Acute nicotine poisoning, known as Green Tobacco sickness, an occupational health risk specific to tobacco farming that occurs when workers absorb nicotine through their skin while having prolonged contact with tobacco plants. Public health research has found dizziness, headaches, nausea, and vomiting are the most common symptoms of acute nicotine poisoning.[94]

In addition, the youth worked in the fields when the neighboring fields were being sprayed with pesticide, they missed school when they worked strenuously over the previous weekend, and several reported not enrolling in school and were unaccompanied undocumented minors.

In 2015, four Democrats introduced Virginia bill HB 1906 that proposed putting important restrictions on children and youth working in tobacco fields.[95] If enacted, it would have changed the legal age to work in the tobacco fields from twelve to sixteen years of age. (Children who were twelve would have continued to be allowed to work in orchards and farms outside of school hours with parental consent.) However, the bill did not pass in the House of Representatives, which was controlled by the Republicans.

The fight for children who work in fields of all kinds must continue. In addition, their parents need stability and deserve the economic compensation that they have earned rather than being consistently shortchanged. A transformation of policies and laws is needed to address the fact that farmworker youth have a high school non-completion rate four times the national average because of their work responsibilities.[96]

POULTRY AND MEAT PROCESSING: DANGEROUS WORK FOR UNDOCUMENTED IMMIGRANTS

The fastest growing areas for undocumented immigrants are in areas where there are meat and poultry industries, oftentimes away from large urban settings.[97] This is also why one of the biggest workplace raids of three hundred undocumented immigrants was in Postville, Iowa, at the Agriprocessors kosher meatpacking plant that employed between one thousand and fifteen hundred workers.[98] When the government inspected fifty-one poultry plants, 100 percent of them had violated labor laws by not paying workers their full hours earned and half of the plants had illegally taken fees from the workers' paychecks.[99] In 2014, more than thirty million beef cattle, one hundred million hogs, two hundred million turkeys, and eight billion chickens were slaughtered in the United States. Government studies tout declines in injuries reported from these industries (5.7 per 100 workers); however the hazardous nature of the industries (particularly of meat plants) remains alarming.[100]

Nonprofit community organizations and other advocacy groups find that injuries are severely underreported and that there is simply great fear in losing a job (or being deported) if one reports an injury. A governmental study found that an on-site nursing station frequently told workers to return to the line when they went to report injuries; in one case, a worker had ninety visits to the nursing station before being referred to a doctor.[101] When advocates have gone to the worksites to test or examine the workers, there were more incidents of injury than were reported by the worksite. For example, The National Institute for Occupational Safety and Health found that at one site, one-third of poultry workers had carpal tunnel syndrome and yet the plant reported only a handful of workers with the condition.[102] This study demonstrated the importance of fieldwork—visiting the worksites and examining workers—as opposed to only relying on reports submitted by companies.

North Carolina Hog Workers

In North Carolina, there are roughly sixty-four hundred workers employed at 938 hog operations that reported hired labor.[103] Researchers at the UNC Gillings School of Public Health reported that workers at industrial hog facilities carried bacteria and staph in their noses up to four days.[104] Children of hog workers were also found to have the strains brought home by their parent(s) or family member. The strains were mostly resistant to antibiotics because of the drugs given to pigs for illness and hormones to help them grow faster.

Nebraska Meatpackers

Researchers and advocates explain that meatpacking workers undergo work that requires mental acuteness and physical exertion. It is one of the most dangerous industries for workers according to a governmental report.[105] This industry is central to Nebraska; it is reported that Nebraska produces one of every five steaks and hamburgers in the country. Nebraska Appleseed, a nonprofit organization that focuses on social justice, administered a survey to 455 meatpacking workers, most of whom were Spanish speakers and 59 percent were men.[106] A majority indicated they were injured last year in incidents such as knife cuts and falling on slick floors. However, the workers did not reference any repetitive motion injuries, which are accumulated over time and cause more long-term harm. Their qualitative responses about experiencing pain on the job indicated most of the workers suffered from this major injury. The report shared:

> Written responses brought a flood of descriptions of swollen hands, pain in the shoulders, back, arms, hands, and fingers. Repetitive motion injuries are a serious and growing concern in meatpacking work. The end result can leave people's limbs curled beyond use and the gradual nature of the injury is insidious. Many disregard the initial pain, not recognizing its seriousness until muscles and tendons are already wasted. In fact, survey responses indicated that many people did not recognize repetitive motion injuries as injuries.[107]

Workers reported the most critical complaints were the accelerated line speed, supervisory abuse, persistently high injury rates, and not being allowed to go to the bathroom. Many workers (91 percent) knew they had rights, but less than 30 percent thought those rights made a difference. Workers' written responses referenced supervisors screaming, employers' apparent indifference to safety concerns, and a failure to treat workers as human beings: "I know of three people who urinated and pooped in their pants and afterwards they just laugh at you."[108]

When workers participating in the survey received the Meatpacking Workers' Bill of Rights, they reflected that the most useful information on it was: "that I am a person" and "that I have the right to go to the bathroom." Basic notions of human dignity are being invoked as newly learned and important, which is significantly delayed considering meatpacking worker legislation and policies have been in place in the state for a decade.

As noted previously, the meat industry was named one of the most dangerous according to a government report.[109] Although this report did not include official statistics related to the experiences of sanitation workers in the poultry and meat industries, analysis of workers' accounts shows that these workers are also vulnerable to the diseases and physical harms that come from working in the plants.

WORKPLACE RAIDS AND DEPORTATION

As we have mentioned, ICE raids have increased since President Trump took office. From February 2017 to August 2018, there were six hundred immigrants apprehended through raids and 109 of them were from California.[110] In the greater New York City region, there have been almost seven hundred ICE raids since 2013; the majority have taken place in Queens (131) and 72 percent of them have taken place since Trump took office.[111] It's important to note that the impact of workplace raids extends beyond labor sites, and such actions directly and negatively impact the family and also terrorize communities.

There is a strong connection between increased ICE raids and rising deportation rates. In 2017, there were fewer apprehensions at the border by Customs and Border Patrol than the year before (a decrease of 24 percent) and more internal removals by ICE (an increase of 37 percent).[112] The ICE raids inflict terror and collateral damage in affected communities. The following are just some of the stories that were reported in 2018.

- In Nebraska, a raid on a tomato greenhouse and potato processing facility yielded 133 arrests in a town of thirty-seven hundred people.[113] The local principal reported that fifty to one hundred children were likely directly impacted since most of the families in the town were employed at the facility.
- In California's agricultural Central Valley region, 232 individuals were arrested before dawn in a multi-county sweep of undocumented workers.[114] The far-reaching raids led family members to discuss safety plans, led some to avoid work, and led yet others to alter their driving patterns. Allegedly, 180 of the migrant workers were categorized as criminals (using a broad definition that includes violations of driving without license, being in removal proceedings, or being returned to the United States after being deported). Some workers were not the original target of an ICE warrant, but were stopped by ICE because they were said to have matched the description of the person on the warrant.
- In Tennessee, over a thousand town members gathered to pray and show unity for ninety-seven workers who had been arrested in a single day.[115] They left behind 160 U.S.-born children who were scared and in need of resources. The business that was raided, Southeastern Provision, had mainly immigrant workers who they required to "kill, skin, decapitate and cut up cattle whose parts were used for, among other things, oxtail soup and a cured meat snack exported to Africa."[116] It was bloody, smelly work. After an informant had reported the oppressive work conditions (e.g., working with chemicals without protection,

fear of complaining), the business was targeted for the raid. By end of day, thirty workers out of the ninety-seven were released and the remainder was sent to immigration detention prisons out of state.[117] A week after the raid, about three hundred people marched through the town to demonstrate solidarity with the arrested workers and draw attention to the plight of the families.

- In North Texas, 157 workers were detained at a trailer factory.[118] Local churches, nonprofit legal agencies, and other advocacy groups came together to support the legal process of those detained, ensure their salaries were paid, and help family members. In one case, a single father worried about the care of his children. In other cases, workers had been living in Texas for decades, raising families, and did not have ties to their birth countries, which made deportation an especially frightening prospect.

Gillian Christensen, a spokeswoman for the Department of Homeland Security who oversees Immigration and Customs Enforcement (ICE), noted she dislikes the term "raids" and prefers to say authorities are conducting "targeted enforcement actions."[119] While employers may know they are under scrutiny through notice of employment audit, the workers typically experience these actions as raids. During the fiscal 2016 year, ICE spent $3.2 billion to identify, arrest, detain, and remove undocumented immigrants.[120]

Each deportation conducted by ICE cost taxpayers an average of $10,854 in fiscal year 2016, which included detention and transportation to another country.[121] To reduce this cost, ICE often tries to work with local law enforcement, and they are met with varying responses, ranging from close cooperation to outright refusal to help the federal agency. ICE maintains that immigration raids target unauthorized immigrants with criminal records. However, with President Trump broadening his definition of "criminality," many more immigrants have been targeted.

Lisa Rein and her colleagues reported on the aftermath of a recent immigration raid:

> David Marin, ICE's field director in the Los Angeles area . . . [said] that 75 percent of the approximately 160 people detained in the operation this week had felony convictions; the rest had misdemeanors or were in the United States illegally. Officials said by Friday night that 37 of those detained in Los Angeles had [already] been deported to Mexico.[122]

Immigration rights activists disputed ICE and stated that nearly one in four of those arrested had no criminal records.[123] (In chapter 6 we will look at the lack of due process that occurs when immigration agents expedite deportations by acting as enforcers, prosecutors, and judges.)

The mere threat of a workplace raid has a chilling effect. Victor Navarro of the UCLA Labor Center explained: "Undocumented workers are much less likely to file a wage theft complaint, talk to inspectors about workplace safety problems, or file a workers compensation claim if they are hurt on the job."[124] Unauthorized immigrants are often vulnerable because employers can get away with failing to pay

Figure 3.2. Undocumented workers often labor in dangerous conditions for employers who do not address their concerns about safety.
Ahsan S., Unsplash

their wages if workers are apprehended through workplace immigration raids and/or picked up by immigration enforcement in their communities or while commuting.

Workers Defense Project (WDP) is a legal advocacy and organizing group in the Texas construction industry—an industry in which more than 50 percent of workers have been undocumented since the early 2000s.[125] Stephanie Gharakhanian, employment and legal services director at WDP, explains that the worker safety laws are engaged through worker complaints. But if workers are afraid to file a complaint, then the laws are meaningless. When states introduce legislation to further tighten relationships between immigration enforcement and local entities, such as law enforcement, then workers are less motivated to complain about injustices. Even in states like New York, where labor support is strong, "a 2014 audit by the state's comptroller found that 17,000 wage-theft cases were still open from 2008."[126]

UNDOCUMENTED PROFESSIONALS: SMART, PERSISTENT, AND COMMITTED TO THE CAUSE

Sergio Garcia made history by not only following his dream to practice law, but by changing the law for other undocumented immigrants.[127] His professional victory was a long time in the making—and it was not an easy road for him to earn the right to practice law. He was born in Mexico and came to the United States as a baby because his father was picking fruit in the orchards of Chico, California. Growing up in Northern California, he recalled feeling like an outsider. At seven years old, the family returned to Michoacán, Mexico. Then, they came back to the United States when Sergio was seventeen and his father, who had become a citizen, petitioned for a visa for Sergio. After eighteen years, Sergio is still waiting his turn in the visa queue. In the meantime, he attended community college, a four-year university, and then attended law school. He then passed the rigorous California Bar Exam. At first, he was granted a license to practice law, but then it was rescinded once his immigration status became known. However, Garcia and his team appealed the decision and he was later granted his law license. California State Bar president Luis J. Rodriguez reflected upon the ruling:

> With today's ruling, the California Supreme Court reaffirms the Committee of Bar Examiners' finding as not a political decision but rather one grounded in the law. . . . The bill, which passed in October and went into effect this week, allows the bar to admit "an applicant who is not lawfully present in the United States (who) has fulfilled the requirements for admission to practice law."[128]

This exciting development in California led to Senate Bill 1159, which required "all 40 licensing boards under the California Department of Consumer Affairs to consider applicants regardless of immigration status by 2016."[129] These professional licenses include those for contractors, nurses, physicians, massage therapists, cosmetologists, architects, psychologists, and acupuncturists. However, unauthorized immigrant youth face significant challenges to reach the high levels of education required of some of the professions. The average high school completion rate for undocumented students is about 50 percent and, of this group, only 5 to 10 percent continue to college.[130]

Unfortunately, undocumented immigrants in other states, such as Georgia, are facing intense anti-immigration laws regarding professions. Because Georgia lawmakers passed a law in 2012 that said all licensed health care professionals must provide their proof of citizenship, many license renewals for doctors, nurses, and pharmacists were not being processed in a timely manner.[131] And, compounding the issue was that staff for the offices processing the paperwork decreased by 40 percent the same year the law was enacted.[132] LaSharn Hughes, director of Georgia's Medical Board, estimated that at least thirteen hundred doctors and other workers in the medical field lost their eligibility to legally work because of delays in the renewal process.

Josefina López is a playwright, novelist, and screenwriter (of works such as *Real Women Have Curves* and *Detained in the Desert*). She is also an activist and strongly influenced by her experience of being undocumented. Her father was part of the Bracero program, so they had deep ties to the United States. Born in San Luis Potosi, Mexico, Josefina came to the United States at five years old.[133] For thirteen years, she was undocumented, and that experience was an important aspect of why she became a writer: to make her voice known, heard, and read. She received amnesty and eventually became an American citizen. Later, Josefina married a Frenchman and lived in France, only to be treated poorly for being an immigrant again—only this time the French thought she was Arab; this was the inspiration for her novel, *Hungry Woman in Paris*.[134] Her career has been spent fiercely advocating for the rights and freedoms of immigrants and women.

Harold Fernandez's parents fled the violence of Medellin, Colombia, to work in the New York City garment industry.[135] Harold and his brother were left with their two elderly grandmothers. At age thirteen, he and his brother flew from his home country and landed in Bimini, Bahamas, where they joined others in a small boat that would land them in Florida. His story, previously profiled in the *New York Times* and other news outlets, is now written in book form: *Undocumented: My Journey to Princeton and Harvard and Life as a Heart Surgeon*. He credited the doctors who came to see one of his very ill grandmothers for inspiring his dreams. While he would never see his grandmothers again, he worked very hard and obtained scholarships to top universities and entered the elite group of heart surgeons. Along the way, he became a U.S. citizen and a practicing heart surgeon in New York. However, he continued to advocate for undocumented immigrants and their rights to health care. He poignantly wrote that lawmakers must improve the conditions for undocumented immigrants because, "You never know: One of those undocumented immigrants may be the surgeon saving your life someday very soon."[136]

Julissa Arce was a whiz at math. She was also undocumented, living in Texas, and extremely driven. Max Abelson of *Bloomberg Business* conducted an extensive profile on Ms. Arce, a former vice president of Goldman Sachs.[137] Legislation in Texas turned in her favor when undocumented people were given the opportunity to attend college and to be considered for in-state tuition. In college, she continued her successful path in finance. Her work ethic guided her through rocky times: her parents returned to Mexico during college and so she took over their funnel cake business on the weekends. With active and supportive social networks, she was able to land a coveted internship at Goldman Sachs. She found her "home" in the world of wealth and finance, but she also held onto a secret: Julissa had obtained false documents (identification and Social Security number) so that she could be employed at Goldman Sachs. No one ever knew about her status. Her friends and peers admitted that they did not think anyone who was undocumented could achieve such success. Despite reaching the high status positions of vice president at Goldman Sachs and director at Merrill Lynch, she felt the gnawing stress of her secret and the deep pain of not being able to see her parents. Through marriage, she eventually became a citizen. Despite knowing that she could continue in the world of high finance and wealth, she shifted gears and joined the efforts of Jose Antonio Vargas, an undocumented Pulitzer Prize–winning journalist whose home country is the Philippines. She is using her unique skillset to help lead the nonprofit and movement called Define American, which was started by Vargas.

As you can see from the examples above, in some cases legislation has allowed undocumented youth to obtain professional jobs that are not "under the table." The Pew Hispanic Research Center found that between 2007 and 2012, the "number of unauthorized immigrants in management or professional related jobs grew by 180,000."[138] With the creation of Deferred Action for Childhood Arrivals (DACA) in 2012 and the granting of a temporary work permit to recipients, there are more undocumented immigrants in white-collar jobs than ever before.

Take the case of Alma, one of our former students. One morning, she arrived a few minutes late to class and looked worried, tired, and was unusually disheveled. After class, she stayed to share her story for the first time. As an undergraduate, she worked thirty hours a week at a twenty-four-hour fast-food restaurant, typically during the nightshift or swing shift. The night before she shared her story, she had worked at the restaurant from 10 p.m. to 4 a.m. She walked home, changed her clothes, and then took two busses to come to the university. However, that morning, the bus had been late and she slept through her first stop, which caused her to walk back to the missed stop. Alma was also involved with campus clubs. We marveled at her ability to excel at work, excel in her classes, and maintain a social life. Around the time of her graduation, she applied for and was granted DACA. She was then able to use her undergraduate degree in sociology with an emphasis in children, youth, and family to apply for a number of positions that could take her out of the restaurant industry and onto a professional pathway. Alma successfully landed a job at a local youth agency that provided afterschool programming. From there, each time we have seen her, she has risen in the ranks, first at her initial organization and then in other, larger agencies. Alma's drive, determination, and intellect were always there.

However, the opportunity to work in an occupation to match her talents was the gift of the temporary work permit given through DACA.

THE ROLE OF VISAS FOR UNDOCUMENTED WORKERS

Some believe that undocumented immigrants should apply for work visas so that they can work legally. Attention has been given to highly skilled immigrants and their ability to work in the United States with the H-1B visa program, which provides employers with high-skilled foreign workers when they can't find qualified domestic workers.[139] It is important to note that *companies* hold the visas and the employees are considered "non-immigrants," with a temporary right to work in the United States. Companies may apply for green cards on behalf of their employees. The top H-1B employers have been: "HTC Global, Wal-Mart, Merrill Lynch, Educational Testing Service, Caterpillar Inc., Credit Suisse, J.P. Morgan Chase & Co., Bank of America, Wells Fargo Bank, and the Mayo Clinic."[140] The following describes the visa's parameters:

> With a statutory limit of 65,000 visa numbers available for new hires—and 20,000 additional visa numbers for foreign professionals who graduate with a Master's or Doctorate from a U.S. university—in recent years demand for H-1B visa numbers has outstripped the supply and the cap has been reached quickly. . . . In seven of the last 10 fiscal years, the H-1B visa cap has been reached in the first five business days. . . . [It] allows employers to petition for highly educated foreign professionals to work in "specialty occupations" that require at least a bachelor's degree or the equivalent.[141]

Additionally, there is an "unlimited" category that is reserved for institutions of higher education, nonprofits, and government research. In 2015, thirty thousand visas were granted in this category.[142] Computer science–related fields have accounted for 60 percent of the requests and the second highest percentage of the requests has been in the science and medical fields.[143]

"America's Got Immigrant Talent!"

The *Wall Street Journal* joined the popular discourse of "immigrants are high performers" with a story with a catchy title, "America's Got Immigrant Talent!"[144] The story focused upon the fact that the children of immigrants often dominate junior science competitions. Stuart Anderson, executive director of the National Foundation of American Policy, studied the 2016 Intel Science Talent Search, a research-based science competition for high school seniors that has been dubbed the "Junior Nobel Prize." He found that, similar to other years, 83 percent of the finalists were children of immigrants. He also found that former H1-B visa holders were "4 times more likely to have a child as a finalist in the 2016 Intel Science Talent Search than were parents who were both born in the United States." Yet, it is important to note the income and educational levels of the immigrant parents of the science search competitors were not comparable to the majority of the children with *undocumented* parents.

Obtaining an H-1B visa is not possible for the majority of undocumented immigrants in this country. First, the educational criteria for obtaining the visa are high and do not reflect the majority of undocumented immigrants' situations. Second, many argue that the conditions in which the employer holds the visa (and the possibility of green card) leads to exploitation and erosion of labor rights, even among highly educated employees. Third, based on current H-1B visa rules, potential employees must reside outside of the United States, which is not the case for undocumented immigrants in this country.

There is an existing guest worker program for agricultural industry, the H-2A program, which does not have any limitations on the number awarded to farms and companies seeking to hire foreign workers on temporary visas. The U.S. Citizenship and Immigration Services Office explains that employers must:

- Offer a job that is of a temporary or seasonal nature.
- Demonstrate that there are not enough U.S. workers who are able, willing, qualified, and available to do the temporary work.
- Show that employing H-2A workers will not adversely affect the wages and working conditions of similarly employed U.S. workers.[145]

Workers with H-2A visas can be in the United States for up to three years and the visa needs to be renewed each year. After three years, the worker must leave the United States and wait three months until she or he can be a contractor for labor again in the United States. Spouses and children under twenty-one may accompany a worker with an H-2A visa, but may not lawfully work in the United States. There are many problems associated with this visa, the most important of which might be that workers must stay with the same company, which leads to exploitation and other labor rights abuses. In 2017, the program "expanded rapidly to more than 165,000 approved jobs"[146] and there was a 27 percent increase in 2018.[147] According to the U.S. Department of Labor, Georgia leads the amount of certified positions under this visa program, following by Florida, Washington, North Carolina, and California. The top areas of work that have been requested by farmers involve berries, general farmwork, tobacco, apples, and melons.

In 2017, Senator Dianne Feinstein introduced the "Agricultural Worker Program Act of 2017."[148] Under the proposed bill, agricultural workers would be given the opportunity to apply for a temporary immigration status (i.e., a blue card) that, after documentation of a certain number of years in the agricultural industry and meeting some other conditions, could lead to applying for lawful permanent residency status, and getting a green card. Families could also be part of the application process. What would be notably different than the guest worker visas was that workers could be employed by more than one company, which might prevent exploitation. In 2018,

Representative Bob Goodlatte introduced the AG and Legal Workforce Act of 2018 that proposed to include agricultural industries and dairy, would use e-verification of immigration status, and would allow for temporary work visas.[149]

At the state level, California governor Jerry Brown signed a new bill that would improve conditions for the wages and hours of agricultural workers.[150] Currently, a "full time" agricultural job is sixty hours a week or ten hours per day. The new bill allows agricultural workers to have a forty-hour workweek as the legal limit and any hours afterwards are considered overtime and must come with compensation. While it still contains flaws, the law is the first for farmworkers in the United States.[151]

An agricultural lobby group, Farm Bureau, recommended providing agricultural workers with a pathway to residency or some other legal status.[152] For example, the San Diego Farm Bureau explained in a news story that the region is experiencing a lack of agricultural workers.[153] Erik Larson, executive director of the San Diego Farm Bureau, recommended making immigration reforms so that farmworkers are "not looking over their shoulders" all the time and farmers can benefit from a strong labor pool. Missing in these recommendations are the voices of the workers themselves to advocate for a socially and economically just system that would create fair working conditions and a pathway to citizenship if desired. Workers' rights groups, such as Farmworker Justice and United Farm Workers, have serious concerns about the health, wages, and safety for farmworkers that work visas or other limited immigration-related policies would not rectify.

PROPOSING A HUMAN-RIGHT-TO-WORK FRAMEWORK

Seeking a better life through better wages has long been the foundation of immigration to the United States.[154] As shown in this chapter, common themes that cut across the experiences of unauthorized immigrant workers include a critical need for work, the widespread fear of deportation, and the challenges of meeting an unreasonably demanding schedule and dealing with harsh working conditions to keep a job. The notion of *individual effort*, *hard work*, and ability to *contribute to society* are elements of the American Dream. While we would argue it is a limiting framework, many undocumented workers fit comfortably within the American Dream. They work hard and contribute to society. In fact, they make society better: there is less crime in immigrant communities[155] and undocumented immigrants are less likely to commit crime than U.S.-born populations.[156]

To honor them, we draw inspiration from political scientists Rachel Meyer and Janice Fine who argue that undocumented immigrants who are participating in the political process—through activism and other civic engagement—are themselves forming a notion of grassroots citizenship.[157] Undocumented immigrants contribute greatly to our economy (and many times at great sacrifice and peril). Until their full inclusion as citizens is achieved, they should be considered economic citizens and be afforded all the rights, services, and safeguards as required by the U.S. Constitution.

4

Educational Dreams and Barriers

Erika excelled in math and science, but rarely spoke in any of her classes. Some of her teachers wondered what else was going on in her life, but in the hectic school day and with forty students in each class, there was rarely time for one-on-one interaction. Erika lived in a two-bedroom apartment with three other families. She shared a bedroom with her mother and three sisters. While she wanted to study more, there was always movement and commotion in her home. Still, she loved being in school and frequently ate lunch quickly so that she could read in the library.

Because of her excellent grades, she was placed in a college preparation track that included a class that had a special counselor to assist students when applying to universities. Even though her high school was predominately low income and Latinx, she was the only Latina in this special class. She often wondered what anyone would say if they knew she was undocumented. When it came time to apply for colleges, she stopped attending that class. She did not know whom to trust with her immigration status and was not sure if any of the workshops were related to her. Of course, she had heard of college, but no one in her family and none of her friends knew about college. Her junior year passed and she began her senior year. Ms. Juarez, an intervention counselor, requested that Erika see her. She also happened to be the only Chicana educator or counselor at the school.

At the meeting, Ms. Juarez began by sharing that she was the first in her family to attend college and her parents worked for decades in the nearby avocado groves. Ms. Juarez told Erika that she saw a lot of potential, reviewed Erika's stellar grades, and learned of her interest in biology. At this point, Erika shared her immigration status and broke down crying. She admitted to Ms. Juarez that she was not sure what she would do after high school graduation. Knowing that the four-year university deadlines had passed, Ms. Juarez immediately accessed the Internet at her desk computer to find the admission page for the local community college. They completed the enrollment at that meeting. Erika left the office like she was walking on air. A week later, she received notification of her acceptance! She recalls that it was the proudest moment of her young life.

Erika represents a relatively small group of undocumented students who were noticed for their potential in high school and were guided to consider higher education. Given the educational outcomes of undocumented students, it is likely rare that a counselor, such as Ms. Juarez, cared deeply and actively orchestrated college enrollment for most of them. Even in Erika's case, she was relatively unnoticed for three years of her high school career and then only because she had stopped attending her college-prep classes. Thanks to large caseloads and a general lack of awareness about their situations, most undocumented students fall through the cracks. The American Immigration Council estimates that half of undocumented students do not finish high school, and just a small fraction (5 to 10 percent) enter college.[1]

While higher education for undocumented immigrants is a contentious political issue, we set the premise of this chapter that education is a basic human right. The United Nations argues that the "inherent dignity and the equal and inalienable rights of all members of the human family is the foundation of freedom, justice, and peace in the world." The UN Convention on the Rights of the Child Article 28 refers to "the right of the child to education, and with a view to achieving this right progressively and on the basis of equal opportunity . . . and make higher education accessible to all."[2] Therefore, this chapter is based on understanding education as a human right that should be afforded to everyone, regardless of immigration status.

Myth: Undocumented students have broken the law, so they should not have the right to education.

Myth Busted: The U.S. Supreme Court protects undocumented students' right to a K-12 education and many states support their right to attend college as well. The leaking educational pipeline makes it difficult for undocumented students to obtain a quality education, but there is increasingly state support to help them do so.

THE (LEAKING) EDUCATIONAL
PIPELINE FOR UNDOCUMENTED STUDENTS

Each year there are about 122,600 undocumented seniors in our high schools and only about two thousand are expected to continue on and graduate with a college degree.[3] Carola Suárez-Orozco and her colleagues conducted a path-breaking immigration study of younger children and found that the undocumented children were among the least academically successful group.[4] In a qualitative study on undocumented children and their experiences of school, children were aware of (and worried about) their undocumented status; yet, they also loved playing school and going to school.[5]

Alejandro Covarrubias and Argelia Lara, Chicanx Studies scholars, warned of the "brown model minority" image of undocumented students; they found this group is—in general —not performing at the same level as their "documented" counterparts. While some media may highlight uniquely resilient and successful undocumented students, many of their cohort peers have been pushed out of the pipeline long before reaching a college or even "college-bound" educational environment.

Covarrubias and Lara analyzed national data to discern the educational attainment rates for undocumented Mexican immigrants.[6] Based on a national sample, they presented one hundred symbolic undocumented students in elementary school. Of one hundred that started elementary school, only forty-nine females and forty males graduated from high school. Of this group, only about sixteen women and twelve men enrolled in college. A small fraction of the group went on to graduate school.

Undocumented students' school experiences are much like those who are first generation, from working poor families, and educated in schools that were under-resourced. For example, in South Carolina, Latinx students (undocumented and documented) represent about 10 percent of the K-12 student population, but only represent 2.5 percent of the population of *any* form of higher education.[7] This makes making the leap to higher education challenging.

Our universities and colleges are failing many of our students. Federal data find that "59 percent of first-time, full-time college students obtain their bachelor's degree *within six years*."[8] Undocumented students are facing a number of barriers that may lengthen their time to graduation and make it difficult. They have similar struggles to their low-income peers, yet they have the additional burden of their unauthorized immigration status. Cesar Montelongo, one of the first undocumented students to be accepted into a joint medical school and doctoral program, explained:

> There are inherent difficulties in being admitted to medical school as an undocumented immigrant student. Students face the challenge of not only lacking a legal immigration status, but many are also members of underrepresented minorities, first-generation college students, children from low income households, members from underserved communities, and may have had minimal access to work or financial aid opportunities during college.[9]

Award-winning Massachusetts educator Nancy Barile shared her despair at witnessing promising and high achieving high school students excluded from higher education because of their immigration statuses. At the end of any given school year, she had ten to twenty students in her classroom "depressed, demoralized, and sometimes even suicidal. They felt that their futures were cut off, despite . . . that they had done everything right by getting good grades and being active and involved school citizens."[10] Given the students' feelings of hopelessness, those of us who are supporters of undocumented youth and families must work toward immigration justice and help bolster the resiliency that youth and families already possess.

For the undocumented students who are poised to make the transition from high school to college, their undocumented status plays a big role. Psychology researcher Ellen Hawley McWhirter and her colleagues found "students who thought they might encounter problems with their immigration status anticipated more external barriers and were less optimistic about their future careers."[11] Additionally, Latinas and older high school students anticipating barriers because of their immigration status were more likely to consider a community college route (versus a four-year university pathway). Overall, the researchers concluded the importance of undocumented students being better informed on the pathways to higher education. Interestingly, for those who anticipated barriers because of their immigration status, an impressive *78 percent* indicated they *still would* continue to higher education of some kind. This research indicates high and meaningful aspiration levels of undocumented students, even in the face of significant challenges.

Financial Barriers and Opportunities

Among the challenges facing undocumented students are financial obstacles. In some states, students are prohibited from receiving in-state tuition, for example, Arizona, Georgia, and Indiana.[12] Others prohibit undocumented students from enrolling in *any* public college or university (post-secondary institution): Alabama and South Carolina. In spite of this, we can see a number of states and a couple of university systems are working to make college more accessible and affordable for undocumented students. According to the National Immigration Law Center, which summarized state and university laws as of June 2018:[13]

- Nine states—California, Maryland, Minnesota, New Jersey, New Mexico, Oklahoma, Oregon, Texas, and Washington, and the District of Columbia—allowed state financial aid to unauthorized students. The University of Hawaii offered financial aid to its undocumented students also.
- Twenty states—California, Colorado, Connecticut, Florida, Hawaii, Illinois, Kansas, Kentucky, Maryland, Minnesota, Nebraska, New Jersey, New Mexico, New York, Oklahoma, Oregon, Rhode Island, Texas, Utah, and Washington—had in-state tuition for undocumented students who qualified through proof of state residency and other eligibility standards. The University of Maryland also allowed for in-state tuition for eligible students at its campuses.
- Four states—California, Connecticut, Minnesota, and Utah—offered scholarships to eligible undocumented students.

When there are no state laws, university systems may ban or encourage undocumented students. For example, the College Board reports that in lieu of a law guiding equitable access to college, "many four-year state colleges in Virginia require applicants to submit proof of citizenship or legal residency and refuse admission to students without documentation."[14]

Despite the perception of some that states are going against federal law when they enact policies that are financially inclusive of undocumented students, the National Immigration Law Center has stated that is most definitely not the case:

Contrary to the claims of immigration restrictionists, federal law does *not* prohibit states from providing in-state tuition to undocumented immigrants. Rather, section 505 of the Illegal Immigration Reform and Immigrant Responsibility Act of 1996 (IIRIRA) prohibits states from providing any higher education benefit based on residence to undocumented immigrants unless they provide the same benefit to U.S. citizens in the same circumstances, regardless of their residence. . . . The states that provide in-state tuition to students who meet certain criteria regardless of their immigration status have fully complied with this provision. The law . . . does not preclude states from providing in-state tuition to undocumented residents of the state as long as nonresidents in similar circumstances also qualify. The tuition equity measures are fully consistent with federal law.[15]

State policies on tuition make a significant impact. Researchers Robert Bozick and Trey Miller found that undocumented youth who were in states without in-state tuition were 49 percent less likely to enroll in a college or university than in states with no explicit policy.[16] Undocumented youth in states offering in-state tuition were 65 percent more likely to enroll in higher education compared to those in states without an explicit policy.[17] States' policies deliver messages to youth about their future educational goals.

Many students' financial responsibilities reach beyond their own schooling to include support for their families. In her research, sociologist Genevieve Negrón-Gonzales shared the situation of a research participant, Zulma, who was a community college student in a rural area of California:

I am responsible for my parents. 'Cause my dad doesn't make a lot of money so I'm responsible for paying like, the water bill, the PG&E [electricity] bill. I was responsible for paying the mortgage last year because my parents were having a hard time. . . . My parents have worked hard. They have paid taxes the whole time they worked because they worked with other people's Social Security numbers. But that money is gone. They don't have anything to fall back on like citizens do, now that they are old and cannot really work.[18]

Zulma's experience is very common; the stress of having such daunting financial responsibilities at a young age can negatively impact students' ability to do well in school and to finish their college degrees. The story of Jose that is shared in Box 4.1 (accompanied by his self-portrait in Figure 4.1) also demonstrates the winding path through the U.S. educational system often necessitated by the many demands on an undocumented student.

Place Matters: Educational Access Driven by Location

As seen in the story of Jose, living in Louisiana versus California significantly impacted his educational opportunities. In sociology, the concept of social location is often used to describe how matters outside of one's control often shape outcomes. For example, being born during a certain time period, in a particular physical location, and of a particular racial, ethnic, and gender background all affect a person's life. Educational opportunities for undocumented students are matters of geography:

Figure 4.1. Portrait of an undocumented student with *canas* (or gray streaks) in his hair, highlighting that some undocumented students are older
Jose Escutia Ruiz

place shapes opportunity. State-level policies have real effects on student outcomes. This is clear when you consider that public policy researcher Stephanie Potochnick found that there was an 8 percent *increase* in high school completion for undocumented students in states that adopted in-state tuition policies.[19]

State legislation and regents' decisions have either created policies to include or explicitly exclude undocumented students. Educational access and the right to education are being held in the hands of political precariousness.[20] Analysts have argued that some states experiencing rapid growth of undocumented immigrants are the ones passing the most draconian laws about education. Senior policy analyst Zenén

BOX 4.1. JOSE'S PATH THROUGH
THE U.S. EDUCATIONAL SYSTEM

Jose's journey to college did not begin right after high school. He does not qualify for any Dreamer legislation. There is no "line" for him to step into for citizenship or residency.

Before immigrating to California, Jose spent his early childhood in Mexico. Jose remembers that they lived in a small shelter by the mouth of a river and tended goats. It was a very remote area and his family was very poor. He came to the United States for a better life, but it has not been easy. Access to education, at times, seemed impossible.

As a middle schooler in San Diego, Jose was exposed to migrant repression in his community. He saw family, friends, and neighbors being targeted by immigration authorities. He recalls: "Immigration officers patrolled main bus stops in my community. One officer would board the bus through the front door, while one or two others waited by the back door to catch anyone that attempted to run." He added, "I would hear friends who had papers talking about how under 'Prop 187,' teachers were going to turn undocumented students over to immigration authorities. This kept me up at night and made me weary of school. I did not know who to trust."

In high school, Jose knew that he was not following the path to college. He grew up thinking that undocumented people were unwanted in the state of California because, at the time, they were prohibited from accessing state resources and from a college education. He also could see his life was different than the college-bound high school students depicted in television shows and movies. The power of media, discussed in chapter 2, shaped and constrained his educational ambitions.

No one in Jose's family had ever stepped foot in a college classroom. His mother did not make it to the first grade. He realizes now that his local schools had been very low resourced, but he internalized this lack of societal commitment to his learning to the idea that he was not college material. He shared, "I barely got through high school. I struggled a lot in English classes. To make up my credits, I took classes where I did not have to write, for example, physical education and art. Taking a foreign language class also helped, since we were all learning the basics." Jose had found a way to meet the credits to graduate from high school, but did not gain the confidence and skills necessary for a college career.

His family had limited resources available to help pay for college. Jose's mother made just enough money cleaning houses to pay the rent and put food on the table. All through his education, he knew that affording the "extras" was difficult.

He shared, "When I first arrived in the [United] States, I attended a predominantly white elementary school. Somehow, I was placed in a music class. I recall the teacher asking me what type of instrument I wanted to play. I had seen President Clinton played the saxophone during his presidential inauguration, so I told the teacher I was interested in playing it. I went home that day and asked my parents for a saxophone. My parents went to shops, but were unable to buy the instrument because of its price. In the end, the music teacher let me borrow an old trumpet to play."

After high school, he had to work full time and left California to find work in Louisiana where friends told him the construction industry was growing. For six years, he joined the ranks of working class undocumented men and women. However, Jose anchored himself to the notion that an education was the only way to move up the social ladder. He had more to offer than his physical labor.

In late 2006, he began researching where undocumented folks in the United States could access a college education. A simple Google search led Jose to discover that California had been providing undocumented college seekers with access to attend college at in-state tuition rates under the AB 540 law since 2001. Jose returned west. With the support of his older brother, Jose enrolled in his first semester at the community college. He recalled, "The enrollment test placed me at the very bottom. I started with English essentials and slowly worked my way up to English 100, which was a requirement to transfer to the university."

Like many students, Jose faced numerous obstacles during his time at the community college. At first, it was adjusting to academic life which left him failing and retaking classes during the summer to maintain his GPA. Moreover, he carried the weight of being undocumented on his own. Jose was expected to navigate college like any other student, but his legal status limited him from fully integrating to the college experience. With no federal or state financial support, Jose found himself attending college part time and working at a sandwich shop to pay for his college tuition. Jose believed in the notion that education was the key to success; this provided him the focus he needed to survive the turbulent waters of college.

In 2013, California began providing undocumented students with state financial aid and scholarships. For Jose, the best part of this *apoyo* [support] was getting connected with a Latina counselor through the Education Opportunity Program (EOP) who saw both his potential and persistence. She helped him navigate his way to a four-year university. His friends and family supported him as well. Also, at the community college, he learned about critical pedagogy, which gave him much inspiration, and he learned about the various structural inequalities confronting many groups in the United States.

At thirty-four years old, Jose dreams of one day teaching sociology courses with a specific focus on migration and education at the university level. He shared, "I am looking at universities outside of the United States like in Mexico, Canada or Australia. Places that want educated Mexicans like myself. I know it will not be easy, but I am going to turn this dream into a reality." The anti-immigration rhetoric of President Donald Trump has reminded him of the xenophobia that he grew up with when he first arrived in California. Nevertheless, Jose continues to devote his energy to his education. He aims to pursue a doctorate and become a professor.

Jaimes Pérez summarized the growth of undocumented immigrants below, many of which passes exclusionary immigrant laws:

> In the new immigrant-receiving states, the undocumented immigrant population makes up a higher share of immigrants than do documented immigrants. Since 1990 to 2008, North Carolina, Georgia, Nevada, Arkansas, Tennessee, South Carolina, Arizona, and Alabama have seen a 200 percent or higher growth in their immigrant populations. In Colorado, Nevada, Georgia, and North Carolina, the undocumented immigrant populations accounted for about half or more of all immigrants.[21]

In the case of Virginia, they have experienced both exclusionary and inclusive legislation within a short time period. In 2014, Attorney General Mark Herring announced that in-state tuition would be available for undocumented students who could show residency, for example, through attending Virginia high schools. Jessica F. Chilin-Hernández contrasted the subsequent anti-immigration policies that have followed:[22]

- HB 1356 and SB 722—outlaws in-state tuition for undocumented students and includes DACA recipients.
- HB 2001—requires universities and colleges to cooperate with immigration enforcement.
- HB 2004—requires governing boards to make public the enrollment of non-citizens and the amount of financial aid they receive.

Importantly, community advocates, students, and legislators have fought back against these restrictions—in many cases by taking Attorney General Herring's refrain and making it their own: "DREAMers are already Virginians."

Anti-immigrant legislation can disrupt students mid-year. In the case of Missouri, the A+ Scholarship had originally granted a two-year college scholarship to students who qualified by near perfect attendance, high grades, and community service hours. Reporter Jenny Simeone-Casas reported on the case of Areli Muñoz Reyes, who was a student at St. Louis Community College and arrived in the United States to begin third grade.[23] The Missouri State Senate Bill 224 changed the criteria for the A+ scholarship to be only for U.S. citizens or legal residents, and they also took away in-state tuition rates for undocumented students. This was a blow to Missouri's fifty-five thousand undocumented population, the over three thousand DACA recipients, and the two thousand future DACA recipients who were in the educational pipeline.[24] In the case of Areli, she was required to pay triple the costs of tuition for in-state students. Despite reports of immigrants leaving the state, Areli and her family stayed and tried to find another path to educational opportunity.[25]

The financial struggle for undocumented students not only stems from their family income, but also from being locked out of federal financial aid of any kind.[26] Even in the few states that offer undocumented students state financial aid, it's not enough. In Marco Murillo's study on urban undocumented students, a participant named Emily shared:

> I think the biggest obstacle is getting into the schools they want to get into and not being able to have the money to get there . . . I don't think in general the packages offered to undocumented students are enough to actually go to a school, [cover] room and board, and pay tuition. I think it covers the tuition for them, but then they're stuck with the other piece. So, they have to be creative figuring out who's going to pay for it, how they're going to pay for it.[27]

Emily had been accepted to prestigious universities, but enrolled at community college because she could not afford the other costs of attending a university (e.g., housing, books). In this same study, educator allies reported calling universities and colleges to see if there were additional scholarships or subsidies that could help their students, but none were identified.[28]

Former secretary of the U.S. Department of Education (DOE) Arne Duncan shared that one of his major disappointments was not creating federal financial aid for undocumented students. He explained: "I meet all the time these amazing students who've worked hard, done great stuff and they're looking at me, what are you going to do to help me in college? I basically say 'I'm so sorry. We're crazy in this country.' It just doesn't make any sense whatsoever."[29] Given the lack of such federal aid, the United States is left with a wide range of state policies. How can states have such variation? The answer is in the landmark Supreme Court cases described below.

IMPORTANT EDUCATION LEGISLATION

In the United States, there have been major Supreme Court decisions that have significantly impacted educational equity and outcomes. These hard-fought civil rights cases include two that were crucial to addressing racial and ethnic segregation in the schools, *Mendez v. Westminster School District* (1946) and *Brown v. Board of Education* (1954).[30] Other legal developments that have been pivotal to discussions of the education of undocumented children in particular, which we discuss below, include *Plyler v. Doe* (1982), the attempts to pass a federal DREAM Act, and the executive action on Deferred Action for Childhood Arrivals (DACA) (2012).

Plyler v. Doe (1982): Guaranteeing Undocumented Children and Youth Public Education

The law that protects undocumented children's rights to attend public K-12 schools in the United States started with two events that happened in Texas in the 1970s.[31] First, Texas legislators in 1975 allowed school districts to require proof of legal admission into the United States to enroll in K-12 schools. Then, in 1977, the Tyler Independent School District decided to charge families $1000 in tuition for any student who could not prove their legal presence in the United States.

Parents sued the school district and the case eventually made its way through the district, appellate, and Supreme Court levels, all of which favored the parents on the basis of the U.S. Constitution's Fourteenth Amendment (1968) that states, "Nor shall any State . . . deny to any person within its jurisdiction the equal protection of the laws."[32] The Supreme Court decision also reasoned that the school district failed to show how providing education to undocumented immigrant children negatively impacted the learning of U.S. citizen children. In its decision to ensure that all undocumented children can attend school, the Supreme Court stated: "By denying these children a basic education, we deny them the ability to live within the structure of our civic institutions, and foreclose any realistic possibility that they will contribute in even the smallest way to the progress of our Nation."[33]

Recently, the *Dallas Morning News* editorial team reflected on the *Plyler* decision and contrasted it with the Texas of today: a state with high Latinx undocumented immigrant populations engaging in some of the most drastic anti-immigration legislation to date.[34] They recalled that in the past even conservative judges on the Supreme Court expressed support for giving undocumented children a chance at success in life. For example, Chief Justice Warren Burger, a conservative judge appointed by President Nixon, wrote: "It is senseless for an enlightened society to deprive any children—including illegal aliens —of an elementary education."[35]

The *Plyler* decision has been tested many times. Most notably was the case of Alabama when a larger piece of anti-immigrant legislation included the following provision: "School administrators [are required] to determine the immigration status of all newly enrolling students, and to submit an annual report to the state Board of Education setting forth all data obtained under the requirement."[36] This had a chilling effect on education in immigrant communities, who thought the requirement for parents to fill out paperwork was because citizenship status was required to attend or enroll in school. While this part of the legislation was blocked, it still had an impact on the state's undocumented population in schools. The American Immigration Council reported that "more than 13 percent of Latino students in the state withdrew from public schools between September 2011 and February

2012—even though immigrants as a whole constituted less than 0.5 percent of students in Alabama schools."[37]

After the incident in Alabama, former attorney general Eric Holder issued a statement from the Obama Administration that clarified public schools must allow all children in their service area to enroll without immigration verification. "Public school districts have an obligation to enroll students regardless of immigration status and without discrimination on the basis of race, color or national origin. . . . We will vigilantly enforce the law to ensure the schoolhouse door remains open to all."[38] Also during the Obama Administration, the U.S. Department of Education pushed back on states, such as Arizona and Alabama, who (unsuccessfully) sought to curtail the right to K-12 education for undocumented students. For example, the DOE released a fifty-page guidebook for educators that explained, "Educators, counselors and principals often serve as informal and trusted advisers to students and families, and thus are uniquely positioned to share critical information and resources for undocumented youth."[39]

The beginning of the Trump Administration marked a change in the federal position on unauthorized migrants to a destructive and inhumane one. In remarks to Congress in May 2018, U.S. Department of Education secretary Betsy DeVos vocally supported public schools' choice to call immigration enforcement agents to report students who "might be undocumented."[40] Following intensive backlash, two weeks later in a Senate hearing, Senator Chris Murphy (D-Conn.) had to ask five times until DeVos definitively stated that teachers and administrators were *not* allowed to call immigration authorities.[41]

For immigrant rights advocates, a major critique of the *Plyler* decision was that it did not include higher education and solely focused on the right to education in the K-12 educational system. In their ruling, the Supreme Court justices reasoned that states should be left to decide on the issue of access to public higher education because it is directly tied to state budgets. However, the higher education system omission in the decision allows states to deny access to community colleges and universities for students who are undocumented. Also, the *Plyler* decision did not address federal financial aid for higher education, which means currently undocumented students in college cannot receive federal aid, work-study funds, or loans. However, as we discussed previously, some states have created legislation to allow for state aid and scholarships. Similar to health care access, which we will discuss in chapter 5, undocumented immigrants' access to college depends on whether states enact inclusive or exclusive policies.

The Federal DREAM Act: A Not-Yet-Realized Pathway for Undocumented Youth

The Development, Relief, and Education for Alien Minors Act (DREAM Act) was legislation first proposed in 2001 by Senators Dick Durbin (Democrat) and Orrin Hatch (Republican).[42] This bill would have granted conditional permanent residency to immigrants with good moral character, who graduated from U.S. high schools, arrived as minors, and had continuously lived in the United States for five years. Applicants would have to wait six years in a temporary status and in the meantime attend college for at least two years before being granted permanent residency. After being in legal permanent resident status for five years, a person could apply for citizenship.

Unfortunately, the bill did not pass and new versions have been introduced many times in Congress and in the House of Representatives over the years, each time with different parameters. Immigration activists have been critical of this approach to immigration and education legislation because it has included extremely punitive actions for non-DREAMer recipients and in general the legislation does not include parents of DREAMers or other adults.[43] Also, some versions have included a pathway to citizenship, which is an ideal outcome; other versions only extended the possibility of legal permanent residency, which would exclude recipients from voting.

Finally, we argue that legislation like the DREAM Act is too stringently focused on who deserves a pathway to citizenship. Far too many undocumented youth are prevented from graduating high school and many do not attend colleges or universities. The scope of intended recipients for proposed DREAM Act legislation is too narrow and leaves out youth and adults who are equally deserving a pathway for citizenship and whose educational promise could be realized through a more hopeful future.

Dreamer Identity

Some undocumented individuals have adopted the notion of "Dreamer" as a personal identity and it stems from the aforementioned proposed legislation. One student shared:

> I've been here for 10 years. I've got a life I've already started to build here. I've got to finish my education. A lot of people ask me, "Once you're done with your education, do you want to go back?" I'm not planning to . . . *I am a Dreamer.* I am a person who is here for my education, and I am fighting for my education.[44]

Many resource centers on college campuses created to support undocumented students have also invoked the notion of "dream" or "dreamers" in their names. For example, California State University Fullerton has over nine hundred undocumented students enrolled at the university; they established The Titan Dreamer Resource Center in order to support these students' educational, emotional, and legal needs.[45] Activist groups have also incorporated variants of "dream/dreamer" into their names, such as the Dreamer Network and United We Dream. On behalf of the National Education Association (NEA), artist Favianna Rodriguez created a welcoming sign for students that states, "Dreamers Welcome," which was held by NEA members at a rally.

Figure 4.2. National Education Association members holding a welcoming sign for undocumented students created by artist-activist Favianna Rodriguez
Pat G. Ryan

However, some have pushed back on the notion that the "Dreamers" label is a good one. First, it takes its name from legislation and lacks the grassroots or humanistic roots that embody immigrant communities. Also, the legislation leaves out significant members of the undocumented population and so the term "Dreamer" could be considered exclusionary to parents and other adults who are undocumented. Poignantly, an undocumented student explained that she was once asked, "As a Dreamer, what is your biggest dream?" She replied: "I want to stop being a Dreamer. I want people to stop telling me that all I can do is dream. I want to make them happen."[46]

Becoming DACAmented: Deferred Action for Childhood Arrivals

While its future is in jeopardy, Deferred Action for Childhood Arrivals (DACA) is still an important opportunity for undocumented youth. President Barack Obama announced this executive order on June 15, 2012, after various failed attempts at comprehensive immigration reform and the passage of a federal DREAM Act. This executive order was meant for youth and young adults. DACA gives recipients a temporary Social Security number and work permit so that undocumented youth can work legally and was designed originally to provide temporary protection from deportation. DACA lasts for two years and recipients can pay to renew for another two years. Currently, it is in its third cycle of renewals. Applicants must assemble a detailed application, pay a $495 fee to the Department of Homeland Security, and pay additional fees to obtain the mandatory biometrics to submit to the federal government. Completing the application is very tricky—any error (even unintentional or minor) could result in rejection and applicants are not allowed to re-apply. The criteria for DACA eligibility can be seen in Box 4.2.

About 1.1 million young people are eligible for DACA and about 70 percent have applied.[47] Mexican immigrants make up the majority of those awarded DACA. Pew Research found that "78% of approved applications—both initial (588,859) and renewals (456,108)—have come from Mexicans."[48] As of March 2017, there were 799,077 DACA requests approved (new or renewals).[49] In 2014, only about 27 percent of undocumented immigrants were awarded DACA.[50]

Because DACA is not a piece of legislation, but an executive order, presidents can eliminate it. Through a public statement by former attorney general Jeff Sessions, President Trump announced the rescission of DACA on September 5, 2017.[51] Strong responses came immediately from undocumented immigrants and allies in favor of the restoration of DACA and the passage of proposed legislation (e.g., Clean DREAM Act) for comprehensive, humane immigration reform. Other responses came from Texas and six other conservative states that brought lawsuits to end DACA on the basis of undue state financial burden.[52] Due to U.S. District Court judge William

---

BOX 4.2: THE CRITERIA FOR DEFERRED ACTION FOR CHILDHOOD ARRIVALS ELIGIBILITY

DACA eligibility requires:

- Arriving in the United States before the age of sixteen
- Proof of presence in the United States as an undocumented person on June 15, 2012
- Being under the age of thirty-one on June 15, 2012
- Proof of continuous presence in the United States since June 15, 2007
- Enrolled in school, graduated, have a GED, serve in the military or a veteran with honorable discharge
- Having no felony convictions, no significant misdemeanor, or no more than three misdemeanors
- Not being considered a threat to national security or the nation
- At the time of application, the applicant must be fifteen years or older.

Source:

Katia Hansen, CEO and President of Unitarian Universalist Refugee and Immigration Services and Education (UURISE) (http://uurise.org/).

Alsup's preliminary injunction on January 9, 2018, DACA was partially restored.[53] Those who have never applied for DACA cannot do so, but renewals may continue. The Department of Homeland Security states: "The DACA policy will be operated on the terms in place before it was rescinded on Sept. 5, 2017."[54] This statement comes after considerable struggle, fear, stress, and activism. The latest available data indicate that as of August 2018, there were 699,350 DACA recipients.[55] Between the January 2018 injunction and August 2018, 153,860 DACA renewal applications were approved.[56] Of the current DACA recipients, 47,480 have pending applications or will be eligible to renew, but this number sharply declines with only a couple of hundred renewing in 2020.[57] The future of DACA remains uncertain.

Several studies on the effects of DACA have revealed that as a program, it has led to better mental health, access to better jobs (in fields related to students' career goals), and more motivation to pursue education for recipients.[58] For example, an undocumented college student in Fullerton, California, who arrived in the United States when he was four years old, shared how he became more motivated after receiving DACA:

> DACA came out one year after I had graduated [from high school]. I had started at a community college, but I think at the time I wasn't really motivated to continue higher education. In addition to finding it really difficult to pay for school—at the time my parents were helping me to pay for tuition and the rest of the school expenses—I didn't have that big of a motivation to continue pursuing a degree. When I received DACA . . . I was able to work and find a job, that helped me, I think, continue on to university.[59]

In the case of North Carolina, students have been able to pursue their professional goals with DACA. More than twenty-nine thousand residents of North Carolina have DACA. In the first two years of DACA (2012–2014), North Carolina had the highest application rate in the nation![60] A documentary about the North Carolina Dreamers shared stories of two college students with DACA.[61] Carolina Siliceo Perez came to the United States at the age of two with her mother. She graduated from Brevard College as an English major. With DACA, she is able to work as a county clerk and hopes to go to graduate school to study the ways that policy impacts people's lives. Melvis Madrigal came to the United States at six years old, is a biochemistry major at Warren Wilson College, and will be the first in his family to graduate from college. He wants to go to medical school and become a doctor. DACA has helped him find work that is flexible with his demanding course schedule.

However, DACA can also lead students into feeling false promises of inclusion. In particular, the Social Security card given to DACA recipients is temporary and only applies to working. So, when students try to use it for any other service, it comes back denied. In Marco Murillo's study of urban undocumented youth, several expressed their confusion and, ultimately, their disappointment with DACA.[62] For example, Danilo explained what it felt like to go through a different process for financial aid (instead of FAFSA, he filled out the CA DREAM FAFSA). He thought that the Social Security number he received through DACA finally gave him access to standard policies and procedures and he would be able to apply for federal financial aid. He compared his experience to that of citizens and shared, "I feel like they're more privileged 'cause they're citizens and all that . . . not like undocumented people, they have to go through a process and *then* get a chance."[63]

Others reported fearing the registration process for DACA. First, one must put the addresses of family members. Second, there is no guarantee of what happens to the information that is registered with the Department of Homeland Security. A student in Southern California explained, "I know all my information, my fingerprints, everything is out there. I would be easy to track."[64] In a research study on rural Central Californian undocumented community college students, researcher Genevieve Negrón-Gonzales presented community members' reactions to the fear of now being "on the radar" of the very government agency they had been trying to avoid. One of her participants, Gabriela, had volunteered at an immigration event to help folks apply for DACA. She recounted:

> [The mother] didn't want to put her real address on her son's DACA application because she was scared of what might happen. She was like, "What if they come for me and my husband?" I had to tell her, like, "Look, if you don't put your real address, they can't send you the approval. . . . They need your real address." But she was scared.[65]

Students often experience the eligibility criteria for DACA (see Box 4.2 on p. 79) as being painfully arbitrary. Recall, to be eligible for DACA, an applicant must have been under sixteen years old when they arrived in the United States and have lived in the United States (continuously) since June 15, 2007. Elizabeth Redden of *Inside Higher Ed* interviewed a student who arrived in the United States as a fourteen-year-old from Mexico one month later, in July 2007, and missed the cutoff date to be eligible.[66] As you can imagine, being that close to eligibility and then finding out she was out of the running for DACA was incredibly frustrating and disappointing for her. This has been the experience of many across the country.

SCHOOL AS A SAFE ZONE: PROTECTION FROM IMMIGRATION ENFORCEMENT

During the Obama Administration, ICE had a policy of discouraging raids in so-called "sensitive" places, which included "churches, hospitals, schools and college campuses, without a supervisor's approval."[67] John Morton, then-director of Homeland Security, elaborated that schools included "pre-schools, primary schools, secondary schools, post-secondary schools up to and including colleges and universities, and other institutions of learning such as vocational or trade schools."[68] He added, "Supervisors should take extra care when assessing whether a planned enforcement action could reasonably be viewed as causing significant disruption to the normal operations of the sensitive location."[69] Under the Trump Administration, the Department of Homeland Security stated that "enforcement actions at sensitive locations, such as schools, hospitals, and places of worship, should generally be avoided" but that it "does not consider courthouses to be a sensitive location."[70]

While attorneys agree that raids *inside* schools and churches have not yet occurred, there have been cases of arrests happening outside of them, such as cases in which a person was arrested when leaving a church's homeless shelter and when another was brought into custody after dropping off a child at school. Traditional media and social media have broadcasted cases when arrests in clinics, hospitals, and court-houses have occurred. Communities acutely feel increased fear due to the intensity of immigration enforcement. A local newspaper in Georgia reported that "police have noticed an alarming drop in 911 calls from an area heavily populated with im-migrants and are hearing reports of parents keeping their kids home from school. Other immigrants are . . . selling off their cars and homes and preparing to return to their native countries."[71] Several states are working on or have passed sanctuary laws where schools would formally be seen as sensitive locations and local law enforce-ment would be prevented from aiding immigration enforcement. Yet, the threats in the community and around schools remain. After a massive ICE work raid in eastern Tennessee, described in more detail in chapter 3, over five hundred students missed school the next day.[72] The Los Angeles Unified School District (LAUSD) has been particularly supportive of undocumented and mixed-status families in the face of these concerns. Monica Garcia, LAUSD board member, stated:

> [Facing deportation is] a particular kind of trauma and disruption. Our schools have been safe places for the children to come. When people at the school sites are aware of the status of the family or an incident of deportation, there are support services, mental health services and interest in supporting that family as best as we can.[73]

The fear of deportation and anti-immigration as a national platform has caused members of immigrant communities to feel what UC Berkeley professor Lisa Garcia Bedolla described as "collective anxiety," and she argued "it's unreasonable to imagine that students can just check that anxiety at the [classroom] door."[74]

University students are also feeling the reach of immigration repression. One morning, a California State University Los Angeles student and immigrant activist disappeared. Claudia Rueda was twenty-two years old, had left her apartment to move her aunt's car, and was immediately surrounded by "three unmarked cars car-rying an estimated nine plainclothes Customs and Border Protection officers who whisked her off to a detention center 130 miles away."[75] Her professors wrote a pow-erful essay that explained Claudia was in the midst of her semester. Her mother had been apprehended the month before and it seemed that Customs and Border Patrol returned for Claudia. Neither mother nor daughter had a criminal record.

Sthefany Flores Fuentes, honor student at Gardner-Webb University in North Carolina and DACA recipient, shared the content of her "notice of deportation let-ter."[76] It arrived in the midst of her finals week and right after she attended a model United Nations weekend event out of town. The March 23, 2017, letter stated, "A review of your file indicates there is no administrative relief which may be extended to you, and it is now incumbent upon this agency to enforce your departure from the United States." Then it ordered Flores Fuentes to: "arrive at 10 a.m. at the federal immigration office in Charlotte with no more than 40 pounds of luggage." It also stated to be "completely ready for removal." Finally, it demanded that she "officially surrender herself in Atlanta where a plane will take her back home." After much social media and activist attention, her deportation order was rescinded. ICE claims there was a clerical error. However, Sthefany worries that they will come back for her again.

Feeling "In Between"

Undocumented students in the United States often feel a sort of "in between" identity. Cecilia Menjívar developed the concept of "liminal identity" to capture a state of neither being from their home country nor the United States.[77] Leisy Abrego added that undocumented youth are (in some states) legally allowed access to public education (and some public services), despite their "illegal" immigration status.[78] Many undocumented youth have grown up in the United States and so only have their birth country as a point of reference. However, their exclusion from so many social institutions leads to their feeling like they are not welcomed in the United States and therefore do not belong.

Social geographers Rebecca Maria Torres and Melissa Wicks-Asbun explored the experiences of undocumented youth living in rural eastern North Carolina, which is one of the most economically disadvantaged regions in the state and in the United States as a whole.[79] A fast growing Latinx population migrated to the area for work in hog farms and poultry plants. The youth in their study were acutely aware of the unfair legislation in their state (i.e., the lack of in-state tuition) and one student explained: "I really actually think it's unfair, you know, they are promoting all this 'America is free, you can do what you want, new opportunities'—but they are limiting you on what you can do. Especially around here, since it is an agricultural environment, a lot of people's parents work in the fields."[80] Participants did not express close affinity with being American or being from their countries of origin when asked about their identities: "Most identified themselves as Latino, Hispanic, or Mexican American but, when asked if they would consider going back to their birth country to pursue a university education, most students talked about feeling uncomfortable."[81] One young participant explained, "I just grew up here and I don't feel like I could stay there very long. I just prefer to be here. I know everything here."[82]

In another case study, Genevieve Negrón-Gonzales conducted an ethnography with community college undocumented students in California's Central Valley, which is home to the world's most productive agricultural region.[83] The region is also home to one hundred thousand undocumented immigrants, and their lives starkly contrast with the region's abundance. The study's participants expressed frustration with the complexities of new, inclusive legislation. For example, Belen had been excited to begin college with the California DREAM Act, legislation that allowed for undocumented students to receive some state aid and financial aid, but noted:

> I thought once the laws changed, it would be more like . . . the people in the financial aid office would be more knowledgeable about stuff, but they are like "What are you talking about? AB540 student? What's that?" . . . And I know it's supposed to be easier now, you know, for undocumented students to go to college, but it doesn't feel very easy.[84]

The participants shared that they could not afford the required pre-college preparations, such as college application fees. One of the participants recalled that the SAT and ACT (college entrance exams) required a Social Security number and were expensive to take. Negrón-Gonzales concluded that even in the most progressive and pro-immigrant state, undocumented students felt *constrained inclusion*, which is the "disconnect between the promise of inclusion embodied in this recent legislation and the reality that citizenship status encumbers their educational experiences."[85] She argued that our educational systems—both the K-12 and higher education systems— have a long way to go to understand the distance between students' aspirations, the information they receive, and ultimately feeling welcomed as a student-scholar.

Studying undocumented students in the Midwest, Aurora Chang and her colleagues interviewed undocumented youth to understand how they viewed themselves.[86] For their particular sample of high academic achievers, top grades could lead to scholarships, but also to making their case for their citizenship pathway, should one open up. Luz explained: "I like school. Doing well in school, I have control over something. I feel like I have control over my life. Generally, I feel like I don't have a lot of control over what happens to me."[87] The researchers discussed the role of *critical hope* among the participants, which is how they strived to maintain good grades and be positive while at the same time "continuing to move forward and push back against the seemingly devastating options before them."[88] It sustained their resistance and resilience.

Returning to the Mexican Education System Through Deportation or Necessity

Investigative journalist Kate Linthicum reported that roughly half a million children enrolled in Mexican schools are U.S. citizens, the majority of whom are presumed to be in Mexico because a parent has been deported.[89] Another half million are Mexican citizens who grew up in the United States and then returned to Mexico.[90] Victor Zuñiga, a sociologist at the Monterrey Institute of Technology and Higher Education, studied undocumented immigrants who migrated to Dalton, Georgia, for work in the carpet mills. His focus was about the way the schools were handling this influx of immigrants' children. However, he soon realized that due to deportation, there were significant numbers of U.S.-born children who were in Mexico and often for the first time in their lives. He shared:

Many students struggled to integrate into Mexican schools because they couldn't read or write in Spanish. Others weren't in school at all because they lacked the necessary accreditations. In all, nearly a third had either been held back a grade or had missed a year or more of school. . . . They suffer so much humiliation. They are invisible.[91]

In another case, Yovany Diaz returned to Mexico, a place he had not been since a child. He had DACA but needed to come to Mexico because his mother was ill.[92] His peers in Mexico, who were undocumented youth from Arizona and Georgia, returned due to stress and fear in the United States. None had been deported and all work at a call center using their English, because their Spanish is not strong. They initially struggled to figure out where they fit in, but are getting closer to having it feel like home.

UNDOCUMENTED VOICES FOR ADVOCACY

Undocumented high school students who are considering college tend to believe in the American Dream—they are working hard and hoping for their efforts to pay off. Social geographers Rebecca Maria Torres and Melissa Wicks-Asbun studied undocumented students in one of the most low-income rural areas of the United States.[93] They found that the students "view higher education as a path to *superarse* (to better oneself) and a way to build a *nueva vida* (new life)."[94] In another study on high school and undocumented immigrants, parents and students often used the refrain "échale ganas" to describe their commitment to education; it translates into try your hardest or put your best effort to move forward.[95] As public advocates, some undocumented students have shared their personal narratives in the form of blogs, newspaper opinion essays, and other first-person accounts. They present riveting and often heart-wrenching stories of resilience.

Cesar Montelongo wrote about how getting into an MD/PhD program was less difficult than obtaining a legal immigration status.[96] He passionately wrote about his family's struggles and the importance of being "given a chance" as an undocumented student. Almost twenty years ago, an uncle petitioned for Cesar and his siblings to become legal permanent residents. However, by the time their notification arrived, Cesar and his sister were in their mid-to-late twenties and no longer considered "family members." This devastating news then was topped with the new reality of once again standing in line for documentation. Cesar explained, "We were told that in five years my U.S.-citizen brother could begin a new family sponsored visa application for us, but it would take an additional 18 or 20 years until a visa could be issued. It will be the year 2040 and I will be 51 years old by then."[97] His voice of advocacy remains focused on comprehensive immigration reform.

Twin sisters, Brizzia and Maria, wrote about their educational journey to the University of Notre Dame and their commitment to fight for the rights of undocumented students.[98] They shared that they were both valedictorians of their high school and received national attention. They wanted to keep their immigration status private. Their peers did not know of their status and, in fact, at times expressed disdain for non-citizens. Trusted educators helped the sisters find a university that was specifically inclusive of undocumented students through scholarships. The sisters attended Notre Dame but were still limited in some of the programs that required U.S. citizenship status. However, faculty and staff at their university offered meaningful substitutions for activities in which they could not participate. For example, instead of studying abroad, they were offered the chance to visit Washington, DC. Their advocacy voices focus on pride for immigration status and educational access.

As seen in Box 4.3 in the first-person account of Dr. Xuan Santos, other advocates emerge through scholarly voices, oftentimes because they have been undocumented at one point in their lives.

BOX 4.3 THE FIRSTHAND PERSPECTIVE OF DR. XUAN SANTOS—IMMIGRANT, ADVOCATE, AND PROFESSOR

I was born in Guadalajara, Jalisco, Mexico. My father worked several jobs such as taxi driver and luchador (wrestler) and my mother was a homemaker. My parents struggled financially. They rented a makeshift room from a relative that was once used as a residential laundry space. My parents decided to migrate to the U.S. after my brother Juan Carlos passed away. They were desperate to afford a proper burial for my brother to avoid having him buried in a community cemetery plot.

When I was a baby, a family friend took me across the U.S./Mexico Border in San Ysidro, California, by using his son's birth certificate. I was reunited with my father who lived with my uncle in Boyle Heights, a small community east of the Los Angeles River. A few months later my mother eventually immigrated into the U.S. As I grew older, my friends learned that I was born in Mexico. They called me "wetback" so often that I thought it was my nickname. I was undocumented for many years. I was discouraged from my family to talk openly about our citizenship status with others. We were afraid of getting deported. We were often referred to as "illegals" by neighbors and would tell us that they would call immigration on us.

My parents petitioned for legal permanent residence after my younger sister was born. We waited seven long years and finally we were asked to travel to the U.S. Consulate General's Office in Mexico City. I was ten years old. I clearly remember meeting the consulate person and she regrettably informed us that we were denied residency because we did not have our paperwork in order. I remember sitting next to my parents and crying because I was not going to be allowed to return to the United States. The consulate person told me

"I'm sorry kid. You are going to have to stay here (in Mexico)." As the person walked out of the office to complete our denial status, my parents anxiously sifted through their piles of paperwork. They found the document we needed. The golden ticket appeared! They provided the consulate with the missing document. When we were granted our green cards and returned to the United States, we no longer felt vulnerable as we did when we were undocumented. However, we still had loved ones who remained fearful. As a *familia*, we could not ignore that other people in my community were being repressed, oppressed, exploited, and threatened.

In college, my immigration consciousness was ignited when I accidentally stumbled on the anti–Proposition 187 march, which dealt with the 1994 California initiative that sought to screen and deny services (e.g., education and health care) to undocumented immigrants. This event galvanized me to become an activist-scholar and to fight for the rights of documented and undocumented immigrants. This newfound consciousness became the catalyst that influenced me to focus on the informal economy and transnational migration. I never forget my immigrant story and I always align myself with this ongoing struggle. This deep-rooted desire to help my community motivated me to continue my activism in the 2006 immigrant rights struggle and other social movements like the struggle against Arizona's SB1070.

I earned my doctorate from the University of California Santa Barbara and I am a tenured professor at California State University San Marcos. I continue to mentor undocumented students and I continue to be involved in the immigrant rights struggle. I am a proud unafraid educator and advocate of our undocumented community.

The Importance of Allies

Within the school and college systems, allies play a crucial role. Allies are considered supporters for and advocates of undocumented students who are not currently undocumented themselves. Allies can be administrators, educators, counselors, financial aid staff, admissions officers, outreach coordinators, and many others who become trusted and empathetic, and also who provide accurate information to students.

In a study on educators and high school students in an urban California school,[99] an undocumented student shared the importance of having a trusted and informed counselor:

> They help you one-on-one. For like the college stuff they make you feel, what do you call it, I guess in a way comfortable . . . if you need help with anything like your Dream Act or stuff like that, they will help you out. I think that's a nice feeling to have. . . .

They help, they research, they help you look for the AB (540), the application for un-documented students. And then, they explain to you how to apply to it and the process that you have to take.[100]

Ideally, these trusted and informed allies become advocates and leaders who strive to make local policy changes and contribute to a positive campus climate for un-documented students. The work of student activists and allies can result in creating safe space resource centers, often called "Dreamer Centers" at university and college campuses.

Two great examples of the creation of Dreamer Centers are from the California State University System. Through its twenty-three campuses, the CSU serves over ten thousand undocumented students.[101] At CSU Sacramento, the student gov-ernment advocated for resources for undocumented students on campus and this resulted in the creation of a Dreamer Center (see Figure 4.3 for its logo). Now, it is staffed and provides "undocu-college success" workshops, legal services, film clubs, policy briefings, ally training, and a general safe space for undocumented students to share and learn.[102]

CSU Fullerton also has a Dreamer Center that emerged after much student activ-ism. Important contributions also came from the then–university president Mildred García and the Titans Hispanic/Latino Alumni. Former Titan Dreamer Resource Center director Henoc Preciado explained: "We're very fortunate that here at Cal State Fullerton we are a campus that is in many ways leading the way in a very public way in supporting undocumented students. We are unapologetic about the fact that we have a resource center specifically for undocumented students."[103]

Peers—other students—can be powerful allies to undocumented students. For example, in the case of University of Georgia, undocumented students have been banned from enrolling. There are documented students who are participants in a club called Undocumented Student Alliance (USA) which "is a service and advocacy organization that works in solidarity with the undocumented community, focusing primarily on equal secondary education opportunities for all students, regardless of legal status."[104] USA member Kevin Ruiz described his club's work as providing tutoring in immigrant communities (K-12) and coordinating with an off-campus advocacy group to help with transportation and other activities that serve undocu-mented youth excluded from college.[105]

In Georgia, ninety students entered three of the universities where undocumented students are banned. They did so on the exact time and day of the fifty-sixth an-niversary of the Greensboro lunch counter sit-in, which was at 3 p.m. on Monday, February 1, 1960. They held classes on the campuses to draw attention to the edu-cational segregation that was occurring based on immigration status.[106] Leading up to this action, members from the 1960s civil rights movement coached the students on how to plan and deliver this powerful form of civil disobedience and provided inspiration based on lessons from the past so that the allies could draw fortitude for engaging in activist work.

Figure 4.3. The logo for the Dreamer Resource Center at Sacramento State University
Erika Perez

School districts sometimes also take a stand and advocate for undocumented immigrants. The Sacramento City School District created and distributed fifty thousand "What to do if ICE comes to your door" cards.[107] The district also placed "Safe Haven" banners at each school. Felix Lopez, a ninth grader, reported that he felt better having the "Know Your Rights" cards. He is a U.S. citizen but is part of a mixed immigration status family. He shared: "I feel that if the president wants, he could do the right thing. He could check their background, and if it's clean, then I think they have the right to come here because it's a free country and sometimes people don't just come here for work, they come here because they're running away from something that they had to live with."[108]

At the K-12 level, it is imperative that school leadership demonstrates knowledge of immigration policies affecting students and their families. Emily Crawford, an educational leadership scholar, outlined the importance of creating a school protocol and policy in the case of immigration enforcement approaching a campus, generating school resources aimed at supporting and protecting undocumented students, and working in collaboration with students and families.[109]

INSPIRING EDUCATIONAL ALTERNATIVES

Freedom University

People have created inspiring alternatives for undocumented students who cannot gain access to higher education—either by legislative bans or life circumstances. For example, Freedom University was born of a dramatic response to U.S. legislation that banned undocumented students from five major public universities in Georgia.[110] It operates with minimal funding and has continued to be a grassroots effort since its beginning in 2011 in Athens, Georgia (it has since been moved to Atlanta). Many people were involved in the founding of the university including four professors from the University of Georgia (Dr. Betina Kaplan, Dr. Lorgia Garcia-Peña, Dr. Pamela Voekel, and Dr. Bethany Moreton), a coalition of undocumented students and allies (e.g., Keish Kim, Gustavo Madrigal, Georgina Perez, Allie McCullen, Claire Bolton, and Juan Cardoza-Oquendo) and human rights activists (Noe and Beto Mendoza and members of the Economic Justice Coalition and Athens Latino Center for Education and Services).[111]

The goal of Freedom University is to serve undocumented university students who have been excluded from various public universities. They drew upon several inspirations that were homegrown, including the Freedom School tradition of engaging black southerners in education, activism, and empowerment during the civil rights movement of the 1960s. They also were inspired by the creation of clandestine schools during American slavery (1700s and 1800s), the labor movement, and the "pedagogy of the oppressed" approach to teaching made popular by Paolo Freire.[112] Additionally, Georgia is home to two Nobel Peace Prize winners who served as inspirations: civil rights leader Martin Luther King Jr. and former U.S. president Jimmy Carter.

Activist and Freedom University volunteer Laura Emiko Soltis was appointed executive director in 2014 and expanded services since then to include college-level courses in "human rights, language arts, biological sciences . . . [along with] college preparation and SAT tutoring, . . . skills-based training in social movement leadership and self-care."[113] She has incorporated students as board members and has done outreach with Georgia private universities so that FU students can continue to achieve their dreams of college graduation. Faculty from different universities come to teach at Freedom University to provide high quality university courses to the students. Soltis is proud to share that one out of five students are awarded a full-ride scholarship.

The *New Yorker* magazine documented the circumstances of Angel, who as an undocumented high school senior had a high GPA but whose education options were significantly limited.[114] His mother shared that Angel had always tried to accomplish a lot and was committed to his education. However, before he discovered Freedom University, Angel felt abject exclusion in a state that had been his home for most of his life. With the help of Freedom University, he received a full scholarship to a historically black institution in Mississippi, Tougaloo College. In a Freedom University film, alumnus Valentina, who is studying biological sciences at Dartmouth with a full scholarship, stated that FU helped her realize that there were options out of state.[115] She stated that FU gave her a sense of community and belonging.[116] While both students have achieved their dreams of attending college, an uncertainty looms. Undocumented students cannot feel peace and focus on their studies because they are worried that their parents will be deported and that the changes in immigration law at the federal, state, and local levels will affect them negatively.

Since the enrollment ban and tuition change, Freedom University has focused on empowerment and college-readiness of undocumented high school students. They enroll to experience high quality college courses, tools for empowerment, and holistic support that includes mental health interventions. Executive Director Soltis believes that education is for liberation—to improve one's self, community, and society. Freedom University is unique because they blend direct and peaceful disruption of the status quo, intellectual rigor, and tangible skill building.

University of the People

In another example of an alternative to the traditional educational system, Shai Reshef, an Israeli entrepreneur, created the University of the People, which is a tuition-free university that is open to anyone and meant to serve those students living in difficult or impoverished conditions.[117] The Distance Education Accrediting Commission accredited the school in 2014. Reshef had already founded several for-profit schools, but he realized that in less developed countries, college was usually out of reach for talented secondary or high school students. The online university has twenty-five hundred students enrolled and a 75 percent retention rate. Students pay a $100 end-of-term fee to support the college.[118] Half of the University of the People's students are from the United States (including undocumented immigrants) and one thousand are refugees.[119] When President Trump called for one of his many travel bans, the University of the People increased its outreach efforts to Syria and other nations that were targeted by the White House administration. The university has corporate supporters and has gained international attention for its humanitarian mission.

BECOMING AN ALLY

For readers who are not undocumented, we hope that after reading this book, you will consider becoming an ally yourself. Being an ally means that you are never done listening and learning. We propose four levels of ally work.[120] We urge you to become more involved and increase your advocacy and leadership over time, as outlined in Table 4.1.

Despite the turmoil (and perhaps because of it), we must look to social action and change on behalf of educational rights. Carolina, an undocumented student and North Carolina resident, stated that she has faith in the community and in the power of social justice. She reminded us: "The power is not with someone sitting in the White House. The power is with each one of us."[121] As chapter 7 will attest to, people of all ages, including very young people, are using their power to lead actions of resistance and social change.

Educator Nancy Barile thinks of students' future contributions to society. She stated, "I believe a country's best resources are its human resources, and we need to

Table 4.1.   Levels of Advocacy and Leadership on Behalf of Undocumented Students

LEVEL 1—Friend	LEVEL 2—Resource
Some understanding of undocumented student experiences so that student is not having to always start from scratch with questions about, for example, why there is no SSN. Empathic. Engaged in ongoing awareness and learning of basic laws, policies, and scholarships related to undocumented students and their families.	Increased knowledge of undocumented students' experience, laws, and policies. Knowing what you don't know. Being able to refer students to others, being able to know the network of services and individuals that can assist undocumented students. Empathic. Engaged in ongoing awareness and learning of laws, policies, and scholarships related to undocumented students and their families.
LEVEL 3—Advocate	LEVEL 4—Leader
Informing others in your area of work about undocumented students' experiences, laws, and policies, and referrals. Being a proactive problem solver if there are problematic areas affecting undocumented students. Active/direct advocacy for undocumented students at the individual level. Empathic. Engaged in ongoing advanced awareness and learning of laws, policies, and scholarships related to undocumented students and their families.	Involved in ally training (facilitating, presenting, organizing). Active and direct advocacy for undocumented students at both the individual and institutional levels. Using leadership role to impact region and beyond. Creating and directing new programs and initiatives. Empathic. Engaged in ongoing, advanced awareness and learning of laws, policies, and scholarships related to undocumented students and their families.

tap into the power that these hardworking students can bring to our country when they are educated."[122] Indeed, Center for American Progress senior analyst Zenén Jaimes Pérez shared that "by 2020, our economy will face a shortage of 5 million educated workers."[123] Continuing their academic progress, enrolling in higher education and graduating from college, expands individuals' human potential.

Undocumented immigrants are powerful advocates, especially when equipped with crucial credentials to change law and policy. In November 2018, Denia Perez, twenty-eight, was the first DACA recipient to be admitted to the Connecticut Bar.[124] Denia arrived in the United States at eleven months of age and her parents supported her educational dreams. Through much struggle and sometimes self-doubt, she completed her undergraduate degree and went on to graduate from the Quinnipiac University School of Law. The *Connecticut Law Tribune* explained that because of Perez and other advocates, the law changed to include DACA recipients.[125] Robert Storace writes that the law eligibility for the bar previously was based on the idea that "the applicant is a citizen of the United States, or an alien lawfully residing in the United States."[126] The new language for the bar eligibility was amended to add, "which shall include an individual authorized to work lawfully in the United States." Education is often a family and community effort, along with individual determination. Coupled with a powerful motivation to change laws for the betterment of others, Denia and other undocumented immigrants are making a lasting impact for future generations.

INCLUDING THE ORIGINAL DREAMERS IN IMMIGRATION REFORM

In the case of Denia above, her mother stood by her during the bar recognition ceremony and has been mentioned in almost every news account as being the key to Denia's resiliency and success. However, what goes unmentioned is the pathway for Denia's mother to obtain permanent lawful status, such as citizenship or residency. In general, in media coverage and in many proposed (and actual) pieces of legislation, well-meaning advocates rationalize that children and youth should not be "punished" for choices made by their parents to cross the border without authorization.

Let's unpack this notion.

The majority of the undocumented youth who would benefit from the educational opportunities, deportation protection, and even a pathway to citizenship also want the same for their parents. When we demonize undocumented parents, we dishonor undocumented youth. The reasons for coming to the United States are many, and most undocumented adults migrate because they seek a better life for their family and are willing to work hard to support their children's future. However, as we read in the previous chapter on work, life in the United States is hard—both physically and emotionally.

As artist Ricardo Levins Morales shares in his artwork: "Nothing about us, without us, is for us."[127] Immigration and educational justice only work when we include all members of the immigrant community.

5

Freefall with No Safety Net: Health

Blanca, a twenty-five-year-old undocumented graduate student, had just moved in with her fiancé Mario and his parents. Once living all together, they commented on how much water she drank and how she seemed to always feel cold, despite the hot and humid August summer days. Four days into living with them, she was out of breath and not able to finish her sentences. Mario took Blanca to a local community clinic. Both were undocumented and did not have regular physicians. On the way to the clinic, Blanca experienced a deep decrease in her energy level; she wanted to be home in her bed and never get out. At the clinic, the nurse immediately told them to go to the emergency room because it looked like Blanca had a mouth infection—her gums were extremely swollen and her mouth was dry.

Blanca does not remember much else. Mario told her that they took her vitals and immediately diagnosed her as diabetic. Her sugar level was extremely high: 520, about five times higher than normal. The hospital staff rushed to find her a room—at that point, Blanca remembers waking up attached to IVs. However, she passed out again and ended up spending five days in the Intensive Care Unit. The ICU doctors said that if Blanca had not gone to the emergency room when she did, she would have likely died within hours.

In the months after the ER visit, Blanca paid out of pocket for her insulin and medical appointments she needed to control her diabetes. She could not consistently pay for either because she could not afford the recommended care plan. Blanca eventually found consistent physician care at a local community clinic and enrolled in a program to purchase her insulin. She has received coverage for conditions related to her diabetes, such as eye care.

While she is extremely worried about her remaining medical bills, Blanca considers herself very lucky to be alive and is working to transform her daily health habits, such as nutrition and exercise. She shared, "I have to pinch [prick] myself every day to check my blood sugar level." Now, Blanca takes insulin every day. She has a strong support system at home—her fiancé helps her manage her medicine and his family supports her good nutrition.

Blanca's story reveals a number of challenges with access to health care for unauthorized immigrants, such as waiting and suffering through symptoms that likely could have been treated early to prevent health emergencies. The lack of access, financial challenges, and the lack of health insurance are themes that run through this chapter. Undocumented immigration status adds another major obstacle to medical care that is manifested through lack of access, delayed or substandard treatment, and subsequent poor health outcomes.

Myth: The health care given to immigrants attracts them to the United States.
Myth Busted: Health care is not the reason for migration and is actually more accessible in immigrants' countries of origin, such as Mexico.

Migrants generally come to the United States to work, not for health care. A national sample of Latinx immigrants found that they arrive in relatively good physical condition—and that stress and work in the United States create mental and physical health challenges for undocumented migrants.[1] Mexican immigrants' health care is guaranteed by the Mexican Constitution, Article 4. The Mexican Secretary of Health's Office also covers health care for unemployed citizens. Open borders and permission to travel to Mexico for medical issues would aid undocumented immigrants who are living in the United States and who need access to health care in Mexico.

Ironically, many Americans flock to Mexico, Costa Rica, and Colombia for medical and dental care. In California, one study found that "approximately 1 million adults in California use medical, dental, or prescription services in Mexico, and nearly half of these are Mexican immigrants living in the United States."[2] Mexican health care costs—clinical care and medicine—are 70 to 90 percent less expensive than in the United States; California is the only state in which some private insurers work with Mexican medical insurers to offer cross-border coverage that is affordable for low-income Mexican immigrants, which is a powerful opportunity for patients.[3] States like California are also making efforts to create legislation and programs to actively enroll undocumented children and youth in health care services.[4]

Finally, despite common misperceptions about undocumented immigrants using health services in the United States, there is no evidence of increased undocumented patient use in states that offer subsidized care. For example, in California, a state that has offered regular dialysis to undocumented immigrants, there has been no significant rise in the undocumented patients enrolling in these services.[5]

Myth: Unauthorized immigrants are illegally using public medical care.
Myth Busted: Unauthorized immigrants are not eligible for most medical and social services. The ones for which they are eligible are dramatically underused.

The federal government has implemented policies that eliminate support for health and social services to undocumented immigrants. The Illegal Immigration

Reform and Immigrant Responsibility Act of 1996 (IIRIRA) and the Personal Responsibility and Work Opportunity Act of 1996 (a major "welfare reform" bill) created the current policy framework that denies health care benefits to undocumented immigrants. These acts added increased border and interior enforcement to the mix, along with taking away states' ability to include undocumented immigrants in many services.[6]

In a review of clinical studies that include undocumented clients, Drs. Lisa Fortuna and Michelle Porche found that the undocumented population *underutilized* all medical and mental health resources.[7] They found that U.S.-born children with undocumented parents also underutilized legally granted services. This is because their parents were far less likely to enroll them in services the children were eligible for, such as child care subsidies, public preschool, and food stamps.

At the state level, anti-immigrant policies that require citizenship negatively impact health care access, not only for undocumented immigrants, but also U.S. Latinx citizens as well. In Alabama, state lawmakers passed the Taxpayer and Citizen Protection Act that required proof of citizenship to receive public benefits. This resulted in U.S. citizen Latinas to underutilize health services, in addition to decrease their "use of services that were exempt from residency proof, such as treatment for sexually transmitted infections."[8] In another example, in Arizona, after state lawmakers passed a now-defunct law, Arizona Senate Bill 1070 (SB 1070), which gave police the power to detain individuals who could not verify citizenship, Toomey and colleagues found Mexican-origin adolescent mothers were less likely to use public assistance or take their U.S. citizen infants to receive medical care.[9]

It is clear that undocumented immigrants are a boon to the U.S. health system.[10] In a landmark study, Leah Zallman and collaborators found that undocumented immigrants pay taxes that go directly to federal health care funds, and that in 2011, they paid "$3.5 billion *more* than they needed in care."[11] The payroll taxes generated by undocumented immigrants contribute to one of the ways that Medicare is funded. For example, the Hospital Insurance Trust Fund (HITH) has received significant funding from immigrant contributions over the past two decades. Zallman and her colleagues' study concluded that had immigrants not contributed from 2000 to 2011, HITH would be insolvent by 2029. Aside from Medicare, "undocumented immigrants incur an estimated $5.5 billion in non-Medicare publicly funded health care expenses annually" but they generate $10.6 billion through state and local taxes.[12] Clearly, the idea that undocumented immigrants are costing U.S. taxpayers money for "free" health care is unfounded; unauthorized immigrants pay nearly twice as much in taxes as the costs they incur for health care expenses.

These crucial contributions have been severely underestimated—or perhaps not considered—by the Trump Administration, which has been considering the creation of additional health care barriers for undocumented immigrants deemed as "public charges" (people who have ever received any form of government assistance).[13]

BOX 5.1: ELISA'S EMERGENCY ROOM NIGHTMARE

Elisa, a thirty-five-year-old undocumented Latina, came to the United States at the age of sixteen. She is part of a mixed-status family. In a family of six, she is the only person who is undocumented. Her five immediate family members have medical insurance through employment or the Affordable Care Act. She applied for and has been waiting for a permanent residence card for sixteen years. Her undocumented status excludes her from the Affordable Care Act. She is unable to afford the $400–$500 per month private medical insurance.

Elisa is in desperate need of medical insurance. She has discovered that she has been suffering from a hyperactive thyroid for the last eight years. Previously, she attributed her symptoms to stress or exhaustion. She never had preventive care as an adult and just continued to live and work through the symptoms. Elisa finally sought medical care after she started having problems with one of her eyes.

She paid $200 to see an endocrinologist who gave her a discount since she was a cash patient. The endocrinologist told her that indeed she had a hyperactive thyroid and that he was surprised that to that point she had not fainted or experienced cardiac arrest. The endocrinologist informed Elisa that she needed to get a lot of blood tests performed, but since he knew Elisa would not be able to afford all the blood tests, he only ordered the minimal amount that would be crucial to her life. Elisa also got a prescription for a drug that is very costly to non-insured patients. In order to have a balanced thyroid she needs to take two to three pills per day, but since they are very costly, she breaks them in half and limits her dosage per day.

On some days, she skips her dosage in order to make it last longer. However, after skipping a few days, Elisa experienced extremely rapid heart palpitations. She thought she was having a heart attack so she went to the emergency room. It took four days in the ER to stabilize her heart, which resulted in a $30,000 hospital bill. Unfortunately, she did not qualify for emergency care that is legally available for undocumented immigrants because the hospital social worker decided that her rapid heart palpitations were not related to a heart attack. This medical assessment excluded her from Emergency Room coverage. Elisa has inadvertently been paying toward this coverage through the payroll taxes that are taken out of her paycheck each week.

Elisa has no medical insurance. She sees her endocrinologist only when necessary due to the high costs of visits. She does not skip her medicine anymore, but she still does not take the daily and required dosages because she cannot afford buying the monthly prescription. Elisa needs specialty care and medicine for the rest of her life, but with her income she can only afford a limited amount.

As told to and written by Flor Saldaña, MA

THE EMERGENCY ROOM:
THE ONLY REMAINING FEDERAL PROTECTION

Elisa's case study in Box 5.1 demonstrates that the only federal medical protection the government gives to unauthorized immigrants is the 1986 Emergency Medical Treatment & Labor Act (EMTALA), which was created to ensure public access to emergency services regardless of ability to pay and immigration status.[14] Services only extend to active emergencies such as active pain, organ failure, and active labor. They do not include routine or preventative care. Medicaid funds are primarily billed for births. It is estimated that only 1 to 4 percent of the state's undocumented population uses emergency room services.[15]

In a report to the City of New York, public health and medical researchers explained that treatment at an emergency room is wholly inadequate for the uninsured.[16] Here is their summary of the limitations of EMTALA care for undocumented immigrants:

- It does not cover supplies or medicine for chronic conditions.
- It does not manage post-ER care.
- It does not include regular appointments or treatments.
- It does not include mental health crises.
- The definition of the "emergency" covered can be too narrow.
- It does not include recovery or rehabilitation: a patient could be released home after heart surgery with no follow-up care or medication included.

Unfortunately, state-by-state definitions of emergencies differ. Public health scholar Michael Rodriguez and his colleagues explained how states interpret the federal Medicare law:

> In some states, outpatient dialysis for renal failure is covered under emergency Medicaid, while in other states, dialysis is covered only when a person goes into diabetic shock and dialysis is required to save his or her life. Once the patient recovers, he or she is discharged to the community without further services until renal failure forces re-hospitalization.[17]

Even in the case of Elisa, who is in a state with inclusive policies for treatment at the emergency room (California), a clinician can decide to assess a medical emergency as eligible according to the Medicare law or not.

At the time of the Affordable Care Act (ACA) rollout, many were glad to see that DACA recipients were included in ACA coverage. However, a few months after the ACA became law, the government revised it and excluded DACA recipients, noting that they were still undocumented immigrants. This occurred despite the fact that DACA includes provisions that give recipients permission to legally work and protection from deportation. However, like other undocumented immigrants, DACA recipients are still eligible to use emergency room services and community clinics.[18]

Most immigrant health advocates consider the changes to the ACA that resulted in minimal health care protection for undocumented youth as a betrayal of them and their societal contributions.

Overall, the limited scope and the extraordinary costs of emergency room care do not make sense—medically or fiscally. In California, for example, $1.7 billion annually is spent on emergency room care.[19] Preventative and routine medical care would only cost the state a fraction of the budget—a budget that unauthorized immigrants actively contribute to through payroll and other state and federal taxes.

In terms of large medical insurance companies, only Kaiser Permanente has a program, Charitable Health Coverage, which provides subsidized health insurance, assistance for premiums, and copays for low-income people.[20] To qualify, families or individuals must be 100 to 300 percent below the federal poverty level, depending on the state. As of 2017, Kaiser offers this program in the following states and regions: Colorado (for people under thirty-five years old), Georgia (for adults), the Mid-Atlantic region (for children and adults), the Northwest region (for children), and California (for children). Having medical insurance available to undocumented immigrants is inclusive. However, the costs of coverage may be prohibitive even when part or most of the insurance is subsidized.

HOW STATES "DO" (OR DON'T DO) HEALTH CARE FOR UNDOCUMENTED IMMIGRANTS

UCLA researcher Michael Rodriguez and his colleagues addressed the levels of health care inclusion for undocumented immigrants across all fifty states and the District of Columbia.[21] The authors examined state laws, mandates, and practices related to health care, work, immigration enforcement, driving laws, and other issues of concern for immigrants. Specific to the area of public health, they measured the extent to which states included or excluded immigrants on the basis of their status in the areas of: children's health insurance, prenatal care, and funding formulas for the Supplemental Nutrition Assistance Program (SNAP, sometimes also referred to as the program it replaced, food stamps).

The researchers graded each state based on the following questions:

- Does the state provide undocumented children health insurance?
- Does the state provide undocumented pregnant mothers with prenatal care?
- Does the state's definition of family size include undocumented family members?

For each question, a state received a +1 for "yes" and a −1 for "no." The states/ regions earning a 3 (meaning a yes for each question) were California, Illinois, Washington, the District of Columbia, New York, and Massachusetts, indicating that they have the most inclusive health care and social service practices for undocumented immigrants. The states that had the most exclusionary practices were Connecticut, Utah, Kansas, Arizona, and Ohio.

Middle-range states have varying degrees of outreach. Reporter Louisa Radnofsky gave an example of how Oklahoma is proactively trying to encourage usage of public health services by undocumented immigrants:

> Oklahoma has a pregnant-women's program aimed at ensuring prenatal care for babies who will become U.S. citizens, named "Soon to be Sooners." This campaign draws on inclusive wordplay using the term "Sooner," which is the state name for people who live in Oklahoma. Historically, the name "Sooner" is derived from people crossing "illegally" in the "light of moonshine" to stake claims on land in the Oklahoma territory after the 1889 Indian Appropriation Act.[22]

Health Care Approaches of Selected States: New York, California, and Texas

New York, California, and Texas are states with some of the largest undocumented immigration populations in the country (the fourth, first, and second respectively). In each state, legislators are responding to the health care needs of marginalized communities in distinctly different ways.

New York—"Lady Liberty's Message"

The Statue of Liberty symbolizes freedom and democracy, and welcomes immigrants with the poem inscribed at the base of the statue. The words chiseled in stone on the statue read: "Give me your tired, your poor, your huddled masses yearning to breathe free. . . . Send [them] to me. I lift my lamp beside the golden door."[23] While there is a complex history of immigration through New York's Ellis Island, this sentiment has been a powerful call for the current advocacy work of community members and legislators to bring resources to undocumented immigrants throughout the years. Yet, in New York, 457,000 unauthorized, uninsured immigrant residents remain ineligible for health care coverage after the Affordable Care Act was signed into law.[24]

Elisabeth Benjamin from the Community Service Society, an advocacy group in New York that is providing ideas for how to expand the state's health care safety net to undocumented immigrants, stated: "We have lots of new Americans in New York State. They contribute substantially in taxes and in providing U.S. great workers and so, it's sort of a matter of justice. It's only fair to treat our immigrant residents equally as other residents."[25] New York City has adopted progressive policies for immigrants, such as city identification cards for all residents, and is working on local voting rights for undocumented immigrants residing in the city.

California—"A Ray of Hope"

In 2015, California became the first state to offer undocumented children public health care through the passage of Senate Bill 4, which "would allow undocumented immigrants to purchase health insurance through Covered California, the state health insurance marketplace created under the Affordable Care Act. Covered California offers Medi-Cal coverage to low-income immigrants who are undocumented."[26] Reshma Shamasunder, executive director of the California Immigrant Policy Center, contextualized this historic moment as taking the "first step toward recognizing that health care truly is a human right."[27] It will go a long way in supporting the "roughly 1.5 million undocumented Californians [who] are without medical care."[28]

The case of California is important because the state has not always been so welcoming of undocumented immigrants. In 1994, Californians passed one of the most anti-immigrant state laws in the country. Proposition 187 aimed to prevent undocumented immigrants from attending school, and denied them social services and medical care. In addition, this proposition increased immigration enforcement and created criminal workplace sanctions for both undocumented workers and employers. While it was eventually overturned, the state's climate became heated during the elections and initial implementation of Prop 187. Researcher Otto Santa Ana conducted a "metaphorical analysis" of immigrants, based on articles published in the *Los Angeles Times*, when the anti-immigration policy was being proposed. He found extremely negative metaphors for immigrants, such as "animals to be hunted."[29] Such blatant and racist stigmatization of immigrant families created a climate of hostility and distrust in the state.

However, California has emerged from those anti-immigrant years to become a leader in innovative, humane, and pro-immigration laws. Governor Jerry Brown supported a bill to make the entire state of California a sanctuary state. Social work researchers Luis Zayas and Mollie Bradlee described legislation that reflected progressive efforts to support undocumented families, including recognizing that services are needed to cope with the mental health issues associated with children caught in the midst of deportation.

> California Assembly Bill 2015 Call for Kids Act (2012) requires law enforcement officers to inform detainees of their rights to make up to three free local phone calls to make child-care arrangements, again limiting situations in which children are suddenly abandoned or left without supervision.
>
> California Senate Bill 1064 (2012) establishes new procedures to assist in the reunification of families, particularly when parents have been removed from the United States. Notably, the bill requires that the California Department of Social Services (CDSS) set forth guidelines by January 2014 that establish best practices of communication with foreign consulates to successfully locate noncitizen parents and arrange for safe reunification of the child and parent in the parent's country of origin.[30]

California is creating many ways for other states to create laws that support and acknowledge undocumented immigrants. Additionally, California state senator Ricardo Lara said of legislation such as Senate Bill 4 that grants undocumented children health coverage: "This is a major investment that California is doing, and it's completely the reverse of what we're seeing at the national level."[31]

Texas—High Need, Oppressive Tactics

Texas has the second highest population of Latinxs in the country. At ten million people, Latinxs comprise nearly 40 percent of the state's population and the third largest immigrant population in the United States.[32] There are counties with extreme poverty and large undocumented populations, particularly by the Mexican border. For example, in Hidalgo County, the average household income is $12,000 per year. There has historically been a fluid relationship along the border for transnational family networks. In terms of medical care, Texas has a crisis over uninsured immigrants and access to health services.

> As of 2013, Texas has the highest uninsured population of any state in the nation at 22% of the population overall. Latinos are more than twice as likely as whites to be uninsured in Texas. . . . Foreign-born Latinos in Texas are more than twice as likely to be uninsured as U.S.-born Latinos. Latinos living in border counties are significantly more likely than those from other racial or ethnic groups to be uninsured and living without health insurance for over a year. Hidalgo County . . . has the highest rate of uninsured people among all metropolitan counties in the nation. The percentage of residents of *colonias* who lack insurance is even higher, ranging from 50–80%.[33]

Guided by conservative politicians, Texans rejected the expansion of adult Medicaid, which "would have insured 1.5 million low-income working adults and provided $90 billion in federal funding to remedy many of the inequality health care gaps in rural areas."[34]

The health care–related concerns for undocumented Latinxs in Texas come at a time when Texas has passed one of the most draconian pieces of state legislation against undocumented immigrants in the nation. Texas State Senate Bill 4, passed on May 7, 2017, punishes elected officials who create sanctuary cities or counties with economic sanctions, fines, and jail time.[35] It also gives expanded rights for law enforcement to enact immigration profiling and allows them to hold undocumented immigrants in jail on behalf of ICE. Strong opposition from legal and immigration advocates, along with elected officials, including sheriffs, resulted in the law being reviewed by both a U.S. District Court and then the 5th U.S. Court of Appeals.[36] Ultimately, the majority of the law was upheld and remains in effect in spite of serious opposition.[37]

As a point of context, states with the fastest growing undocumented immigrant populations are in the South and Midwest, and include states such as Alabama, South Carolina, Tennessee, and Kentucky. By 2050, Nebraska expects its Latinx population to triple.[38] Some states, similar to Texas, have enacted reactionary and xenophobic responses to growing undocumented communities, which will be discussed later in this chapter.

The Difference a County Makes

Despite state level politics and laws, counties and local services can make a difference. In a national survey of the twenty-five counties with the largest unauthorized

immigrant populations, twenty have programs that pay for the low-income uninsured to have doctor visits, shots, prescription drugs, lab tests, and surgeries at local
providers.[39] As an extension of our discussion of Texas, we will examine counties
within Texas to understand how undocumented immigrants navigate health care.
Political affiliation can make a difference in how immigrants are viewed and treated
in a given county. A Democratic county official, Clay Jenkins in Dallas County,
stated his philosophy: "There are 2.5 million people that live here, and they're all
important and they're all deserving of respect and medical care."[40] In contrast, in
Tarrant County, which includes part of neighboring Fort Worth, all patients are required to prove legal immigration status before receiving medical care. The decision
to exclude undocumented immigrants from services was made because the county
was struggling to pay for U.S. citizens.

However, there is evidence that indicates that providing health services to immigrants can actually cut state costs. An example of this is in Montgomery County,
Maryland. Expanding services to include undocumented immigrants there resulted
in "a 41% reduction of behavioral-health emergency-room visits and a 67% reduction in trips related to chronic conditions."[41] Clearly, smart policies that emphasize
prevention and early treatment of chronic disease and other health problems save
money in the long run by cutting down on the need for emergency services.

In rural counties in Texas, women are often unable to access any social services to
report or prevent harassment or domestic violence. This lack of access is especially
true when the county is saturated with immigration enforcement, which fuels fear
of all authorities. Ana Rodriguez DeFrates of the National Latina Institute for Reproductive Health described the conditions in Texas:

> Many women live on the outskirts of communities where there is not even a bus service.
> . . . You have to walk at least 45 minutes to get to the bus. And that 45-minute walk ex-
> poses you to Border Patrol agents and an increase in Department of Public Safety Texas
> agents. . . . What you have is a recipe for people too fearful of immigrant consequences
> to travel the great distances that are required for getting the care you need.[42]

Public health research compares the health care behavior of pregnant undocumented Latinas in immigration-friendly counties versus less welcoming counties.
Scott Rhodes and his team of collaborators used mixed methods (i.e., statistical
analysis of public records and focus groups) to focus on South Carolina, a state with
growing anti-immigration legislation.[43] They studied seven counties that intention-
ally linked county law enforcement resources with (federal) immigration enforcement through a program called, "Section 287(g) [which] authorizes Immigration
and Custom Enforcement (ICE) to enter into agreements with state and local
law enforcement agencies to enforce federal immigration law during their regular,
daily law enforcement activities."[44] The experience of these women in heavy anti-
immigrant enforcement counties was contrasted with the experiences of women
participants living in seven "sanctuary" counties, which explicitly rejected the Section
287(g) arrangement.

Interestingly, they found that county lines were not significant when they examined use of health care services between the two groups. In general, undocumented Latinas sought out *less or no* maternal health care before their babies were born, compared to U.S.-born Latinas, regardless of the county in which they resided. This points to the general fears immigrants feel, possibly derived from media depictions of harsh penalties and law enforcement activities targeting immigrants. Also, it is possible the actual practices of so-called sanctuary counties are not strong enough to dissuade fear of a penalty for seeking health care. Participants did not know if they lived in a county with a Section 287(g) agreement or not. The researchers found that overall, regardless of the county, "participants reported fearing immigration enforcement policies, avoiding health services, and thus sacrificing their own health and the health of members of their families."[45]

THE CRUCIAL ROLE OF COMMUNITY CLINICS

Sweeping exclusion denied undocumented immigrants access to the federal Patient Protection and Affordable Care Act (ACA) of 2010. Researcher Omar Martinez and his colleagues reasoned that "healthcare safety net hospitals and clinics, which are the main providers of health care and services for undocumented immigrants, might face funding and reimbursement challenges by ACA, making it impossible to continue providing services to undocumented immigrants."[46]

Community clinics are important health care resources for undocumented immigrants.[47] Public health researchers Alexander Ortega and his colleagues report that "Latinos account for more than 35% of patients at community health clinics (CHCs) nationally, and they are the majority of CHC users in many states."[48] For most undocumented individuals, the community clinic is their only legitimate avenue to health care and serves as an important social network site for the community.

A North Carolina study of undocumented immigrants and their attitudes about medical insurance found that most were very receptive to the importance of medical care. However, because none had health insurance, they used community clinics.[49] In fact, many of the participants in the study credited the outreach efforts of local community clinics for their ability to access health care. Community clinics are usually located in the heart of immigrant communities and frequently operate on donations, grants, and other "soft money." Profiles of community clinics across the country demonstrate that many function as the only trusted, affordable health care option.

In Philadelphia, the community clinic *"Puentes de Salud"* (Bridges to Health) has been volunteer run since 2006. Reporter John Hurdle profiled the program and founder Dr. Steve Larson, and it was the topic of a 2017 award-winning HBO documentary, *Clínica de Migrantes: Life, Liberty and the Pursuit of Happiness.*[50] The program focuses on health services for low-income undocumented Latinx clients, offering them everything from dental care to family-planning advice to oncology referrals for as little as $10 per visit. *Puentes de Salud* had been operating out of borrowed spaces—business offices, the back room of a mechanics shop, and church basements. However, they have a comprehensive office that offers preventive medical services and attorneys, along with financial literacy and cooking classes. While parents have appointments, tutoring and other services are offered to their children. *Puentes de Salud* also serves as a bridge to resources for clients who need treatment for major illnesses, such as leukemia. The program also supports helping the families of deceased clients to make travel arrangements to bury their loved ones in their homeland. The program runs on volunteers but recently has started to hire staff funded by donations and other sources of income. Dr. Larson and his team focus on the needs of the community, trying to prevent illness and disease. In this context, this program treats undocumented immigrants with respect guided by an ethic of humane service.

Planned Parenthood, a national organization, has clinics that serve low-income communities. Their funding is under attack in the Republican-controlled government because of their abortion services. Yet, abortion is only a very small part of what Planned Parenthood does in terms of reproductive health for both women and men. Planned Parenthood serves clients beyond the important services related to reproductive health and does preventive screening for blood pressure, diabetes, and other chronic illnesses. Vanessa Gonzalez-Plumhoff, director of Latino Leadership & Engagement at Planned Parenthood, explained: "Defunding Planned Parenthood—and thus reducing the availability of quality, trusted healthcare providers—would strike yet another blow to undocumented women's already limited access to reproductive health care."[51]

Projecto Salud (Health Project) in Montgomery County, Maryland, runs a successful program, "Montgomery Cares," that funds community clinics serving thousands of undocumented immigrants. Directed by Dr. César Palacios, it is "housed in a government building in Wheaton close to a metro station, fast-food franchises and an apartment complex."[52] Project Salud's services include treatment plans for diabetes, orthopedic injuries, and anxiety disorders. Community clinics like this serve a critical need in immigrant communities and ultimately save money through preventative health practices that lower the need for expensive emergency care.

Dr. Cristina Gamboa is an obstetrician at a community clinic called *Salud Para La Gente* (Health for the People) in the agricultural coastal region of Watsonville, California.[53] She is committed to providing pre-natal and birthing care for immigrant women. She has noticed an increase in cases of high blood pressure and notes that the pregnant women are very stressed about intensive immigration enforcement. She notes that the expectant mothers are also indicating higher levels of depression and anxiety than they have seen in the past. The clinic provides a safe haven for families to access health care, but can do little to protect people from the external political and enforcement activities.

The effectiveness of community clinics can be jeopardized due to gentrification. For example, the California Immigrant Policy Center reported on a health care program in San Francisco that is among the most robust in the state.[54] Its aim was to help ease the unjust exclusion of undocumented residents from federal health care reform. However, the rapid invasion of high-tech companies and professionals into traditionally immigrant communities have forced clinics to relocate. In a historically Latinx and immigrant neighborhood called the "Mission District," over the last ten years, the immigrant population fell by 28 percent and the U.S.-born population increased by 11 percent.[55] Gentrification has high costs to undocumented immigrants' health and well-being. A report on the city showed that the lowest income immigrants, likely undocumented, are experiencing the most residential displacement during the process of gentrification. If low-income and undocumented people cannot afford to live in the city, then the progressive work of the health care programs located there will be unused by the very population that could use them most.

BOX 5.2: JUAN'S EXPERIENCE OF WORKPLACE INJURY AT A CONSTRUCTION SITE

Juan, a thirty-six-year-old Latino, has been living in the United States for fifteen years as an undocumented immigrant. His immediate family members are all in Mexico and he only has a couple of relatives in the United States. He lives with four other Latino males, who are also undocumented immigrants from Mexico. They share a two-bedroom apartment and they all work in the construction industry.

Juan's first jobs upon arrival in the United States were factory jobs that paid the minimum wage. He wanted a job that would pay more, but with his high school education and undocumented status the only option for work was in the construction industry. He had friends who worked in construction and they invited him to work with them. Even though Juan knew that construction work was dangerous, he reasoned that the pay made up for it.

Juan had heard and seen people have really bad accidents on construction worksites. But he never thought it would happen to him. Then one day at work a heavy, steel beam fell on his right shoulder. He felt some pain, but continued working. In the days following the incident, his pain became worse and he had to wear support bands and apply pain ointments or take over-the-counter pain medication. He was reluctant to tell his supervisors because he was afraid of being fired or being perceived as weak. Further, he thought that if a workers' compensation case were filed, his undocumented status would be disclosed.

His pain got unbearable and started to affect his physical movement. Unable to withstand it, Juan finally decided to inform the supervisor. The supervisor did not believe him, but Juan told him that he had witnesses to his incident. Juan recounts that the project managers would mock him in various ways: accusing him of lying, moving his shoulder to see if he was really in pain, and telling him insults in English. The supervisor told Juan that if he wanted to open a workers' compensation case then everybody in the construction industry would know and never hire him again. At that point, Juan did not care if he was never hired again in the construction industry, because his physical pain was torture.

Almost two months passed before Juan could see a doctor through workers' compensation. The construction company dragged out and delayed processing the claim. The doctor found sprains in his wrists and shoulder, damage to his arm tendons, and his right clavicle bone was dislocated. However, Juan's medical treatment for these serious conditions has been subpar. He leaves the doctor visits frustrated because the doctor says that he is getting better, but Juan does not feel improvement. The doctor has never taken Juan off work, but has advised the supervisors to give him lighter work. So, Juan has to keep working in pain with poor medical treatment. He is also upset with the medical office translators: he can tell that they do not translate what he says and that at times, they are not listening to him. Juan just wants to be physically healthy again, but feels hopeless due to the carelessness, disregard, and inhumane treatment he experiences from the workers' compensation doctor and office staff personnel.

—As told to and written by Flor Saldaña, MA

EFFECTS OF IMMIGRATION POLICIES: BAD FOR HEALTH

As you see in Juan's story in Box 5.2, living as an undocumented immigrant in the United States is often detrimental to one's physical and emotional health, because of the multiple levels of exclusion and oppression stemming from immigration policy and a climate of fear around that policy. Undocumented immigrants do not have firm legal standing, respect, and inalienable human rights in the United States. Undocumented immigrants' vulnerable health stems from being excluded from most social and medical systems, having their labor exploited, and the constant fear of actual or perceived threats from immigration enforcement.

Undocumented immigrants are usually in good health upon arrival in the United States. In general, public health researchers find that there is a "new immigrant" health bonus— immigrants benefit from their country of origin's unprocessed food habits and less sedentary activity—but these effects fade with the conditions of living and working in the United States.[56] In fact, the more assimilation (e.g., speaking English), the higher the risk factors for poor health outcomes for immigrants.[57]

Undocumented immigrants must find multiple sources and resources for their health needs.[58] In a recent study of immigrant youth in California, 71 percent "currently need access" to a doctor; however, 69 percent did not have health insurance, 53 percent had not seen a doctor in over a year, and 58 percent had relied on the Internet as a source of care.[59] Findings from this study also indicated that 50 percent of immigrant youth delayed getting medical care due to finances, access, and fear.[60]

Medical expenses in the United States are exorbitant for most people, and especially for a population who lives near or below the poverty rate without health insurance. Immigrant youth, in a study called, *Undocumented and Uninsured*, explained the choices their families made:

- I have a blood disease, and I have to constantly look for ways to stay healthy. My family stopped taking me to the hospital because it was getting expensive, and we couldn't pay.
- It's a struggle because we either pay our rent or go to the clinic, and the rent is our first priority.
- I broke my arm and had to tolerate the pain for three days until I had to go to the emergency room to help with the pain.[61]

Undocumented immigrants are in a double bind—their previous and current lives compound to create medical hardships. Medical researcher Fernando Holguin and his collaborators found that there are many overlooked health challenges for migrants who move to allegedly better developed countries than their countries of origin.[62] They find that "migrants suffer from medical conditions typical of other populations (e.g., asthma, tobacco-related disease, sleep-disordered breathing), but also have conditions relevant to the nature of their living circumstances, including infection (e.g., tuberculosis) and malnutrition."[63]

Undocumented immigrants' lack of access to nutritious food adversely affects their health.[64] Undocumented immigrants often live in poor communities, many of which are characterized as being "food deserts": places with little fresh food and few supermarkets and many liquor stores and fast-food restaurants.

While dangerous work conditions are discussed in another chapter in this book, they are central to our consideration of serious health concerns related to occupational health and safety. Francesca Gany and her colleagues conducted an extensive review of studies about health and undocumented workers in urban settings. They found that Latino immigrant workers experience the highest fatality and injury rates while at work, and they have the lowest rate of reporting injuries.[65] In 2007, 44 percent of recorded immigrant occupational fatalities involved Mexican workers.[66] Regardless of immigration status, workers' compensation covers medical care.

In this same review, they found the highest injury rates for Mexican workers in urban, low-paying, potentially hazardous occupations including manufacturing, construction, restaurants, moving, and cleaning. Both men and women are affected.

Mexican women often work in cleaning but also in urban factories as food processing packagers, garment sewers and cutters, and assembly line workers. Health

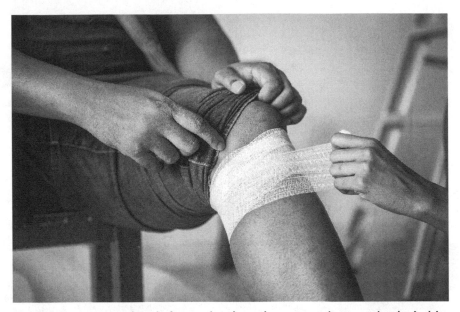

Figure 5.1. Many workers in low-paying, hazardous occupations sustain physical injuries on the job.
rawpixel, Unsplash

concerns for women working in factories include: "repetitive motion injuries, poor working conditions, and insufficient provision of personal protective equipment and safety training." Men in construction and day labor report similar injuries, along with being denied lunch and dinner breaks. Restaurant work yields similar injuries for men and women: burns, cuts, punctures, sprains, and respiratory problems.

The researchers also discovered that the same employers are cited and are repeat offenders—in complaints of occupational injury and death. Therefore, repeat offenders continue inhumane, careless, and dangerous work practices for primarily undocumented immigrant workforces. In yet another study, Michael Flynn and colleagues found that working in construction for a small company (which represents 89 percent of all companies in the United States) increases young men's likelihood of injury and fatality due to lack of safety training and pressure to work harder and faster.[67] Among the many challenges in caring for these workplace injuries are that employers often do not offer health insurance and workers often do not have personal insurance. Undocumented immigrants are not eligible for public health care—even though their paychecks withhold Social Security, workers' compensation, and disability benefits that they likely will never collect. However, the research team also summarizes additional key reasons for poor health outcomes for immigrants. Other reasons cited include "reluctan[ce] to seek health care as a result of numerous barriers including culture, language, hours of operation of medical facilities, and lack of transportation and child care."[68]

Public health researchers Jacqueline Torres and Steven Wallace surveyed sixteen hundred Latinx immigrants in the United States and found that undocumented immigrants' pre-immigration lives included trauma, violence, and economic hardship.[69] The decision and process of migration also created challenges:

> Having to migrate is generally indicative of a lack of perceived personal control over migration decision-making, which may contribute to past and current levels of stress and in turn influence outcomes of psychological distress and self-assessed physical well-being.[70]

Specific groups of undocumented immigrants may have additional health risks from experiences in their home countries. For example, "61 percent of undocumented trans[gendered] Latinas reported that they came to the United States because they were running away from physical, social, psychological, and/or economic violence."[71] They may bring undiagnosed health issues with them when they migrate to the United States.

Omar Martinez and his research team reviewed 325 studies related to undocumented immigrants and their health.[72] Several important trends emerged. They found a "direct relationship between anti-immigration policies and their effects on access to health services" and that lack of health care access causes symptoms of "depression, anxiety, and post-traumatic stress disorder."[73] Many undocumented immigrants already have unique and possibly negative health factors stemming from their home country, their journey to the United States, and/or their experiences in the United States because of their immigration status. Martinez and his colleagues explained:

> Undocumented immigrants originate from countries with long-term war or civil unrest, or in some cases they migrate for particular economic, cultural, social, and political reasons. Undocumented immigrants have often experienced multiple pre- and post-migration stressful events, including imprisonment, rape, ethnic cleansing, physical violence, economic distress, torture, and more.[74]

Even in the few counties or states that allow some use of health care (HIV, pre-natal, serious injury) for immigrants, this research found that "they were hesitant to go to health centers or to receive emergency care due to potential retaliation and fear of deportation."[75] The tactics used in states that prohibit undocumented immigrants from seeking any public, affordable, medical care are numerous. For example, in Indiana and North Carolina:

> Undocumented immigrants are prevented from using vital health services such as HIV screening and prenatal care by creating barriers including . . . asking for documentation before accessing health services and the use of police checkpoints in front of health departments.[76]

In addition, when unauthorized immigrants do seek out services that are legally available to them, intake and medical staff treat them poorly. In a study based in Montreal, Canada, of over one thousand hospital staff and clinicians, researchers found *staff members* held restrictive and biased attitudes toward undocumented immigrants who were in fact entitled to medical health care.[77] In the United States, another study found that "two-thirds of primary care providers demonstrated implicit biases against Latinos even as they explicitly reported egalitarian attitudes toward the group."[78] Discrimination is clearly another barrier to health care access for undocumented people.

A number of studies have shown that there is a chilling effect on undocumented immigrants when anti-immigrant laws are passed at the state levels. In one study, researchers examined the obesity rates across twenty-one states.[79] They found a positive link between obesity and states that had explicitly passed legislation that restricted or excluded undocumented immigrants from access to health care. Based on in-depth qualitative interviews, the authors found that undocumented immigrants were in fact too scared to go outside and exercise for fear of ICE deportations, which increased their obesity rates.

Public health researchers examined the effects of undocumented women seeking health care after Alabama passed one of the broadest anti-immigration laws, House Bill 56: The Alabama Taxpayer and Citizen Protection Act (HB 56).[80] At the time, Alabama was the second fastest growing undocumented immigrant population (after South Carolina, which also enacted broad-reaching anti-immigration legislation). This bill had the effect of reducing the already limited health services in the state, and giving local law enforcement the ability to inquire about citizenship during any type of encounter with individuals. Perhaps not surprisingly, the passage of HB 56 adversely affected health care access for undocumented women. Undocumented mothers—even ones with U.S. citizen children—encountered negative treatment by staff while seeking health care. Among all the mothers, there was general confusion as to what was still available to their children. Women who had recently given birth went to the hospital for the delivery—a time that is already stressful—and reported feeling enormous fear about immigration enforcement. One woman shared:

> When I started going to my [prenatal care] appointments, I was worried, and said to myself . . . "only God knows if I am going to return home or not." There in the hospital, too, I heard stories and people told me, "They picked up my friend" or "my brother-in-law" and things like that. It was a very tense time.[81]

Omar Martinez and his team of researchers concluded:

> The presence of anti-immigration rhetoric . . . impacted health providers' attitudes and behaviors towards serving the health needs of undocumented immigrants. Some providers, in localities where these anti-immigration policies were implemented, discriminated against undocumented immigrants by denying services and saw them as the "other."[82]

The research of Elizabeth Moran Fitzgerald and her nursing colleagues provided evidence of racial bias by health care providers.[83] However, they argued that nurses have a professional and ethical commitment to treat each patient fully and fairly. They presented the following case study, based on their supervision experience:

> Ms. Ximena Martinez is a Guatemalan national who is pregnant and has been admitted to the Mother Baby Unit in a local hospital to deliver her child. She is accompanied by several members of her extended family who do not speak English. During shift report, a nurse complains of being sick and tired of "illegal aliens" coming to the United States and "dropping their babies" so their children can become U.S. citizens. To her co-workers this nurse states, "If these people are living in the United States they need to learn to speak English." Another co-worker nods in agreement and attributes rising unemployment to "illegals taking jobs that Americans need." Two other nurses and the nursing student assigned to Ms. Martinez remain silent during this dialogue. Later, the student learns that Ms. Martinez is a U.S. citizen, has a graduate degree, and is employed by a large corporation.[84]

The authors offered solutions based on Joseph Badaracco's tenets of Quiet Leadership to help nurses not be bystanders to biased treatment and to find constructive, direct, and respectful ways to address injustices.[85] Ultimately, they called on nurses "to hold one another accountable for adherence to the [American Nursing Association's 2015] code of ethics which clearly prohibits any show of disrespect toward a patient or any group of people under their care."

Negative experiences with health care have dramatic consequences during public safety crises. For example, in the case of the Flint, Michigan, water crisis, Ana Aparicio reported:

> An estimated 1,000 Latino immigrants in Flint would not open their doors to National Guard troops bringing bottled water. Nor do Latino immigrants have easy access to clean water if they leave their homes. Weeks ago, troops began giving out water and filters at Flint fire stations. Officials asked for identification—and turned away immigrants who didn't provide one.[86]

In addition, language barriers and a disregard for the Latinx community were apparent when English-only warnings and resources were provided to the residents. In Flint, many who needed this life-or-death information were prevented from receiving complete information due to language barriers. Similarly, the personal safety of North County San Diego farmworkers, many of whom were undocumented, was threatened in the face of serious wildfires in the region.[87] The key to achieving trust and providing health care to the undocumented community is a truly community-based outreach and educational program. In a California Immigrant Youth survey, "42 percent reported that they initially turned to friends and family for guidance and support in accessing medical care" instead of turning to medical authorities, which signals how unwelcoming they view the system.[88]

We can conclude that active and impending laws prohibiting use of public health resources, lack of appropriate language, fear of detection (and deportation) when attempting to access public health services, and negative treatment when using the services contribute to the overall low usage of public health care by undocumented immigrants in the United States.

UNDOCUMENTED CHILDREN AND YOUTH

Unless families live in an inclusive state, undocumented children often have very little recourse for health care. This leaves parents of undocumented children with hard choices due to the lack of health insurance, low financial resources, or not knowing where to turn for trusted medical care. In a study of an impoverished region of Texas,[89] a parent reflected on what happened after her little girl was injured:

> Like one time my girl, who doesn't have Medicaid, fell. She was playing, running, and she banged into a chair and got a bump that swelled up and almost burst open. You know it's something that is worth going to the doctor for, but then you don't have money for it. All you can do is try to get the swelling to go away. It's better to put Vick's [VaporRub ointment] or something like that on it to bring down the swelling. For a heavy blow like that, you have to get x-rays. If that happened to someone with Medicaid you would immediately go to the doctor, because you know your insurance will cover it.[90]

Researchers consistently find that undocumented children experience the most serious of health challenges. Additionally, they experience a variety of mental health conditions: "Undocumented children experience significant trauma, and . . . particularly . . . to the development of symptoms of PTSD."[91]

Children who are U.S. citizens of undocumented parents are also suffering. Currently, 5.1 million children in the United States live with at least one unauthorized immigrant parent.[92] Social work scholars Luis Zayas and Mollie Bradlee created a path-breaking study on this population: children of mixed immigration status families.[93] They revealed tragic truths about the treatment of citizen children. Deportation practices have created circumstances where children are put in foster care or are detained along with their parents and subsequently deported so that the family stays intact. There was a memorandum of understanding from John Morton, former director of Homeland Security, to use discretion for humanitarian cases such as keeping families together and not prioritizing unauthorized immigrants without criminal histories. However, this MOU did not prevent a record high number of deportations under the Obama Administration, and with the overt hostility toward immigrants on the part of the Trump Administration, it is now null and void.

Zayas and Bradlee explained that because parents are often scared to use social services on behalf of their children (who have access), they are deemed neglectful by doctors and social workers. This often leaves these parents caught up in the complex web of child protective services. Additionally, when a parent is deported, children display a number of traumatizing outcomes:

- disruption of eating and sleeping habits, sadness, anger, guilt, and anxiety;
- economic instability, which leads to inadequate education and delayed cognitive development; and,
- the change to an unfamiliar and possibly dangerous environment carries other consequences to the child's life expectancy, quality of education, vulnerability to discrimination, and social networks, among other factors.[94]

One group of researchers studied children who had a parent deported or in deportation proceedings in the United States and children who were in Mexico with their parents because they were removed from the country.[95] Most of these children exhibited signs of depression, often related to incidents of family domestic violence that led a parent to be deported. The children who were in Mexico lost trusted networks back in the United States and had negative perceptions of Mexico. Overall, the study found that *perceived threat* of parental deportation powerfully shaped the emotional well-being of the children in their study.

Both undocumented and U.S. citizen children worry about their parents who are undocumented. Diana García-Mellado, as part of her master's thesis research, asked children of both legal statuses to take photographs of what was important to them and share their interpretations of them with her.[96] The children had a startling awareness of political conditions that were anti-immigrant and verbalized heartbreaking fears about their parents' safety. For example, an eleven-year-old child who was a U.S. citizen explained:

My family is important because like I am the only one in my family like who was born here and, well, they are gonna kick them out, so who's gonna pay for all this stuff now? So I get really scared because I'm gonna be the only one here with my *tio* [uncle], if my family, like, goes to Mexico. We are gonna be the only ones here. So that's why I think my family should be together with me and it's important that we are together as a family.

The child continued to share:

I . . . realize like how much they go through to stay here. It makes me feel like my family is not safe and it worries me a lot that they can't do much like go out and stuff or drive. And with the whole thing that's happening here in [her town]. There's the Border Patrol. They are everywhere here now, so like my parents and whole family that doesn't have any papers, are always looking out. And so many people are affected here and a lot of people have been taken out, like, just these past weeks because of that.[97]

García-Mellado concluded that, "children in mixed immigration status families conceptualize deportation and the separation aspect of it through fear of being separated from their families. The anguish of idealizing the separation between them and their parents generates a form of emotional violence as they develop feelings of sadness displayed in their responses."[98] Her study highlighted the misconception that children are unaware of anti-immigrant policy and practices. There is no "innocence" about the reach and threat of immigration enforcement.

Another study confirmed the stressful role of deportation in the lives of children. Scholars conducted a study in Texas that included children in three groups: those whose parents were deported, those whose parents were in deportation proceedings, and those whose parents were in neither category but were undocumented.[99] Parents were asked to complete a Child Behavior Checklist translated into Spanish. They found that "children with a deported parent were more likely to demonstrate elevated levels of internalizing and externalizing problems than children without a deported parent."[100] Therefore, researchers and advocates argued for the reconfiguration of laws pertaining to immigration and families.[101]

DENTAL CARE: URGENT NEED AND FEW RESOURCES

In the United States, 25 percent of the overall population has reported that they cannot afford to see a dentist and have put off a needed appointment in the last year as a result.[102] Proper dental care is crucial to overall medical well-being. Poor oral health can decline into poor general health due to untreated infections, and there is a social stigma regarding extracted or missing teeth that also affects psychological health.[103]

In a study about the effects of immigration status and health care among Los Angeles families, Urban Institute researcher Julia Gellat found that undocumented children have a very high likelihood of not having seen a dentist within the last year.[104] Interestingly, in the case of dental access, children who are U.S.-born but have undocumented parents (i.e., they are in mixed-status families) have the same rates of going to the dentist as children with U.S. citizen parents. In some cases, dental care is offered in community sites, such as flea markets. A participant in an anthropological study of medical care in rural Texas shared:

> There is a dentist at the flea market. Seriously, we are in such an extreme [circumstance], we are resorting to this type of care. In the back there is a chair, and you are directed to enter the doctor's "office," well, it is outdoors. You don't want to think about it, full of dirt and everything, open air. All they have there is a chair and they do it [dental work].[105]

In this same study, community members explained that dental providers in Mexico apply for a Border Crossing Card and do house calls on the U.S. side of the border.

There are few dental clinics in the United States that serve undocumented immigrants. St. Paul Children's Dental Clinic in Tyler, Texas, is one of them. They describe their services as providing top-notch pediatric dental care including dental check-ups, dental cleanings, fillings, sealants, stainless steel crowns, extractions, and emergency care.[106] They also serve the community through a medical clinic, food pantry, and clothing closet. Similar to the community medical clinics described in this chapter, the dental clinic is staffed with mostly volunteers. It is coordinated by a foundation, which is part of the St. Paul United Methodist Church.

Public health initiatives providing dental care for undocumented immigrants have also had success in providing outreach and services in a culturally competent way. An example of a successful intervention is *Boca Sana, Cuerpo Sano* (Healthy Mouth, Healthy Bodies), led by San Diego State University researchers and members of the National Latino Research Center at California State University San Marcos.[107] A team of twenty-two community leaders (*líderes comunitarias*) were trained to conduct outreach to better understand the challenges and beliefs that undocumented immigrants—including gardeners, nannies, day laborers, and agricultural workers—have about dental care. They discovered that immigration status was the biggest barrier to seeking dental care (because of fear of immigration enforcement) and, despite their proximity to Mexico, their unauthorized status prohibits them from easily crossing the border for affordable, familiar dental care. The research also revealed the lengthy process of simple dental cleaning at a local dental clinic:

> I come from Mexicali, and that's where I would go to my dentist and because of reasons with immigration, I could not leave now. And when I had to go there, to the cleaning, I did not like that they put you in four cleaning sessions. I was accustomed to well, going and getting your cleaning in one day, in one session. . . . But they told me that because they are community clinics, they have to do it that way, in four sessions, that because this gives time for them to attend to other patients.[108]

Echoing the experiences of other undocumented patients, the participants in the *Boca Sana* project describe very negative treatment from the staff at clinics, very long wait times, transportation challenges due to bus riding schedules, and a lack of Spanish language facility among the dentists and dental assistants. All of these factors create a barrier for trust and mutual respect between undocumented clients and health care providers. Given the importance of dental hygiene and periodontal disease, inclusion of dental care in medical services for undocumented immigrants is crucial.

CREATION OF A MENTAL HEALTH CRISIS

Our knowledge is increasing about the mental health of undocumented immigrants. This topic has been less researched compared to the topic of physical health in general, but the number of immigrant removals from the United States in the last decade has spurred a focus on mental health issues for affected populations. Interestingly, public health researchers find that mental health for young undocumented youth—not physical health—is significantly associated with their immigration status. Research suggests that life circumstances will take a toll on their mental health as these youth age.[109] Paula's experience with anxiety and depression (described in Box 5.3) is indicative of the sorts of mental health challenges that are prevalent in the undocumented immigrant community.

BOX 5.3: PAULA'S EXPERIENCE WITH IMMIGRATION AND MENTAL HEALTH CHALLENGES

Paula is a twenty-one-year-old Latina living in California. She is an undocumented immigrant and has been living in the United States for three years. She came to the United States looking for better economic opportunities, leaving her parents and sister behind in Mexico. She lives with her uncle and cousins. Paula is a bookkeeper for an accountant, and reflects on her "blessing" to have an office job as an undocumented immigrant.

When Paula first arrived in the United States, she was healthy and her health had never been an issue. A few months after her arrival, she began to feel moments of sadness and desperation, but thought they were normal symptoms. She thought about consulting a doctor, but mentions that she did not know where to seek help, was embarrassed to ask family members for help (she did not want to be a burden to her relatives), and could not afford paying a doctor. Paula continued to have recurring symptoms for over a year and thought that they would eventually go away. However, she could feel the situation getting worse.

One early Tuesday morning, while Paula was preparing her lunch before going to work, she started to feel her heart palpitating really fast and then she passed out right on the floor. Her cousin, Gisela, who was going to give her a ride to work that morning, found her lying flat on the kitchen floor. Then, Gisela performed CPR. Paula became responsive and Gisela offered to take her to the emergency room. Paula said that she was feeling dizzy, but otherwise fine and that she did not want to have an enormous medical debt, because she had no medical insurance. She stayed home that day from work.

Paula, as an undocumented immigrant, does not have a primary doctor or any source of preventive care. In the following days after her incident and at the urging of her relatives, Paula decided to call a clinic that a family member found for her. The clinic gave her an appointment almost a month away from the time she called. She was diagnosed with depression, anxiety, and high blood pressure. The doctor told her that she needed to see a mental health professional, but to this day Paula cannot afford personal therapy. Paula also needs ongoing preventive care with a primary doctor, but she is hesitant to go because she needs someone to go with her to interpret and help her fill out forms. The costs, even if they are considered low in a clinic, add up and are a hardship to include in monthly expenses.

Every day, Paula deals with depression and anxiety. She relies on home remedies to deal with her high blood pressure. She hopes that one day she will save enough money to afford therapy or even buy medical insurance. She has not had an appointment for depression or anxiety and only goes to the doctor when it is an urgent matter. Continuous preventive care is not an option that Paula can afford.

—As told to and written by Flor Saldaña, MA

Overall, there is a strong need to address mental health in immigrant communities. For example, in a public health study of an immigrant Latinx community in Chicago, it was found that an estimated 10,500 individuals in the community suffer from some kind of mental illness and that only 3,100 people seek or receive some type of service.[110] Drs. Fortuna and Porche found that undocumented immigrant patients exhibit significant multiple psychosocial stressors associated with trauma, anxiety, and stress compared to U.S. residents and U.S. citizen patients.[111] Sometimes cultural norms may prevent undocumented Latinxs from seeking help. Reporter and cultural worker Stephanie Manriquez interviewed a young woman in Chicago whose family has various mental health issues, such as alcoholism and bipolar disorder. Manriquez reflected:

> Many immigrants disregard their own mental wellness; especially if they come from communal cultures, where it is not accepted or expected to focus on themselves as a single individual. Instead, the vital focus is the family as a whole.[112]

Stephanie Manriquez also reports on the work of Mirna Ballestas, who is a clinical psychologist and part of the Roots to Wellness coalition of mental health providers. These providers work in Chicago's predominantly Latinx neighborhoods and offer culturally sensitive services that extend to the entire family. Dr. Ballestas describes the main challenge of helping immigrant families: "There is a lot of pain and trauma in the community."[113]

In rural Florida, mental health challenges are also experienced by undocumented immigrants who are socially isolated and have few medical or psychological resources.[114] Health researchers presented a case study of Ms. A, a thirty-year-old mother of three U.S. citizen children. Her life since arriving to the United States at thirteen years of age was characterized by home instability, poverty, and fear. Her depression and suicide attempts were direct consequences of her hopelessness and feeling like she could not fulfill the needs of her children because of her undocumented status. The researchers detailed the elements that also shaped Ms. A's life: lack of community, discrimination, stressful family dynamics, lack of belonging, and poverty.

In a study on farmworker Latinas in North Carolina, researchers also found depression that was linked to general economic hardships.[115] Poverty was an even more significant factor than the abject hard work of farm labor and older age in accounting for high rates of depression.[116] Finally, rural undocumented individuals, especially youth, experience discrimination when they do access health care of some kind.[117]

Mental Health and Youth

For undocumented youth, there are additional issues of fitting in with peers and achieving goals that are norms in the United States. Often, these youth are prevented from feeling like they belong because of their immigration status. Many times, this group is considered the 1.5 generation, who arrived in the United States at a very

Figure 5.2. Mental health challenges, such as depression and anxiety, are related to the stressors that unauthorized immigrants experience.
Anh Nguyen, Unsplash

young age. As they grow older, their responsibilities may increase but, because of their legal status, their opportunities may not. They experience a great amount of worry, sadness, and fear related to their undocumented status. Social science researchers, drawing on multiple studies, found that undocumented young people experience chronic stress due to managing their immigration status:[118] "As they learned to live with such restrictions, these external barriers were progressively internalized, starting to function as an internal boundary, or border, with implications for almost every aspect of their lives, extending beyond the immigration barrier itself with deep implications for their identity, mental health, and well-being."[119]

Undocumented youth try various strategies to manage information about their status (and that of their parents), but the long-term effects negatively impact their behavior and cognitive functions, such as mood, problem solving, and memory. In this large study, feelings of grief and chronic stress led to excessive drinking and engaging in arguments for some youth. For others, the stress of undocumented status manifested in poor sleep, over- or under-eating, anxiety, and a "desire to never get out of bed."[120] However, club participation in school activities and trusting relationships served as protective factors for many participants. Participants reported they "found a sense of purpose and a role" that resulted in them feeling more hopeful.[121]

Another study found undocumented students who were finishing college experienced depression, sadness, and thoughts of suicide.[122] These recent undocu-grads felt that they could not join in the joy of graduation, an important and hard-earned rite of passage. Instead, they felt "bittersweet" about graduating. One participant in the study shared: "On graduation day, I was happy but also experienced moments of depression and had thoughts of suicide. I did walk in my graduation. I even delivered the commencement speech."[123] Graduates explained that they removed themselves from social media, noting that their lives shifted dramatically after graduation. Several participants characterized themselves as top of their class or very driven in the days as an undergraduate, but after graduation, they felt a distinct lack of career opportunities due to their status. Often they began working minimum wage jobs, sometimes with parents at their "under the table" jobs, or they did not work at all. These undocumented youth explained that their experiences were in stark contrast to their college peers, who were starting their careers, "taking time off to travel," or going to graduate school. In general, the loss of student status coupled with the lack of workforce opportunity leads to social isolation and contributes greatly to increased risk for anxiety and depression for undocumented college graduates.

Being undocumented can be profoundly isolating. The undocumented status carries with it a legal rejection and with that, anti-immigrant sentiments that are intensifying under the Trump Administration. Youth and other undocumented immigrants experience negative societal forces—outspoken politicians combined with conservative news media—that also invoke rejection and stoke ethnic and racist fears. Yet, resistance and social action have become a cornerstone of the undocumented immigration youth movement, as is discussed in chapter 7.

Being in a mixed-status family creates tension and stress. For example, Angelica Manriquez and her brother are both undocumented. She qualified for DACA and he did not. Because of the hyper-surveillance of young men of color and other related factors, her brother was in deportation proceedings. Angelica shared: "Thinking about my brother and the proceedings my family went through while his case was solved, emotionally [drains] me."[124]

Not only do anti-immigration policies affect access to health care and medical health outcomes, but mental health is also negatively impacted. "In localities and jurisdictions with anti-immigration policies, the prevalence of negative mental health outcomes is even higher when compared to locations and jurisdictions in the same country with neutral or welcoming policies towards immigrants, including 'sanctuary cities'."[125] Therefore, the campaign to create sanctuary cities and states could positively impact public health.

HARMFUL FOR HEALTH:
RAIDS, DETENTION, AND DEPORTATION

The constant increasing and looming threats of deportation and immigration enforcement negatively impact undocumented immigrants' seeking health care. Merely knowing someone was deported increases the probability of reporting poor health.[126] Researchers in the *Undocumented and Uninsured* report call this phenomenon "self-monitoring," where immigrants tend to think about when they go out, where they are going, and the urgency of their needs—often forgoing social and medical encounters for fear of immigration enforcement.[127] For immigrant youth, 83 percent reported that they "self-monitor."[128] In this same report, immigrant youth report very low levels of medical and mental health access: only 27 percent have access to counseling services.[129]

Raids have immediate negative effects on the health and wellness of an immigrant community. William López and his research team initially set out to understand the health determinants of a Latino community in the midwestern state of Michigan.[130] (Note that while Michigan does not have sweeping anti-immigrant laws, it is also not a trailblazer for immigration advocacy at the state level.) They collected surveys from 325 Latinxs. However, three months after the surveys were completed, there was a major immigration raid in an old warehouse that served both as a mechanic shop and a place where families lived in the second story. The research team completed an additional 151 surveys after the raid, which allowed them to compare the mental health status of those taking the survey before and those taking it after the enforcement raid. After the raid, most participants reported increased immigration enforcement stress and lower self-rated health scores.

The Michigan raid negatively affected the health and well-being of all the community members—both undocumented and U.S. citizens. They found—not surprisingly—that community members who took the survey after the raid felt "less free to interact with their social networks, less able to use government services, and increasingly fearful of the consequences of deportation."[131] They also reported lower self-rated health scores. Community members who had children and those who were undocumented had the highest levels of stress and fear. The researchers argue that this was a community that already was underresourced in terms of health care options, and now this need would be exacerbated. Those needing medical services would feel less inclined to access them due to fears about immigration enforcement, while at the same time, the raids increased the need for mental health services.

Finally, reporter Xatherin Gonzalez covered the repercussions involving a woman arrested by ICE during a community clinic visit.[132] She had checked in to the clinic with her eight- and twenty-two-year-old daughters. Her crime? Using a false driver's license to check into her appointment. After two hours of waiting for her appointment, she was called for what she thought was her medical appointment. She left her daughters behind only to be apprehended by a sheriff who had been called by clinic front desk staff. The sheriff told the daughters, who were extremely distraught, that their mother was being arrested for false papers and was "going to be deported." Clearly, this situation created an emotional toll on the entire family and they are now even more frightened to access even the most basic health services.

Detention Centers: Troubling Solution, Terrifying Health Effects

As we discuss at length in the next chapter, immigration is an administrative process. Previously, the only thing "illegal" about immigration was when someone was detected crossing over the border without permission—and it was only considered a misdemeanor. Therefore, the creation of detention centers for those who are in the United States without current authorization is a troubling solution and creates inhumane conditions for undocumented families. The effects of detention for immigrants are terrifying and take an emotional and physical toll on the health of those detained. Martinez and colleagues state: "a clear correlation was shown to exist between conditions in immigration detention centers and increased anxiety, depression, and overall stress."[133]

In addition, reports from detention centers reveal that inhumane treatment has led to unnecessary deaths.[134] In particular, the for-profit detention centers are dangerous environments for detainees as they have less oversight, less public accountability, lax requirements for employment, and a cavalier culture of neglect.[135] Activist and writer Mary Turck summarized several cases of immigrants who died waiting to have their cases tried in a for-profit immigration detention center due to medical negligence: no response to desperate pleas for help from an immigrant suffering from a stroke, an immigrant needing medical help and never being seen by a doctor while unknowingly having HIV, and a person with blood in her vomit and stool that was disregarded as a sign of stomach cancer.[136] For-profit detention centers are human warehouses that profit off detention while neglecting the medical concerns of detained undocumented persons, including families.

Children in Detention: Inflicting More Harm

In a battle to prevent children from being held in immigration detention centers, Human Rights First filed an *amicus* brief[137] that drew upon research about the detrimental effects of children in detention. The brief was based on reports by experts from the American Academy of Child and Adolescent Psychiatry and the National Association of Social Workers.[138] It also relied (unsuccessfully) on the precedent set by the *Flores* settlement, which mandated the release of children because it causes undue harm to unaccompanied minors. Specifically, pediatrician Dr. Alan Shapiro stated that immigration detention "leads to isolation, helplessness, hopelessness, and serious long-term medical and mental health consequences for children."[139] Staff who work in the detention facilities are not allowed to physically comfort or touch children in their care. The separation of children from their parents when they present themselves at the border has been in the spotlight and is the focus of strong opposition from multiple sources, including the American Psychological Association and immigrant rights groups.[140]

U.S.-born children are gravely affected by their parents' deportation. A leading scholar in the field, Dr. Lisseth Rojas-Flores, and her team of clinical researchers studied the impact of deportation on ninety-one children.[141] The children in the study exhibited signs of post-traumatic stress syndrome as noted by parents and clinical sources. U.S.-born children internalized the fear and uncertainty felt by their undocumented parents. Anecdotally, we are learning that more and more undocumented adult family members are having difficult conversations with their children about contingency plans and safety measures in case of sudden deportation.

DOCTORS' MORAL COMPASSES AND PROFESSIONAL ETHICS

Some of the strongest support for health care or for undocumented immigrants comes from leaders in the medical field. Indeed, one study assessed the attitudes of health care clinicians and staff and found general support of a human right to health care for all people. However, the results were more divisive when asking about undocumented immigrants.[142] Whereas clinicians were more likely to embrace full access to health care as a fundamental human right for undocumented immigrants, the staff members were much less likely to support this idea.

Doctors with a passion to provide health care services to immigrants have founded community clinics. Dr. Steve Larson, director of *Puentes de Salud*, a community health clinic in Philadelphia, explained: "I'm a health-care provider. I signed an oath that didn't have anything to do with geographic boundaries or anything but a life."

Dr. Sural Shah, a volunteer at *Puentes De Salud*, shares a case about Ana, a young mother—undocumented and low income—who initially came to the community clinic for a sore throat but was diagnosed with a troubling heart murmur.[143] Despite the help of a nurse filling out paperwork and a heart ultrasound from the local hospital, the wait for enrollment into Medicare took months. Typically, Dr. Shah explained, undocumented patients are only covered by Medicare for emergency surgeries or acute care—not preventative or sustaining care. However, she pointed out that "emergency" can be defined as "medical condition with symptoms that, if left untreated, would put his or her life in serious jeopardy or result in serious impairment to bodily function or serious dysfunction of any body organ or part." Ana fit this expanded definition of eligibility, yet months went by before she received any notification. In the meantime, her condition worsened and she had to undergo emergency heart surgery. Thankfully, Ana came through the operation and is healing, but she did not have health insurance coverage at the time of her illness.

Dr. Shah reflects on the high number of patients who do not have the support of a community clinic, caring nurses, and a generous hospital. And, even in the best of circumstances, with all those supports, Ana still ended up with emergency surgery. Dr. Shah concluded:

> For the sake of patients like Ana and her young family, and for my own sake as a physician bearing witness to the consequences of our restrictive system, I can only hope [that states] would extend coverage to this population and recognize not only their contribution to our society, but also their value as fellow human beings.

Southern California doctor Dr. Abraar Karan wrote about the need for patients to have regular physician visits so that conditions can be diagnosed before they become a medical emergency.[144] Dr. Karan noted the human and economic costs of systematically excluding undocumented immigrants. Dr. Karan reasoned that when undocumented immigrants only rely on emergency care for medical treatment, their immediate health crisis is addressed but "their health outcomes end up being significantly worse, and their cost to the hospital and healthcare system are far greater."

Preventative treatment makes a huge difference in health outcomes and cuts the costs of emergency treatment dramatically. Dr. Karan explains the case of Mr. Gomez, who worked as a landscaper. For months, he had been experiencing abdominal pain but was too scared to seek treatment at a local clinic. He tried to treat his symptoms with herbs and other home remedies. It turned out he had "diverticulosis, which is a condition in which the colon develops out-pouchings which can become clogged with stool." He went to the emergency room once his pouches became infected and he had recurrent bouts of fever. An operation cured Mr. Gomez, but the lack of humane conditions to access basic health care was apparent and the costs involved for his hospitalization were far greater than if he had been able to access preventive health care.

Finally, in the case of organ transplant patients, undocumented immigrants are able to *provide* organs, but many times are unable to receive them. Dr. Vanessa Grubbs explained the controversy as she treated an ideal kidney organ transplant patient who is undocumented.[145] She argued that the cost effectiveness of helping the 1 percent of undocumented immigrants who have dialysis-requiring liver disease receive transplants makes sense. After the first year of the transplant (approximately $1 million in cost), the medical costs are $30,000 compared to $70,000 of yearly dialysis. But, even more compelling is the need for humanity in immigration law related to making life and death decisions about medical care. As an African-American female doctor, Dr. Grubbs stated, "I just want to take care of the patient in front of me in the way that I know is best for him." [146]

"Salud, Dignidad, y Justicia" (Health, Dignity and Justice)

—slogan for the National Latina Institute for Reproductive Health

Health advocates for undocumented immigrants urge the United States to consider the lack of access to medical and mental health resources, the poor quality and treatment when they do access health care, and the many challenges facing immigrants in their daily lives that affect both their physical and emotional health. Imelda Plascencia and her colleagues at the UCLA Labor Center reminded us that the "incorrect assumption that low-income communities already have adequate access to services leads to the belief that poor health is a personal choice. Health care is a collective concern—not a personal issue."[147]

Health anthropologists Heide Castañeda and Milena Andrea Melo conceptualized the exclusion of undocumented immigrants from health care by using the concept of "legal violence" developed by Leisy Abrego and Cecilia Menjívar.[148] "Legal violence" is defined as "laws that protect the rights of some [but] simultaneously marginalize other groups, leaving them unprotected and ultimately more vulnerable"[149] Castañeda and Melo argued that "violence is especially devastating when it restricts practices at the core of family dynamics (via ideas of, e.g., "good parenting").[150] An example of this is the ability of parents to access resources for children when they are ill. Exclusion from legally accessing basic human rights and fear of deportation shape the health of undocumented parents and individuals, along with U.S. citizen children. In the "DACAmented Voices in Healthcare" study, undocumented youth in Arizona recommended the following for supporting expansion of state services: clear indicators of accepting undocumented patients in community clinics and the inclusion of undocumented and youth constituents to decision-making bodies in health care.[151]

The Center on Reproductive Rights called for a "rights affirming policy solution" approach to reform that specifically includes: "equity, non-discrimination, participation by impacted communities, transparency, and accountability."[152] The discourse on unauthorized immigrants and health care must be based on a simple concept: that all humans have the right to health, dignity, and justice.

6

Legal Issues, Detention, and Deportation

Two Immigration and Customs Enforcement (ICE) agents went into an Ann Arbor, Michigan, restaurant and ordered breakfast in May 2017. After eating the breakfast, they went into the kitchen and questioned the cooks who made their meal. The agents arrested three of the cooks who did not have their papers, even though they had been looking for an employee who was not at the restaurant that day.[1]

In Stewart Detention Center in Lumpkin, Georgia, in 2014, detained immigrants contended with "maggots in food, no medical care, sweltering temperatures, and in many cases no communication with staff due to no translators on site."[2] In one case after a detainee named Ismael had a stroke, went to the hospital, and was released back to ICE, he received no more medical attention at Stewart. He had a second stroke a month later and they did not provide him with any treatment or rehabilitation beyond headache medication. Due to this medical neglect, he felt forced to sign self-deportation papers simply to get out of the facility.[3]

Eighteen-month-old Mariee Juárez died after being detained along with her mother Yazmin Juárez at the South Texas Family Residential Center in Dilley, Texas. Her mother says Mariee was a happy, healthy child when they arrived at the U.S. border in March to seek asylum. They were sent to Dilley. Six weeks after being discharged, her mother says, she died of a treatable respiratory infection that began during her detention.[4]

In 2017 in Baltimore, Maryland, a criminal defense attorney, Christos Vasiliades, was caught on tape encouraging a rape victim not to testify against her alleged perpetrator due to the current anti-immigrant climate in the United States. He insinuated that she would be deported if she went to court and offered her $3,000 not to show up at the court and testify against his client.[5]

Myth: Alleged unauthorized immigrants in the United States are subject to fair detention and deportation procedures and principles of decency enshrined in the law.

Myth Busted: Current immigration law enforcement in the United States today challenges the principles often thought of as cornerstones of the country—fairness and equality. This is because immigration law enforcement is motivated in large part by a combination of nativist and government and business concerns.[6] Anti-immigrant biases as well as governmental and business financial interests are built into the immigrant detention and deportation systems, but are hidden behind a focus on migrants who "break the law."[7] Yet, a deeper look at the stories behind immigration law and its enforcement easily reveals the truth about what drives the United States' dependence on detention and deportation.

The news events summarized at the beginning of this chapter show how people assumed to be unauthorized immigrants are treated when law enforcement agents attempt to apprehend, detain, and in many cases, deport them. The collateral damages of a punitive immigration enforcement system are clear. Stories such as these provide evidence that makes observers question how the traditional U.S. immigration system, which is rooted in civil law, involves procedures and punishments that are similar, if not worse, than the ones experienced by those accused of criminal acts.[8] Given that the civil immigration law was designed to be less punitive than criminal law, how is it that the two systems are merging together into what many now call a system of "crimmigration"?[9]

CRIMMIGRATION AND THE
IMMIGRATION INDUSTRIAL COMPLEX

Crimmigration = The Criminalization of Migrants

To understand the relatively new term *crimmigration* (a combination of the words *criminalization* and *migration*) requires a familiarity with what scholars call the *immigration industrial complex*. Sociologist Tanya Golash-Boza explains that the immigration industrial complex involves "private and public sector interests in the criminalization of undocumented migration, immigration law enforcement and the production of 'anti-illegal' rhetoric."[10] The immigration industrial complex is one that operates like the prison industrial complex by socially controlling groups that are considered "dangerous" or "risky" by dominant power holders in our society.[11] Politicians and activists use mainstream news and entertainment media to spread stereotypes about immigrants as irresponsible or criminal. At certain stages in history, these stereotypes are used to fuel moral panics (exaggerated widespread fears about immigration and immigrants) that lead to tough-on-immigration laws and policies.

When people define immigrants as "illegal," they are able to strip them of their rights. Legal scholar César Cuauhtémoc Hernández García explains that "to be deemed an 'illegal' is to be cast out of the space of law and placed in that vulnerable space where rights, including the right to breathe, think, or speak, do not exist."[12]

This allows the government to detain individuals simply because they are considered undesirable "non-citizens." They are typically denied access to free legal counsel and have little chance to have meaningful due process under the law.[13] Social scientists Cecilia Menjívar and Leisy Abrego explain that unauthorized immigrants are subjected to "legal violence," the use of the law to question their existence, threaten their humanity, and demean them.[14] A number of different entities benefit from this form of violence: state agencies such as the Department of Homeland Security are expanded, companies that make surveillance technology and other social control tools experience increased business, and private prison companies and associated industries, such as detention center food and health care providers make enormous profits.[15]

The immigration industrial complex promotes the interests of U.S. employers inside and outside of the country while limiting the ability of workers to protest and improve their conditions. As noted by scholar Nicholas De Genova, policies of deportation in the United States can never actually result in the deportation of the over eleven million undocumented people that are living in the country in any given year.[16] What the deportation system can and does do is to scare workers with the knowledge that they can be deported at any time. This threat encourages workers to keep their heads down and meet the needs of employers even when they are being mistreated and/or abused.[17] In spite of this some people do resist in multiple and creative ways, a subject we examine in chapter 7.

The Effect of "Free" Trade Agreements

The North American Free Trade Agreement (NAFTA), which was passed in 1994, created a trade agreement between Canada, the United States, and Mexico that removed most tariffs and taxes on imports and exports on the goods traded between the countries. Ten years later, the Central American–Dominican Republic Free Trade Agreement (CAFTA-DR) expanded NAFTA to five Central American countries: El Salvador, Guatemala, Costa Rica, Nicaragua, and Honduras, as well as the Dominican Republic. As a result of NAFTA, the United States filled the Mexican market with U.S. corn and other crops (often subsidized by the government), and multinational corporations that paid little attention to the demands of workers.[18]

These changes negatively affected the agricultural and manufacturing sectors of the Mexican economy. As noted by sociologist Nicole Trujillo-Pagán, NAFTA created a situation in which workers became the main export of their country, yet at the same time U.S. immigration policies and laws related to migrant laborers became strict tools of surveillance and control.[19] CAFTA has resulted in a similar effect on Central American workers as well. Economic instability in the region has fueled drug- and gang-related violence, and is a factor in the increased migration of people from Central America to the United States.[20] Yet, as in the Mexican case, U.S. immigration policies are not usually constructed to take the big-picture factors related to immigration into account.

Debunking the Criminal Immigrant Stereotype

Efforts to equate immigrants, legal or undocumented, to "criminals" are off the mark because historically immigrants have been less likely to commit serious crimes than native-born people.[21] Yet, immigrants are subjected to tougher rules about criminal behaviors that do not match those applied to U.S. citizens.[22] These folks are labeled as "criminal aliens," yet as researchers Walter Ewing, Daniel E. Martínez, and Rubén Rumbaut found, most immigrants who are detained and deported have not committed the serious offenses that the general public is led to believe (e.g., murder, assault, rape, robbery, burglary). Instead, they are generally detained and removed from the country for what the Department of Homeland Security labels "immigration offenses," such as unauthorized entry or re-entry into the United States, drug offenses (including possession of marijuana), and/or criminal traffic offenses, which include driving under the influence and hit-and-run incidents.[23] Researchers from Syracuse University found that *80 percent* of people in ICE custody as of June 2018 had either no criminal record or only a minor record with an offense such as a traffic violation.[24]

Imperfectly Addressing Immigrant Victimization: The U-Visa and T-Visa

In addition to the criminalization of undocumented immigrants, those in power rarely address their victimization. Two exceptions are the use of the U-Visa Program and the T-Visa Program, which were first implemented as part of the Victims of Trafficking and Violence Protection Act of 2000. The U-Visa Program allows undocumented victims of crime who suffered physical or mental harm to apply for a non-immigrant visa if they agree to provide helpful information to law enforcement about the crime. A law enforcement agent must be willing to sign a form stating that an applicant has aided in the investigation or prosecution of the crime as part of the application. This program provides limited relief to a subset of crime victims and their close family members. The maximum number of applicants who can be granted the U-Visa per year is ten thousand, and in 2015 the number of petitions submitted was over thirty thousand.[25] The waiting time for petitioners is now up to over eight years! In addition, the likelihood of finding out about the U-Visa and applying for it successfully varies depending on where a person lives.[26] When people live in big, diverse cities like New York or Los Angeles, officials are more likely to encourage migrant victims of crime to apply for the U-Visa and to help them fill out the application than officials are in a small city or a large city openly hostile to immigrants.[27]

Like the U-Visa, the T-Visa program allows people who have been trafficked and their immediate families to apply for temporary U.S. residency. It requires that the victims of the trafficking help law enforcement build a case against the traffickers. Unfortunately, enforcement officers are reluctant to pursue such cases, which makes it hard for victims to apply for relief.[28] The annual limit on the number of U-Visas that can be granted is five thousand. Given that the estimated number of people trafficked into the United States each year is between fourteen thousand and eighteen thousand people and there are already trafficked people living in the United States, it is clear that the limit falls short of the demand for this type of relief.[29]

The U-Visa and T-Visa programs help a portion of the subset of undocumented immigrants who are crime victims, witnesses, or trafficked people obtain legal status, but these efforts are eclipsed by the many other government-backed efforts to criminalize, detain, and deport immigrants. Immigrant advocacy agencies and attorneys have noted an uptick in the detention and deportation of crime victims who have applied for U-Visas and T-Visas during the Trump Administration. In addition, there has been a significant decrease in the number of people who are applying for these visas under the Trump Administration.[30] ICE claims there have not been any official changes to policies for U-Visa applicants,[31] but the U.S. Citizenship and Immigration Services (USCIS) has officially changed its procedures to trigger deportation of applicants immediately if they are denied a T-Visa.[32] This is a move that ultimately weakens the ability for the government and the victims to stand up against sex traffickers. Trafficked people are less willing to have their cases heard than they were before because they know if it does not go perfectly they will be marked for deportation.[33]

THE SCOPE AND ENFORCEMENT METHODS OF CUSTOMS AND BORDER PROTECTION AND IMMIGRATION AND CUSTOMS ENFORCEMENT

The two agencies primarily responsible for questioning people about their legal status and detaining them if U.S. citizenship cannot be determined are Customs and Border Protection (CBP) and Immigration and Customs Enforcement (ICE). Both of these agencies, along with USCIS, are part of the U.S. Department of Homeland Security. CBP is charged with focusing on the borders of the United States and ICE is charged with focusing on the interior region of the country.

Customs and Border Protection and the 100 Air-Mile Zone

Customs and Border Protection agents arrest people at the border, ports of entry, and up to 100 air-miles inland for alleged criminal activity, unlawful entry into the United States, or presence without status.[34] They are allowed to place alleged unauthorized migrants into short-term detention facilities.

According to 8 U.S.C.§1357(a)(3), Customs and Border Protection can stop and search vehicles, trains, aircraft, or vessels near the border of the United States. The term "near the border" may seem broad, and it is. Since 1953 the CBP's jurisdiction has been defined in the Immigration and Naturalization Act (INA) as 100 air-miles from any border unless the chief agent in charge deems a shorter distance more appropriate.[35] This makes it possible for CBP to conduct checkpoints that are far from the border and pull people over based on "reasonable suspicion" of an immigration violation or crime, although the enforcement of immigration law in the interior of the country is usually the responsibility of ICE.

If CBP officers claim to have probable cause to investigate a potential violation, they do not need a warrant to search vehicles within the 100 air-mile zone.[36] According to the American Civil Liberties Union, this has widespread consequences because eleven states are contained completely within 100 air-miles from the border: Connecticut, Delaware, Florida, Hawaii, Maine, Massachusetts, Michigan, New Hampshire, New Jersey, Rhode Island, and Vermont, as well as many major U.S. cities (e.g., Chicago, Houston, Phoenix, San Diego, Los Angeles, San Antonio, San Jose, Philadelphia, and New York).[37] It is important to note that the border zone is home to about 65 percent of the entire U.S. population and 75 percent of the Latinxs in the United States.[38] CBP can also search private properties within twenty-five miles from the border without a warrant (except in the case of dwellings).

The Customs and Border Patrol is also tasked with the policing of the see-through border barriers that run along parts of the 1,954-mile U.S.-Mexico border. (There are no such fences on the U.S.-Canada border, in spite of the fact it is 5,500 miles in distance and the longest border between two countries in the world.[39]) The barriers take the form of pedestrian fences or vehicle barriers along the borders of California, Arizona, and New Mexico.[40] Although Texas makes up half the border, it has very few border barriers in place. The Trump Administration's aim to make a "big, fat, beautiful border wall" inspired the call from CBP for proposals from contractors to build border wall prototypes.[41] Although eight prototypes were eventually built in the desert between San Diego and Tijuana, Congress has not approved enough funding for the Trump Administration to build the promised wall.[42] Instead, CBP is still patrolling the busiest border crossing in the world in San Ysidro, California, and focuses much of its attention on the primary border fence established in 1994 during the Clinton Administration's Operation Gatekeeper[43] and the secondary fence established around 2008.

Use of Force Claims Against the CBP

The practices of CBP have led to concerns about their potential abuse and the lack of constitutional protections for community members. For example, in Rochester, New York, hundreds of legal residents were arrested and released due to a Border Patrol arrest incentive program between 2006 and 2010.[44] And, in Tucson, Arizona, a CBP agent reportedly came to the room of a woman giving birth in the hospital and stayed through the delivery.[45] The Southern Border Communities Coalition estimates that the Border Patrol was involved in the deaths of at least fifty people and the injuries of at least twenty people between 2010 and 2016.[46]

CBP itself has acknowledged that the agency has not been forthcoming about its use of force.[47] A report by outside evaluators showed that CBP did not do an adequate job in investigating sixty-seven shootings that occurred between 2012 and

2014.[48] Its most recent statistics show that use of force increased 29 percent from the 2015 fiscal year to 2016 fiscal year.[49] They claim that the increase can be attributed to less lethal weapons being used against multiple people at a time.[50]

In 2017, the Supreme Court considered a case about a CBP cross-border use of force in which Agent Jesus Mesa shot and killed a fifteen-year-old Mexican boy named Sergio Adrián Hernández Güereca who was with his friends in a dry river bed in the Rio Grande River between Texas and Mexico. The Supreme Court considered the question of whether Hernández's family could sue Mesa for civil damages for the death of their son under the Fourth and Fifth Amendments. The justices sent the case back to the 5th Circuit Court of Appeals who had originally considered the first appeal, and in 2018 that court stated again that the victim's family could not sue the government or Agent Mesa because Hernández was killed in Mexico.[51] The ruling is extremely controversial because it implies that federal agents and agencies can harm people living in bordering countries with no implications.[52]

Immigration and Customs Enforcement and Interior Enforcement

Immigration and Customs Enforcement (ICE) focuses on issues of interior immigration law enforcement, and agents are meant to enforce the law against "those who encourage and rely on unauthorized workers" and to find, and possibly remove from the country, "illegal aliens who are criminals, fugitives, or recent arrivals."[53] They use a Priority Enforcement Program (PEP) (replacing their former Secure Communities Program), in which they spell out their enforcement priorities.[54] Detainees are held in federal prisons, state prisons, private prisons, and county jails to maintain the long-term U.S. immigration detention system.[55]

The Department of Justice, which screens people in jail for immigration violations, shares data with ICE. As a result, ICE agents routinely ask local law enforcement to hold people suspected to be unauthorized migrants so they can pick them up and place them in custody. In addition, ICE trains some state and local law enforcement officers to enforce federal immigration law under the 287(g) program. This program has significantly impacted the number of people who have been placed in ICE custody. For example, in sociologist Amada Armenta's book, *Protect, Serve, and Deport*, she shows that in Nashville, Tennessee, there were about ten to fifteen people held under ICE detainers per month (about 120–180 per year) prior to the enactment of the 287(g) program.[56] This increased significantly when local officials were able to start using traffic stops and patrolling to identify suspected unauthorized immigrants; approximately ten thousand people, mostly Latinx men, were placed in ICE custody during the five years the program was in effect in Nashville.

ICE uses a variety of methods that raise constitutional concerns, including the use of cellphone trackers, known as "Stingrays" or "Hailstorms," that act like cellphone towers.[57] When ICE uses these trackers, they are collecting information from any number of phones of people in a given region. Critics cite this as invasive technology that is questionable not only for the purposes of detention and deportation,

Figure 6.1. **The zero tolerance stance of ICE during the Trump Administration has had a chilling effect on Latinx immigrant communities.**
U.S. Immigration and Customs Enforcement, Flickr

but because of its effect on the greater public.[58] In Nashville in 2010, ICE agents in SWAT gear conducted a warrantless raid at night on a primarily Latinx apartment complex with no probable cause or reasonable suspicion. The agents wielded guns and threatened the apartment tenants with racist slurs. At the end of it all, no criminal charges were filed. The residents filed a lawsuit, *Escobar v. Gaines*, against the agency and the Metropolitan Nashville Police Department for discriminatory conduct and conspiracy to violate their right to be free of searches and seizures. The case was settled for a substantial amount of money and protected those plaintiffs who were undocumented from deportation for seven years.[59]

Chilling Changes in ICE's Policies and Enforcement

There is a heightened concern that ICE's approaches to the apprehension of undocumented individuals will lead to unreported crimes of all types and a less safe society for all. In 2011 during the Obama Administration, ICE's director, John Morton, wrote two memos about immigration priorities. In the first, often referred as "the Morton Memo," he instructed lawyers and agents to use discretion and to avoid interrogating or arresting non-citizens with strong family ties in the United States who were not threats to national security and were not involved in serious criminal activity. This memo guided federal immigration law for five years until the election of Donald Trump as president.

When President Trump went into office, he signed two executive orders on Immigration Enforcement during his first week in office that communicated his intention to expand the federal agencies' priorities for detention and deportation.[60] Now anyone who has committed even a minor crime, has been charged with a crime (without a determination of guilt), or has done something that *could have been* charged as a crime even if it was not, is eligible for deportation. In addition, anyone who has an outstanding removal order, has engaged in any misrepresentation of themselves to a government agency, has abused a public benefit program, or who is deemed a threat to the safety of the United States in the eyes of a given immigration officer is also eligible for deportation. This very broad understanding of deportability makes it so anyone who is undocumented could be chosen for deportation by virtue of living in the country.[61]

The change in immigration enforcement that has occurred since late 2016 has had serious repercussions. In El Paso, Texas, ICE went into a courthouse and arrested an undocumented woman who was filing a protective order against a person who had been abusing her. This occurred even though the woman was in the presence of a victim's advocate from the domestic violence shelter where she was living[62] and was the victim of a crime. This went against the longstanding policy of ICE established by Director John Morton in his second 2011 memo, which stated that absent "special circumstances or aggravating factors, it is against ICE policy to initiate removal proceedings against an individual known to be the immediate victim or witness to a crime."[63] In Los Angeles, California, the police chief of the LAPD, Charlie Beck, stated the fear of federal immigration enforcement was strongly related to the 25 percent decrease in sexual assault reporting among the Latinx population in early 2017 compared to the same time period the year before.[64] This pattern was also apparent in Houston, Texas, where reports of rapes in 2017 decreased 40 percent from the number of reports the previous year.[65]

Federal agents' disregard for undocumented victims and witnesses was reinforced by the Trump Administration's creation of a Victims of Immigration Crime Engagement (VOICE) Office within Immigrations and Customs Enforcement. The Department of Homeland Security justified this new office by claiming, "criminal aliens routinely victimize Americans and other legal residents," and stating that advocacy for the victims of crimes by undocumented immigrants is essential to a safe society.[66] As discussed earlier in this chapter, the data on crime and immigration do not support this broad characterization of immigrants as criminals. Nevertheless, President Trump has chosen to emphasize this harmful mischaracterization in both his executive orders and his tweets. The Department of Homeland Security followed his lead and stated that they will take all funds that have been used to support services for undocumented immigrants and use them for this new office.[67]

Apprehensions in Formerly Protected Places and of Formerly Protected People

A number of judicial officials have raised opposition to federal immigration agents in uniforms or in street clothes who are in or around courthouses looking to find and arrest undocumented immigrants. In Colorado in early 2017, an attorney confronted and videotaped ICE agents who were out of uniform and attempting to blend in as they looked to apprehend someone in a Denver courthouse.[68] This video went viral and created a panic about immigration agents in communities across the country. In April 2017, several high-ranking officials in Denver asked ICE *not* to arrest people near courthouses or schools.[69] Local ICE officials responded that they would continue to apprehend people in the courts. True to their word, in May 2017, ICE agents arrested two men—one inside the courthouse and one outside,[70] once again igniting concern across the country about ICE tactics.

In March of 2017, the chief justice of California wrote a letter to the U.S. attorney general and the secretary of the Department of Homeland Security, requesting that the practice be stopped. She asserted:

> Enforcement policies that include stalking courtrooms and arresting undocumented im-
> migrants, the vast majority of whom pose no harm to our public safety, are neither safe
> nor fair. They not only compromise our core value of fairness, but they undermine the
> judiciary's ability to provide equal access to justice.[71]

In April 2017, the chief justice of the New Jersey State Court followed suit as he requested that the Department of Homeland Security put a halt to the arrests of unauthorized immigrants while they are visiting courts, because these arrests have a chilling effect on crime witnesses, crime victims, families, and children who need legal services, and defendants in state criminal cases.[72] In his claim, the justice stated that courtrooms should be treated as one of the "sensitive locations" that federal immigration officials traditionally have considered off limits for arrests—such as hospitals, schools, and places of worship.[73] Others in the state testified at a special government hearing on the matter two months later, stating that the problem is even more serious than the chief justice claimed. They testified that the courtroom arrests were negatively affecting *all* of the courts, not just the criminal courts.[74] Similarly, letters from the chief justice of the Connecticut State Supreme Court and a Washington State Supreme Court justice were also sent to DHS making strong arguments for the courts to be treated as sensitive locations.[75]

Although some state judges are hoping that courts will be classified as sensitive locations, it appears that under the Trump Administration, in spite of official talk to the contrary, there may not be any more sensitive locations or situations that are off limits to federal immigration actions. Even at the beginning of his term when President Trump told Deferred Action for Childhood Arrival (DACA) recipients[76] that they should "rest easy," federal immigration officials' actions were sending the opposite message. For example, on February 17, 2017, federal immigration agents questioned twenty-three-year-old Manuel Montes in Calexico, California, as he waited for a ride.[77] Montes had lived in the United States since he was nine years old. He was enrolled in DACA for the second time, but because he did not have his wallet with his identification or his DACA card on him, he couldn't show proof of his status to the CBP agents. He was deported to Mexico *less than three hours later* and was the first DACA recipient in the United States to be deported during the Trump Administration.[78] Other DACA recipients have been targeted for detention deportation as well, including an activist in Mississippi (Daniela Vargas) and a young Seattle, Washington, man (Daniel Ramirez Medina) who was detained in an immigration raid that was aimed at his father.[79]

In Los Angeles, California, Claudia Rueda, a California State University college student and immigration activist who was eligible for DACA but did not have the fees to apply, was arrested in front of her house and put into detention in 2017. Given her history she would normally not be a priority for detention and deportation, but she was targeted in what federal authorities said was a drug raid. Nevertheless, she and the seven other people targeted were arrested for alleged immigration violations, not drug offenses.[80] Rueda had been protesting the detention of her mother in a drug raid that had occurred the month before prior to her arrest, and activists and friends believed Rueda's detention was a retaliatory move on the part of federal authorities.[81]

Other indications that sensitive locations named by ICE are being encroached upon by immigration agents include arrests outside religiously operated programs and houses of worship and schools. For example, in Virginia in February 2017, six Latino men exiting Fairfax Church's hypothermia shelter were questioned by ICE and at least two of the men were arrested when they did not have proof of citizenship or green cards.[82] The same month in Los Angeles, ICE officials arrested a man who was with his wife dropping off his teenager at school. His daughter, along with other students at the school, were deeply troubled by the event and the school administrators called an assembly that day to discuss fears related to immigration enforcement and ways to create safety plans with their families. Undocumented parents who heard about the arrest remain wary about taking their children to school because it is not clear that school is still a safe place for them.[83]

Federal Budgeting for Increased Detection, Detention, and Deportation

The incredible increase in the federal budgets of Customs and Border Protection and Immigration and Customs Enforcement over the course of the twenty-first century tells a powerful story about the demonization of undocumented immigrants. CBP's budget increased from $5.06 billion in 2002 to $16.39 billion in 2018, while ICE's budget increased from $2.4 billion in 2002 to $7.94 billion in 2018.[84] In his first year in office, President Trump committed to hiring ten thousand more ICE agents and five thousand more CBP agents.[85] Although this number of hires has not come to pass due to a lack of support by the Congress (and the difficulty of hiring qualified people who will stay on the job), the Trump Administration has amped up the arrest and detention of unauthorized immigrants. In a period of less than six months after Donald Trump was sworn into the presidency in late January 2017, immigration agents arrested over 41,300 people. This was equivalent to about four hundred people a day across the country, and was 38 percent higher than during the same time period in 2016.[86] In the summer of 2018, right before hurricane season, the Trump Administration shifted almost $10 million from the Federal Emergency

Management Agency (FEMA) to ICE for the increased detention and deportation of migrants.[87] In light of FEMA's flawed response to the Puerto Rican crisis after Hurricane Maria in September 2017, this shift in funding priorities was widely criticized.

AN OVERVIEW OF THE REMOVAL PROCESS

There is a series of steps established by the Executive Office for Immigration Review (EOIR) within the U.S. Department of Justice (DOJ) that is typically followed when the federal government is attempting to remove people from the country. Individuals who are targeted for deportation, known as respondents, are either mailed or handed a document by an immigration officer called a "Notice to Appear" (NTA) that lists their alleged immigration violations. The respondents are required to indicate on the form whether they are an "arriving alien"—someone who has just been stopped at the border or port of entry; "an alien present in the U.S. who has not been admitted or paroled"—as in the case of a person who entered into the country without being inspected by an immigration agent beforehand; or whether they have been allowed into the country previously but have overstayed their permitted time in the United States (e.g., they overstayed a visa or have been convicted of a deportable crime[88]). The factual allegations against the respondents and the rationale for removability are listed on the NTA. The form states that respondents can hire a lawyer if desired and must provide the court with address updates if they move. The NTA may include the date and place for a first master calendar hearing in immigration court, which is when the respondents or their lawyers must respond to the government's charges; if the form does not include that information a separate hearing notice is provided to them.[89]

When respondents go to their immigration court hearings, a federal immigration judge decides their cases; there are no juries involved in the process.[90] The respondents may deny that they should be deported and may state that they want "relief from removal." Then another hearing, known as a merits hearing, is scheduled and the burden is on the Department of Homeland Security's attorneys to show that the respondents are not citizens. When the people summoned to court are legal residents that the government is claiming committed deportable crimes, the government attorneys must prove their case by showing "clear and convincing evidence."[91]

If the respondents are shown to be removable, they can request that their judge grant them relief from deportation in the form of voluntary departure (i.e., paying for themselves to go back to their birth country or another country if allowed); cancellation of removal (based upon time of residence in the country, good behavior with no aggravated felonies and other requirements); asylum (based on a well-founded fear of persecution or torture upon return to their birth country); or adjustment of immigration status to that of a permanent resident (petitions are often filed by a family member or employer in these cases).[92]

Ultimately, respondents are either deported by the government or receive some form of relief from removal along with instructions about the steps they need to take to stay in the country. Judges are required to ask respondents if they want to reserve the right to appeal their decision. If they do, they must file a notice of appeal to the Board of Immigration Appeals (BIA) within thirty days and pay a fee (or apply for a fee waiver).[93] The original decision may be upheld or overturned in the decision by the BIA judge or panel of three judges in some cases. Occasionally, these decisions will be appealed again at the federal circuit court level and a panel of three judges will decide the case. Very rarely, cases will go up for review in front of the highest appellate court of the land, the U.S. Supreme Court.

In a standard proceeding, when immigration judges order people to be removed from the country who are not in immigration detention, they get to go home while the government arranges their deportation out of the country. They may receive a letter that tells them when and from where they will leave the United States and how much baggage they can bring with them. When people do not receive such a letter or when they ignore their letters, they are then considered fugitives.

These procedures above occur in a different context for people who have been arrested and held in detention. People are often detained in circumstances in which the government validates their identification and/or runs background checks on them. This traditionally occurs after re-entering the United States after traveling abroad; being interviewed by law enforcement agents while in jail or prison; applying for citizenship or a security clearance or renewing a green card and providing fingerprints; or after workplace or home raids.[94] People who have a criminal record or an immigration violation are often detained. Sometimes they are given the right to have a bond (bail) hearing that would allow them to go home and report to court on their next hearing date. However, this is not always the case, as demonstrated in the *Jennings v. Rodriguez* case highlighted in box 6.1.

Operation Streamline: Moving Immigration Matters to the Criminal Courts

Defense attorneys, U.S. prosecutors and marshals in dark blue suits stand in groups talking quietly. And then, seven men and women are led into the courtroom through a side door by a U.S. Border Patrol agent. They are dressed in orange jumpsuits. The laces of their shoes have been removed, the tongues folded out so they fit like slippers. The seven U.S. marshals walk them up to the front where they stand in front of a judge. Each person is questioned by the judge and then sentenced. Four minutes later, seven more are brought in and the process repeats itself.[95]

The federal criminal court procedures described above in a Tucson, Arizona, criminal court are a far cry from the typical procedures unauthorized immigrants face in civil immigration court. This is because they are part of a set of procedures put into place under "Operation Streamline," an approach to border enforcement that dates back to George W. Bush's presidential administration. (It continued in Barack Obama's administration, and is expanding in magnitude during Donald Trump's administration.) Operation Streamline plays a significant role in the criminalization of

BOX 6.1: CHALLENGING THE DENIAL OF BOND HEARINGS: ALEJANDRO RODRÍGUEZ

In the case *Jennings v. Rodriguez*, the lead plaintiff in the case, Alejandro Rodríguez, claimed that he was denied a bond hearing as a detained lawful permanent resident during the span of his immigration case. A long-term resident of California since the age of one when his parents brought him from Mexico, Rodríguez was a dental assistant and the father of two. He had an old joyriding conviction on his record and was put into detention after pleading guilty to a misdemeanor drug possession offense at age twenty-four. He was denied a bond hearing for the entire three years that he was in detention. He was released in 2007 and then the ACLU connected him with others with similar detention experiences in a class action lawsuit. This lawsuit challenged the lack of bond hearings for detainees who are kept under mandatory detention and for detained asylum seekers. Rodríguez ultimately received a cancellation of removal.

The case made its way to the U.S. Ninth Circuit Court of Appeals, which held that people in detention should be given bond hearings every six months and that the government needs to be able to justify their detention with "clear and convincing evidence" that they are a danger to society or a flight risk. The Obama Administration and ICE challenged the decision and asked for review by the Supreme Court. In 2018, the Supreme Court ultimately reversed the decision of the Ninth Circuit Court by stating that the Immigration and Nationality Act does not give detainees the right to periodic bond hearings during detention even in the case of people seeking asylum and those with no criminal records. They sent the case back to the lower appeals court to hear it again. The Supreme Court decision in this case is considered a negative development in terms of civil rights that will shape the face of detention and deportation in the United States for years to come.

Sources:

Reichlin-Melnick, Aaron. 2016. "Supreme Court Considers Challenge to Detention of Immigrants Without Bond Hearing." Immigration Impact, December 1. American Immigration Council. (http://immigrationimpact.com/2016/12/01/supreme-court-considers-challenge-detention-immigrants-without-bond-hearings/).

Thompson, Christie. 2016. "The Crucial Immigration Case About to Hit the Supreme Court." The Marshall Project, November 29. (https://www.themarshallproject.org/2016/11/29/the-crucial-immigration-case-about-to-hit-the-supreme-court#.rqEjO31aR). *Rodríguez v. Robbins*, 804 F.3d 1060 (9th Cir. 2015). *Jennings v. Rodríguez, 583 U.S.(2018).*

migrants.[96] It is an effort on the part of both the Department of Homeland Security (with the aid of CBP and ICE) and the U.S. Justice Department. This approach to unauthorized U.S. border crossers makes it so they are charged with a criminal offense in federal court rather than processed through the civil immigration court. Prior to Operation Streamline, the criminal prosecution of migrants was reserved for people with criminal histories or histories of prior deportations. With the creation of Operation Streamline, those with no records or former deportations were targeted for criminal prosecution.[97]

Customs and Border Patrol started Operation Streamline in the federal border patrol sector of Del Rio, Texas, in 2005.[98] CBP claimed that they needed to make a change because of the rising numbers of immigrants and the inability to house those whom they apprehended in detention. At that point, agents were able to remove unauthorized Mexican migrants through "voluntary returns," documenting their border crossing, taking fingerprints, and subsequently walking them across the border. But, they were not able to quickly remove the high number of unauthorized border crossers that came from other countries, so they developed a new approach.[99]

As indicated by its name, Operation Streamline involves changing the normal due process procedures given to unauthorized immigrants in the past in the name of streamlined mass trials in federal criminal court. CBP agents refer unauthorized border crossers to the U.S. Attorney's Office and they are charged with misdemeanor illegal entry (and sometimes charged with having a fraudulent visa as well) if it is their first time going through the system, or felony re-entry if they have been deported in the past. Then federal prosecutors, or in some cases, Border Patrol attorneys considered special assistant U.S. attorneys, prosecute migrants in groups in U.S. district court.[100]

Defendants do not have a chance at getting much legal advice from the federal public defenders, who typically meet with them for about thirty minutes before the hearing. Most people plead guilty, which shortens the federal prison sentences that they receive (up to six months for the misdemeanor and between two and twenty years for the felony), and sometimes their time served is waived for their first offense. They are deported immediately after their incarceration. The Operation Streamline procedures are critiqued as "assembly line justice."[101] They shut down avenues for people to make asylum claims, criminalize migrants, divert taxpayer funds to private prisons, and are at odds with the immigration system of the United States, which is rooted in civil and administrative law.

Operation Streamline was expanded from Del Rio, Texas, to seven other Customs and Border Patrol sectors in Arizona and Texas for a time (Yuma, Arizona; Tucson, Arizona; Las Cruces, New Mexico; El Paso, Texas; Laredo, Texas; Brownsville, Texas; and McAllen, Texas), but was scaled back to only three sectors by 2014—Del Rio, Laredo, and Tucson. California never implemented Operation Streamline until the San Diego sector started to do so in the summer of 2018.[102] The use of the program has been increased since late 2017—in Tucson, they prosecuted eighty-five hundred people through the program between October 1, 2017 and April 19, 2018, compared to the five thousand people prosecuted the year before during the same period.[103]

Separating Families

> If you cross this border unlawfully, then we will prosecute you. . . . If you are smuggling a child, then we will prosecute you and that child may be separated from you as required by law.
>
> —Attorney General Jeff Sessions, May 7, 2018[104]

In keeping with the ramped-up criminalization priorities of Operation Streamline, the Department of Homeland Security increased the number of migrant families being separated at the U.S.-Mexico border in late 2017 and early 2018. Because adults entering the country were increasingly charged with a crime upon entering, the U.S. Border Patrol would then detain them, separate them from their children, and label the children as unaccompanied minors and hand them over to the Office of Refugee Resettlement.[105]

Subsequently, the parents would be in one detention center and the children were placed away from them in a variety of different places such as group homes, foster families, and with sponsors or relatives. Children and infants, including *newborns* and toddlers younger than three years old, have been called to immigration court to appear on their own.[106] In fact, one immigration lawyer remembered having a judge ask for a crying infant to be taken out of the courtroom, and she had to tell the judge that the baby was the respondent for the next case and asked if her grandmother could speak instead.[107]

In spite of the absurdity of having children represent themselves in immigration court, one federal immigration judge testified in a trial that he taught immigration law to kids as young as three and four years old successfully—the implication being fair legal proceedings could include them, but they would need to be slowly paced.[108] Developmental psychologists disagreed with this claim.[109]

During their separations from their children, parents were sometimes deported. Some have claimed that they were offered reunification with their children if they signed voluntary deportation forms. For example, the *Texas Tribune* covered the story of a young man named Carlos, who paid $7,000 to a smuggler to get out of Honduras due to threats to his safety related to gang activity and organized crime.[110] He and his six-year-old daughter came into the United States from Mexico on a raft across the Rio Grande. They turned themselves into Border Patrol and made a plea for asylum, but Carlos did not pass the credible fear test. They were separated and held in separate locations—in an adult detention center outside of Houston, Texas, and in a children's shelter somewhere in Arizona. After Carlos received the offer to be reunited with his daughter, he signed the deportation papers and dropped his asylum claim. He thought they would be deported together, but quickly regretted his decision when he learned she would likely be kept in the shelter she was placed in in Arizona, while he would be sent back to Honduras.

The case of Carlos and his daughter is typical of the more than six thousand migrant family separation cases that Amnesty International estimates occurred between April 2018 and August 2018.[111] National outrage around the separation practices quickly grew and protestors noted that they often violated the *Flores* settlement, which states children should not be detained in facilities that have not been licensed by a child welfare entity, nor should they be held in any family detention centers for more than twenty days.[112]

On June 20, 2018, Donald Trump signed an executive order called "Affording Congress an Opportunity to Address Family Separation"[113] and changed the policy. The order stated that unauthorized migrants crossing the border should be kept together after they have been detained and placed on military bases even if they have asylum claims. The due date for family reunification was July 23, 2018, but three months after the due date there were hundreds of parents who were separated from their children.[114] About four hundred Central American parents were deported without their children, and nonprofits have been leading the effort to find the parents in their countries of origin and discussing next steps.[115] Because the government is adamant about not paying to bring the parents back to the United States, they are faced with the choice of letting their children pursue asylum alone in the United States or bringing them back to their dangerous home countries.

DETENTION

Over the last few decades, the number of people detained in U.S. immigration detention while awaiting a decision about their legal status or possible deportation has increased dramatically. The Global Detention Project estimates that there were about eighty-five thousand people held in immigration detention in 1995, and by 2012, there were over 477,000 people detained.[116] Although this number declined by 2016, there was still a huge number of people in immigration detention—approximately 352,000[117]—at an estimated cost of $150 per person per day.[118]

ICE uses over two hundred facilities for immigration detention, including local jails, private detention facilities, field offices, "family residential centers," and juvenile detention centers. Since 2010 Congress has required that ICE have approximately thirty-four thousand beds reserved for immigrant detainees in its centers each day. This is the result of a controversial mandate that was placed into the 2010 Department of Homeland Security Appropriations Act without any public debate.[119] Every year that followed (except for 2017) a number of detention beds have been set aside for immigrant detainees in the congressional appropriation process.[120] After the presidential election of Donald Trump in late 2016, there has been talk that the Department of Homeland Security may want to increase the "bed quota" to eighty thousand people per day.[121] Although that number seems unbelievably large, by mid-2018, ICE was already detaining slightly over forty-four thousand individuals per day. Guatemalans, Hondurans, and El Salvadorans collectively made up 43 percent of the detainees, while 25 percent were Mexican, 5 percent were Indian, and 5 percent were Cuban (all other nationalities only made up 1 percent of the detainees each).[122] The vast majority, five out of six detainees, were men and 30 percent of the detainees were held in the state of Texas.[123]

Table 6.1 shows data from TRAC Immigration researchers that demonstrate how deeply entangled the private prison industry is in immigration detention. Private for-profit correctional corporations were involved in the operation of the ten U.S. detention centers with the most detainees as of mid-2018.[124]

Table 6.1. For-Profit Correctional Corporations and the Ten Most Populous Detention Centers in the United States

	Facility	*Location*	*Company Operating*	*Approximate # of Detainees*
1	Stewart Detention Center	Lumpkin, GA	CoreCivic (CCA)	1,839
2	Adelanto ICE Processing Center	Adelanto, CA	GEO	1,831
3	South Texas ICE Processing Center	Pearsall, TX	GEO	1,815
4	Eloy Federal Contract Facility	Eloy, AZ	CoreCivic (CCA)	1,500
5	South Texas Family Residential Center	Dilley, TX	CoreCivic (CCA)	1,300
6	Tacoma ICE Processing Center	Tacoma, WA	GEO	1,300
7	Montgomery County Jail	Conroe, TX	GEO	1,150
8	Port Isabel SPC	Los Fresnos, TX	Ahtna Technical Services (staffed by)	1,150
9	LaSalle ICE Processing Center	Jena, LA	GEO	1,150
10	Houston Contract Detention Facility	Houston, TX	CoreCivic (CCA)	1,000

Source: TRAC Immigration. 2018. "Profiling Who ICE Detains—Few Committed Any Crime." Syracuse University, October 9. (http://trac.syr.edu/immigration/reports/530/).

The Supreme Court has supported the detention of unauthorized immigrants as a guarantee that individuals will appear for their removal hearings and as a means of preventing the detainees from harming anyone.[125] Although there are other ways of making sure that people show up to their immigration proceedings, such as the Alternatives to Detention Program that is run by ICE for low-risk individuals (using home visits, electronic ankle monitors, and voice recognition tools), immigrant detention is still relied upon heavily.[126] There is little evidence that detention is particularly helpful in ensuring public safety as ICE has estimated that the vast majority of their detainees are neither violent nor high security risks.[127]

The State of Detention Centers

> People who say this is not a prison are lying. . . . It's a prison for us and children, but none of us are criminals.
>
> —Yancy Maricela Mejia Guerra, a detainee in Dilley, Texas[128]

Detention centers for those alleged to have defied immigration laws are not supposed to be prisons, yet the experiences of those held there are often similarly dehumanizing. As noted previously, ICE contracts with large correctional corporations, such as CoreCivic (known prior to 2016 as Corrections Corporation of America) and the GEO Group, to run the majority of the detention centers in the United States. These companies are paid an enormous amount of money to provide services to ICE—for example, in 2012 Corrections Corporation of America received $208 million and the GEO Group received $208 million.[129] As a means of protecting their interests, the private prison companies lobby Congress each year to support increased immigration enforcement through legislation and budgeting.[130]

ICE officials hold the power to determine whether a detention center is safe and healthy for the detainees. ICE provides the detention center with advanced notice of when their inspection of the facility will occur.[131] Investigators typically use a checklist of what is provided at each facility to write their reports rather than conducting interviews with detainees and visitors that would provide detailed information about the quality of life in the detention centers.[132] If a facility fails to pass investigation twice, ICE is required to shut it down.

ICE inspectors often overlook violations of policy and law and allow their contracts with offending facilities to be maintained. For example, in 2012 when ICE inspectors examined Eloy Federal Contract Facility in Arizona, they were aware that there had been five detainee suicides there since 2003.[133] When they examined the suicide watch room, they noted that there were structures and small objects in the room that could be used in suicide attempts, yet they passed the facility on the inspection item for suicide prevention.[134] In another example, inspectors claimed two facilities with no outdoor recreation areas at all satisfied that standard because their rooms in the center had "natural light and air circulation."[135]

A surprise inspection of the Adelanto Detention Center by the Department of Homeland Security's Office of Inspector General (OIG) in May 2018 was one of the rare examples in which inspectors noted serious problems. In fifteen of the twenty rooms they examined, inspectors found "nooses" made from twisted bed sheets hanging from the vents. The OIG discovered that staff did not bother to take them down in spite of the fact that multiple detainees had tried to commit suicide in the detention center in recent history.[136] The inspectors also found that detainees were segregated from the group for no justifiable reason and they were not providing adequate dental or health care. They ordered ICE and GEO Group, the private prison company that runs the detention center, to immediately address these issues.[137]

The U.S. Civil Rights Commission found that both public and private detention centers in the United States violate the detainees' right to proper medical care, hamper their ability to contact lawyers, and ignore their claims of rape and sexual assault.[138] They also found that they prevent Muslim detainees from observing Ramadan and harm transgender detainees.[139] The American Civil Liberties Union found that although all detention centers mistreat detainees, the private detention centers have more of a problem with a lack of transparency, and less meaningful oversight and accountability than their public counterparts.[140] There are also fewer educational and medical care opportunities in private detention centers than there are in public ones.[141]

In spite of the blatant disregard for them by many detention facility officials, undocumented people have rights that have been asserted by the highest court of the land. The U.S. Supreme Court has noted that the Fifth Amendment protection of due process extends to people who are not citizens who reside in the United States.[142] In the case *Zadvydas v. Davis* (2001), the Supreme Court ruled that detainees should not remain in immigration detention more than 180 days (approximately six months) after receiving a final order to be removed from the country unless the government proves special circumstances are relevant or that they will be removed in the foreseeable future.[143] If the government cannot enforce the removal order, the detainee is required to be released. In addition, the Supreme Court has ruled in more than one case that the First Amendment to the Constitution protects the rights of detainees to engage in hunger strikes while in detention, as they are forms of free speech.

The detention of families in so-called family residential centers (also known as "baby jails" by critics) has been controversial for years. In 2009, community members convinced the Obama Administration to stop detaining families in the Hutto Detention Center in Taylor, Texas, based on claims of mistreatment including sexual abuse.[144] For some years after that, only the Berks Family Residence Facility in Pennsylvania still detained families.[145] Yet, in the summer of 2014, the federal government opened several privately owned family detention centers in response to over seventy thousand Central American children and families fleeing violence in their home countries.[146] One center was opened in Artesia, New Mexico; one was in Karnes, Texas; and one was in Dilley, Texas.

The U.S. Citizenship and Immigration Services found that approximately 90 percent of all women and children held in U.S. family detention facilities qualified to seek asylum in the United States. As a representative of the United Nations Refugee Services noted, "The flight of people escaping life-threatening violence in El Salvador, Honduras and Guatemala continues unabated. Those who manage to make it to the United States are not illegal migrants. They are refugees."[147] Yet for all intents and purposes, the Central Americans who crossed the border into the United States that summer were treated as undocumented migrants. Observers of the Artesia, Karnes, and Dilley detention centers found that detention damaged the ability for detainees to effectively move forward with their asylum cases and found that detention was physically and mentally harmful to the women and children housed there.[148]

The Texas Department of Family and Protective Services (TDFPS) attempted to get their two family detention centers in Dilley and Karnes licensed as child care providers. The regulation that was going to be used to justify the child care licensing was especially lenient and made it so the companies running the centers (CoreCivic [formerly CCA] and Geo Group) would not have to comply with the typical standards that needed to be met.[149] For example, under Texas law child care facilities should not have children sharing bedrooms with unrelated adults, but the detention centers there did not meet this requirement. Under the lax regulations established for the family detention center licensing, this issue would not be seen as an obstacle.

Detained mothers in the Dilley and Karnes centers and the nonprofit Grassroots Leadership recognized this, along with many other serious problems, and filed a case against the TDFPS and the companies running the centers.[150] At the heart of their case was the claim that the detention centers were run more like prisons than child care centers, and therefore the Texas Department of Family and Protective Services had no right to be licensing them. If they were licensed with a lack of basic protections put into place, it would only hurt the children and increase their time locked in the facilities. The judge hearing the case agreed, and she ruled that the TDFPS could not license the family detention centers as child care providers.

Without child care licenses, family detention centers should no longer be detaining children.[151] None of three currently opened family detention centers in Texas or Pennsylvania have active child care licenses: they were revoked for Berks and Karnes and Dilley was never issued one. This is a violation of the 1997 *Flores* settlement that was a response to years of lawsuits about the treatment of unaccompanied migrant children. The settlement requires that children should be detained in facilities with licensed child care.[152] Although four hundred women and children were released from the South Texas Family Residential Center in Dilley in late 2016, it was still the case that children were being detained in all three existing family detention centers well into 2018.[153]

The Financial Benefits of Detention

Although at first glance it may not seem as though the social control of immigrants through detention and deportation serves the needs of U.S. business owners, when we look more closely we can see that this is the case. Despite the apparent downside of locking up a subset of their workers, many U.S. business owners benefit from the revolving temporary labor force that stems from the enforcement of immigration law.[154] When their workers are labeled as "illegal" they have more freedom to pay the laborers less, avoid paying for safe business practices and equipment, and neglect to provide them with benefits. (See the discussion in chapter 3 for more details about these oppressive conditions for undocumented workers.) The decentralization of government services over the past several decades allows the government to subcontract with companies to provide services related to detection, detention, and deportation. Ultimately, there is very little oversight of any of these providers because of the decentralization—in other words, nobody is watching the watchers very closely.

At the public level, law enforcement agencies earn millions of dollars by housing federal immigration detainees in county jails, and in light of the Trump Administration's promises to increase detention and deportation, they see money-making opportunities on the horizon. For example, in California in 2017, Sheriff Sandra Hutchins was successful in her plea to expand the immigrant detention in the Orange County jails, and as a result one thousand more people will be detained in the county. Orange County will receive around $36 million a year for housing immigrant detainees.[155] The concerns of critics—that one of the primary jails that would be used as a detention center has been shown to be unsanitary; that detainees are fed spoiled lunchmeats; and that they have been subjected to solitary confinement with no exercise or visitors allowed—made little impact on the Orange County Board of Supervisors who approved the expansion.[156] The Board of Supervisors justified their decision as one that would let detainees in Orange County have the opportunity to be detained close to home.[157] Also relevant to the decision was the fact that one of the cities in the county, Santa Ana, had recently moved to phase out its involvement in immigration detention, which led to ICE's early termination of their contract and a loss of revenue for the county.[158] (Important fact: Santa Ana Jail was the only detention center in the country that had a module for transgender detainees before it was closed.[159] The transgender women who were housed there were moved to the Cibola County Detention Center in New Mexico, which now has the only transgender pod.)[160]

ICE runs "Housekeeping and Voluntary Work Programs" in their detention facilities. In these programs, they use detainees to work up to eight hours a day and forty hours a week doing tasks like cleaning the detention center and serving meals. They typically pay workers $1 a day, which was the rate approved for voluntary labor in immigration detention centers by Congress in *1950*.[161] In some family detention centers, detainees are paid $3 a day for what is labeled as voluntary labor.[162] Given that the food and goods that the detainees can purchase in the detention center is up to seven times more expensive than it would be at Walmart, the pay is insignificant and the bulk of it goes right back to the detention center.[163] Critics of this program state that the labor is anything but voluntary and it allows the companies to exploit the detainees and avoid paying outside laborers minimum wage.

The government, which forbids everyone else from hiring people without documents, has effectively become the biggest employer of undocumented immigrants in the country.

—Carl Takei, ACLU National Prison Project attorney[164]

A federal class action lawsuit against the GEO Group on behalf of over sixty thousand current and former detainees claims that they were often forced to do janitorial, clerical, or landscaping work at the Aurora Correctional Facility in Colorado for no pay or $1 a day, or they would face solitary confinement.[165] The plaintiffs also claim that they should have been paid market wages for the work that they were doing in the facility. The lawsuit states that requiring civil detainees to work against their will is a violation of the Victims of Trafficking and Violence Protection Act, which is designed to prevent slavery and forced labor.[166] Unlike prisoners who are imprisoned as a criminal punishment, those who are detained in immigration detention are not there to be punished—they are there to wait for a determination of their legal status or civil deportation. The plaintiffs in this lawsuit are standing up against their social and economic exploitation. Unfortunately, it is expected to take years for this case to make its way through the legal system.

DEPORTATION

Legal Roots of the Modern Era of Deportation

The modern era of deportation followed the passage of two pieces of federal legislation under the Clinton Administration in 1996. The first, the Illegal Immigration Reform and Immigrant Responsibility Act (IIRIRA), expanded federal immigration agents' ability to detain and deport immigrants for many nonviolent and minor criminal offenses. It made it much harder for people to wage a defense against their immigration violation charges, and limited the ability for people to apply for asylum.[167] It also created the administrative process of *expedited removal*. The second, the Antiterrorism and Effective Death Penalty Act of 1996 (AEDPA), was a response to the Oklahoma City Federal Building bombing and it made it easier to detain and deport undocumented immigrants and long-term legal residents.[168] AEDPA is known for being the first act to "fast-track" immigration proceedings. As a result, today we have several deportation processes that occur in a quicker manner than standard court cases, and they are often critiqued for taking a shortcut around due process protections. There is an enormous backlog of pending cases in immigration courts that helps drive the use of fast-track procedures. In fact, by 2017, the average time that a person waited to have their case determined in immigration court was over 650 days![169] The backlog has only intensified since then with ten of the thirty-one states that have immigration courts experiencing a massive backlog of 746,049 cases as of July 2018.[170]

Deformalized Methods of Deportation

As outlined by legal scholar Daniel Kanstroom, there are several deformalized methods of deportation.[171] The first, expedited removal, has traditionally been used for people who have been stopped by a federal immigration agent within one hundred miles of the border who cannot prove that they have been in the United States for longer than fourteen days. In these removal cases, federal officials can deport people without giving them a chance to explain their case to an immigration judge. Following the Trump Administration Executive Order on Border Security, the Department of Homeland Security has announced that it will expedite deportation for a much larger group of people—those questioned *anywhere* in the nation who have not been in the country continuously for *two years*.[172] People who have credible fears of torture or persecution in their home countries and have not been in the United States more than a year may be able to get an asylum hearing with a judge in lieu of expedited removal, but the bulk of the people questioned can be automatically removed.

The second type of fast-track procedure is administrative removal. There are no court hearings associated with this type of removal either—if people have committed an "aggravated felony" an administrative immigration official can notify them of their upcoming removal from the country. People have ten days to respond to the letter and there is little in the way of legal protection to stop their deportation from occurring. The third type of fast-track procedure is reinstatement of removal, which applies to people who have previously been deported and have returned to the United States during the time period in which they have been forbidden to (e.g., five years to life depending on their deportation order). Their prior removal order can be reactivated in these cases and they can be promptly deported. In the fourth type of expedited removal, people may decide to sign stipulated orders of removal in situations that they have formally been charged with an immigration violation. Similar to a plea bargain (but usually without the guarantee of a government-provided lawyer), they forgo their right to a hearing, agree to deportation, and are barred from re-entering the United States. Many people who are in detention sign these agreements at ICE agents' request in spite of the fact they may not fully understand what they are signing due to language barriers or a lack of familiarity with the consequences.[173]

The final method of voluntary departure is a very common one in which people voluntarily agree to deportation, but may not be barred from legally re-entering the country one day if they have not been undocumented in the United States for more than a year. If they have been in the country for longer than a year, they will have a ten-year ban on entering the country again.

"Deporters in Chief" and Zero Tolerance

Things are now quickly shifting in terms of deportation policy. During President Obama's two terms in office, he was labeled by many as the "deporter in chief" due to the high number of people who were deported, especially at the beginning of his

Figure 6.2. The Trump Administration has been heavily critiqued for its reliance on deportation.
Rochelle Brown, Unsplash

first term. Yet, an analysis published by the Migration Policy Institute shows that Obama has a mixed legacy related to immigration.[174] His administration focused heavily on removing undocumented people who had recently crossed the border and people with criminal records. He intensified the use of the Secure Communities Program, a program that involves allowing officers in jails and prisons to ask about immigration status and to hold undocumented inmates and discharge them to ICE.

At the same time, the Obama Administration significantly decreased the number of removals of people without a criminal record who had been in the country for many years compared to both the Bush Administration and the Clinton Administration. Under his administration, fewer people were deported in total (5,281,115) than in the Bush Administration (10,328,850) or the Clinton Administration (12,290,905). In spite of this, it is clear that his administration deported millions of people and disrupted millions of families. Obama's support of Deferred Action for Childhood Arrivals (DACA) in 2010 and Deferred Action for Parents of Americans and Lawful Permanent Residents (DAPA) in 2014 indicated his intent to shield many people from deportation, at least temporarily.

As noted throughout this chapter, the Trump Administration is taking a zero tolerance approach to deportation and expanding what scholar Nicholas De Genova calls the "deportation regime."[175] ICE is tracking around 970,000 immigrants who have previously received deportation orders and 82 percent of them have no criminal record.[176] In addition, they appear to be focusing on the 2.3 million people who have standing check-in arrangements with the Department of Homeland Security, and two million of those people have no criminal record.[177] These groups of people are seen as the most easily targeted for deportation because they will not get a lot of time in the courts. Cases of people going to their yearly check-in with ICE and then being deported are becoming more common under the president's mass deportation campaign.

In addition, ICE has reported that more than forty-three former DACA recipients have been deported under the Trump Administration due to alleged criminal behavior and another 676 former DACA recipients are facing deportation. At least ninety of them are in detention centers.[178] This move to focus on DACA recipients began at the end of President Obama's term when there was a tremendous increase in applications prior to the presidential election and has been amped up by the Trump Administration.[179] Ultimately, as Tanya Golash-Boza explains in her book *Deported: Immigrant Policing, Disposable Labor and Global Capitalism*, the outcome of this deportation machine is a system of gendered and racialized removal that disproportionately affects black and Latinx men.[180]

Legal Representation in Deportation Cases

Unlike in criminal cases, historically immigrants in this country have not been provided with free legal representation by the government when called to immigration court, even if they are without financial means to hire an attorney. As noted previously, immigration issues have traditionally been considered matters of civil law rather than criminal law, even though detention and deportation procedures involve many restrictions that mirror those placed on criminal defendants. Without free legal assistance, people faced with possible deportation have a limited chance of gaining a successful outcome in their cases and being able to remain in the country. In fact, people who have their cases heard in immigration court have been shown to have successful case outcomes only 3 percent of the time.[181] Recent research has shown that when people have an immigration attorney represent them, they are five times more likely to have their asylum cases resolved favorably than those who do not have such assistance.[182] In many cases the very presence of an immigration lawyer, regardless of the quality of their courtroom advocacy, can be beneficial to respondents.[183]

Legal nonprofits often provide limited assistance to people who do not have lawyers for their immigration cases, such as filling out paperwork, but the Department of Justice Executive Office of Immigration Review tried to put a stop to this help in 2017 by sending cease and desist letters to some practitioners.[184] A federal court in Seattle temporarily blocked this request, but the message remains: the federal government does not want immigration respondents to have free legal help.

Although the federal government will not provide legal help, a handful of cities and states have created or are in the process of creating government-assisted legal aid programs for people with cases in federal immigration court. The first one of its kind began with a $500,000 commitment by the New York City Council in 2013, which was enough to fund legal representation for a subset of the population who needed it. The New York City Council significantly increased their funding for the New York Immigrant Family Unity Project (NYIFUP) to almost $5 million in 2014, which allowed them to provide legal representation to any immigrant considered to be poor or indigent who had an immigration case pending in the New York City courts and two other upstate courts. In April 2017, it was announced that the coalition between nonprofit organizations, such as the Vera Institute of Justice; the Immigration Clinic at Cardozo Law School; and Democratic senators in New York inspired the state to fund public defenders for *all* eligible people facing deportation in the state of New York.[185]

The rationale behind the government funding the program was based in part upon the idea that if free immigrant legal defense was provided to the people who need it in New York (with a cost of about $7.4 million or 74 cents per personal income taxpayer per year), not only would it uphold universal human rights, but it would save the state of New York a good deal of money in the long run.[186] Researchers at the Center for Popular Democracy (CPD) estimated that it would generate significant cost savings in the areas of social services such as foster care and health care for children whose parents would be detained or deported.[187] They also found that public immigration legal assistance would save private employers money that they would otherwise spend replacing detained or deported employees, and would save the government an enormous amount of money in detaining and deporting non-citizens. In addition, CPD found it would protect the future earning potential and tax contributions of youth who would not have to drop out of school in light of the detention and/or deportation of their parents or guardians.

Following New York's lead, Alameda County, California (which includes the cities of Berkeley and Oakland), also began funding legal counsel for a legal defense fund as part of its coalition to protect individuals and families from deportation. Research on the immigration hearing outcomes in the Bay Area by Stanford University researchers demonstrated the need for support of free or affordable legal support; they found that detained people with legal representation from nonprofits are 70 percent more likely to be successful in resisting their deportation than detained people without legal counsel.[188]

In nearby San Francisco, Mayor Ed Lee and the Board of Supervisors provided nonprofits in their city with funds to represent over thirty thousand people who were not detained but were facing deportation proceedings in late 2016.[189] In response to pressure from legal nonprofits, in 2017 they began to extend this legal counsel to include those in immigrant detention as well.[190] Although the funding allotted to the Public Defender's Office is short of what is needed to fully do the job, advocates see their city as moving in the right direction.

Lawmakers in the state of California followed Alameda County and San Francisco's lead and agreed in June 2017 to dedicate $45 million of the state budget to fund immigrant legal defense.[191] The funding supports collaborative efforts between immigrant rights groups, legal services groups, and OneCalifornia, a faith-based group, to provide legal help to those threatened with deportation through the year 2020.[192] This effort will build on the Department of Social Services' existing legal assistance program that helps people apply for citizenship and for DACA status.

Although many attorneys do a wonderful job of representing their clients in immigration court, it is also the case that some do not. In fact, some may increase their clients' likelihood of removal from the country if they are unprepared, unfamiliar with the intricacies of immigration law, or simply unprofessional. As a result of this, the Executive Office of Immigration Review (EOIR) punishes lawyers who have been determined to be sub-par in their representation of their clients by suspending them for practice either for a specific amount of time or indefinitely, or disbarring them altogether. A list of these attorneys can be found on the EOIR's website and is often posted in immigration courts as well.[193]

The American Bar Association warns about the work of *noratorios* or immigration consultants who are not licensed attorneys but illegally take on immigration cases.[194] The American Immigration Lawyers Association writes that "many noncitizens find out that they will never get their green card or other immigration benefits because an unqualified immigration consultant or *notario* unlawfully working as an immigration lawyer destroyed their dreams."[195]

Deportation Hearings in Detention Centers

The difficulties that characterize immigration hearings in immigration courts are multiplied many times over in detention centers. As seen in Table 6.2, the U.S. Department of Justice Executive Office for Immigration Review reported that in

Table 6.2. Immigration Courts with the Highest Percentages of Cases That Ended in Deportation (in 2015)

1. Stewart Detention Facility Court in Georgia (98.2%)
2. Oakdale Detention Center Court in Louisiana (96.2%)
3. Saipan, Northern Mariana Islands Court (95.2%) (Not in a detention center)
4. Florence Service Processing Center Court, Arizona (92.9%)
5. El Paso Service Processing Center Court, Texas (92.5%)
6. Otay Mesa Detention Center Court, California (91.5%)
7. Ulster Correctional Facility Court, New York (91%)
8. Adelanto Detention Center Court, California (90.2%)
9. Fishkill Correctional Facility Court, New York (90.1%)
10. Eloy Detention Center Court, Arizona (89.0%)

Source: Thompson, Christie. 2016. "America's Toughest Immigration Court." New York: The Marshall Project, December 12. (https://www.themarshallproject.org/2016/12/12/america-s-toughest-immigration-court#.hAAkz75Ke).

the fiscal year of 2015, the majority of the ten immigration courts with the highest percentages of cases that ended in deportation were in detention centers or service processing centers:

When compared to the courts with the lowest percentages of total cases ending in deportation, the contrast is striking. The percentage of deportation outcomes for cases in the New York City Immigration Court was 30.6 percent, 42.0 percent in the Honolulu Immigration Court in Hawaii, and 44.2 percent and 44.8 percent respectively in the Phoenix Immigration Court in Arizona and the San Diego Immigration Court.[196]

There are multiple barriers that detainees face when trying to wage an effective claim against deportation. Often the locations of the detention centers where they are placed makes it very difficult to find a lawyer. For example, #1 on the list of courts with the highest percentage of cases ending in deportation, the Stewart Detention Center, is located in Lumpkin, Georgia, near the border with Alabama. The court is in an isolated area about 140 miles from Atlanta and is forty miles from Columbus, which is the nearest town with hotels and Internet service.[197] Lawyers have found it highly inconvenient to get there, and highly inconvenient to work on cases in the center because there was no access to the Internet or even a fax to use. As a result few lawyers today are willing to go there, and if they are they generally charge fees that are higher than the detainees can afford.[198]

Some private detention centers like Stewart make rules that make it virtually impossible to build a defense for clients—for example no free phone calls are given to the detainees to call their lawyers; they have to save up money for a calling card. Only very recently did many detention centers add videoconferencing to their centers, and video is often used for hearings where the immigration judge is in a court in another city. Detainees are moved around the country to different detention centers with little notice. This means they might be working with a lawyer near their detention center when they are transferred to a detention center somewhere else, possibly even another state, and the working arrangement may no longer work. As in the traditional immigration court, language issues and access to quality translation are hard to come by in deportation center courts.

In addition, judges are often rotated around the detention center courts, so one judge usually does not hear a single case from its start to its end.[199] This means attorneys who represent detained clients have a difficult time knowing how to prepare a case for a particular judge. Cases are often hurried in some of the newer detention centers, such as LaSalle Detention Center in Louisiana, and detainees are expected to find an attorney within two days of being detained, which is often impossible for them because of limited phone access and the limited availability of qualified lawyers.[200]

All of these barriers, when combined with the overall lack of cleanliness and prison-like atmosphere in detention centers, cause many clients to give up resisting the process. Pro-bono attorney Jeremy Jong's description of his clients' reaction to the LaSalle Detention Center in *The Guardian* newspaper summarizes the cumulative effect of all of these barriers, "Detention there drives a lot of people crazy, to the point where a lot of people would rather go [back] to a place they know is dangerous, where they have no family, where they might be tortured."[201]

Veterans and Deportation

> After manning a machine gun on a combat helicopter as a U.S. Marine during the liberation of Kuwait, Antonio Romo came back to the United States traumatized by the death and carnage he saw. He says he turned to alcohol and narcotics to try to quiet the nightmares, and made multiple suicide attempts. With addiction, he fell into dealing, and was arrested for selling cocaine. And after getting out of prison, Romo was deported in 2008 to Mexico, from where he had migrated to Lynwood, California, illegally at age 12.[202]

As shown in the *Chicago Tribune* excerpt above, military service can take a toll on its members for many years after it has ended. Most people know about this, yet not everyone realizes the U.S. military benefits from the labor power of many people who are not citizens. A little-known fact about the U.S. military is that on most days there are up to eighteen thousand undocumented people serving as military members, and about five thousand legal permanent residents (green card holders) sign up to serve each year.[203] When many people sign up to serve in the military, they are under the impression that they will be able to become citizens. They often do not realize that military service does not guarantee that a person will be granted citizenship. Nor do they realize that if they do apply, it will be difficult to complete the complicated series of required steps while deployed.[204]

The U.S. government has long used citizenship as a promise to increase military enlistment, such as in World War I and World War II.[205] The government stopped offering naturalization during the Vietnam War, but reinstated the practice in

2001.[206] It has been estimated that over one hundred thousand service members have become naturalized citizens.[207] Yet, many veterans encounter hardships when they try to become citizens and have found that the U.S. government does not come to their aid in the way they expected.

This is illustrated in the case of Joaquin Sotelo, whose story was highlighted by NBC News.[208] Sotelo, a former member of the U.S. Navy who served in the Persian Gulf, was a green card holder who was told he would receive citizenship when he was recruited at age nineteen. He filled out and turned in the paperwork for his citizenship during his service and was under the impression it had been processed. Former president George W. Bush announced a program for the naturalization of noncitizen military members at that time and Sotelo believed he was granted citizenship. He left the Navy with an honorable discharge six years later. Later, he was convicted of a drug possession charge and domestic violence charge and was imprisoned.

After he served his time, he found out he would be deported because he committed an aggravated felony, which is considered any crime with a punishment of one year or longer in prison (crimes which include acts such as petty theft and failing to appear in court). After his sister reached out to others in the community with connection to immigration attorneys, a San Francisco lawyer, Etan Newman, came to the aid of Sotelo and accompanied him to his hearing. He worked with Sotelo to provide documentation to the judge about Sotelo's strong ties to the United States and the military's failure to provide him with needed services after leaving the Navy. The judge was convinced to give him bail due to the fact he was not a flight risk nor dangerous to other people. Rather than being deported immediately, he was given another hearing.

Because veterans often face mental health challenges after their military service, the policy of no second chances for those who have committed crimes is a punitive one. The mental health problems that veterans experience have been shown to be related to the likelihood they will commit nonviolent crimes, particularly in the case of male veterans experiencing family or substance abuse problems.[209] Given the large number of the armed forces who experience post-traumatic stress disorder (PTSD) after their service and the lack of services for veterans, it is no surprise that many undocumented veterans have been cited for violation of immigration law policies. In their report, *Discharged and then Discarded*, the ACLU claims that the U.S. military abandons lawful permanent resident veterans and banishes them to their birth countries right at the time when they need assistance from the country that they served the most.[210] As a result, they are not able to use the medical benefits and social services that the military is supposed to provide for all of its veterans. In addition, their deportation exacerbates their mental health challenges by separating them from family members and their established social networks.

There is no official count of the veterans who have been deported, but it is estimated to be at least 239 people, who have been sent to thirty-two countries.[211] Some government officials are beginning to pay attention to the plight of deported veterans. For example, Democratic members of the U.S. House of Representatives and the Hispanic Congressional Caucus went to Tijuana, Mexico, to visit the Deported Veterans Support House in June 2017. The support house, founded by Hector Barajas-Varela, a deported Army veteran, is a place where deported veterans who live in the border city can network and form a sense of community.

As more attention gets placed on deported veterans in the news media and online, legislators are starting to put forward suggestions to address their situation. For example, in 2016 Raúl Grijalva, the Democratic U.S. representative from Arizona, introduced a congressional bill that instructs the Department of Homeland Security to allow the majority of deported veterans to return back to the United States and to stop deportation processes underway for current and former military service people.[212] Also, Juan Vargas, a Democratic representative of California, reintroduced a deported veterans' bill package in 2017 that would require deported veterans to get access to medical care, establish naturalization centers at military training sites, and prevent veterans from being deported.

At the state level, legal momentum is also underway. Arizona and California legislators have introduced legislation that supports deported veterans in various ways—such as allowing those convicted of nonviolent or minor crimes to return home and creating a fund to help deported veterans.[213] California's Governor Brown granted Hector Barajas-Varela, Erasmo Apodaca Mendizabal, and Marco Antonio Chavez pardons for their past crimes in April 2017.[214] Subsequently, Chavez regained his green card and Barajas-Varela became a U.S. citizen.[215] Although these are helpful developments for these three men, they do not address the many other veterans who have been deported.

In October 2017, the U.S. Department of Defense made changes that make it harder for non-citizens to serve in the military and foreign nationals to apply for naturalization. Background checks now must be completed before lawful permanent residents serve in any capacity in the military.[216] Non-citizens have to serve at least six months of active duty service or a year of reserve service to apply for a certification of honorable service and apply for expedited naturalization (instead of the old requirement of service for one day). By mid-2018, a number of military recruits with special language and medical skills were cut from the Army before being able to apply for citizenship. Lucas Calixto, an Army reservist who was born in Brazil and moved to the United States when he was twelve, sued the Defense Department when he was suddenly dismissed from the military. He told the *New York Times*, "It was my dream to serve in the U.S. military. Since America has been so good to me I wanted to give back and served in the U.S. Army. . . . I know this is not coming from my military unit. They have been very nice to me. It seems as if the decision is being made by higher-ups who don't know me and are just trying to complicate things."[217]

The web of detention and deportation laws and practices in the United States is so complex that we have only scratched its surface in this chapter. These are not static subjects; immigration laws and policies are being changed quickly in the current era, and people in this country find themselves in shifting legal statuses over time or find that their legal status has different consequences than it did previously. The impact on families is particularly devastating as it is common for families to have members with different immigration statuses, which result in complicated situations and difficult choices.[218] Parents who fear that they will be detained and deported must have frank discussions with their children about emergency plans in the event they are targeted by immigration enforcement.[219] DACA enrollees must decide if they will go with their parents to another country if their parents are deported and must decide what to do themselves if DACA is permanently phased out and they are deported.[220] After the deportation of a family member, transnational families must figure out how to bridge their physical distance through the use of technology, financial support, and gifts to one another in spite of the costs and obstacles involved.[221] Deportees must make their way outside of the United States in a country where they may have few connections or resources.[222]

Taking all of this into consideration, it is clear to see that the path forward for people affected by detention and deportation is often challenging, and more often than not, unjust. Yet, as we will see in the next chapter, many migrants and their allies are strengthened and inspired through their collective social actions geared toward changing this path into a more just one.

7

Resistance and Social Change

In 2013, the Los Angeles band, La Santa Cecilia, wrote the song "ICE/El Hielo"[1] to draw attention to the impact of immigration enforcement on the lives of unauthorized immigrants and their families. The title of the song is a play on the acronym for Immigrations and Customs Enforcement (ICE) and the words for "the ice" in Spanish, *el hielo*. The band members collaborated with the National Day Labor Organizing Network (NDLON) to create a song and video for their #Not1More (deportation) campaign.[2] La Santa Cecilia band members were uncomfortably familiar with the risk that everyday people take as they go to work and the complications that come with being criminalized; a founding member of the band is undocumented and the band takes extra measures on the road to support his safety. The song reflects the group's passionate interest in using music to support the immigrant rights movement.

The video for the song is especially powerful. Filmmaker Alex Rivera and several undocumented community members and activists act out scenarios of everyday working people getting caught up in an immigration raid (and one activist played the role of an ICE officer arresting others).[3] The video ends with a powerful message stating that at least two people in the video, and one child's parents, are in the process of being deported.[4] The final scene is of the #Not1More slogan—a reminder of the need to organize with others to stop deportations. The message of the song is to keep asserting one's human rights and, ultimately, immigrant justice. The inspiring news is that so many people are indeed doing just that.

Myth: Unauthorized Latinx immigrants are scared to speak up against immigration policies and practices.

Myth Busted: Immigrants of all legal statuses, including unauthorized, play a central role in the immigrant rights movement.

"¡*Si, se puede*!" (Yes, we can!)
"Undocumented, unafraid, and unapologetic!"
"Obama, Obama, do not deport my mama!"
"Trump, stop the hate—we are here to stay!"
"¡Aquí estamos, and no nos vamos!" (Here we are, and we are not going!)
"No ban! Abolish ICE! No wall!"
"No baby jails! Families belong together!"

The slogans above have been some of the rallying cries at the center of recent social actions by undocumented Latinxs. Although catchy and short, the pleas for change are significant. In the face of multiple forms of repression, unauthorized Latinxs in the United States have a long history of taking action in the name of social justice.[5] This reality is diametrically opposed to the idea that being undocumented means always being paralyzed by the fear of speaking truth to power.

Like many other social movement actors before them, undocumented Latinx activists and their allies have spread their messages about the need for change in many creative ways. In spite of an increasingly vocal anti-immigrant contingent in the United States, and the overt anti-immigrant positions of many political leaders, they persevere. Time and time again, unauthorized Latinxs put their futures on the line in the name of a bigger cause. Many of their efforts have resulted in concrete changes that have made what seemed politically impossible at one point possible.

Myth: Only Latinx young adults who are undocumented are involved in today's immigrant rights movements.

Myth Busted: Unauthorized Latinx immigrants of all ages are involved as well as family and allies from multiple generations.

On the first weekend of June, 40 children lined up on the front steps of the New York offices of U.S. Immigration and Customs Enforcement holding picket signs in their small hands. On each, the same message, "I am a Child." An homage to the 1968 "I am a Man" protest led by Martin Luther King Jr., the signs were meant to send a message to lawmakers who, creator Paola Mendoza said, seemed to have lost sight of the fact that the children crossing the U.S.-Mexico border with or without their parents were still, in fact, children.[6]

Protesting alongside teenagers . . . was 86-year-old Armony Share of Sherman Oaks [California], who [stated] . . . "The Jews were turned away [from America] when they were able to escape from Europe in World War II. . . ." "Are we doing the same thing to these people? When you're against one group, you're against all of them." Share's parents, who are Russian and Polish, fled brewing anti-Semitism in the 1920s. She was born in Mexico and eventually found her home in the U.S. in 1941.[7]

The well-known saying "age is just a number" is a fitting description of the age demographic of people out on the streets and behind closed doors working toward immigration reform. Similar to the participants in the Keep Families Together rallies of June 30, 2018, described above, people of all ages, from children to elders, are involved in social actions related to immigration. Some of the most powerful voices of resistance have been those of children and young adults. Not only is it common to see young people at rallies and marches with their parents, but as we discuss below, there has even been a six-year-old child who has made a compelling speech about immigration justice in front of hundreds of thousands of marchers! Youthful voices draw attention to important causes, and middle-aged adults and elders strengthen these same causes with their invaluable socio-historical insights and knowledge.

Unauthorized youth activists are uniquely positioned in society as those who often have spent much of their lives in the United States and are familiar with its institutions, but live with the threat of serious repercussions if they freely express themselves through protest. They have been told in school that the United States is a country of free speech, but if they speak freely about their legal statuses they could be in danger of deportation.[8] As a result, they often experience internal conflict: they socially identify with U.S. institutions and practices, but find that they are legally defined as outsiders.[9] Undocumented youth and young adults are often motivated by this conflict to get involved in social activism.[10] They are also motivated by friends and peers who are already involved, and by a desire to see specific political issues addressed,[11] such as legal and racialized violence.[12] As sociologist Roberto Gonzales points out, undocumented youth might be "left out, but [they are] not shut down."[13]

Middle-aged undocumented adults and elders often continue the community work that they were involved in during their youth. Like their younger counterparts, they remain motivated by the strain between their familiarity with U.S. institutions and the numerous obstacles that stand in their way from participating fully in them. Experienced adults share the basics of social movement organizing and personal knowledge of the past events that influence today's immigration battles. Although the younger generation of activists is at the forefront of using new technologies for social change[14] (our previous chapters highlight some examples of these methods), other methods that we cover in this chapter are often taught to the younger generation of activists by more experienced ones. Indeed, the social actions of the twenty-first century have all been influenced by their predecessors, such as the Chicanx movements of the 1960s and 1970s and their revitalization in the 1990s, and the Central American asylum and amnesty struggle of the 1980s.[15]

KEY GROUPS WORKING FOR SOCIAL CHANGE

There are many key groups who engage in social actions related to immigration issues in general and issues of unauthorized immigration specifically. The main types of groups involved include:[16]

- small service organizations and nonprofits (such as local legal support offices, day laborer centers, and ethnic organizations);
- national organizations (such as Fair Immigration Reform Now, the National Council of La Raza, National Immigration Project of the National Lawyers

Guild, National Immigration Law Center, CARECEN, the Mexican American Legal Defense and Education Fund [MALDEF], the American Civil Liberties Union, United We Dream, UndocuBlack Network, National Immigrant Youth Alliance [NIYA]);

- faith-based organizations (e.g., American Friends Service Committee, Unitarian Universalist Refugee and Immigrant Service and Education [UURISE], Catholic Charities);
- state and city advocacy organizations (such as California Rural Assistance League, Coalition for Humane Immigrant Rights of Los Angeles [CHIRLA], Arizona Coalition for Migrant Rights, New York Immigration Coalition, Tennessee Immigrant and Refugee Rights Association, Las Americas Immigrant Rights Association [El Paso, Texas], RAICES [Texas], Organized Communities Against Deportation [OCAD] (Chicago, Illinois), Immigrants Rising (Oakland, California);
- research and educational centers and groups (e.g., Harvard Immigration and Refugee Clinical Program, National Latino Research Center—California State University San Marcos, University of California Undocumented Legal Services Center, UCLA Labor Center, *Movimiento Estudiantil Chicanx de Aztlan* [M.E.Ch.A];
- and trade unions and labor federations (e.g., Change to Win, United Farm Workers [UFW], the American Federation of Labor-Congress of Industrial Organizations [AFL-CIO], Service Employees International Union [SEIU], the United Food and Commercial Workers [UFCW], and UNITE HERE).[17]

If you look collectively at these groups as a whole, it is clear that they draw upon people from all walks of life. Undocumented and formerly undocumented members are a driving force behind all of them, if not as members, as inspirations for the work being done. As you will see in Box 7.1, involvement in social action becomes

BOX 7.1 A LOOK AT ONE
WOMAN'S PATH TO SOCIAL ACTION

As we begin this chapter about social resistance and activism, it is important to realize that involvement in immigration-related causes is often a natural outgrowth of other community involvement. The empowerment that comes from becoming informed often leads people to expand their social circles and to share the knowledge that they have gained with others. The path of Raquel, an undocumented Latina from Southern California, demonstrates this pattern.

Raquel is the mother of two children, a boy and a girl. She emigrated from Mexico in 2004 with her children on a tourist visa. The reason why she came to this country was because she feared for her family's safety in Mexico City.

The crime wave in that part of the country was reaching alarming heights at that time. Raquel and her children came to the United States, overstayed their visas, and lived in this country for over a decade.

The fact that Raquel had overstayed her tourist visa and rumors she heard from other family members led her to worry that she could not show it in case she was ever stopped by law enforcement. Since she had no Social Security number or work permit, she started to participate in the informal economy. She worked as a cashier in a mini-market, helped a family member clean houses, and babysat. She shared that she took care of children for a week and she was never paid. The woman told her, "*No te voy a pagar, porque eres una ilegal en este país*" (I won't pay you because you are an illegal in this country). This was Raquel's first encounter with abuse by an employer who never paid her for work.

In 2006, she started to engage in organizations in her children's school as well as in the community. She also started attending school to learn English, and obtained her GED as well as other occupational certificates from her local college. Raquel became interested in immigration-related activism when she witnessed a march that took place near a local university. She said, "I won't get anything done sitting at home." She participated in the DREAM Act movement and in the DACA movement in 2012. She worked with a community group to educate potential candidates for DACA to start getting their evidence ready so when the bill was enacted they would be ready to apply. By 2013 she began to learn about the AB60 bill, which would provide driving licenses to immigrants who met certain requirements. Although it did not become active until January 2, 2015, she started to plan, by studying to take her exam and helping other people.

Raquel was one of the first unauthorized immigrants who received her license/driving permit in California. She explained, "I guess it was destiny or something but somehow I started teaching classes to prepare people before taking the DMV written exam." The class first started at a small conference room at her apartment complex. After the first class was successful, more people were interested and now she gives these classes in multiple libraries as a volunteer.

Raquel has a three-ring binder where she has been collecting the many awards she has received from her children's schools, her church, the ACLU, UURISE, and other organizations in which she has volunteered her time to stay active and bring about change in the community. She has collected evidence of her good moral character so when the time for immigration reform comes she will be ready to be one of the first ones to apply, just like she was when she applied for her driving license. "I have taken these eleven years of living as undocumented in this country as an opportunity to learn the culture, assimilate it, be involved and learn how the system works."

—As shared with Isaias E.

somewhat contagious; once people get involved in one group they are often inspired to join several!

STRATEGIZING FOR CHANGE

There are many strategies that people have used to challenge mainstream misconceptions about unauthorized immigration and immigrants. Those involved in social change work have used just about every well-known social movement strategy under the sun, as well as a few new ones developed specifically for immigration-related causes (e.g., self-deportation).

Flipping the Script: The Use of Frame-Shifting Strategies

As alluded to previously in this book, one of the most effective methods to generate social change on behalf of a marginalized group is to "flip the script" or transform the public discussion about the group and its members. This concept is referred to in social movement terms as *reframing* or *counter framing* an issue.[18] When a group is effective in taking back negative meanings or characterizations related to them and framing their experiences and claims in a different way, they increase their ability to spread their message and gain support from outsiders. Depending on the political and social opportunities available, this can lead to concrete gains for the movement.[19]

For example, Genevieve Negrón-Gonzales[20] found that undocumented youth activists involved in federal DREAM Act organizing in California reframed the mainstream narrative that cast them as non-citizens without rights to one as people with rights to create social change in their country. These young people challenged their status as political outsiders and asserted their right to political inclusion. They cited what they learned in U.S. schools about the civil rights movement and other historical evidence of how social change takes place as they asserted their ability to influence policy. Youth looked to social movement leaders of the past, such as Martin Luther King Jr., as examples of how to achieve their goals against all odds. They began referring to themselves as "undocumented, unafraid, and unapologetic," a catchphrase that inspired their courageous actions.

In their analysis of the Immigration Youth Justice League (IYJL) in Chicago, Illinois, Tania Unzueta Carrasco and Hinda Seif[21] explained that 1.5 generation undocumented young people used a number of different framing methods to challenge the idea that only some people are worthy of a pathway to citizenship. They used online petitions, rallies, letters to the government, and public statements as a means of stopping and/or drawing attention to many threatened deportations. They also shared their "coming out" stories as unauthorized migrants. These different methods allowed them to shift focus from the worthiness of a particular individual to a wider questioning of how the federal government was prioritizing some lives over others. IYJL noted that the federal government considered undocumented college students a less threatening presence than other unauthorized immigrants. As a result, they decided that their group's resistance strategies had to assert the rights of all to stay in the United States. This counter frame challenged the government's notion that only role models should be safe from deportation. As one IYJL activist noted, "The people being deported who are called 'criminals' are our parents, our neighbors, our local store owners, and our classmates. We see them disappear everyday. ICE does this in silence, and we are challenging them to do it publicly."[22] IYJL activists decided to de-emphasize claims privileging education status or year of arrival in the United States when possible (sometimes they were still used strategically), and emphasize the needs of the undocumented community as a whole. This included putting an emphasis on the importance of keeping families and communities intact and healthy.

Fast-forward to January 21, 2017, and we saw this same frame being used by six-year-old Sophie Cruz as she spoke about the immigrant rights movement at the Women's March on Washington. Sophie, whose parents are unauthorized immigrants, made her claims in both Spanish and English as she stood on the stage in front of over four hundred thousand people:[23] "We are here together making a chain of love to protect our families. Let us fight with love, faith and courage so that our families will not be destroyed."[24] Sophie's claim that the destruction of families is at the heart of the deportation threat posed by Donald Trump and his supporters received a great deal of attention online and was the subject of magazine and newspaper articles across the country in publications such as *USA Today*, *People* magazine, and the Huffington Post.[25]

Other reframing efforts used by immigration organizers in recent years are that undocumented people in states that are overtly hostile to them are the *targets* of ignorance and racism rather than victims;[26] and a broadened discussion of who is worthy of protection that includes lesbian, gay, bisexual, transgender, and queer (LGBTQ) people,[27] indigenous migrant youth,[28] and older adults.[29] All of these efforts challenge the mainstream characterization of undocumented immigration and immigrants as "problems" to be solved, emphasize the complexity of immigration issues, and acknowledge the ability of people to resist oppression.

As you can imagine by reading these examples, the act of creating and sharing these new frames related to undocumented immigration with the public involves the use of many social action methods. Some of the most popular methods that Latinx youth and adults have used to spread the word about their concerns and social movement goals include marches and protests, sharing *testimonios* (testimonies) and storytelling, civil disobedience and direct action, and art.

Marching for Justice

> Don't be a marshmallow. Walk the street with us into history. Get off the sidewalk.
> . . .
>
> —Dolores Huerta, 1975[30]

As indicated by the quote above by iconic Latinx social movement organizer Dolores Huerta, getting out on the street has long been seen as essential to any social movement concerted with changing history. In the case of the undocumented struggle, marches, rallies, and protests are effective ways to spread the word about injustices and actions that could be taken to lessen their negative impact or eliminate them altogether. These public events are a way for people to share their voices on political issues, which is particularly powerful for undocumented people who are not allowed to share them officially by voting in U.S. government elections.[31]

When people march, they not only help reframe an issue through the signs people hold and the chants they say in unison, but they also demonstrate who cares about immigration issues. People may hear that others are concerned about the punitive trends in immigration law and might understand the movement intellectually, but when they actually see bodies out on the streets, the message is undeniable. Because of this important reason, it is no wonder that individuals and groups are willing to dedicate their precious time to publicly join with others and emphasize the importance of their cause, rain or shine.

In the twenty-first century, some of the best-known examples of this strategy were the marches of March, April, and May 2006 (often called the *Mega Marchas)* against H.R. 4437, which occurred in over 160 cities in states around the country (e.g., Illinois, California, Arizona, Georgia, Massachusetts, Florida, Nevada, South Carolina, Utah, Washington, Oregon, Colorado, Nebraska, Tennessee, and New York).[32] It is estimated that between *3.5 million to 5.1 million* Latinxs participated in the marches.[33] H.R. 4437 was a punitive bill passed by the House of Representatives in 2005 that would criminalize undocumented immigrants, roll back a number of social services, and strip their due process rights. Millions of people around the country marched in the name of rejecting the bill and replacing it with comprehensive immigration reform. Chants of "*Sí, se puede!*" and "Today we march, tomorrow we vote!" emphasized the power of the people to stop the passage of anti-immigrant legislation and the future possibility of the full political participation of all. The popular chant, "We didn't cross the border, the border crossed us!" reminded observers of the big picture and the socio-historical forces that shaped the immigration debate.[34] In addition, marchers chanted, "¡Aquí estamos, and no nos vamos!" (We are here and we are not leaving!) to assert the presence and power of the immigrant community as a whole.[35] Many marchers wore white shirts as a symbol of peace. It was common to see participants carrying flags—sometimes U.S. flags and sometimes flags that honored their countries of origin.[36]

The marches were driven by a group of Latinx intellectuals and leaders who had a long history of organizing, and they motivated U.S.-born and migrant Latinxs to successfully rise up and challenge the House bill.[37] Spanish-language radio personalities inspired older adults to participate in the marches, and the younger generation used social media tools to organize and participate.[38] The spectacle of the anti-immigrant group, the Minutemen, a group consisting of mostly white men who had filmed themselves "policing" the southern border of the United States, also served as fuel for the resistance.[39]According to political scientist Alfonso Gonzales,[40] for a time the marches successfully shifted the national discussion from one about how migrants should be criminalized and punished by the federal government to one that humanized migrants and considered paths to citizenship.

Recent examples of pro-immigrant marches and rallies include the many that have occurred before and during the presidential administration of Donald Trump. In one example *hundreds of thousands* of people across the United States marched in Families Belong Together rallies to protest the zero tolerance policy for unauthorized immigrants, which resulted in the separation of immigrant children from their parents.[41] Rallies were held on June 30, 2018, in places known for immigrant activism, such as Washington, DC, New York, California, and Illinois, as well as in states that are not traditionally thought of as activist hubs, such as Connecticut and Oklahoma. Protestors communicated messages by carrying signs with messages such as "Keep Families Together" and "Abolish ICE" and by creating symbols such as dolls in boxes that looked like jail cells[42] and dolls in cages, representing the incarceration of migrant children.[43]

"Coming Out" through *Testimonios* and Truth-Telling

> We came out because we are tired of the mistreatment. We are tired of waiting for change and we know that it never comes without risk or without sacrifice.
>
> —No Papers, No Fear, 2012

A technique that has been central to a number of the different social actions related to immigration in recent years is the use of personal *testimonios* (testimonies). This tactic has been especially popular among undocumented teens and young adults in their twenties and thirties in spite of the danger involved.[44] After being defined as "illegal" and "alien" by the government, activists who share their stories related to legal status may be punished and/or deported after publicly sharing their stories. They are increasing their vulnerability and decreasing their sense of safety by giving government officials and others who could harm them this information.[45] Yet, there is power in numbers and the individuals who boldly share their testimonies vividly convey how social and legal decisions are negatively affecting them. The *testimonios* also shatter stereotypes by demonstrating that unauthorized immigrants share a lot in common with other members of society and make vital societal contributions.[46] They are a means of empowering the narrator's own voice and they inspire people to become leaders of social movement organizations.[47] Perhaps most importantly, *testimonios* allow truth-tellers to resist being silenced by and excluded from mainstream society.[48]

The notion of "coming out" to the public about being undocumented borrows language from the LGBT community and their movement strategies. "Coming out of the shadows" and sharing the truth about one's legal status parallels the use of the term "coming out of the closet" by LGBT individuals who publicly share their sexual and/or gender identities. Some observers, such as anthropologist Nicholas de Genova, also see these immigration activists as using the same oppositional stance as queer political organizers. De Genova notes that the popular chant, "We are here, we are queer, get over it!" is mirrored in a different context by undocumented activists when they share their legal status at public events and assert their presence and determination to stay in the United States.[49] Immigrant Youth Coalition activist Tania Unzueta created "Coming out of the Shadows Day" in Chicago.[50] On March 10, 2010, people in states across the nation, including New York, California, Texas, Wisconsin, Colorado, and Arizona, took part in events in which they revealed that they were undocumented and communicated their support for the DREAM Act. Many people revealed their status in person, or posted coming out stories online.[51] Unzueta explained that the tactic of coming out "connected us, created community, and allowed us to organize in ways we hadn't before.[52] Due to its success, the day-long event was transformed into Coming out of the Shadows month in March. In 2012, forty undocumented people from all walks of life built on the momentum by "coming out" on their No Papers, No Fear bus ride across the United States.[53] The activists rode the "undocubus" from Arizona through New Mexico, Colorado, Texas, Louisiana, Alabama, Georgia, and Tennessee, ultimately ending their trip in North Carolina, where the Democratic Convention was being held.[54] They created a website and a blog to help tell their stories along the way.

The role of *testimonios* and storytelling has been helpful to the movement. Because of these methods, organizers realized over time that they wanted to highlight a more diverse group of voices in the movement. For example, Tania Unzueta explained that the Immigrant Youth Justice League chose to rename themselves Organized Communities Against Deportations based on what they learned about storytelling. She noted, "Our politics have changed. We've seen the limits of telling our stories as 'good' undocumented students, because it doesn't work for others. . . . There is a limit to how much change can happen by justifying your own existence to a system that's built to oppress you."[55]

Transgressing Through Civil Disobedience and Direct Action

> About two dozen immigrant rights advocates and religious leaders were arrested Monday outside the White House as they participated in a civil disobedience action aimed at calling on President Barack Obama to stop deportations. They prayed and sang in front of the White House, refusing to leave until police officers moved in to arrest them. Those participating in the civil disobedience action included two United Methodist bishops and family members of undocumented immigrants who are currently in detention. They were loaded into white vans and taken away.[56]

Often used in conjunction with peaceful protests, the tactic of civil disobedience is used by activists to draw additional attention to their causes. Sometimes immigration activists place their bodies on the line by refusing to obey governmental laws, policies, and/or procedures.[57] Some of the many types of civil disobedience immigration activists have used are sit-ins, infiltration of detention centers, and hunger strikes. Due to the fact that undocumented migrants are at risk of being deported, acts of civil disobedience can have serious implications for them if interrogated or arrested by law enforcement; yet, many bravely challenge the status quo in spite of this.[58] As you can see from the above news excerpt on the civil disobedience in early 2014 aimed at stopping deportations, it is not uncommon for people to be arrested in a demonstration, even if they are simply praying, singing, and/or chanting. Yet, those who use civil disobedience to gain attention to their causes are motivated by the fact that a long line of social justice movement leaders, such as Mahatma Gandhi and Martin Luther King Jr., successfully employed the tactic against incredible odds.

Sitting-In and Staying Put

The use of sit-ins by young activists in the 2000s followed the use of less confrontational methods, such as lobbying, letter writing, and marches for which they had applied for permits.[59] The first of such moments occurred on May 17, 2010, when the group of young people now known as the DREAM 5—Lizbeth Mateo (from California), Yahaira Carillo (from Kansas), Tania Unzueta (from Illinois), Mohammed Abdollahi (from Michigan), and Raul Alcaraz (from Arizona)—went to sit in former Arizona senator John McCain's office in Tucson, Arizona, wearing graduation caps and gowns.[60] They demanded that he support the passage of the DREAM Act and end the criminalization of immigrants.[61] Ultimately, four of the activists were arrested for refusing to leave his office (one was outside speaking with the press); three of those arrested were undocumented and they were placed in removal proceedings. Eventually, their charges were dropped and the removal proceedings were ended.[62] This act was followed in July 2010 with a sit-in at the U.S. Capitol in which twenty-one DREAMers from around the country wearing caps, gowns, and signs saying "What now?" continued to press the federal government to pass the DREAM Act. This act was a very visible one that garnered a great deal of publicity as well as some backlash from politicians.

In another example of the use of sit-ins, Arizona residents have shown their dismay and concern about the expansion of Border Patrol policing by conducting a number of sit-ins at checkpoints. For example, in Arivaca, Arizona, a group called People Helping People in the Border Zone started sitting near the checkpoints on Arivaca Road in 2014 and on Arizona State Route 286 in 2016.[63] The residents who take part in the sit-ins wear safety vests and take detailed notes about the number of cars going through the checkpoint and how many cars are stopped, the ethnicity or race of the driver when possible, the length of their questioning, and whether Border Patrol agents require the drivers to go through a secondary inspection. They note multiple reasons for their approach,

> We monitor the checkpoint for three reasons: 1) to act as a deterrent [of] Border Patrol misconduct at the checkpoint as a third-party witnessing presence, 2) to record data on the activities of BP at the checkpoint as the agency has yet to make any data collected on individual checkpoint operations available to the public, 3)

to keep our opposition to the checkpoint visible to the public. Our message to the Border Patrol is this: we are watching.

—People Helping People in the Border Zone[64]

People Helping People take a peaceful approach to their sit-ins, but refuse to move when the Border Patrol asks them to sit farther away because it would prevent them from making their observations. The information gathered from People Helping People's sit-ins is used to make sure the Border Patrol is accountable for its practices and to make a case to the Department of Homeland Security for the removal of all internal checkpoints. The group argues that not only are these checkpoints unnecessary (they are responsible for very few of the arrests in the greater Tucson area), but they create a zone of racial profiling and violence in their community that must be stopped.[65] In conjunction with the sit-ins, they have held rallies and sent petitions to their congressional representative, asking him to organize an ad hoc congressional hearing to explore the militarization of rural areas. The data they collected were used in a report by the ACLU of Arizona about law enforcement abuse and widespread acts of impunity in the interior areas of southern Arizona.[66]

Some of the most notable sit-ins related to immigration policy have been occurring since Donald Trump was declared president-elect of the United States in November 2016. Large sit-ins occurred across the country in order to show a lack of support for his anti-immigrant threats,[67] and sit-ins at airports followed his first executive order to ban refugees and prevent travel between the United States and seven predominantly Muslim countries (making it so many lawful permanent residents were detained or turned away from the border at airports).[68] Sit-ins also occurred in 2018 after the U.S. Supreme Court upheld a revised version of the travel ban that targeted nationals from Iran, Libya, Somalia, Syria, Yemen, North Korea, and government officials from Venezuela.[69]

Infiltrating Detention Centers

One group who employed the tactic of civil disobedience was the National Immigrant Youth Alliance (NIYA). Young adults associated with NIYA used multiple forms of civil disobedience to address the jailing of undocumented people in detention centers and the inhumanity of the immigration system. The mission of NIYA was threefold and included empowerment, education, and escalation. They justified their use of escalation as a necessity given the severity of the threats against the undocumented community: "We have reached a point where lobbying alone is not adequate to accomplish our mission. We strongly believe that our movement needs to escalate and we will use mindful and intentional strategic acts of civil disobedience to be effective."[70]

In order to learn more about the detention centers and to help inform the people inside of the detention centers about their rights and possible sources of relief, five undocumented members of NIYA got themselves arrested so they could be held at a detention center in Pompano Beach, Florida.[71] This detention center, the Broward Transitional Center, is one of many owned by a private correctional company, the GEO Group. Carlos Saavedra worked with men in the men's section of the facility, while Viridiana Martinez worked with the women in the women's section. Outside of the facility, Mohammed Abdollahi and other NIYA colleagues used the information that Saavedra and Martinez shared with them over the detention center's payphones to inform the media about the experiences of the detainees and the factors that warranted their release.[72] Martinez and Saavedra also got the word out about what was going on in detention by conducting interviews with media outlets such as *Telemundo* and *Univision* via telephone while they were inside Broward. NIYA members contacted family members of some of the people inside who appeared to be eligible for release. They provided them with the rationale to challenge their loved one's detention, such as they had low-priority cases and should not have been detained by Immigration and Customs Enforcement, they were eligible for relief under the Violence Against Women's Act, and/or they had U.S. citizen children who needed their care. Saavedra and Martinez were released after the authorities figured out what they were doing. But, they were able to free at least forty people from detention afterwards using the information they gathered in Broward with the help of lawyers, family members, and the media.[73]

Hunger Striking Against Injustice

One of the detained individuals whose case was being publicized by NIYA members, Claudio Rojas, began a fast at the end of Martinez's and Saavedra's time there. He did his first fast for spiritual reasons rather than political ones, but the weekend after the release of the activists, he organized a hunger strike and hundreds of detainees joined him.[74] NIYA members spread the word to media sources on the outside with a march and a banner. Shortly thereafter, more detainees began to be granted bond and released on a daily basis. Rojas was one of them.[75]

When activists use hunger strikes as a means of promoting social change, they are relying on the message about morality that they are trying to convey and the publicity for their message that follows once the strikes are announced.[76] As scholar Ralph Armbruster-Sandoval points out, a hunger strike, "is designed to make people 'wake up' and see suffering misery."[77] It is a serious strategy that demonstrates how important the cause is to those who are refusing to eat; the most dire consequence one can imagine might occur if fasting is taken to the extreme—the loss of their lives. When people engage in hunger strikes in detention centers, as many detained migrants from varied ethnic and racial backgrounds have in recent years,[78] they make claims about the substandard food that they are provided, which often makes them sick; the lack of medical care; the restrictions on their freedom; and the threat that they will be deported, often to dangerous situations.[79] Detainees who participate in hunger strikes are often subjected to disciplinary measures and solitary confinement.[80] The advocacy group, #Not1More, found that detainee hunger strikers have experienced

extreme sleep deprivation, severe communication restrictions, and increased deportations as consequences for their behavior. In some cases, such as in the detainee
hunger strikes of late 2015/early 2016 in the Krome Service Processing Center in
Miami, Florida, correctional officers force-fed protestors to interrupt their actions
and deter others from starting hunger strikes.[81]

In 2018, a number of immigrant parent detainees who had been separated from
their children launched hunger strikes in detention centers. A group of mothers at the
Port Isabel Service Processing Center in Texas participated in a rolling hunger strike to
protest their lack of phone calls with their children. A small group of women would
not eat for a few days, then when they resumed eating, another group of women
would stop.[82] Following this, a group of immigrant fathers who were reunited with
their children and placed in Karnes County Residential Center in Texas together went
on a hunger strike, while some of their children protested their detention by refusing
to engage in activities.[83] Then over two hundred detained immigrants participated in
prisoner hunger strikes across the country in late August 2018.[84] The hunger strikers
demanded attention be paid to their unjust situations (and those of other prisoners
across the United States) and asked for the detention centers to be closed.

ICE officials generally downplay the magnitude of the hunger strikes and
sometimes their very existence. Social movement organizations that advocate for
immigrant rights, such as the Northwest Detention Center Resistance in Tacoma,
Washington, challenge ICE's claims by presenting written statements from detainees
about why they are striking.[85] In other cases, journalists have been able to interview
detainees and spread the word about their hunger strikes.[86]

The experiences of those who participate in hunger strikes in public settings are,
unsurprisingly, a little different than those in detention. One of the primary ways
they differ is that activists have interactions with others who see them. When five
mothers who were part of the group Dreamers' Moms USA fasted across from the
White House in Lafayette Square for ten days and nights in 2014, they had others
who would stop by.[87] They had folks come by from a church who would play music,
a doctor who would check their vital signs, and federal park police who would make
sure they were obeying the rules about space management and tidiness.[88] Although
the public fasters enjoyed these distractions, they also had the challenge of dealing
with the weather, which was especially harsh at night in Washington, DC. Dreamers'
Moms fasted in the name of asking President Obama to provide relief for undocumented adults, just as he did for some young people with the Executive Order for
DACA in 2010. Shortly after they ended their strike, President Obama announced
his plan for Deferred Action for Parents of Americans and Lawful Permanent Residents (DAPA) in November 2014 (which never actually went into effect).

Boycotting Consumption and Companies

> After so much sacrifice, pain, trauma, and hard work, we think it is time for our
> community to try something new. Sustained mass non-cooperation. Widespread
> boycotts. A general strike.

Figure 7.1. People rallied in response to the rescission of Deferred Action for Childhood Arrivals (DACA) in New York City on September 9, 2017.
Rhododendrites, Wikimedia Commons

We come from cultures that have a rich tradition of popular struggle and movement building. Along with so much else, we bring these stories of resistance to the U.S. when we migrate. They live in each of our communities.

We are fighting for a new day of justice, reconciliation and unity for our immigrant communities. We are fighting for permanent protection, dignity, and respect.

—Cosecha, 2017[89]

As leaders of the undocumented immigration social movement out of Boston, Massachusetts, *Cosecha* (Harvest) explain that boycotts are often used to bring attention to an issue when traditional methods have not fully worked. *Cosecha* activists center their approach squarely in the tradition of the many social activists and farmworkers who have struggled for justice over the course of history, such as the boycott of California grapes starting in the 1960s to support living wages for migrant workers. They have long used boycotts, withholding purchases as a form of protest, in order to demonstrate the economic power of the immigrant community and to hurt the powerful in the one place it counts—the wallet. *Cosecha*'s response to the anti-immigrant rhetoric and punitive executive orders signed by Donald Trump in the first week of his presidency in January 2017 was to strategize a series of acts that led up to their participation in *Un Día Sin Inmigrantes* on May 1, 2017 (following the tradition of the May 1, 2006 Great American Boycott and the February 16, 2017 Day Without Immigrants[90]). Participants did not go to work or make any purchases that day to show what happens when the daily economic and societal contributions of immigrants can no longer be relied upon.[91]

The Coalition of Immokalee Workers (CIW) made powerful use of the boycott over the course of over twenty years to highlight the unjust treatment of migrant tomato pickers in the fields of Immokalee, Florida.[92] Latinx workers from Mexico and Guatemala, along with their non-Latinx coworkers from other countries such as Haiti, joined together in a number of actions to highlight their abuse, exposure to pesticides, and poor pay for backbreaking labor. A number of the workers were undocumented, so they could not rely on waging complaints to the higher-ups, although some tried. While limited positive changes came after telling the farmers about their concerns, they eventually decided to go straight to the top and challenge the large corporations who were buying most of the tomatoes. In the early 2000s, CIW decided to focus on Taco Bell, and with the help of outside organizers who started a group called the Student/Farmworker Alliance and religious leaders, they convinced over twenty high schools and colleges to quit contracting with Taco Bell. Their protests and boycotts lasted over four years, and then the company that owns Taco Bell (and Pizza Hut, Kentucky Fried Chicken, and Long John Silver's), Yum Brands, agreed to pay workers a higher price for tomatoes (one penny per pound). They quickly expanded their campaign to other companies and food suppliers including McDonald's (2007); Whole Foods, Burger King, and Subway (2008); Sodexo and Aramark (2010); Chipotle and Trader Joe's (2012); and Walmart and Fresh Market (2015), and they all agreed to pay a bit more per pound of tomatoes and to improve farmworker conditions.[93] In 2016 they began boycotting Wendy's, the fast-food chain that quit buying tomatoes in Immokalee, Florida, and began buying them instead in Mexico as a means of avoiding support reforms.[94] The Fair Food Program that the CIW has established has spread to other states as well, has eliminated a good deal of the abuses and injustices tomato pickers face, and protects their jobs if they do speak their minds about their concerns.

Creating and Distributing Art

> Art has the power to shape thoughts and change hearts. Art also has the power to shape law and to change society.
>
> —Favianna Rodriguez, 2013, from the online
> documentary, *Migration Is Beautiful*[95]

Another strategy that has been harnessed for positive changes related to immigration and immigrants is the creation and distribution of art. As noted in the quote above, art is a powerful transformative tool. Art can be used to influence people's minds about the complex relationship of migration, globalization, and legal status, and simultaneously be used for tasks such as decorating flyers to publicize a march, sit-in, or other social action and creating educational pamphlets or documents.[96]

The Fair Immigration and Reform Movement emphasizes, "there has never been a movement of social change without the arts—posters in particular being central to that movement. Protest posters flaunt their politics and court discussion. They can deepen compassion and commitment, incite outrage, elicit laughter, and provoke action."[97] Favianna Rodriguez, a well-known artist and the creator of CultureStrike, a national pro-migrant arts association, notes that art and other cultural strategies are important to a movement because they touch people's emotions.[98] When people are moved emotionally about the injustices that a group of people face, they are more likely to support their causes. She has popularized the image of a butterfly in her artwork, which is a symbol for the immigrant rights movement. She pairs her graphic of a butterfly with the statement, "Migration is beautiful." The monarch butterfly, a beautiful insect that flies over human-made borders when it migrates to survive, represents the beauty of the people who also migrate to survive. The symbolism of the butterfly continues to spread; for example, prior to the rash of pro-immigrant and women's rallies in January 2017, people were sharing online directions for creating butterfly wings that they could wear to the events to send a pro-migrant message.[99]

The artists associated with CultureStrike have also created a project called Visions from the Inside, in which they work with social movement groups who have collected letters from and interviews of migrants inside and outside of detention centers in the United States, such as *Mariposas Sin Fronteras* (Butterflies without Borders), End Family Detention, Northwest Detention Center Resistance, Familia Trans Queer Liberation Movement, and Families for Freedom.[100] The artists take those letters and turn scenes into illustrations in order to emphasize the effects of the for-profit system that benefits from holding human bodies captive. David Long also used the power of art to make a statement about migrant detention in a society dominated by the prison industrial complex. He created a mural that served as a stopping point for a rally and march of over two hundred people on the Northwest Detention Center in Tacoma, Washington, in November 2015.[101] He explained that through his mural, "he wanted to amplify the voice of the people who are organizing from the inside and from outside."

Another artist, Julio Salgado, collaborated with three of his friends from college to create Dreamers Adrift, which is a collective of artists and writers who are undocumented.[102] He calls himself an "undocuqueer artivist" and his work has brought attention to the complex experiences of those in the undocuqueer community:

> What does "undocuqueer" mean to me? In the image that I made of myself [on my own poster], I mention that I use two identities that are supposed to make me weak and empower myself. As an undocumented person, I am seen as a criminal. As a queer person, I am seen as somebody who is going to go to hell. So how do you turn that [around]? For me, through the art, I turn that [around] by showing ourselves in dignified ways that embrace the terms that make us feel like we are less than human.[103]

Salgado does many forms of art in the name of pro-migrant causes, but he is especially well known for the artwork he created for the "I Exist!" series related to the Dream Act, the "Liberty for All" online comic strip about life for an undocumented college graduate, and the "I am Undocuqueer!" posters that he illustrated in collaboration with United We Dream's Queer Undocumented Immigrant Project.[104] Salgado has gained national acclaim for his online "Undocumented and Awkward" videos, which demonstrated the awkward situations that undocumented people face on a daily basis. His reputation was further cemented when he was featured on the June 25, 2012, cover of *Time* magazine with other undocumented change makers.

Another way that art is central to social action and resistance is because it is often sold to fundraise for immigrant programs and services. The Unitarian Universalist humanitarian campaign in Tucson, Arizona, No More Deaths/*No Más Muertes*, for example, held an online auction of donated art to raise money to provide water, food, and medical help to people crossing the border.[105] In Memphis, Tennessee, where the Latinx population is one of the fastest growing in the United States, the L. Ross Gallery held an exhibit "Art of Resistance" to fundraise for immigrant legal services in the city, which coincided with the #HeretoStay National Day of Action on January 14, 2017.[106]

Josefina López, an accomplished playwright known for her play *Real Women Have Curves*, became involved with Border Angels (*Angéles de la Frontera*), a San Diego–based group that does multiple forms of migrant outreach.[107] She brought her artistic skills to the group that drops off water in the desert in order to help prevent migrant deaths, establishes border rescue stations, and supports a migrant shelter at *Parque de la Amistad* (Friendship Park). López participated in water drops in the desert and worked with other volunteers to place crosses on the makeshift graves of migrants in the desert that had the words "*No Olvidado*" (not forgotten) on them.[108] She created a play called *Detained in the Desert*, which she eventually turned into a film of the same name. Her work drew upon the Border Angels' activism as well as founder Enrique Morones' debates with anti-immigration activists and former Arizona sheriff Joe Arpaio.[109]

As explained by journalists Michelle Téllez and Alejandra Ramírez, art related to the U.S.-Mexico border can help better understand the complex and dangerous experiences that occur when people cross over into the United States unauthorized. They state that border art helps us "reimagine where an alternative discussion of the border would begin"[110]—in other words, the art helps us challenge the mainstream dialogue about immigrants as criminals and people who are "getting one over" on the government, and question the very notion of the border itself. Powerful acts of border art have been created over the decades, including Chicano artist Gronk's giant eraser placed at the border in 1981, Marcos "ERRE" Ramirez's 33-foot sculpture *Toy an-Horse*, a two-headed Trojan horse that was placed on the international border straddling Mexico and the United States in the late 1990s,[111] and Ana Teresa Fernández's attempt to erase the border visually by painting part of the San Diego–Tijuana border wall blue in 2012.[112] San Diego–based artists such as Guillermo Gomez-Peña, Victor Ochoa, and David Avalos have held a number of border art workshops and created a number of art pieces related to migration over the last three decades as well as inSite, a public art project in the San Diego–Tijuana border region.[113]

After the Trump Administration allowed eight border wall prototypes to be put next to the border fence in Otay Mesa, California, local artists created protest art on and around them. For example, artist Perry Vasquez and his Southwestern College art students collaborated with Jill Holslin and Andrew Sturm to project their artwork onto the prototypes. The projection had the effect of making it look like a hammer was knocking down the wall, or that the wall prototype itself had been transformed into an elevator used to transport families over it.[114] In another type of border art, Max Herman's photography of the work that humanitarians and volunteers do to prevent migrant deaths in the southern Arizona desert was included online in a photo essay for LatinoUSA.[115]

Another form of art that is vital to activism in the immigrant rights movement is music. As we discussed at the beginning of this chapter, songs and videos that send a message about the immigrant experience powerfully impact listeners both emotionally and intellectually. Although a book this size cannot do justice to all the songs about immigration that artists have created, it is important to be familiar with some of the Spanish-language immigration songs that have had an impact over the years. See Box 7.2 for a selection of some of these compelling songs.

Self-Deporting and Asserting the Right to Entry

> You don't have social change by keeping people comfortable. You have to escalate and escalation doesn't mean putting a suit and tie on and lobbying corrupt politicians. . . . Escalation means raising the levels of audacity and courage within the movement.
>
> —Roberto Lovato, co-founder Presente.org, on the use of self-deportation[116]

The strategy of self-deportation is arguably the most daring and specific to the cause of the immigrant justice movement. Three of the undocumented young adults, members of the group now known as the DREAM 9 (Lulu Martinez, Lizbeth Mateo, and Marco Saavedra), used this strategy to get themselves deported to Mexico while Congress was debating immigration reform.[117] Six of the other Dreamers had already been forced to go to Mexico due to life circumstances. They created their plans and turned themselves into federal authorities at the border in Nogales, Arizona, on July 22, 2013. As in other actions in support of the passage of a federal DREAM Act, the students wore graduation caps and gowns to emphasize the juxtaposition of being educated in the United States, yet remaining labeled as legal outsiders. Nine religious leaders accompanied them when they made their request for humanitarian parole, which was rejected. They then asked for political asylum and were taken to the detention center in Eloy, Arizona. Eight of the nine members were eventually granted asylum by the Department of Homeland Security, surprising many observers.[118] The fact that over thirty members of Congress wrote letters

BOX 7.2 POWERFUL SPANISH-LANGUAGE IMMIGRATION SONGS

As shown in this chapter's opening, music is another powerful art form that inspires and organizes people in the immigrant communities and their allies. There have been a multitude of Spanish-language songs that have addressed the plight of Latinx immigrants, both authorized and unauthorized, over the centuries. As noted by Spanish teacher and blogger Elisabeth Alvarado, these are some of the most powerful recent songs about immigration:

Pobre Juan by Maná
Fronteras by Gaby Moreno
Un Besito Más by Jesse y Joy
ICE El Hielo by La Santa Cecilia
Ave Que Migra by Gaby Moreno
A Las Tres by Enanitos Verdes
Mis Dos Patrias by Los Tigres del Norte (she notes they have many other songs about immigration as well such as *Jaula de Oro*)
Papeles Mojados by Chambao
Pa'L Norte by Calle 13
El Inmigrante by Calibre 50
El Mojado by Calibre 50
"Shock" in Arizona by Ana Tijoux
Lagrimas del Corazon by Grupo Montéz de Durango
Bandera by Aterciopelados
Clandestino by Manu Chao

Source: Spanish Mama. 2018. Spanish Songs About Immigration, March 26. (https://spanishmama.com/spanish-songs-about-immigration/).

encouraging their release was likely one of the factors that helped their cause. The DREAM 9's courageous planning of their plea for re-entry and their willingness to be detained have left an indelible mark on the immigrant social justice movement in the United States.

Creating Spaces of Sanctuary

One strategy that is used to improve the lives of undocumented immigrants in the United States is the creation of sanctuary spaces and places. The "new" sanctuary movement took hold around 2007 as a coalition of activists and faith-based commu-

Figure 7.2. A young woman who is proud of being undocumented. She wears her *sin papeles* (without papers) t-shirt and blue butterfly wings.
Jose Escutia Ruiz

nities chose to support community members through legal, financial, and spiritual means while they were facing deportation proceedings.[119] The movement followed the lead of the sanctuary movement of the 1980s in which more than five hundred religious congregations housed immigrants and refugees who were usually fleeing death squads in El Salvador, Honduras, and Guatemala, in churches and synagogues across the United States.[120]

Sanctuary movements challenge what its members see as unjust governmental policies and immigration laws. As explained by sociologist Grace Yukich, sanctuary movements challenge stereotypes about undocumented immigrants by framing them as "brothers and sisters" (rather than culturally inferior "strangers"), and cast them as deserving of shelter and protection.[121] Modern day sanctuary efforts have been used a lot more in the mid-2010s as people across the country face threats of deportation.

Often lawyers, religious leaders, and other activists encourage people who are facing final deportation orders to hold press conferences and then take sanctuary in a church or other religious institution. ICE policies restrict officers from arresting people in places of worship. Then, religious practitioners of a given congregation speak up in favor of the people who have sought sanctuary and often phone ICE officials and write letters to the Department of Homeland Security pleading for stays of deportation for them. Sometimes they are granted. Churches like the Unitarian Universalists provide webinars and other information about how congregations can become sanctuary congregations.[122] People involved in the sanctuary movement had a week of action in January 2017 in which they engaged in press conferences, prayer vigils, training, and social media outreach in the name of protecting undocumented immigrants and refugees. Sanctuary participants powerfully vocalized support for their cause and the need for programs like DACA to continue to protect over seven hundred thousand immigrant youth.[123]

Although sanctuary for immigrants is usually spoken of as a good thing, even a good thing can go too far when people are stuck in churches or places of worship indefinitely. (It is also a problem when officials call their city a place of sanctuary, but do not provide real sanctuary—see, for example, the story about Chicago, Illinois in Box 7.3.) In 2018, *Colectivo Santuario*, a coalition of immigrants, immigrant advocates, attorneys, and people in faith-based communities from seven states (Virginia, Texas, Missouri, Ohio, Pennsylvania, North Carolina, and Colorado) was created.[124] Leaders of the group include Juana Luz Tobar Ortega, a woman who fled Guatemala in the 1980s due to death threats and was later denied asylum. After living in the United States for over twenty years, in 2017 she was ordered out of the country. The American Friends Service Community helped her find sanctuary in St. Barnabas Episcopal Church in North Carolina. Ortega's perspective on sanctuary is a complicated one:

> I'm grateful to be here, but it's a certain kind of suffering being stuck in one place. I call it a "golden cage." So many good people help us, we are never lacking food, shelter; we have everything we need, but we can't leave. Others in sanctuary understand these feelings and we talk about it in our calls and try to lift each others' spirits.[125]

Colectivo Santuario works to pressure state lawmakers to support the immigrants who are in sanctuary by pressuring federal officials to advocate for them. They highlight the details of the specific stories of people who are in sanctuary and use them to draw attention to the flaws of the current immigration system. They state their hope is to free the people who are incarcerated in the churches, to stop their deportations, and to allow them to stay in the country. The people who are involved in the movement are bravely working together to address their cause. Along with Juana Ortega, four other leaders, Pastor Jose Chicas, Edith Espinal, Samuel Oliver-Bruno, and Hilda Ramirez, left their places of sanctuary in order to meet for a three-day training in Durham, North Carolina, on social organizing.[126] They bravely risked deportation to meet with well-known immigration activists and lawyers with roots in groups such

BOX 7.3 ORGANIZED COMMUNITIES AGAINST DEPORTATIONS (OCAD): CHALLENGING THE MEANING OF THE "SANCTUARY CITY" DESIGNATION

The group Organized Communities Against Deportations (OCAD), based in Chicago, Illinois, has used art to cleverly challenge what it means to be a "sanctuary city." Dismayed that Chicago was officially a sanctuary city, yet still enacted policies and practices that encourage the deportation of immigrants, OCAD created a life-size bar graph comparing the city's 2017 spending on police to that of public health; planning and development; and family and support services. They placed their art installment on a public street with a sign stating, "This is how Chicago spends your dollars." The twelve-foot-high dollar bill that represented police funding dwarfed the representations of the funds given to other areas (which were twelve cents for planning, two cents for public health, and five cents for family services).

They also created a number of silhouettes of black and brown people standing around a representation of a gang database, along with a sign protesting the police academy the city wanted to fund. OCAD used this installation to draw attention to the practice of adding black and Latinx men to gang databases, which may lead to the deportation of those who are unauthorized immigrants. In many cases, people who are not involved in gangs are added to the database in error, because there is little oversight or fact checking of the process. OCAD also created a number of coffins with bodies laying on them and a tombstone stating "88% of Chicagoans killed by police are Black and Brown." OCAD's different forms of street art had the cumulative effective of drawing connections between the immigration and criminal justice systems that were rarely discussed amidst the passage of Chicago officials' Welcoming City ordinance earlier that year. OCAD's actions aimed to draw attention to big-picture factors that make it so migrants need to find places of sanctuary: mass deportation, the existence of Immigration and Customs Enforcement, and the surveillance of communities of color.

Sources:

Organized Communities Against Deportations. 2017. "Breaking: Life Size Graphs Blocking Streets Outside City Hall Show Why Chicago Is Not a Sanctuary City for Black and Brown People. OCAD, October 10. (http://organizedcommunities.org/whychicagoisnotasanctuarycity/).

Huynh, Van and Tania Unzueta. 2017. "Opinion: Mayor Emanuel Falls Behind Gov. Rauner in Protecting Immigrants." *Chicago Sun-Times*, September 20. (https://chicago.suntimes.com/opinion/mayor-emanuel-falls-behind-gov-rauner-in-protecting-immigrants/amp/).

as DreamActivist, *Alerta Migratoria*, Grassroots Leadership, and the former National Immigrant Youth Alliance to share experiences and plan actions for the future.

As this chapter demonstrates, unauthorized immigrants and their allies harness creativity and community to create positive social change in the face of adversity. Their use of multiple social movement methods allows them to garner attention for immigrant rights and creates momentum around their causes. It is important to note that Latinx activists are also networking with immigration activists from other communities. The alliances of resistance and campaigns that result from these collaborations are powerful ones that shake up the establishment. As noted by Mark and Paul Engler,

> Social movements change the political weather. They turn issues and demands considered both unrealistic and politically inconvenient into matters that can no longer be ignored; they succeed, that is, by championing the impractical. . . . Outbreaks of hope and determined impracticality provide an important rebuttal to the politics of accommodation, to the idea that the minor tweaking of the status quo is the best we can expect in our lifetimes.[127]

8

Conclusion

We have painted a portrait of unauthorized Latinx immigrant experiences in the United States that is multidimensional. We highlighted studies and stories related to media, work, education, health, detention and deportation, and social action. Now we conclude this book with some recommendations related to each of these topics and a consideration of global migration trends to further contextualize the dynamics of immigration in the United States.

All signs indicate that people who are growing up today in the United States are going to be the impetus behind a shift toward more humane policies and an inclusive society for immigrants and their families. Children, teens, and young adults in this country are increasingly demonstrating support for a more inclusive society. In fact, a 2016 national poll of the now biggest generation in the United States, Millennials (eighteen-to-thirty-four-year-olds), demonstrated that 68 percent support a pathway to citizenship for undocumented immigrants.[1]

In another study, Carlos Santos and colleagues interviewed Arizona youth after the passage of anti-immigrant law SB 1070. They found that when youth were aware of the anti-immigrant law, they experienced a significant dip in the sense of being "American" and lower levels of self-esteem, compared to those who were not aware of the law.[2] Something important about this study was that youth of *all racial and ethnic backgrounds* (not just immigrant or Latinx youth) who were aware of the anti-immigration law were negatively impacted by it.

Cecilia Menjívar, one of the authors of the study, noted that the connections young people are building across color and ethnic lines may explain this finding—if students' Latinx friends and neighbors are being targeted by the law, the youth may feel a shared sense of injustice and internalized negative feelings.[3] Although it is distressing to read that young people's emotional states are negatively affected by exclusionary laws, it does hint at the idea that youth in diverse cities may develop a sense of empathy for others that fuels interracial and interethnic coalitions for immigrant justice in their teen and adult years.

RECOMMENDATIONS

Our recommendations for improving the treatment of unauthorized immigrants range from working on long-term goals incrementally, creating collaborations between multiple entities, and implementing organizational and individual-level changes. As sociologists, we know that multiple levels of change must be addressed for significant and long-lasting transformation to occur. Recall, social institutions create norms and behaviors for a given society. However, we humans embody these social institutions. We establish these institutions and their rules of behavior, and have the power to change them when needed.

Media

As scholar Leo Chavez claims in his book, *The Latino Threat: Constructing Immigrants, Citizens, and the Nation*,[4] the conversation about undocumented immigration needs to be broadened to transcend stereotypes and racist propaganda that attract media coverage, like that of the anti-immigrant group the Minutemen. There needs to be an active effort for those in the news and entertainment media to challenge the myth of all Latinx immigrants as dangerous threats. One way to work against these threats is to replace them with portrayals about the realities of immigration and the contributions of Latinx immigrants. As Chavez challenges: "For over four hundred years, Latinos have been contributing to the social, economic, and cultural life of what is now the U.S. Southwest. Where are the media spectacles celebrating those contributions?"[5]

Although there has been some progress in the accurate coverage of immigration, there is room for improvement in English-language media. The word "illegal" must be replaced with undocumented and unauthorized. The Race Forward Center for Racial Justice Innovation has resources to begin a "Drop the 'i' Word" campaign.[6] The campaign has had success with some major media sources; for example the Associated Press pledged to stop using the word "illegal" to describe undocumented immigrants.

Mainstream news and entertainment network executives need to hire more Latinxs and other people of color who are concerned about immigrant justice. We recommend that they support them in creating programming that dissects and counters myths about unauthorized immigrants. For example, well-researched immigration studies (e.g., Leisy Abrego's work on transnational families[7]) could be presented in the format of television news specials or online video podcasts in order to expose the general public to truths about undocumented immigration.

It is important for the creators of popular media to include more undocumented characters in feature films, television shows, and comic books as well. The more realistic portrayals of the undocumented experience that there are, the more likely it is that the understanding of the complex experiences of the undocumented will be reinforced. This is why the production of documentary films on unauthorized immigration is particularly important: they open a window to people's realities that some are not privy to otherwise. The continued creation of websites by immigrant advocacy groups like UnitedWeStay (www.unitedwestay.org) that combine daily news about undocumented immigration with videos and blogs by undocumented immigrants sharing their stories is crucial. Concerted efforts by educators to expose students to alternative online media is essential at the high school and college level, so that they learn to counter the hateful narratives about immigrants that they are exposed to elsewhere. Media literacy should increase awareness of how to be critical consumers of media regarding human rights and immigration issues. User-generated media forms are among the most popular today, and we recommend that undocumented people and their allies continue to use them and social media to share information about social and legal developments related to undocumented immigration. We also recommend that entrepreneurs continue to invest in the creation of innovative phone and computer apps that undocumented people can use to establish a network of allies and support.

Figure 8.1. The monarch butterfly is often a symbol of the immigrant rights movement and represents the potential of all to freely move across borders.
Alex Guillaume, Unsplash

Work

Work is closely connected to many immigrants, undocumented or not. The opportunity to work for better wages is the "pull" that attracts immigrants to the United States; the lack of economic opportunities in the home country is the "push" that propels them. We list our work-related recommendations below ranging from the most ambitious and overarching—the farthest moonshot—to those that would be small, but important, steps to improving current realities.

Ultimately, we believe in an *open border*, which means that immigrants can work and live where they wish. Although this is unimaginable to some people, it is important to note that over 75 percent of all border walls and fences were created after the year 2000, and both literal and figurative borders can always be torn down.[8] For those economically minded, consider that the world would be a lot richer as a result.[9] For those who wish to settle and formalize their stay, there should be a direct path to apply for citizenship and access to all social services granted to citizens. Chapter 3 illuminated that undocumented immigrants already contribute a great deal more than they receive in terms of their taxes and production. Interestingly, when looking back at the period with the most open border in the last century (i.e., the 1960s), 85 percent of the immigrants eventually returned to their home countries.[10]

Amnesty allows people who are undocumented to apply for citizenship. There are typically requirements and criteria as to who is selected for amnesty. The American Immigration Council summarized the economic and social benefits for the last major amnesty program, the Simpson-Mazzoli Act (1986) during the Reagan Administration, for those who received amnesty: increased wages (which led to higher tax revenues), increased home ownership, and increased educational attainment.[11]

We note, that this legislation included other costs and harm to immigrants:

> The Simpson-Mazzoli Act (1986) was introduced as a way to end illegal border crossings once and for all. It had three parts: Give amnesty to those who had been in the country for at least five years, crack down on employers who hire people who can't legally work here, and pump up border security to prevent future illegal crossings.[12]

Therefore, we recommend creating a widely encompassing "amnesty" program to remove barriers regarding time spent in the United States, educational attainment, and work or professional occupations. We also support "clean" comprehensive immigration legislation, meaning humane immigration laws that do not contain elements of immigration enforcement.

We also recommend significant changes in the law, which often reflects the idea that undocumented immigrants are single males. Undocumented immigrant women are *half* of the undocumented population.[13] They are concerned with family reunification and often work in jobs that put them in vulnerable contexts.[14] Additionally, about 7 percent of the undocumented population or about eight hundred thousand are under sixteen years old.[15] There are 5.9 million children who have at least one undocumented parent, meaning they are in a mixed-status family.[16]

Therefore, we need to understand that undocumented immigration is a family affair. The Center for American Progress argues that states need to pay attention to mixed-status families. For example, they estimated that California has the highest number of people in mixed-status families with 4.7 million or 12 percent of the state's population.[17] Other states have high and/or growing mixed-status families: Arizona, Colorado, Nevada, New Jersey, New Mexico, New York, South Dakota, Wyoming.[18] Policies and laws must reflect supporting a more complex and comprehensive population of undocumented individuals and their loved ones.

Workers of all ages and genders should be free of fear and be compensated with decent wages. The enforcement of workers' rights and workers' compensation needs to limit the harm to the workers themselves (e.g., retaliation at work) and to focus on overall better safety and respect in the workplace (i.e., rewards, priority, and subsidies for exceptional workplace culture). Following the lead of states like Illinois where the "Fight for $15" campaign was successful, we recommend that the state and federal minimum wage levels be raised to $15 an hour. The Migration Policy Institute estimates that about 85 percent of undocumented workers participate in lower-income or seasonal industries such as retail, food, care services, agricultural labor, and construction.[19] The increase in minimum wage would also support DACA recipients, because the majority are working in non-professional occupations.[20] Additionally, loopholes allowing minors to work in agriculture need to be closed as well.

Nebraska legislators, working with an immigrant worker rights group, created a Meatpacker's Bill of Rights and created a workers' rights coordinator position to help enforce them. These rights included:

(a) The right to organize;
(b) The right to a safe workplace;
(c) The right to adequate facilities and the opportunity to use them;
(d) The right to complete information;
(e) The right to understand the information provided;
(f) The right to existing state and federal benefits and rights;
(g) The right to be free from discrimination;
(h) The right to continuing training, including training of supervisors;
(i) The right to compensation for work performed; and
(j) The right to seek state help.[21]

We recommend that other states adopt expanded versions of this bill of rights that include all major forms of labor undertaken by undocumented workers, such as construction, factory work, agriculture, and restaurant and food industry labor. The coordinator of these programs should be bilingual in both English and the primary language of the workers in a given state. Also, unlike in Nebraska, where the coordinator is appointed by the governor, in the case of the expanded workers' bill of rights implementation, coordinators should be selected by and from community workers' rights groups.

Education

Although in *Plyler v. Doe* (1982) the Supreme Court decided that states cannot deny undocumented children a public elementary or secondary education, access to an affordable college education remains difficult for many undocumented people across the country. States have created barriers to higher education for undocumented students by barring enrollment (e.g., South Carolina, Alabama, Georgia, and North Carolina community college only) and undocumented students from in-state tuition (e.g., Arizona, Georgia, and Indiana).[22] There are twenty states that offer undocumented students in-state tuition, but only ten (and the District of Columbia) that offer state financial aid (California, Maryland, Washington, Oregon, New Mexico, Texas, Minnesota, Connecticut, Oklahoma, and New Jersey). The University of Hawaii Board of Regents granted eligible undocumented students in-state tuition at their six public community colleges and four universities.[23] In states offering financial aid, the promising news is that more undocumented students have applied for it and been awarded it than ever before. This assuages a bit of fear that immigrant advocates and allies had in terms of undocumented students shying away from higher education due to hateful anti-immigrant national politics. Lupita Cortez Alcalá, the executive director of the California Student Aid commission, publicly exclaimed "We are on Cloud Nine right now," because there were about thirty-six thousand financial applications by immigrants in March 2017 compared to thirty-four thousand in 2016.[24]

Unfortunately, tuition and admission policies can change during a student's college career. Arizona opened in-state tuition for undocumented students with DACA in 2015, but on June 20, 2017, the Arizona Court of Appeals reversed this policy and rescinded their in-state tuition eligibility, leaving two thousand community college and 240 university students having to pay annual tuition of $26,470 (non-resident students) versus $10,640 (residents).[25] Many of these Arizona undocumented students would have easily qualified as in-state residents because they attended high school in Arizona, if it were not for their immigration status.

Because federal law allows in-state tuition and enrollment in higher education for undocumented students,[26] current laws and policies prohibiting undocumented students' right to college should be dismantled. Undocumented students should be allowed to apply for and receive federal aid. We understand that these are enormous challenges that advocates would have to work extraordinarily hard for due to the conservative majority in Congress and Trump's strident anti-immigrant stance.

Luckily, we find much promise in focusing on where undocumented students do have a right to education: the K-12 system. In schools with large immigrant populations, there must be a hiring focus on talented teachers who are bilingual and have a passion for undocumented students and their families. Educator and author Alma Ruiz Pohlert recommends that teachers adopt a nurturing family climate in classrooms that have newcomers.[27] Partnering with teacher education programs and recruiting ideal candidates should become routine. Professional development should be provided to educators, counselors, and administrators so that they can incorporate best practices when supporting undocumented students and their families.

In terms of the educational pipeline, elementary school is one of the brightest spots with low push-out rates and many opportunities for interventions. Educators who are working with undocumented students report feeling isolated in terms of being the "only one" in the school who supports undocumented students; therefore more institutional support is required so that more educators are sources of support and schools adopt a positive campus climate for undocumented students and their families.[28] Efforts to support undocumented students must start in grades K-12 and should be unabashedly proactive. Sometimes educators are unsure about how to approach undocumented populations, and there are elementary school sites where undocumented parents feel unsafe, unwelcome, and excluded. The district-level leadership must enact changes so that the serving population feels safe, welcomed, and included. Holding immigration rights events at the school will demonstrate support for *familias* and an understanding of the challenges they face. Adopting a community center–based approach to elementary schools serves the neighborhood and enhances the relationships between family and school, which includes creating a welcome center for immigrant families. Local and state funding must be allocated to give schools the fiscal ability to implement these innovations.

The next priority should be similar efforts that focus on middle schools and high schools. From a research perspective, we know very little about middle schools and undocumented students, beyond the fact that there is still a low push-out rate at this stage in the educational process.[29] High schools, the last educational level where undocumented students are guaranteed access, experience a high push-out rate with about 50 percent of undocumented students leaving high school before graduation. There is much work to be done for successful advocacy at both of these levels, and we recommend that resources be provided to administrators, educators, and researchers to continue to explore ways to best serve their undocumented students. According to the Migration Policy Institute, only 37 percent of undocumented students from ages eighteen to twenty-four are enrolled in school.[30] We must find multiple ways to ensure crucial human potential is not lost.

We recommend that the diverse members of any K-12 school or institute of higher education convey a collective interest and a coordinated approach to their success. This includes creating professional development training across all units and departments and visible, easily accessible, and centralized resources—both online and in the physical form at a resource center on school grounds. We also recommend that school officials encourage community and advocacy groups to join campus or school efforts to support undocumented students' and their families' success. For example, on our university campus, a diverse group of faculty, staff, administrators, and student advocates have invited immigration attorneys to hold mini–legal consultations, community activists to conduct "Know Your Rights" workshops and ally trainings, and social workers to explain the deportation safety planning process.

We recommend that budget and resources be allocated to all education institutions to support these endeavors in a systematic and proactive way. In tandem with collaborations between schools and their community partners, we recommend that advocates for undocumented students build strong coalitions between their schools and colleges in their region. This will help create a regional pipeline of support that spans the educational pipeline and benefits undocumented students and their families at the K-12, community college, and university levels.

The community college is key for access to many groups of undocumented students. The largest proportion of undocumented immigrants in higher education attends community college. For example, in California, two-thirds of the undocumented students applying for financial aid came from community college students. The mission of open access and the large population can be politically powerful: In 2013, the Maricopa Community College (MCC) system, one of the largest systems in the United States, stated that they would allow students with DACA to pay in-state tuition. Unfortunately, they were sued by the state of Arizona, and the Arizona Supreme Court eventually ruled in 2018 that DACA recipients are no longer eligible for in-state tuition at MCC.[31] Depending on the political and social context of a given state, the campaign for financial aid for undocumented community college students may be successful. This was the case in New Jersey; a month after the Arizona decision, Governor Phil Murphy signed a bill allowing qualifying undocumented students financial aid.[32] We believe it is essential for all states to have such financial support in place to support undocumented students in higher education.

It is important to realize the immense scope of community colleges. A relatively small group of undocumented students attend with the goal of transferring to a four-year university, and it is important to ensure they are receiving high-quality and culturally competent classes and advising. Many more undocumented students are taking non-credit courses (e.g., GED, citizenship class, English as a Second Language (ESL), basic education, adult high school) or are in career education, which used to be known as vocational education (e.g., mechanics, child development, food services, welding). While counseling faculty and student support staff might be trained as allies, students taking these courses do not traditionally seek out their services. Therefore, faculty members in these areas of the community college need to invite specialists into their classrooms to provide information and support to undocumented students. A systematic and proactive approach in outreach, retention, and resources is crucial.

Finally, undocumented students at all educational levels will benefit from the practice of *validation theory* at their school or campus. Validation theory encompasses the need to have *culturally relevant and supportive elements* in academic programs, student services, and co-curricular programs to further the success of low-income students and other students who have been historically marginalized in the university.[33] Validation helps students become active agents and consumers along their educational journey. Undocumented students experiencing validation theory in action come away from a class, event, or meeting believing: "I matter," "Somebody cares about me," and "I am a capable person."

Health

At the policy level, it's clear that federal mandates must guide states to include undocumented immigrants in public health and social programs. Again, we point to the notion of basic human rights: food, shelter, and safety. These basic needs should not be "earned," but are inalienable rights; human rights are what everyone should have as a birthright. Immigrant health advocates argue that allowing undocumented immigrants to receive preventative health services would greatly reduce the emergency room costs billed to the federal government. Frank Rodriguez, president of the Latino Health Care Forum, reasons: "Those [emergency room] bills could've been drastically reduced. . . . There are no preventative health measures, so they [undocumented, uninsured immigrants] end up having to use emergency care."[34]

Also, federal authorities should define stringent inclusion of unauthorized immigrants so that there is less leeway for exclusionary policy and practices at the state level. Undocumented immigrants should be included in every policy that applies to the general population. Attorney Akiesha Gilcrist wrote about the rights afforded to undocumented immigrants under the U.S. Constitution.[35] She reminds us that:

> The Fourteenth Amendment provides that "[n]o State shall . . . deprive any person of life, liberty, or property, without due process of law; nor deny to any person within its jurisdiction the equal protection of the laws". . . . Aliens, even aliens whose presence . . . is unlawful, have long been recognized as "persons" guaranteed due process of law.

Similar to the essential right to education granted to undocumented youth in the U.S. Supreme Court *Plyler* decision, equitable health care for undocumented immigrants should also be treated as an essential human right and a benefit to society.

At the practitioner level, there are several approaches that would benefit undocumented families. First, practitioners should understand that undocumented immigrants likely have experienced significant trauma and so treatment needs to be trauma-informed.[36] Also, undocumented patients are negotiating and weighing trust in terms of revealing their immigration status, so treatment must be culturally sensitive. For example, the type of language used ("undocumented" instead of "illegal"), the awareness of the multitude of challenges affecting the community (e.g., needing to take the bus instead of driving could result in late arrivals to appointments), and operating from a strength-based approach (e.g., recognizing the resiliency it takes to live in the United States as a person who is undocumented) can make a world of difference in making undocumented patients feel comfortable. It is important that bilingual medical and mental health providers be hired as well, so patients can fully communicate their needs.

Immigration reform is key to encouraging undocumented youth to thrive in the educational pipeline and enter the workforce of medical and mental health professions. Angelica Velazquillo, a doctoral student at the University of Chicago who is studying health and immigrant communities, shared that the current and future generations give her hope: "We'll have general practitioners, social workers, doctors, school counselors, anyone within the healthcare field, or like myself, pursuing a master's in social service administration. . . . Our professionals will have our cultural background and experience as more young immigrants enter the workforce."[37]

Finally, researchers who reviewed over three hundred studies on undocumented immigrants and health produced several important policy recommendations:[38]

1. We must promote a national and local culture of "access to health for all."
2. Remember that health care providers have an ethical and professional obligation to care for the sick, regardless of immigration status.
3. Cultural diversity and linguistic competency training and education for health professionals is needed, which should include awareness, respect, evidence-based research, and capacity-building components.

Special consideration should be paid to the mental health of those who endure trauma related to immigration enforcement and detainment. In particular, this focus must extend to children and youth, along with those who are U.S. born and members of mixed immigration status families.

Legal Issues, Detention, and Deportation

It is clear that banning people from traveling to the United States, building walls, increasing surveillance, housing migrants in detention centers, and using deportation to remove immigrants from the United States is never going to address the global and national factors that drive undocumented immigration. In addition, the reliance on incarcerating migrants and turning them back to often dangerous or untenable situations in their countries of origin is simply inhumane. As shown by anthropologist Lauren Heidbrink's research with deported youth in El Salvador, the criminalization of undocumented immigrants in the United States is mirrored in the public's reaction to youth after deportation to their home country. As a result, after deportation youth are ostracized, and they internalize their deportation as individual failures that exacerbate the negative effects of the state violence they have experienced.[39] Other scholars have similarly found that the social costs that deportees face are harsh ones that include law enforcement abuse, social stigmatization, and employment discrimination.[40]

In light of these and other findings, we recommend that the United States reduce its participation in policies and practices that create "legal violence"[41] against immigrants. Politicians and officials should abide by the country's agreement to enforce the Universal Declaration of Human Rights and sharply reduce the number of people who are being deported and detained in the United States today. Immigration agents should not be able to kill people without any consequences. Children should

Figure 8.2.   Keeping immigrant and mixed-status family members free from legal violence increases their health and happiness.
Jhon David, Unsplash

never be held in cages, or incarcerated in facilities that harm them, and families should not be torn apart in the name of expediency. The fact that people are *dying* in detention, such as thirty-three-year-old transgender detainee Roxsana Hernandez in May of 2018,[42] before having their immigration hearings is a testament to the dangerous path we are on that needs to be reversed. The cries to abolish Immigration and Customs Enforcement (ICE) are getting stronger and stronger in light of documented abuses of power.[43] Given that the agency was created in 2002 and does not have a long historical presence in the country,[44] it is not difficult to argue that its mission could easily be changed or eliminated.

We recommend comprehensive immigration reform that includes pathways to citizenship for undocumented people. Unfortunately, we realize that the current federal administration has all but abandoned any such plan for reform of this kind. Therefore, until the political climate of the federal government changes, we recommend that it fund competent legal counsel for those who are called to court for a removal hearing and cannot afford a lawyer. States like New York and California are beginning to foot the bill for immigrant legal counsel, but because the federal government is treating immigrants as quasi-criminals, we believe the financial responsibility to provide legal help should be borne by the federal government. It is unfair to deny people a lawyer to help them navigate their cases when the consequences of being removed from the country are so serious.

Additionally, undocumented people may be eligible for relief that they are un-aware of because of the complexity of immigration law, and only qualified legal advocates can help them adequately prepare for a case.[45] Without this system in place, some immigrants will continue to hire *notarios* or others that cannot represent them in court. An economic analysis of the benefits of having legal representation in the state of New Jersey found that the $2 million that they have set aside for legal representation for immigrants in the state pales in comparison to the $1.6 million that is lost and the $18 million in wages lost by the detention of people and their loss of work.[46] Private donor efforts, such as the Catalyst Fund in California, award grants to public universities and community colleges, in part to have legal services provided on campus for undocumented students and their loved ones, which is a move in the right direction.[47]

In cases in which migrants face actual criminal charges in criminal courts under Operation Streamline, they need to be provided with the normal due process that other defendants experience. Their time with the public defender needs to be suf-ficient for them to receive sound legal advice, and the practice of group trials needs to be ended. In California, the most recent state to implement Operation Streamline in the federal courts, attorneys with the Federal Defenders of San Diego vehemently opposed the procedures that had migrants being charged and sentenced in a special courtroom all during one visit.[48] The federal court in San Diego has begun mak-ing small changes to the procedures to increase due process, such as making it so defendants cannot enter a plea the first time that they come to court.[49] These small changes are important ones while Operation Streamline is in operation; however, the elimination of the program altogether, as well as the zero tolerance approach fueling it, are necessary to bring immigration back into the civil and administrative realms.

In addition, we recommend that the Department of Homeland Security treat courthouses as "sensitive locations" off-limits for apprehensions and arrests of sus-pected undocumented immigrants and maintain the traditionally protected sensitive locations as well (e.g., schools, houses of worship, and hospitals). We also recom-mend that the federal government eliminate the congressional mandate for how many people must be detained per day in detention facilities. To require thirty-four thousand beds to be filled in a given day is unprecedented worldwide and a viola-tion of the human right to be free of unnecessary incarceration. Eliminating that mandate would also expedite a sharp reduction in immigrant detention that could be further reduced by closing down all of the detention centers run by private cor-rectional corporations.

If detention must be used, alternatives to detention can be more humane. The re-lease of immigrants and asylum seekers into the custody of community organizations or families, release on recognizance, and non-monetary parole are all alternatives to detention that should be used. Unfortunately, the Trump Administration recently ended such a program: the Family Case Management program had an outstanding record with almost 100 percent of their clients going to their asylum hearings.[50] As Amnesty International points out, Congress, the U.S. Department of Homeland

Security, and the Department of Justice must institute a number of changes in order for the immigration system to begin to stem the flow of injustices affecting undocumented asylum seekers.[51] An external body, not beholden to political parties and changes of administrations, must be created to monitor human rights abuses for all migrants. It is legal to seek asylum and people doing so should not be subjected to physical and emotional abuse through militarized violence and tear-gassing at the border.[52]

Resistance and Social Movements

The lesson learned from activism about undocumented immigration is that we must keep advocating and fighting for immigration reform. We strongly support movements that are led by undocumented immigrants. We also support organizations that partner with undocumented immigrants to help amplify the needs and voice of immigrants. There is room for everyone at the local, national, and global levels to enact positive social change. Sociologist and activist Jose Ruiz Escutia remarks that organizers must realize that individuals who are undocumented may not be ready or have the time (due to work) to march in the streets, and that organizations must get creative about including diverse members of the impacted communities.[53]

We detailed an assortment of methods in chapter 7 to challenge misconceptions about undocumented immigration and highlight the effects of the immigration industrial complex on a large proportion of the U.S. population. The variety of techniques that are being used appeal to a range of people who may want to be involved, such as an undocumented person living far from live activism, the compassionate person with relative privilege who wants to donate resources, the mild-mannered person who may want to attend a rally, and the brave-hearted advocates who infiltrate detention centers. This increases the number of social actors on the ground working for change, which cannot be ignored. We recommend that immigration activists continue to use social media tools to connect with other organizations that are fighting for immigrant justice as well.

We recommend that immigrants and their allies generate public discussions about these large-scale factors that are driving migration. Free trade agreements, such as NAFTA and CAFTA-DA, hurt the manufacturing and agricultural industries of less-developed partner countries, and spur on unauthorized migration to the United States.[54] (The new NAFTA, now called the United States-Mexico-Canada Agreement or USMCA, was signed into effect in October 2018 and the results are yet to be seen.[55]) As a result, many frame their social change campaigns as efforts to transform and/or dismantle the forces that encourage violence against unauthorized migrants—global capitalism and racism.[56] The notion of free trade—if it cannot be altered or suspended altogether for the good of the workers who are at the center of production—should include migration and the free movement of people.

Finally, if you would like to get involved in the immigrant rights movement, we recommend that you examine the social media resources of any of the groups that we have written about in this book. Discover the different campaigns that are being organized in your area and reach out to movement organizers to get started. Challenge the myths about unauthorized immigration when you hear them. If you are not undocumented, learn about how to be an ally in chapter 4.

If you are undocumented, consider the recommendation from communication scholar and activist Dr. Antonio De La Garza: "Participation in organizing and activist work is a crucial form of self defense for undocumented people. Membership fights isolation by building community. Activism educates people on their rights and connects them to resources to manage daily conflicts. Most importantly, the struggle against injustice is redemptive. It brings dignity and works toward a more just future."[57]

THE RELEVANCE OF GLOBAL MIGRATION PATTERNS

In the introduction to this book, we contextualized our book's focus as part of the larger issue of unauthorized immigration as a whole in the United States. Now we conclude by turning our attention to the even bigger context of global migration.

According to the International Organization of Migration's (IOM's) 2018 report on global migration trends, the United States was (by far) the destination with the most resident migrants, followed by Germany, the Russian Federation, Saudi Arabia, the United Kingdom, the United Arab Emirates, Canada and France (tie), Australia, and Spain.[58] The country with the most migrants living in another country was India, followed by Mexico, the Russian Federation, China, Bangladesh, Pakistan and Ukraine (tie), the Philippines, the Syrian Arab Republic, and the United Kingdom.[59]

The number of global unauthorized migrants (which IOM refers to as irregular migrants) is difficult to estimate.[60] One of the most recent available estimates was that there were at least fifty million unauthorized migrants around the world in 2010. By looking at existing reports IOM found that there were about five to six million unauthorized migrants in the Russian Federation in 2011, three to six million undocumented migrants in South Africa in 2010, and 11.3 million undocumented people in the United States in 2016.[61]

By the end of 2017, there were forced displacements (including people seeking asylum, people internally displaced in their own countries, and refugees who fled to other countries) of 68.5 million people due to human rights violations, persecution, and conflict—the largest number ever recorded.[62] Five countries—the Syrian Arab Republic, Afghanistan, South Sudan, Myanmar, and Somalia—were the source countries for over two-thirds of the world's refugees in 2017.[63] The major host countries for refugees at the end of 2017 were Turkey, Pakistan, and Uganda.[64] The migrants suffer from poor conditions of refugee camps, which are better described as carceral spaces.[65] Critical refugee studies scholar Dr. Mohamed Abumaye explains that Somalis in the largest refugee camp in the world (Dadaab, Kenya) are subject to police abuse, limited food and other basic resources, limited options for work, and an overall system of corruption and bribery.[66] Asylum claims increased the most noticeably in the United States, with 331,700 claims of asylum—double the amount of asylum claims in 2015.[67] Most of these claims were by Salvadorans, Guatemalans, and Hondurans. Germany had 198,300 asylum claims in 2017, the second most in the world, yet experienced a major decrease from the 722,400 claims that were made the year before.[68]

To stop and imagine the movement of all the people around the world in a given year and the social forces behind their international migration is truly staggering. If we do imagine it, we can see the human desire to thrive, or at a minimum to survive, is strong enough for people to risk health, family separation, incarceration, and even death. In the United States, we see the completion of the often-dangerous journeys that migrants undertake and we fail to pay attention to their stories. In 2014, people in Murrieta, California, protested the transport of Central American youth and adults to a Border Patrol station in the area, and despite the presence of some supporters of the migrants, the protesters forced their bus to turn around.[69] With a rabid anti-undocumented-immigrant fervor, the protesters ignored the trauma the migrants—including many children—faced that drove them to travel for months to the United States.

As we conclude this book in the fall of 2018, migrant caravans are walking hundreds of miles to escape instability and violence in their Central American countries (e.g., Honduras and El Salvador).[70] They are being characterized as dangerous threats worthy of military intervention at the U.S.-Mexico border. Donald Trump stoked the fires of anti-migrant panic when he tweeted, "Many Gang Members and some very bad people are mixed into the Caravan heading into our Southern Border. . . . This is an invasion of our Country and our Military is waiting for you!"[71] In contrast, migrants share that they are leaving their home countries for a better future for their children, a chance to work, and safety.[72] Additionally, members of the LGBTQ Caravan from Central America arrived seeking economic opportunities and better civil rights.[73]

The ongoing criminalization of unauthorized migrants is powerful and when combined with a disregard for global affairs, it is a recipe for almost rabid support for the punitive treatment of the undocumented. We agree with the American Immigration Council's suggestions to address the root causes of the caravans and mass migration, which include addressing the root causes of Central America's instability; improving oversight and accountability of U.S. Customs and Border Protection; helping Mexico improve their asylum system; increasing refugee admissions; and resuming in-country refugee processing for Central American children.[74]

We close this book with some ideas about resiliency, hope, and fierce determination. Undocumented immigrants and advocates in the United States and around the world display complex understandings of global and national issues. Anthropologist Laura Corrunker studied anti-deportation movements in the United States and globally and found evidence of this: "Undocumented activists are aware of the profit their labor provides for the global capitalist economy, as well as the paradox between free trade agreements and the extraordinary global flows of capital, commodities, information, and jobs on one hand, and the concomitant criminalization of immigration on the other."[75] Social activists around the world share their knowledge with one another via social media and sometimes in person, and continue to strategize ways to promote immigrant justice.[76] The future is bright in this regard, but the struggle for immigrant dignity and justice must continue.

It is up to each of us to do what we can and then do even a bit more. Undocumented immigration is one of the major civil rights battles of our times. It is helpful to remember what Martin Luther King Jr. told the students at Barratt Junior High School in Philadelphia on October 26, 1967, during his speech entitled *What Is Your Life's Blueprint*: "If you can't fly, run. If you can't run, walk. If you can't walk, crawl. But by all means, keep moving."[77] We hope that our book on undocumented immigration has empowered you to consider what you can do to move us all toward a more just and humane nation.

Notes

ACKNOWLEDGMENT

1. Elise, Sharon and Xuan Santos. 2017. "Department Statement: Standing Up for Social Justice." Department of Sociology, California State University San Marcos, September 25, 2017. (https://www.csusm.edu/sociology/index.html).

CHAPTER 1

1. Burnett, John. 2018. "Finally Reunited with Her Child, Migrant Mother Has a Warning for the Caravan." National Public Radio, November 15. (https://www.npr.org/2018/11/15/668380488/finally-reunited-with-her-child-migrant-mother-has-a-warning-for-caravan).

2. American Civil Liberties Union. 2017. "The Constitution in the 100-Mile Border Zone." (https://www.aclu.org/other/constitution-100-mile-border-zone).

3. Pulitano, Elvira. 2013. "In Liberty's Shadow: The Discourse of Refugees and Asylum Seekers in Critical Race Theory and Immigration Law/Politics." *Identities: Global Studies in Culture and Power* 20(2): 173.

4. Pérez Huber, Lindsay. 2009. "Challenging Racist Nativist Framing: Acknowledging the Community Cultural Wealth of Undocumented Chicana Students to Reframe the Immigration Debate." *Harvard Educational Review* 79(4): 704–29.

5. López, Gustavo, Kristen Bialik, and Jynnah Radford. 2018. "Key Findings About U.S. Immigrants." Pew Research, September 14. (http://www.pewresearch.org/fact-tank/2018/09/14/key-findings-about-u-s-immigrants/).

6. Passel, Jeffrey S. and D'Vera Cohn. 2017. "20 Metro Areas Are Home to Six-In-Ten Unauthorized Immigrants in the U.S." Pew Research Center, February 9. (http://www.pewresearch.org/fact-tank/2017/02/09/us-metro-areas-unauthorized-immigrants/).

7. Passel, Jeffrey S. and D'Vera Cohn. 2016. "Overall Number of U.S. Unauthorized Immigrants Holds Steady Since 2009." Pew Research Center, September 20. (http://www.pewhispanic.org/2016/09/20/overall-number-of-u-s-unauthorized-immigrants-holds-steady-since-2009/).

8. Ibid.

9. Passel, Jeffrey and D'Vera Cohn. 2018. "U.S. Unauthorized Immigrant Total Dips to Lowest Level in a Decade." Pew Research Center, November 27. (http://www.pewhispanic.org/2018/11/27/u-s-unauthorized-immigrant-total-dips-to-lowest-level-in-a-decade/).

10. Passel and Cohn, "20 Metro Areas."

11. Passel and Cohn, "Overall Number of U.S. Unauthorized Immigrants."

12. Passel, Jeffrey S. and D'Vera Cohn. 2017. "As Mexican Share Declined, Unauthorized Immigrant Population Fell in 2015 Below Recession Level." Pew Research Center, April 25. (http://www.pewresearch.org/fact-tank/2017/04/25/as-mexican-share-declined-u-s-unauthorized-immigrant-population-fell-in-2015-below-recession-level/).

13. American Immigration Council. 2018. "Temporary Protected Status: An Overview." August 1. (https://www.americanimmigrationcouncil.org/research/temporary-protected-status-overview).

14. American Immigration Council, "Temporary Protected Status."

15. U.S. Citizenship and Immigration Services. 2018. "Temporary Protected Status." (https://www.uscis.gov/humanitarian/temporary-protected-status).

16. Miroff, Nick. 2018. "What Is TPS, and What Will Happen to the 200,000 Salvadorans Whose Status Is Revoked?" *Washington Post*, January 9. (https://www.washingtonpost.com/news/worldviews/wp/2018/01/09/what-is-tps-and-what-will-happen-to-the-200000-salvadorans-whose-status-is-revoked/?utm_term=.7618a7e01037).

17. Migration Policy Institute. N.d. *Profile of the Unauthorized Population: United States.* (https://www.migrationpolicy.org/data/unauthorized-immigrant-population/state/US).

18. Passel and Cohn, "U.S. Unauthorized Immigrant Total Dips."

19. Moyles, Trina and K. J. Dakin. 2016. "Female Migrant Farmworkers Push Back Against Machismo and Abuse in California's Wine Country." *YES! Magazine*, June 21. (http://www.yesmagazine.org/people-power/female-migrant-farmworkers-push-back-against-machismo-and-abuse-in-californias-wine-country-20160621).

20. Gelatt, Julia and Jie Zong. 2018. *Settling In: A Profile of the Unauthorized Immigrant Population in the United States.* Migration Policy Institute, November. (https://www.migrationpolicy.org/research/profile-unauthorized-immigrant-population-united-states).

21. Migration Policy Institute, *Profile of the Unauthorized Population.*

22. Chishti, Muzaffar and Fay Hipsman. 2015. "In Historic Shift, New Migration Flows from Mexico Fall Below Those from China and India." Migration Policy Institute, May 21. (http://www.migrationpolicy.org/article/historic-shift-new-migration-flows-mexico-fall-below-those-china-and-india).

23. Passel and Cohn, "U.S. Unauthorized Immigrant Total Dips."

24. Montagne, Rene. 2014. "U.S. Is Home to 1.5 Million Undocumented Asian Immigrants—Interview with Immigration Attorney Muzaffar Chishti." National Public Radio, November 28. (http://www.npr.org/2014/11/28/367154343/u-s-is-home-to-1-5-million-undocumented-asian-immigrants).

25. Siegel, Robert and Selena Simmons-Duffin. 2017. "How Did We Get to 11 Million Unauthorized Immigrants?" National Public Radio, March 7. (http://www.npr.org/2017/03/07/518201210/how-did-we-get-to-11-million-unauthorized-immigrants).

26. Acuña, Rudy. 2015. *Occupied America: A History of Chicanos* (Eighth Edition). Boston: Pearson.

27. Florido, Adrian. 2017. "How Trump Criminalized 11 Million with a Stroke of His Pen." NPR.com, January 28. (http://www.npr.org/sections/codeswitch/2017/01/28/512040631/how-trump-criminalized-11-million-with-a-stroke-of-his-pen?sc=tw).

28. American Immigration Council. 2016. "Why Don't They Just Get in Line? There Is No Line for Many Unauthorized Immigrants." Fact Sheet, August 12. (https://www.americanimmigrationcouncil.org/sites/default/files/research/why_dont_they_just_get_in_line_and_come_legally.pdf)

29. Warren, Robert and Donald Kerwin. 2017. "The 2,000 Mile Wall in Search of a Purpose: Since 2007 Visa Overstays Have Outnumbered Undocumented Border Crossers by a Half Million." *Journal on Migration and Human Security* 5(1): 124–36.

30. Heyer, Cole. 2016. "Over 4.5 Million Are Waiting for Green Cards—Over 100,000 of Them Are Employment-Based." *National Law Review*, January 12. (http://www.natlawreview.com/article/over-45-million-are-waiting-green-cards-over-100000-them-are-employment-based).

31. American Immigration Council, "Why Don't They Just Get in Line?"

32. Siegel and Simmons-Duffin, "How Did We Get to 11 Million?"

33. American Immigration Council, "Why Don't They Just Get in Line?"

34. Castaneda, Heide and Milena A. Melo. 2014. "Health Care Access for Latino Mixed-Status Families: Barriers, Strategies, and Implications for Reform." *American Behavioral Scientist* 58(14): 1891–1909.

35. Buiano, Madeline. 2018. "ICE Data: Tens of Thousands of Deported Parents Have U.S. Citizen Kids." Center for Public Integrity, October 12. (https://www.publicintegrity.org/2018/10/12/22333/ice-data-tens-thousands-deported-parents-have-us-citizen-kids).

36. Siegel and Simmons-Duffin, "How Did We Get to 11 Million?"

37. California Immigrant Policy Center. 2017. *Resilience in the Age of Inequality: Immigrant Contributions to California.* (http://www.haasjr.org/sites/default/files/resources/Immigrant-Contributions2017-CIPC-USC.pdf).

38. Berger, Peter L. 1963. *An Invitation to Sociology*. New York: Doubleday/Anchor Books.

CHAPTER 2

1. Valdivia, Angharad N. 2010. *Latina/os and the Media.* Cambridge, UK: Polity Press.

2. *Washington Post* Staff. 2015. "Full Text: Donald Trump Announces a Presidential Bid." *Washington Post*, June 16. (https://www.washingtonpost.com/news/post-politics/wp/2015/06/16/full-text-donald-trump-announces-a-presidential-bid/?utm_term=.9a5286fc1750).

3. Ross, Janell. 2016. "From Mexican Rapists to Bad Hombres, the Trump Campaign in Two Moments." *Washington Post*, October 20. (https://www.washingtonpost.com/news/the-fix/wp/2016/10/20/from-mexican-rapists-to-bad-hombres-the-trump-campaign-in-two-moments/?utm_term=.076e4dc0887d).

4. Surette, Ray. 2010. *Media, Crime, and Criminal Justice: Images, Realities, and Policies* (Fourth Edition). Belmont, CA: Wadsworth.

5. Swan, Richelle S. 2018. "Popular Culture, Media, and Crime." In Dan Okada, Mary McGuire, and Alexa Sardinia (Eds.), *Critical Issues in Crime and Justice* (Third Edition). Thousand Oaks, CA: Sage Publications, 125–40.

6. Kim, Sei-Hill, John P. Carvalho, Andrew G. Davis, and Amanda M. Mullins. 2011. "The View of the Border: News Framing of the Definition, Causes, and Solutions to Illegal Immigration." *Mass Communication and Society* 14(3): 292–314.

7. Schneider, Anne and Helen Ingram. 1993. "Social Construction of Target Populations: Implications for Politics and Policy." *American Political Science Review* 87(2): 334–47.

8. Leah, Rachel. 2018. "Laura Ingraham Enforces Racist Stereotypes About People of Color as She Laments Demographic Changes." Salon, August 9. (https://www.salon.com/2018/08/09/laura-ingraham-enforces-racist-stereotypes-about-people-of-color-as-she-laments-demographic-changes/).

9. Cohen, Stanley. 1972. *Folk Devils and Moral Panics*. London, England: MacGibbon & Kee; Goode, Erich and Nachman Ben-Yehuda. 2009. *Moral Panics: The Social Construction of Deviance* (Second Edition). Malden, MA: Wiley-Blackwell.

10. Cohen, *Folk Devils and Moral Panics*; Goode and Ben-Yehuda, *Moral Panics*.

11. Chiricos, Ted, Kathy Padgett, and Marc Gertz. 2000. "Fear, TV News, and the Reality of Crime." *Criminology* 38: 755–85; Potter, Gary W. and Victor E. Kappeler. 2012. "Introduction. Media, Crime and Hegemony." In Denise L. Bissler and Joan L. Conners (Eds.), *The Harms of Crime Media: Essays on the Perpetuation of Racism, Sexism, and Class Stereotypes*. Jefferson, NC: McFarland and Company, 3–17.

12. Clark-Ibáñez, Marisol, Bettina Serna, and Rhonda Avery-Merker. 2014. "In/Visibility of Undocumented Latino Immigrants in the News Media." Conference presentation at the 2014 Pacific Sociological Association in Portland, OR, March 27.

13. Lopez, Cristina G. 2015. "Latino Voices Call on Media to Improve Hispanic Representation." *Media Matters for America* (Blog), September 21. (http://mediamatters.org/blog/2015/09/21/latino-voices-call-on-media-to-improve-hispanic/205684).

14. Barreto, Matt A., Sylvia Manzano, and Gary Segura. 2012. *The Impact of Media Stereotypes on Opinions and Attitude Towards Latinos*. National Hispanic Media Coalition. (http://www.nhmc.org/nhmcnew/wp-content/uploads/2013/03/american_hate_radio_nhmc.pdf).

15. Barreto, Manzano, and Segura, *Impact of Media Stereotypes*, 3–4.

16. Barreto, Manzano, and Segura, *Impact of Media Stereotypes*, 4.

17. Barreto, Manzano, and Segura, *Impact of Media Stereotypes*, 22.

18. Dixon, Travis L. and Charlotte L. Williams. 2014. "The Changing Misrepresentation of Race and Crime on Network and Cable News." *Journal of Communication* 65(1): 24–39; Wilson, Clint C., Felix Gutiérrez, and Lena M. Chao. 2003. *Racism, Sexism and the Media: The Rise of Class Communication in Multicultural America*. Thousand Oaks, CA: Sage Publications.

19. Santa Ana, Otto. 2013. *Juan in a Hundred: Representations of Latinos on Network News*. Austin: University of Texas at Austin Press.

20. USC Annenberg Norman Lear Center's Media Impact Project and Define American. 2018. *Immigration Nation: Exploring Immigrant Portrayals on Television*. Los Angeles: The Norman Lear Center, October. (https://defineamerican.com/tvstudy/).

21. Negrón-Muntaner, Frances and Chelsea Abbas. 2016. *The Latino Disconnect: Latinos in the Age of Media Mergers*. The Center for the Study of Ethnicity and Race, Columbia University, and National Hispanic Foundation for the Arts. (http://www.columbia.edu/cu/cser/Documents/TheLatinoDisconnect.pdf).

22. Negrón-Muntaner and Abbas, *Latino Disconnect*.

23. Guo, Lei and Summer Harlow. 2014. "User-Generated Racism: An Analysis of Stereotypes of African Americans, Latinos, and Asians in YouTube Videos." *Howard Journal of Communications* 25(3): 281–302.

24. Guo and Harlow, "User-Generated Racism."

25. Chavez, Leo. 2013. *The Latino Threat: Constructing Immigrants, Citizens, and the Nation* (Second Edition). Stanford, CA: Stanford University Press. Kindle Edition: 23.

26. Santa Ana, Otto. 2002. *Brown Tide Rising: Metaphors of Latinos in Contemporary American Public Discourse.* Austin: University of Texas at Austin Press.

27. Chavez, *Latino Threat.*

28. Chavez, *Latino Threat*, 53.

29. Kalaw, Martine. 2016. "Is the Face of the Undocumented Immigrant Still Mexican." Huffington Post, March 21. (http://www.huffingtonpost.com/martine-kalaw/is-the-face-of-the-undocumented-immigrant-still-mexican_b_9512842.html).

30. Mendoza, Sylvia. 2015. "Building False Crisis: The Role of the Media Covering Undocumented Immigrants." *Hispanic Outlook in Higher Education*, June 15: 10. (https://www.hispanicoutlook.com/articles/building-false-crisis-the-role-of-the-media-coveri).

31. Rumbaut, Rubén and Walter A. Ewing. 2007. "The Myth of Immigrant Criminality and the Paradox of Assimilation: Incarceration Rates Among Native and Foreign-Born Men." Washington, DC: American Immigration Law Foundation.

32. Jones, Reece. 2014. "Border Wars: Narratives and Images of the US-Mexican Border on TV." *ACME: An International E-Journal for Critical Geographies* 13:530–50.

33. Santana, Arthur D. 2015. "Incivility Dominates Online Comments on Immigration." *Newspaper Research Journal* 36(1): 92–107.

34. National Hispanic Media Coalition. 2012. "American Hate Radio: How a Powerful Outlet for Democratic Discourse Has Deteriorated Into Hate, Racism and Extremism." (http://www.nhmc.org/nhmcnew/wp-content/uploads/2013/03/american_hate_radio_nhmc.pdf).

35. National Hispanic Media Coalition, "American Hate Radio," 4.

36. National Hispanic Media Coalition, "American Hate Radio," 6.

37. Bussert-Webb, Kathy. 2015. "Parrying the Pathologization of a Strong, Unified Mexican American Community." *Creative Approaches to Research* 8(2): 46–69.

38. Bussert-Webb, "Parrying the Pathologization."

39. Santa Ana, *Brown Tide Rising*, 72.

40. Santa Ana, *Brown Tide Rising*, 73.

41. Santa Ana, *Brown Tide Rising*, 78.

42. Menjívar, Cecilia. 2016. "Immigrant Criminalization in Law and the Media: Effects on Latino Immigrant Workers' Identities in Arizona." *American Behavioral Scientist,* 60(5-6): 597–616.

43. Menjívar, "Immigrant Criminalization."

44. Weiner, Rachel. 2013. "AP Drops 'Illegal Immigrant' from Stylebook." *Washington Post,* April 2. (https://www.washingtonpost.com/news/post-politics/wp/2013/04/02/ap-drops-illegal-immigrant-from-stylebook/?utm_term=.1989c32bef43).

45. Sen, Rinku. 2015. "Let's Drop the I-Word Again." Colorlines, November 6. (https://www.colorlines.com/articles/lets-drop-i-word—again).

46. Race Forward. n.d. "Drop the I-Word." *Race Forward.* (https://www.raceforward.org/practice/tools/drop-i-word).

47. Kim, Sei-Hill, John P. Carvalho, Andrew G. Davis, and Amanda M. Mullins. 2011. "The View of the Border: News Framing of the Definition, Causes, and Solutions to Illegal Immigration." *Mass Communication and Society* 14(3): 292–314.

48. Kinefuchi, Etsuko and Gabriel Cruz. 2015. "The Mexicans in the News: Representation of Mexican Immigrants in the Internet News Media." *Howard Journal of Communications* 26(4): 333–51.

49. Chuang, Angie and Robin Chin Roemer. 2015. "Beyond the Positive-Negative Paradigm of Latino/Latina News-Media Representations: DREAM Act Exemplars, Stereotypical Selection, and American Otherness." *Journalism* 16(8): 1045–61.

50. Schmidt, Samantha. 2018. "Rachel Maddow Breaks Down in Tears on Air While Reading Report on 'Tender Age' Shelters." *Washington Post,* June 20. (https://www.washingtonpost.com/news/morning-mix/wp/2018/06/20/rachel-maddow-breaks-down-in-tears-on-air-while-reading-report-on-tender-age-shelters/?utm_term=.0e507546ebd7).

51. Grimm, Josh. 2015. "Tenacity of Routine: The Absence of Geo-Ethnic Storytelling in Constructing Immigration News Coverage." *Howard Journal of Communications* 26(1): 1–20.

52. Kinefuchi and Cruz, "The Mexicans in the News."

53. Branton, Regina and Johanna Dunaway. 2008. "English- and Spanish-Language Media Coverage of Immigration: A Comparative Analysis." *Social Science Quarterly* 89(4): 1006–22.

54. Negrón-Muntaner, Frances, Chelsea Abbas, Luis Figueroa, and Samuel Robson. 2014. *The Latino Media Gap: A Report on the State of Latinos in U.S. Media.* The Center for the Study of Ethnicity and Race, Columbia University, and National Hispanic Foundation for the Arts. (http://www.columbia.edu/cu/cser/downloads/Latino_Media_Gap_Report.pdf).

55. Jenkins, Henry. 2015. "Important Reminder: Superman Was an Undocumented Immigrant." Fusion.net. (http://fusion.net/video/103908/superheroes-are-undocumented-immigrants-and-the-other-way-around/).

56. Abed-Santos, Alex. 2017. "Superman Saved Undocumented Workers from a Racist—and Conservative Media Is Mad About It." Vox.com, September 17. (https://www.vox.com/culture/2017/9/15/16307794/superman-undocumented-workers-white-supremacist-action-comics).

57. Konstantinides, Anneta. 2015. "New Captain America Comic Sees Superhero Sam Wilson Take On and Defeat Anti-Immigration Vigilantes." DailyMail.com, October 18. (http://www.dailymail.co.uk/news/article-3278524/Captain-America-defeats-anti-immigration-vigilantes-new-Marvel-comic.html); Marcotte, Amanda. 2015. "Sorry Fox News: Captain America Has Long Been a Liberal, Anti-Nationalist Character." Salon.com, October 20. (http://www.salon.com/2015/10/20/sorry_fox_news_captain_america_has_long_been_a_liberal_anti_nationalist_character/).

58. Konstantinides, "New Captain America Comic."

59. Terror, Jude. 2016. "Will the Falcon Be Deported in Captain America: Sam Wilson #17?" BleedingCool.com, December 29. (https://www.bleedingcool.com/2016/12/29/will-falcon-deported-captain-america-sam-wilson-17/).

60. Framke, Caroline. 2015. "For Years, TV Has Treated Immigrants as Punchlines. These Shows Are Fighting Back." Vox.com, December 3. (http://www.vox.com/2015/12/3/9843124/tv-immigrants-stereotypes-asian-american).

61. Rivas, Jorge. 2010. "Why 'Ugly Betty' Was a Really Big Deal." Colorlines, April 20. (http://www.colorlines.com/articles/why-ugly-betty-was-really-big-deal).

62. Sowards, Stacey K. and Richard D. Pineda. 2011. "*Latinidad* in *Ugly Betty:* Authenticity and the Paradox of Representation." In Michelle Holling and Bernadette M. Calafell (Eds.), *Latina/o Discourse in Vernacular Spaces: Somos de Una Voz?*, Lexington Press, 123–43; Sowards, Stacey K. and Richard D. Pineda. 2013. "Immigrant Narratives and Popular Culture

in the United States: Border Spectacle, Unmotivated Sympathies, and Individualized Responsibilities." *Western Journal of Communication* 77(1): 72–91.

63. Sowards and Pineda, "Immigrant Narratives and Popular Culture."

64. Primeau, Jamie. 2017. "America Ferrera's Women's March Speech Spreads a Powerful Message About Immigrants." *Bustle.* (https://www.bustle.com/p/america-ferreras-womens-march-speech-spreads-a-powerful-message-about-immigrants-32061).

65. Moreno, Carolina and Roque Planas. 2015. "'Jane the Virgin' Pauses Mid-Episode to Drive Home the Need for Immigration Reform." Huffington Post, January 22. (http://www.huffingtonpost.com/2015/01/22/jane-the-virgin-immigration-reform_n_6518768.html).

66. Moreno and Planas, "'Jane the Virgin' Pauses."

67. Carlin, Shannon. 2015. "'Jane the Virgin' Deals with Immigration Reform in an Important Way." *Bustle*, November 11. (https://www.bustle.com/articles/123223-jane-the-virgin-deals-with-immigration-reform-in-an-important-subtle-way).

68. Blake, Meredith. 2011. "America Ferrera Talks About Playing an Illegal Immigrant on 'The Good Wife'." *Los Angeles Times,* March 30. (http://latimesblogs.latimes.com/showtracker/2011/03/america-ferrera-talks-about-playing-an-immigrant-on-the-good-wife.html).

69. Brissey, Breia. 2015. "The Good Wife Recap 'The Next Month'." *Entertainment Weekly*, March 2. (http://ew.com/recap/the-good-wife-season-5-episode-8/2/).

70. Leeds, Sarene. 2018. "How 'One Day at a Time' Brilliantly Captures the Effect of Trump's America on One Latinx Family." Mic, January 30. (https://mic.com/articles/187694/how-one-day-at-a-time-brilliantly-captures-the-effect-of-trumps-america-on-one-latinx-family#.IKioFExNE).

71. Yandoli, Krystie Lee. 2018. "'One Day at a Time' Season 2 Addresses Donald Trump Without Ever Using His Name." BuzzFeed, January 31. (https://www.buzzfeednews.com/article/krystieyandoli/one-day-at-a-time-season-2-donald-trump).

72. Lee, Esther Yu-Hsi. 2014. "How Cultural Depictions Are Changing the Way We Think About Undocumented Immigrants." ThinkProgress. (http://thinkprogress.org/immigration/2014/05/01/3425260/jose-antonio-vargas-documented/).

73. Reichard, Raquel. 2016. "Diego Luna's Film 'The Journey' Illustrates the Struggles and Triumphs of Immigrants." *Latina*, October 21. (https://www.latina.com/entertainment/movies/diego-luna-film-journey-trailer).

74. Lee, "How Cultural Depictions Are Changing."

75. Lee, "How Cultural Depictions Are Changing."

76. Sinn, Jessica. 2010. "'The Other Side of Immigration:' Q & A with Documentary Filmmaker." *University of Texas at Austin News*, February 1. (https://news.utexas.edu/2010/02/01/fighting_immigration).

77. *Democracy Now!.* 2013. "Who Is Dayani Cristal?: Gael García Bernal Traces Path of Migrant Worker Who Died in Arizona Desert." *Democracy Now!.* (https://www.democracynow.org/2013/1/25/who_is_dayani_cristal_gael_garcia).

78. Reichard, Raquel. 2015. "Immigrants' Rights Activist Angy Rivera Talks Documentary, 'No Le Digas a Nadie'." *Latina*, September 16. (http://www.latina.com/lifestyle/our-issues/immigrants-rights-activist-angy-rivera-talks-documentary).

79. Reichard, "Immigrants' Rights Activist Angy Rivera."

80. Reichard, "Immigrants' Rights Activist Angy Rivera."

81. Reichard, "Immigrants' Rights Activist Angy Rivera."

82. Korhonen, Greyson. 2016. "A Visceral Portrait of Life at the U.S.-Mexico Border." *The Atlantic*. (https://www.theatlantic.com/video/index/472707/a-visceral-portrait-of-life-at-the-us-mexico-border/).

83. Korhonen, "A Visceral Portrait."

84. Main, S. J. 2012. "Actor Demián Bichir Talks Hollywood, Scarlett, Oscars & Being Latino." Huffington Post, April 28. (http://www.huffingtonpost.com/sj-main/post_3033_b_1301097.html).

85. Santos, Xuan. 2016. "Spare Parts." *Contemporary Justice Review* 19(1): 164–67.

86. Ibañez, Armando. N.d. *UndocuTales: A Web Series about a Queer Undocumented Immigrant Living in Los Angeles*. (https://www.undocumentedtales.com).

87. Ibañez, *UndocuTales*.

88. Zimmerman, Arely. 2016. "Transmedia Testimonio: Examining Undocumented Youth's Political Activism in the Digital Age." *International Journal of Communication* 10: 1886–1906.

89. Costanza-Chock, Sasha. 2014. *Out of the Shadows, Into the Streets! Transmedia Organizing and the Immigrant Rights Movement*. Cambridge, MA: MIT Press.

90. Zimmerman, "Transmedia Testimonio."

91. Costanza-Chock, *Out of the Shadows*, 137.

92. Presente.org. N.d. BastaDobbs.com. (http://bastadobbs.com/facts/).

93. Stelter, Brian and Bill Carter. 2009. "Lou Dobbs Abruptly Quits CNN." *New York Times*, November 11. (http://www.nytimes.com/2009/11/12/business/media/12dobbs.html).

94. Costanza-Chock, *Out of the Shadows*.

95. Montgomery, David. 2010. "Trail of Dream Students Walk 1,500 Miles to Bring Immigration Message to Washington." *Washington Post*, May 1. (http://www.washingtonpost.com/wp-dyn/content/article/2010/04/30/AR2010043001384_pf.html).

96. Pacheco, Gaby. N.d. "Case Study: Trail of Dreams." *Beautiful Trouble: A Toolbox for Revolutionaries*. (http://beautifultrouble.org/case/trail-of-dreams/).

97. Cuen, Leigh. 2015. "#WeAreSeeds Campaign Has People Talking Immigration, Racism." Vocativ, May 31. (http://www.vocativ.com/culture/media/weareseeds-twitter-hashtag-immigration-racism/).

98. Costanza-Chock, *Out of the Shadows*.

99. Park, Minyoung. 2017. "5 Must-Have Apps for Undocumented Immigrants." CNN, March 30. (http://money.cnn.com/2017/03/30/technology/immigrant-apps/).

100. Lapowsky, Issie. 2017. "A Portable Panic Button for Immigrants Swept Up in Raids." *Wired*, March 10. (https://www.wired.com/2017/03/portable-panic-button-immigrants-swept-raids/).

101. Park, "5 Must-Have Apps."

102. Park, "5 Must-Have Apps."

103. Lyons, Joseph D. 2017. "This 'Guadalupe Garcia' Tweet Shows How Donald Trump's Immigration Law Will Tragically Affect Families." *Bustle*, February. (https://www.bustle.com/p/this-guadalupe-garcia-tweet-shows-how-donald-trumps-immigration-law-will-tragically-affect-families-36780).

104. *CBS This Morning*. 2018. "'Psychological Trauma': Ex-Employee Describes Facilities for Separated Immigrant Children." *CBS This Morning*, June 29. (https://www.youtube.com/watch?v=8-wtqAMRc3w).

105. *LatinoUSA*. 2015. "The Dream9." National Public Radio, October 16. (http://www.npr.org/programs/latino-usa/513279638/the-dream-9).

106. Thompson, Ginger. 2018. "Listen to Children Who've Just Been Separated from Their Parents at the Border." ProPublica, June 18. (https://www.propublica.org/article/children-separated-from-parents-border-patrol-cbp-trump-immigration-policy).

107. Engleberg, Stephen. 2018. "DHS Chief Is Confronted with ProPublica Tape of Wailing Children Separated from Parents." ProPublica, June 18. (https://www.propublica.org/article/kirstjen-nielsen-homeland-security-crying-children-white-house-press-briefing).

CHAPTER 3

1. Scenario adapted from: Canseco, Omar. 2017. *Cruces Violentos, Violent Crossings: Undocumented Mexican Migration and Deportation Narratives.* Master's thesis, California State University San Marcos. (https://csusm-pace.calstate.edu/handle/10211.3/191105).

2. Connell, John. 1993. "Kitanai, Kitsui, and Kiken: The Rise of Labor Migration to Japan." Sydney, Australia: University of Australia as cited in Flynn, Michael A., Donald E. Eggerth, and C. Jeffrey Jacobson Jr. 2015. "Undocumented Status as a Social Determinant of Occupational Safety and Health: The Workers' Perspective." *American Journal of Industrial Medicine* 58(11): 1127–37.

3. Elk, Mike. 2017. "Spike in Latino Workplace Deaths Has Many Worried About Trump Era." Payday Report, January 25. (http://paydayreport.com/spike-in-latino-workplace-deaths-has-many-worried-about-trump-era/).

4. Gee, Lisa Christensen, Matthew Gardner, Misha E. Hill, and Meg Wiehe. 2017. "Undocumented Immigrants' State & Local Tax Contributions." Institute on Taxation and Economic Policy (ITEP), March. (https://itep.org/wp-content/uploads/ITEP-2017-Undocumented-Immigrants-State-and-Local-Contributions.pdf).

5. Gee, Gardner, Hill, and Wiehe, "Undocumented Immigrants'."

6. Gee, Gardner, Hill, and Wiehe, "Undocumented Immigrants'," 4.

7. Gee, Gardner, Hill, and Wiehe, "Undocumented Immigrants'."

8. Gee, Gardner, Hill, and Wiehe, "Undocumented Immigrants'."

9. Rodney, Jon. "Resilience in an Age of Inequality: Immigrant Contributions to California." *California Policy Center.* (http://www.haasjr.org/sites/default/files/resources/Immigrant-Contributions2017-CIPC-USC.pdf).

10. Rodney, "Resilience in an Age of Inequality."

11. Cummings, Bill. 2017. "Study Shows Value of Undocumented Immigrants." *Connecticut Post*, February 26. (https://www.ctpost.com/local/article/Study-shows-value-of-undocumented-immigrants-10959317.php).

12. Hill, Misha E. and Meg Wiehe. 2018. *State & Local Tax Contributions of Young Undocumented Immigrants.* Institute on Taxation & Economic Policy, April. (https://itep.org/wp-content/uploads/2018DACA.pdf).

13. Hill and Wiehe, *State & Local Tax Contributions.*

14. Campbell Fernández, Alexia. 2016. "The Truth About Undocumented Immigrants and Taxes: They're Contributing Billions of Dollars a Year to Social Security, but May Never Reap Any Retirement Benefits from It." *The Atlantic*, September 12. (http://www.theatlantic.com/business/archive/2016/09/undocumented-immigrants-and-taxes/499604/).

15. Campbell Fernández, "The Truth About Undocumented Immigrants."

16. Campbell Fernández, "The Truth About Undocumented Immigrants."

17. Campbell Fernández, "The Truth About Undocumented Immigrants."

18. Passel, Jeffrey S. and D'Vera Cohn. 2009. "A Portrait of Unauthorized Immigrants in the United States." Pew Hispanic Center, April 14. (http://www.pewhispanic.org/files/reports/107.pdf).

19. Cooperativa Latino Credit Union. 2000–2018. "Latino Community Credit Union." (http://latinoccu.org).

20. Self-Help Federal Credit Union. N.d. "Economy Opportunity for All." (https://www.self-helpfcu.org).

21. Khimm, Suzy. 2014. "The American Dream, Undocumented." MSNBC, August 28. (http://www.msnbc.com/msnbc/american-dream-undocumented).

22. Reyes, Carrie B. 2014. "ITIN Mortgages for Homebuyers Without Social Security Numbers." *FT Journal*, December 18. (http://journal.firsttuesday.us/itin-mortgages-for-homebuyers-without-social-security-numbers/39420/).

23. Jordan, Miriam. 2008. "Mortgage Prospects Dim for Illegal Immigrants." *Wall Street Journal*, October 22. (http://www.wsj.com/articles/SB122463690372357037).

24. Gonzales, Richard. 2017. "Tax Filings Seen Dipping Amid Trump Crackdown on Illegal Immigration." National Public Radio, April 17. (http://www.npr.org/2017/04/17/523634144/tax-filings-seen-dipping-amid-trump-crackdown-on-illegal-immigration).

25. Gonzales, "Tax Filings Seen Dipping."

26. Gonzales, "Tax Filings Seen Dipping."

27. Shih, Kevin. 2017. "Want a Stronger Economy? Give Immigrants a Warm Welcome." *The Conversation*, February 22. (http://theconversation.com/want-a-stronger-economy-give-immigrants-a-warm-welcome-73264).

28. Shih, "Want a Stronger Economy?"

29. Kitroeff, Natalie and Geoffrey Mohan. 2017. "Wages Rise on California Farms. Americans Still Don't Want the Job." *Los Angeles Times,* March 17. (http://www.latimes.com/projects/la-fi-farms-immigration/).

30. Elias, Thomas. 2017. "Farmers Fear Immigration Raids." *Record Searchlight*, April 3. (https://www.redding.com/story/opinion/columnists/tom-elias/2017/04/03/farmers-fear-immigration-raids/99986002/).

31. Rienzo, Cinzia. 2013. "There Is a Positive and Significant Association Between Increases in the Employment of Migrant Workers and Labour Productivity Growth. *The London School of Economics and Political Science* (Blog), November 27. (http://blogs.lse.ac.uk/politicsandpolicy/labour-productivity-and-immigration-in-the-uk-whats-the-link/).

32. California Department of Industrial Relations. 2007. "In California, Restaurant Workers Have Rights." (Flier) (https://www.dir.ca.gov/dlse/Publications/WorkersRightsFlyer-Restaurant-English.pdf).

33. Molandes, Lucas. 2017. April 8. "If the Undocumented Continue to Work in These Conditions, It Could Create a Security Threat to the U.S.'s Food Supply." *MITU*, April 8. (https://www.wearemitu.com/things-that-matter/report-finds-that-poor-treatment-of-undocumented-farm-workers-would-have-consequences-for-all-americans/).

34. Passel, Jeffrey S. and D'Vera Cohn. 2015. "Share of Unauthorized Immigrant Workers in Production, Construction Jobs Falls Since 2007: In States, Hospitality, Manufacturing and Construction Are Top Industries." Pew Research Center, March 26. (http://www.pewhispanic.org/2015/03/26/share-of-unauthorized-immigrant-workers-in-production-construction-jobs-falls-since-2007/).

35. Charles, Dan. 2016. "Inside the Lives of Farmworkers: Top 5 Lessons I Learned on the Ground." National Public Radio, July 15. (http://www.npr.org/sections/thesalt/2016/07/15/484967591/inside-the-lives-of-farmworkers-top-5-lessons-i-learned-on-the-ground).

36. Kossek, Ellen E. and Lisa B. Burke. 2014. "Developing Occupational and Family Resilience Among U.S. Migrant Farmworkers." *Social Research* 81(2): 359–72. (http://search.proquest.com.ezproxy.csusm.edu/docview/1551709197?accountid=10363).

37. Kossek and Burke, "Developing Occupational and Family Resilience."

38. Glatz, Julianne. 2014. "Cheap Food I: Illegal Immigrants." *Illinois Times*, June 26. (http://illinoistimes.com/article-14108-cheap-food-i:-illegal-immigrants.html).

39. Glatz, "Cheap Food I."

40. AJ+. *The Unheard Story of America's Undocumented Workers.* Films for Action. (http://www.filmsforaction.org/watch/the-unheard-story-of-americas-undocumented-workers/).

41. United States Immigration and Customs Enforcement. 2018. *Fiscal Year 2017 ICE Enforcement and Removal Operations Report.* (https://www.ice.gov/removal-statistics/2017#wcm-survey-target-id).

42. Elias, Thomas D., 2017. "Immigration Raids Scare California Farmers, Not Just Their Workers." *Los Angeles Daily News*, April 10. (http://www.dailynews.com/opinion/20170410/immigration-raids-scare-california-farmers-not-just-their-workers-thomas-elias).

43. Horton, Sarah B. 2016. *They Leave Their Kidneys in the Fields: Injury, Illness, and Illegality Among U.S. Farmworkers.* Oakland: University of California Press.

44. Campoy, Ana. 2016. "Mistaken Identity: Immigrant 'Ghost Workers' Are Lining Their Bosses' Pockets in a Whole New Way." Quartz, June 30. (http://nr.news-republic.com/Web/ArticleWeb.aspx?regionid=1&articleid=67751880).

45. Davidson, Lee. 2014. "Will Work for Pay: Utah Day Laborers Lining Up at Home Depot." *Salt Lake Tribune,* April 22. (http://archive.sltrib.com/story.php?ref=/sltrib/politics/57806652-90/contractors-customers-depot-guards.html.csp).

46. Davidson, "Will Work for Pay."

47. Davidson, "Will Work for Pay."

48. Abel, Valenzuela, Jr., Nik Theodore, Edwin Meléndez, and Ana Luz Gonzalez. 2006. *ON THE CORNER: Day Labor in the United States.* UCLA's Center for the Study of Urban Poverty.
    (http://www.sscnet.ucla.edu/issr/csup/index.php).

49. Abel Jr., Theodore, Meléndez, and Gonzalez, *ON THE CORNER.*

50. Wang, Hansi Lo. 2017. "Maine's Immigrants Boost Workforce of Whitest, Oldest State in U.S." National Public Radio, April 20. (http://www.npr.org/2017/04/20/524536237/maines-immigrants-boost-workforce-of-whitest-oldest-state-in-u-s?sc=tw).

51. Wang, "Maine's Immigrants Boost Workforce."

52. Passel, Jeffrey S. and D'Vera Cohn. 2017. "Immigration Projected to Drive Growth in U.S. Working-Age Population Through At Least 2035." Pew Research Center, March 8. (http://www.pewresearch.org/fact-tank/2017/03/08/immigration-projected-to-drive-growth-in-u-s-working-age-population-through-at-least-2035/).

53. Wang, "Maine's Immigrants Boost Workforce."

54. Ruiz, Ariel G., Jie Zong, and Jeanne Batalova. 2015. "Migration Policy Institute: Immigrant Women in the United States." March 20. (http://www.migrationpolicy.org/article/immigrant-women-united-states).

55. Ruiz, Zong, and Batalova, "Migration Policy Institute."

56. Ruiz, Zong, and Batalova, "Migration Policy Institute."

57. Flippen, Chenoa A. 2014. "Intersectionality at Work: Determinants of Labor Supply Among Immigrant Latinas." *Gender & Society* 28(3): 408. (http://gas.sagepub.com.ezproxy. csusm.edu/content/28/3/404.full.pdf+html).

58. Flippen, "Intersectionality at Work."

59. Burnham, Linda and Nik Theodore. 2012. *Home Economics: The Invisible and Unregulated World of Domestic Work.* National Domestic Workers Alliance. (http://www.domestic-workers.org/pdfs/HomeEconomicsEnglish.pdf). Cited in: We Belong Together, "Immigration Reform Is Central to Women's Equality: A Fact Sheet."

60. Hondagneu-Sotelo, Pierrette. 2007. *Doméstica: Immigrant Workers Cleaning and Caring in the Shadows of Influence.* Oakland: University of California Press.

61. Romero, Mary. 2011. *The Maid's Daughter: Living Inside and Outside of the American Dream.* New York: NYU Press.

62. Guerrero, Jean, Maureen Cavanaugh, and Megan Burke. 2016. "San Diego Janitors, Security Guards March Against Workplace Sexual Assault." KPBS Radio, March 8. (http:// www.kpbs.org/news/2016/mar/08/san-diego-janitors-march-raise-awareness-about-wor/#).

63. Guerrero, Cavanaugh, and Burke, "San Diego Janitors."

64. Hinkley, Sara, Annette Bernhardt, and Sarah Thomason. 2016. "Race to the Bottom." UC Berkeley. Labor Center. March 8. (http://laborcenter.berkeley.edu/pdf/2016/Race-to-the-Bottom.pdf).

65. Moyles, Trina and K. J. Dakin. 2016. "Female Migrant Farmworkers Push Back Against Machismo and Abuse in California's Wine Country." *Yes! Magazine*, June 21. (http://www.yesmagazine.org/people-power/female-migrant-farmworkers-push-back-against-machismo-and-abuse-in-californias-wine-country-20160621).

66. Moyles and Dakin, "Female Migrant Farmworkers Push Back."

67. Bauer, Mary and Monica Ramirez. 2010. *Injustice on Our Plates.* SPLC Southern Poverty Law Center, November 7. (https://www.splcenter.org/20101108/injustice-our-plates).

68. Bauer and Ramirez, *Injustice on Our Plates.*

69. Bauer and Ramirez, *Injustice on Our Plates.*

70. Bauer and Ramirez, *Injustice on Our Plates.*

71. Bauer and Ramirez, *Injustice on Our Plates.*

72. Bauer and Ramirez, *Injustice on Our Plates.*

73. Ontiveros, Maria. 2003. "Lessons from the Fields: Female Farmworkers and the Law." *Maine Law Review* 157, 169. Cited in the Southern Law Poverty Center report, *Injustice on Our Plates.*

74. Buckley, Madeline. 2017. "Unauthorized Immigrants Can Sue for Workplace Injury, Court Rules." *Indystar*, May 5. (http://www.indystar.com/story/news/2017/05/05/unauthorized-immigrants-can-sue-employers-court-rules/101322798/).

75. Buckley, "Unauthorized Immigrants Can Sue."

76. Morales, Lauren. 2016. "The Costs Behind a Migrant Crisis: Unaccompanied Minors in the Hands of Traffickers." *Fronteras*, June 10. (http://www.fronterasdesk.org/content/10334/costs-behind-migrant-crisis-unaccompanied-minors-hands-traffickers).

77. Morales, "The Costs Behind a Migrant Crisis."

78. Morales, "The Costs Behind a Migrant Crisis."

79. Heidbrink, Lauren. 2014. *Migrant Youth, Transnational Families and the State: Care and Contested Interests.* Philadelphia: University of Pennsylvania Press.

80. Morales, "The Costs Behind a Migrant Crisis."

81. Morales, "The Costs Behind a Migrant Crisis."

82. Morales, "The Costs Behind a Migrant Crisis."

83. Morales, "The Costs Behind a Migrant Crisis."

84. Samuels, Robert. 2017. "After Trump's Immigration Order, Anxiety Grows in Florida's Farm Fields." *Washington Post*, February 25. (https://www.washingtonpost.com/politics/after-trumps-immigration-order-anxiety-grows-in-floridas-vegetable-fields/2017/02/25/1539c4be-f915-11e6-be05-1a3817ac21a5_story.html?utm_campaign=buffer&utm_content=bufferc4e77&utm_medium=social&utm_source=twitter.com&utm_term=.9c9ef8db4c7c).

85. Samuels, "After Trump's Immigration Order."

86. Samuels, "After Trump's Immigration Order."

87. Human Rights Watch. 2010. *Fields of Peril: Child Labor in US Agriculture*. May: 10. (https://www.hrw.org/sites/default/files/reports/crd0510_brochure_low_0.pdf).

88. "Under Alabama Code § 16-28-6(4), children who are legally employed under the state child labor code are not obligated to attend school. Because Alabama's child labor law (Ala. Code § 25-8-33) exempts agriculture, children employed in agriculture are not required to attend school in the state." Cited on page 30 of the Southern Law Poverty Center report, *Injustice on Our Plates*.

89. Sanchez, Teresa F. 2015 "Gendered Sharecropping: Waged and Unwaged Mexican Immigrant Labor in the California Strawberry Fields." *Journal of Women in Culture and Society* 40(4): 917–38.

90. Kearney, Gregory D., Guadalupe Rodriguez, Sara A. Quandt, Justin T. Arcury, and Thomas A. Arcury. 2015. "Work Safety Climate, Safety Behaviors, and Occupational Injuries of Youth Farmworkers in North Carolina." *American Journal of Public Health* 105(7):1336–43.

91. Human Rights Watch, *Fields of Peril*.

92. Human Rights Watch, *Fields of Peril*.

93. Human Rights Watch, *Fields of Peril*.

94. Human Rights Watch, *Fields of Peril*.

95. Virginia's Legislative Information System. 2015. (http://lis.virginia.gov/cgi-bin/legp604.exe?151+ful+HB1906).

96. Human Rights Watch, *Fields of Peril*.

97. Government Accountability Office. 2016. *Workplace Safety and Health: Additional Data Needed to Address Continued Hazards in the Meat and Poultry Industry*. Report GAO-16-337 to Congress. April. (http://www.gao.gov/products/GAO-16-337).

98. Reinitz, Jeff and Jens Manuel Krogstad. 2008. "ICE Raid Is Largest Ever in Iowa." *The Courier*, May 13. (http://wcfcourier.com/news/local/ice-raid-is-largest-ever-in-iowa/article_d497d1f9-8935-5891-becc-f1452c79e96b.html).

99. Bauer and Ramirez, *Injustice on Our Plates*.

100. Government Accountability Office, *Workplace Safety and Health*.

101. Government Accountability Office, *Workplace Safety and Health*.

102. Government Accountability Office, *Workplace Safety and Health*.

103. Nadimpalli, Maya, Jessica L. Rinsky, Steve Wing, et al. 2014. "Persistence of Live-stock-Associated Antibiotic-Resistant *Staphylococcus aureus* Among Industrial Hog Operation Workers in North Carolina Over 14 Days." *Journal Occupational and Environmental Medicine* 72: 90–99.

104. UNC Gillings School of Public Health. 2014. "Hog Workers Carry Drug-Resistant Bacteria Even After They Leave the Farm." September 9. (http://www.jhsph.edu/news/news-releases/2014/hog-workers-carry-drug-resistant-bacteria-even-after-they-leave-the-farm.html).

105. Government Accountability Office, *Workplace Safety and Health*.

106. Nebraska Appleseed. 2009. "'The Speed Kills You'—The Voice of Nebraska's Meatpacking Workers." Report, 113. (https://neappleseed.org).

107. Nebraska Appleseed, "'The Speed Kills You'."

108. Nebraska Appleseed, "'The Speed Kills You'."

109. Government Accountability Office, *Workplace Safety and Health*.

110. Government Accountability Office, *Workplace Safety and Health*.

111. Kelley, Ryan. 2018. "New Research Shows Nearly 100 ICE Raids in Queens Since President Trump Took Office." Queens Borough News QNS.com, August 14. (https://qns.com/story/2018/08/14/new-research-shows-nearly-100-ice-raids-queens-since-president-trump-took-office/).

112. United States Immigration and Customs Enforcement. 2018. *Fiscal Year 2017 ICE Enforcement and Removal Operations Report*. (https://www.ice.gov/removal-statistics/2017).

113. Flynn, Meagan. 2018. "ICE Raid Targeting Employers and More Than 100 Workers Rocks a Small Nebraska Town." *Washington Post*, August 29. (https://www.washingtonpost.com/news/morning-mix/wp/2018/08/09/ice-raid-targeting-employers-and-more-than-100-workers-rocks-a-small-nebraska-town/?noredirect=on&utm_term=.e28896854a42).

114. Castillo, Andrea. 2018. "ICE Arrests Farmworkers, Sparking Fears in the Central Valley Over Immigrants and the Economy." *Los Angeles Times*, March 31. (http://www.latimes.com/local/lanow/la-me-farmworkers-ice-20180316-htmlstory.html).

115. Jordan, Miriam. 2018. "ICE Came for a Tennessee Town's Immigrants. The Town Fought Back." *New York Times*, June 18. (https://www.nytimes.com/interactive/2018/06/11/us/tennessee-immigration-trump.html).

116. Jordan, "ICE Came for a Tennessee Town's Immigrants."

117. Jordan, "ICE Came for a Tennessee Town's Immigrants."

118. Aguilar, Julián. 2018. "After ICE Raid in North Texas, Immigrants Face Uncertain Futures." *Texas Tribune*, September 6. (https://www.texastribune.org/2018/09/06/after-ice-raid-north-texas-immigrants-face-uncertain-futures/).

119. Rein, Lisa, Abigail Hauslohner, and Sandhya Somashekhar. "Federal Agents Conduct Immigration Enforcement Raids in At Least Six States." *Washington Post,* February 11. (https://www.washingtonpost.com/national/federal-agents-conduct-sweeping-immigration-enforcement-raids-in-at-least-6-states/2017/02/10/4b9f443a-efc8-11e6-b4ff-ac2cf509efe5_story.html?utm_term=.1588cd8f817b).

120. Blanco, Octavio. 2017. "How Much It Costs ICE to Deport an Undocumented Immigrant." CNN Business, April 13. (http://money.cnn.com/2017/04/13/news/economy/deportation-costs-undocumented-immigrant/index.html).

121. Blanco, "How Much It Costs ICE."

122. Rein, Hauslohner, and Somashekhar, "Federal Agents Conduct Immigration Enforcement Raids."

123. Samuels, "After Trump's Immigration Order."

124. Miller, Justin. 2017. "Trump's Immigration Crackdown Is Dangerous for Workers (Not Just Immigrants)." *American Prospect*, January 31. (http://prospect.org/article/trump's-immigration-crackdown-dangerous-workers-not-just-immigrants).

125. Miller, "Trump's Immigration Crackdown Is Dangerous."

126. Miller, "Trump's Immigration Crackdown Is Dangerous."

127. Layton, Leslie. 2012. "Semantics Important to Immigrants' Struggle, Garcia Argues." New America Media, June 22. (http://newamericamedia.org/2012/06/semantics-important-to-immigrants-struggle-garcia-argues.php).

128. Shoichet, Catherine E., and Tom Watkins. 2014. "No Green Card? No Problem— Undocumented Immigrant Can Practice Law, Court Says." CNN, January 3. (http://www.cnn.com/2014/01/02/justice/california-immigrant-lawyer/).

129. Huang, Josie. 2014. "How Americans Are Redefining 'American' in Southern California: Immigrants Without Legal Status Able to Apply for Professional Licenses in CA." *Multi-American,* KPCC Radio. September 29. (http://www.scpr.org/blogs/multiamerican/2014/09/29/17360/immigrants-professionally-licensed-california/).

130. American Immigration Council. 2010. "The DREAM Act: Creating Opportunities for Immigrant Students and Supporting the U.S. Economy." Fact Sheet published on July 13, 2010. (https://www.americanimmigrationcouncil.org/research/dream-act).

131. Burress, Jim. 2012. "Georgia Immigration Law Trips Up Doctors and Nurses." National Public Radio, November 11. (http://www.npr.org/sections/health-shots/2012/11/12/164950641/georgia-immigration-law-trips-up-doctors-and-nurses).

132. Burress, "Georgia Immigration Law Trips Up."

133. Hispanic Lifestyle. N.d. "Profile of a Latina of Influence—Josefina López." (http://www.hispaniclifestyle.com/articles/latina-of-influence-josefina-lopez).

134. Santiago, Eduardo and Pen Center. 2014. "Josefina Lopez Talks Immigration Ahead of Book Signing." *USA Today.* July 12. (https://www.usatoday.com/story/life/entertainment/books/2014/07/10/josefina-lopez-idyllwild-immigration-murrieta/12496287/).

135. Fernandez, Harold. 2016. "Undocumented & Unhealthy: Why We Should All Want to Care for Immigrants Who Lack Legal Papers." *Daily News,* November 30. (http://www.nydailynews.com/opinion/undocumented-unhealthy-confronting-immigrant-care-crisis-article-1.2891811).

136. Fernandez, "Undocumented & Unhealthy."

137. Abelson, Max. 2015. "How an Undocumented Immigrant from Mexico Became a Star at Goldman Sachs." *Bloomberg Businessweek,* February 25. (https://www.bloomberg.com/news/articles/2015-02-25/how-an-undocumented-immigrant-from-mexico-became-a-star-at-goldman-sachs).

138. Passel and Cohn, "Share of Unathorized Workers."

139. Wolf, Connor D. 2017. "How Talented Immigrant Children Are Shaping the Country." Inside Sources, March 15. (http://www.insidesources.com/talented-immigrants-children-shapingcountry/?utm_content=bufferc0afe&utm_medium=social&utm_source=twitter.com&utm_campaign=buffer).

140. American Immigration Council. 2016. "The H-1B Visa Program: A Primer on the Program and Its Impact on Jobs, Wages, and the Economy." (https://www.americanimmigrationcouncil.org/research/h1b-visa-program-fact-sheet).

141. American Immigration Council, "The H-1B Visa Program."

142. Department for Professional Employees. 2017. "Guest Worker Visas: The H-1B and L1." DPE Research Department. June 15. (http://dpeaflcio.org/programs-publications/issue-fact-sheets/guest-worker-visas-the-h-1b-and-l-1/#_edn6).

143. U.S. Citizenship and Immigration Services. 2016. *Characteristics of H-1B Specialty Occupation Workers: Fiscal Year 2015 Annual Report to Congress.* U.S. Department of Homeland Security, March 17. (https://www.uscis.gov/sites/default/files/USCIS/Resources/Reports%20and%20Studies/H-1B/H-1B-FY15.pdf).

144. *Wall Street Journal* Editors. 2017. "America's Got Immigrant Talent. Children of Immigrants Are Dominating U.S. Scientific Contests." *Wall Street Journal,* March 7. (https://www.wsj.com/articles/americas-got-immigrant-talent-1488847644).

145. U. S. Citizenship and Immigration Services. 2018. "H-2A Temporary Agricultural Workers." (https://www.uscis.gov/working-united-states/temporary-workers/h-2a-temporary-agricultural-workers).

146. Goldstein, Bruce. 2017. "Sen. Feinstein's New Bill to Shield Farmworkers from Deportation, Though Imperfect, Deserves to be Passed." Alternet, May 11. (http://www.alternet.org/food/sen-feinsteins-new-bill-shield-farmworkers-deportation-though-imperfect-deserves-be-passed).

147. Farm Bureau. 2018. "Eye-Popping H-2A Figures Posted in FY2018." (https://www.fb.org/market-intel/eye-popping-h-2a-figures-posted-in-fy2018).

148. United States Senator for California. Dianne Feinstein. (https://www.feinstein.senate.gov/public/_cache/files/a/a/aadb14f1-bc2a-459a-9695-f9f6ea0bcf60/71DC9ADF97CD1394AD3BE1288A64CAF1.blue-card-bill.pdf).

149. U.S. House of Representatives. 2018. *H.R. 6417-AG and Legal Workforce Act.* (https://www.congress.gov/bill/115th-congress/house-bill/6417/text).

150. Mitric, Julia. 2016. "Why California's New Farmworker Overtime Bill May Not Mean Bigger Paychecks." National Public Radio, August 30. (http://www.npr.org/sections/thesalt/2016/08/30/491944679/why-californias-new-farmworker-overtime-bill-may-not-mean-bigger-paychecks).

151. Mitric, "Why California's New Farmworker Overtime Bill."

152. Farm Bureau. 2018. "Agriculture Labor Reform." (http://www.fb.org/issues/immigration-reform/agriculture-labor-reform/).

153. Brooke, Ruth and Maureen Cavanaugh. 2017. "How Increased Immigration Enforcement Could Impact San Diego County Farms." KPBS, February 23. (http://www.kpbs.org/news/2017/feb/23/san-diego-county-farms-could-be-impacted-increased/?utm_medium=social-media&utm_campaign=kpbsnews-twitter&utm_source=t.co).

154. Siegel, Robert and Selena Simmons-Duffin. 2017. "How Did We Get to 11 Million Unauthorized Immigrants?" National Public Radio, March 7. (http://www.npr.org/2017/03/07/518201210/how-did-we-get-to-11-million-unauthorized-immigrants).

155. Ewing, Walter, Daniel E. Martínez, and Rubén G. Rumbaut. 2015. "The Criminalization of Immigration in the United States." American Immigration Council, July 13. (https://www.americanimmigrationcouncil.org/research/criminalization-immigration-united-states).

156. Riley, Jason L. 2015. "The Mythical Connection Between Immigrants and Crime." *Wall Street Journal,* July 14. (https://www.wsj.com/articles/the-mythical-connection-between-immigrants-and-crime-1436916798).

157. Meyer, Rachel and Janice Fine. 2017. "Grassroots Citizenship at Multiple Scales: Rethinking Immigrant Civic Participation." *International Journal of Politics, Culture and Society* 30(4): 323–48.

CHAPTER 4

1. American Immigration Council. 2010. "The DREAM Act: Creating Opportunities for Immigrant Students and Supporting the U.S. Economy." July 13. (https://www.americanimmigrationcouncil.org/research/dream-act).

2. United Nations Human Rights Office of High Commissioner. *Convention on the Rights of the Child.* (http://www.ohchr.org/EN/ProfessionalInterest/Pages/CRC.aspx).

3. Pérez, Zenén J. 2015. "Denying Higher Education to Undocumented Students Is a Roadblock to Future Economic Growth." Huffington Post, March 31. (https://www.huffingtonpost.com/zenen-jaimes-perez/denying-higher-education-to-undocumented-students_b_6976300.html).

4. Suárez-Orozco, Carola, Hirokazu Yoshikawa, Robert T. Teranishi, and Marcelo M. Suárez-Orozco. 2011. "Growing Up in the Shadows: The Developmental Implications of Unauthorized Status." *Harvard Educational Review* 81(3): 438–72.

5. Clark-Ibáñez, Marisol and Rhonda Avery-Merker. 2015. "Elementary School: The Beginning and the Promise." In *Undocumented Latino Youth—Navigating Their Worlds*. Boulder, CO: Lynne Rienner Publishers, Chapter 3.

6. Covarrubias, Alejandro and Argelia Lara. 2014. "The Undocumented (Im)Migrant Educational Pipeline: The Influence of Citizenship Status on Educational Attainment for People of Mexican Origin." *Urban Education* 49(1): 75–110.

7. Torres, Rebecca M. and Melissa Wicks-Asbun. 2014. "Undocumented Students' Narratives of Liminal Citizenship: High Aspirations, Exclusion, and "In-Between" Identities." *Professional Geographer* 66(2): 195–204.

8. Anderson, Nick. 2016. "Students to Education Dept.: Small Changes Can Make Big Payoffs in Graduation Rates." *Washington Post*, March 22. (https://www.washingtonpost.com/news/grade-point/wp/2016/03/22/students-to-education-dept-small-changes-can-make-big-payoffs-in-graduation-rates/).

9. Montelongo, Cesar. 2015. "As an Undocumented Immigrant, It's Easier to Get My MD-PhD Than a US Visa." Huffington Post, November 13. (http://www.huffingtonpost.com/cesar-montelongo/undocumented-immigrant-mdphd-visa_b_8538018.html).

10. Barile, Nancy. 2015. "Undocumented Students: A Teacher's Perspective." Huffington Post, December 10. (http://www.huffingtonpost.com/nancy-barile/undocumented-students-a-t_b_8759510.html).

11. McWhirter, Ellen H., Karina Ramos, and Cynthia Medina. 2013. "'¿Y Ahora Qué?' Anticipated Immigration Status Barriers and Latina/o High School Students' Future Expectations." *Cultural Diversity and Ethnic Minority Psychology* 19(3): 293.

12. The Best Colleges. 2018. *College Guide for Undocumented Students* (2018 Edition). The Best Colleges. (https://www.thebestcolleges.org/resources/undocumented-students/).

13. National Immigration Law Center. 2018. "Basic Facts About In-State Tuition for Undocumented Immigrant Students." June 1. (https://www.nilc.org/issues/education/basic-facts-instate/).

14. College Board. N.d. "Advising Undocumented Students." (https://professionals.collegeboard.org/guidance/financial-aid/undocumented-students).

15. National Immigration Law Center, "Basic Facts."

16. Bozick, Robert and Trey Miller. 2014. "In-State College Tuition Policies for Undocumented Immigrants: Implications for High School Enrollment Among Non-Citizen Mexican Youth." *Population Research and Policy Review* 33(1): 13–30.

17. Bozick and Miller, "In-State College Tuition Policies."

18. Negrón-Gonzales, Genevieve. 2017. "Constrained Inclusion: Access and Persistence Among Undocumented Community College Students in California's Central Valley." *Journal of Hispanic Higher Education* 16(2): 116.

19. Potochnick, Stephanie. 2014. "How States Can Reduce the Dropout Rate for Undocumented Immigrant Youth: The Effects of In-State Resident Tuition Policies." *Social Science Research* 45: 18–32.

20. Nguyen, David H. K. and Gabriel R. Serna. 2014. "Access or Barrier? Tuition and Fee Legislation for Undocumented Students Across the States." *The Clearing House* 87: 124–29.

21. Pérez, Zenén J. 2014. *Removing Barriers to Higher Education for Undocumented Students.* Washington, DC: Center for American Progress: 14. (https://www.luminafoundation. org/files/resources/removing-barriers-for-undocumented-students.pdf).

22. Chilin-Hernández, Jessica F. 2016. "Undocumented Virginians in the Age of Trump." *Virginia Policy Review* 10(1): 20–25. (http://www.virginiapolicyreview.org/uploads/5/5/9/2/55922627/chilin_final.pdf).

23. Simeone-Casas, Jenny. 2017. "Between State and National Policy, Undocumented Students Brace for Uncertain Future." St. Louis Public Radio, January 19. (http://news. stlpublicradio.org/post/between-state-and-national-policy-undocumented-students-brace-uncertain-future#stream/0).

24. American Immigration Council. 2017. "Immigrants in Missouri." October 13. (https://www.americanimmigrationcouncil.org/research/immigrants-in-missouri).

25. American Immigration Council, "Immigrants in Missouri."

26. Velez, Angel Luis. 2016. "Inaccessible Dreams: Undocumented Students' Financial Barriers to College Attainment." Office of Community College Research and Leadership, October 5. (http://occrl.illinois.edu/our-products/current-topics-detail/current-topics/2016/10/05/inaccessible-dreams).

27. Murillo, Marco A. 2017. "Undocumented and College-Bound: A Case Study of the Supports and Barriers High School Students Encounter in Accessing Higher Education." *Urban Education*: 17.

28. Murillo, "Undocumented and College-Bound," 1–29.

29. Brown, Emma. 2015. "Days from Leaving Office, Education Secretary Arne Duncan Talks About Successes, Failures." *Washington Post*, December 17. (https://www.washingtonpost.com/news/education/wp/2015/12/17/days-from-leaving-office-education-secretary-arne-duncan-talks-about-successes-failures/)._

30. United States Courts. N.d. Supreme Court Landmarks (http://www.uscourts.gov/about-federal-courts/educational-resources/supreme-court-landmarks).

31. American Immigration Council. 2016. *Public Education for Immigrant Students: Understanding Plyler v. Doe.* Fact Sheet. October 24. (https://www.americanimmigrationcouncil. org/research/plyler-v-doe-public-education-immigrant-students).

32. United States Senate. N.D. Civics. (https://www.senate.gov/civics/constitution_item/ constitution.htm).

33. American Immigration Council, *Understanding Plyler v. Doe.*

34. *Dallas Morning News* Editorial. 2017. "Remembering the Supreme Court Case out of Texas That Saved Classroom Seats for Undocumented Children." *Dallas Morning News.* June 12. (https://www.dallasnews.com/opinion/editorials/2017/06/12/remembering-plyler-v-doethe-supreme-court-case-texas-saved-classroom-seat-undocumented-children).

35. *Dallas Morning News Editorial*, "Remembering the Supreme Court Case."

36. American Immigration Council, *Understanding Plyler v. Doe.*

37. American Immigration Council, *Understanding Plyler v. Doe.*

38. Gomez, Alan. 2014. "White House: Don't Discourage Undocumented from Schools." *USA Today*, May 8. (http://www.usatoday.com/story/news/nation/2014/05/08/obama-immigration-undocumented-students/8840289/).

39. Camera, Lauren. 2015. "In the Classroom, and in the Country Illegally." *US News*, October 20. (http://www.usnews.com/news/articles/2015/10/20/education-department-issues-guide-to-help-schools-serve-students-in-the-country-illegally).

40. Balingit, Moriah. 2018. "Can Educators Call ICE on Students? Betsy DeVos Finally Answers." *Washington Post*, June 5. (https://www.washingtonpost.com/news/education/wp/2018/06/05/can-educators-call-ice-on-students-betsy-devos-finally-answers/?utm_term=.2ddb971d27f6).

41. Balingit, "Can Educators Call ICE?"

42. American Immigration Council. 2017. "The Dream Act, DACA, and Other Policies Designed to Protect Dreamers." American Immigration Council, September 6. (https://www.americanimmigrationcouncil.org/research/dream-act-daca-and-other-policies-designed-protect-dreamers).

43. Benevento, Maria. 2017. "Keep 'Dream Act' Free of Strings, Activists Say About Childhood Immigrants." *National Catholic Reporter*, October 19. (https://www.ncronline.org/news/justice/keep-dream-act-free-strings-activists-say-about-childhood-immigrants).

44. Redden, Elizabeth. 2017. "California Dreamers—and Their Nightmares." *Inside Higher Education*, April 14. (https://www.insidehighered.com/news/2017/04/14/dreamers-grapple-increased-stresses-and-challenges).

45. Redden, "California Dreamers."

46. Redden, "California Dreamers."

47. Krogstad, Jans Manuel. 2017. "Unauthorized Immigrants Covered by DACA Face Uncertain Future." Pew Hispanic Research, January 5. (http://www.pewresearch.org/fact-tank/2017/01/05/unauthorized-immigrants-covered-by-daca-face-uncertain-future/).

48. Krogstad, "Unauthorized Immigrants Covered by DACA."

49. U.S. Department of Homeland Security. 2017. "Number of Form I-821D, Consideration of Deferred Action for Childhood Arrivals, by Fiscal Year, Quarter, Intake, Biometrics and Case Status Fiscal Year 2012–2017." March. (https://www.uscis.gov/sites/default/files/USCIS/Resources/Reports%20and%20Studies/Immigration%20Forms%20Data/All%20Form%20Types/DACA/daca_performancedata_fy2017_qtr2.pdf).

50. Pérez, *Removing Barriers to Higher Education.*

51. Trump, Donald J. 2017. Press Release on Immigration, September 5. (https://www.whitehouse.gov/briefings-statements/statement-president-donald-j-trump-7/).

52. National Immigration Law Center. 2018. "Status of Current DACA Litigation." November 9. (https://www.nilc.org/issues/daca/status-current-daca-litigation/).

53. National Immigration Law Center, "Status of Current DACA Litigation."

54. U.S. Department of Homeland Security. N.D. *Deferred Action for Childhood Arrivals.* (https://www.dhs.gov/deferred-action-childhood-arrivals-daca).

55. U.S. Department of Homeland Security. 2018. *Report: Approximate Active DACA Recipients.* August 31. (https://www.uscis.gov/sites/default/files/USCIS/Resources/Reports%20and%20Studies/Immigration%20Forms%20Data/All%20Form%20Types/DACA/DACA_Population_Data_August_31_2018.pdf).

56. U.S. Department of Homeland Security. 2018. *Report: DACA Recipients Since the Injunction.* August 31. (https://www.uscis.gov/sites/default/files/USCIS/Resources/Reports%20and%20Studies/Immigration%20Forms%20Data/All%20Form%20Types/DACA/DACA_Receipts_Since_Injunction_August_31_2018.pdf).

57. U.S. Department of Homeland Security. 2018. *Report: DACA Expiration Date.* August 31. (https://www.uscis.gov/sites/default/files/USCIS/Resources/Reports%20and%20Studies/

Immigration%20Forms%20Data/All%20Form%20Types/DACA/DACA_Expiration_Data_ August_31_2018.pdf).

58. For example, Gonzales, Roberto G., Basia Ellis, Sarah Rendón-Garcia and Kristina Brant. 2018. "(Un)authorized Transitions: Illegality, DACA, and the Life Course." *Research in Human Development* 15 (3-4): 345–59; Swan, Richelle S. and Marisol Clark-Ibáñez. 2017. "Perceptions of Shifting Legal Ground: DACA and the Legal Consciousness of Undocumented Students and Graduates." *Thomas Jefferson Law Review* 39(2): 67–92.

59. Redden, "California Dreamers."

60. Gill, Hannah and Sara Peña. 2017. "The Deferred Action for Childhood Arrivals (DACA) Program in North Carolina: Perspectives from Immigrants and Community-Based Organizations." The Latino Migration Project. Chapel Hill: University of North Carolina at Chapel Hill.

61. *Citizen-Times.* 2017. "Undocumented Immigrants in the DACA Program Face Uncertainty Under President Trump." April 18. (http://www.citizen-times.com/videos/news/ local/2017/04/18/daca-immigration/100595134/).

62. Murillo, "Undocumented and College-Bound," 1–29.

63. Murillo, "Undocumented and College-Bound," 21.

64. Redden, "California Dreamers."

65. Negrón-Gonzales, "Constrained Inclusion," 115.

66. Redden, "California Dreamers."

67. Henderson, Tim. 2017. "Cities, States Move to Calm Fear of Deportation." *Governing—The States and Localities*, May 10. (http://www.governing.com/topics/politics/stateline-Cities-States-Fear-of-Deportation.html).

68. Morton, John. 2011. "Memorandum: Enforcement Actions at or Focused on Sensitive Locations." U.S. Department of Homeland Security, U.S. Office of Immigration and Customs Enforcement, October 24. (https://www.ice.gov/doclib/ero-outreach/pdf/10029.2-policy.pdf).

69. Morton, "Enforcement Actions."

70. U.S. Department of Homeland Security. "Myth versus Fact." August 28. (https://www. dhs.gov/myth-vs-fact).

71. Redmon, Jeremy and Mario Guevera. 2017. "Anxiety Grips Immigrants in Georgia During President Trump's Crackdown." *Atlanta Journal-Constitution*, March 13. (http://www. myajc.com/news/national-govt--politics/anxiety-grips-immigrants-georgia-during-president-trump-crackdown/XrNalP7TxTTEjgjfwYhk3N/).

72. Shoichet, Catherine E. 2018. "ICE Raided a Meatpacking Plant. More Than 500 Kids Missed School the Next Day." CNN.com, April 12. (https://www.cnn.com/2018/04/12/us/ tennessee-immigration-raid-schools-impact/index.html).

73. Nicosia, Mareesa. 2016. "Deportation Fears Taking a Toll on Immigrant Children's Education." *Los Angeles School Report*, February 2. (http://laschoolreport.com/lausd/).

74. Nicosia, "Deportation Fears."

75. Baker, Beth and Alejandra Marchevsky. 2017. "Immigration Agents Came for Our Student." *Los Angeles Times*, June 8. (http://www.latimes.com/opinion/op-ed/la-oe-baker-marchevsky-rueda-deportation-20170608-story.html).

76. Walton, Beth. 2017. "DACA Student Might Face Deportation, Asked to Meet with ICE." *Citizen-Times / USA Today*, April 17. (http://www.citizen-times.com/story/ news/2017/04/17/daca-student-might-face-deportation-meet-authorites/100561990/).

77. Menjívar, Cecilia. 2006. "Liminal Legality: Salvadoran and Guatemalan Immigrants' Lives in the United States." *American Journal of Sociology* 111(4): 999–1037.

78. Abrego, Leisy J. 2008. "Legitimacy, Social Identity, and the Mobilization of Law: The Effects of Assembly Bill 540 on Undocumented Students." *Law & Social Inquiry* 33(3): 709–34.

79. Torresand Wicks-Asbun. 2014. "Undocumented Students' Narratives," 195–204.

80. Torres and Wicks-Asbun, "Undocumented Students' Narratives," 200.

81. Torres and Wicks-Asbun, "Undocumented Students' Narratives," 201.

82. Torres and Wicks-Asbun, "Undocumented Students' Narratives," 201.

83. Negrón-Gonzales, "Constrained Inclusion," 105–22.

84. Negrón-Gonzales, "Constrained Inclusion," 106.

85. Negrón-Gonzales, "Constrained Inclusion," 118.

86. Chang, Aurora, Mark Anthony Torrez, Kelly N. Ferguson, and Anita Sagar. 2017. "Figured Worlds and American Dreams: An Exploration of Agency and Identity Among Latinx Undocumented Students." *Urban Review* 49: 189–216.

87. Chang, Torrez, Ferguson, and Sagar, "Figured Worlds and American Dreams," 209.

88. Chang, Torrez, Ferguson, and Sagar, "Figured Worlds and American Dreams," 210.

89. Linthicum, Kate. 2016. "Nearly Half a Million U.S. Citizens Are Enrolled in Mexican Schools. Many of Them Are Struggling." *Los Angeles Times*, May 14. (http://www.latimes.com/world/mexico-americas/la-fg-mexico-return-migration-schools-20160913-snap-story.html).

90. Linthicum, "Nearly Half a Million."

91. Linthicum, "Nearly Half a Million."

92. Frederick, James. 2016. "What Is Home? Going Home and Struggling to Fit Back In." 2016. *LatinoUSA*, December 6. (http://www.npr.org/2016/12/09/504989799/going-home-and-struggling-to-fit-back-in).

93. Torres and Wicks-Asbun, "Undocumented Students' Narratives," 195–204.

94. Torres and Wicks-Asbun, "Undocumented Students' Narratives," 200.

95. Clark-Ibáñez, Marisol. 2015. *Undocumented Latino Youth—Navigating Their Worlds.* Boulder, CO: Lynne Rienner Publishers.

96. Montelongo, "As an Undocumented Immigrant."

97. Montelongo, "As an Undocumented Immigrant."

98. Munoz Robles, Brizzia and Maria Munoz Robles. 2015. "We Were High School Valedictorians, but We Weren't Sure We'd Make It to College Because We're Also Undocumented Immigrants." *Washington Post*, May 19. (https://www.washingtonpost.com/posteverything/wp/2015/05/19/we-were-high-school-valedictorians-but-we-werent-sure-make-it-to-college-because-were-also-undocumented-immigrants/).

99. Murillo, "Undocumented and College-Bound," 1–29.

100. Murillo, "Undocumented and College-Bound," 14.

101. The University of California system has less than two thousand. It is important to note that better resourced campuses in the University of California system, such as Berkeley and Los Angeles, have led the way in establishing centers, advocacy, and research. The California Community College system serves over twenty thousand undocumented students.

102. Sacramento State Dreamer Resource Center. N.D. "Welcome." (http://www.csus.edu/sernacenter/dreamer%20resource%20center/welcome.html).

103. Redden, "California Dreamers."

104. Undocumented Student Alliance. 2016. "About." (https://uga.collegiatelink.net/organization/USA/about).

105. Castillo, Walbert. 2015. "Undocumented Students Work for Support, Reform." *USA Today*, January 17. (http://college.usatoday.com/2015/01/17/undocumented-students-work-for-support-reform/).

106. Freedom University. 2016. "Who We Are in 2016." (https://www.youtube.com/watch?v=7w3yEAg-QPg).

107. Moffitt, Bob. 2017. "Sac City Unified Launches Program to Protect Undocumented Students." Capitol Public Radio, March 7. (http://www.capradio.org/91610).

108. Moffitt, "Sac City Unified Launches Program."

109. Crawford, Emily R. 2017. "The Ethic of Community and Incorporating Undocumented Immigrant Concerns into Ethical School Leadership." *Educational Administration Quarterly* 53(2): 147–79.

110. Freedom University. 2018. "History." (https://freedom-university.org/timeline).

111. Freedom University. 2018. "Timeline." (https://freedom-university.org/timeline).

112. Teaching for Change. "Teaching About Freedom Schools." (http://www.teachingfor-change.org/teaching-freedom-schools).

113. Freedom University Homepage (https://freedom-university.org/home).

114. *New Yorker*. 2017. "Georgia's Underground University for Undocumented Students." (https://www.youtube.com/watch?v=d3NW5AOQQYw).

115. Freedom University, "Who We Are in 2016."

116. Freedom University, "Timeline."

117. University of the People. 2018. (http://www.uopeople.edu).

118. Sanchez, Claudio. 2015. "The Online College That's Helping Undocumented Students." National Public Radio, October 26. (http://www.npr.org/sections/ed/2015/10/26/449279730/the-online-college-thats-helping-undocumented-students).

119. Sanchez, "The Online College That's Helping."

120. Created by Arturo Ocampo, Sandra Carrillo, and Marisol Clark-Ibáñez at California State University San Marcos, 2015.

121. WCNC. 2017. "A Citizen of Nowhere Living in North Carolina." (https://www.wcnc.com/article/news/a-citizen-of-nowhere-living-in-north-carolina/427738117).

122. Barile, "Undocumented Students: A Teacher's Perspective."

123. Pérez, "Denying Higher Education to Undocumented Students."

124. Nunez, Lissette. 2018. "Local Woman Becomes First DACA Recipient to Be Admitted to Connecticut Bar." Fox 61 News, November 2.
(https://fox61.com/2018/11/02/local-woman-becomes-first-daca-recipient-to-be-admitted-to-ct-bar/).

125. Storace, Robert. 2018. "This Young Attorney Is the First DACA Recipient Admitted to Practice Law in Connecticut." *Connecticut Law Tribune*, November 2. (https://www.law.com/ctlawtribune/2018/11/02/this-young-attorney-is-the-first-daca-recipient-admitted-to-practice-law-in-connecticut/?slreturn=20181006133839).

126. Storace, "This Young Attorney."

127. Morales, Ricardo Levins. N.d. "Nothing About Us." (http://www.rlmartstudio.com/product/nothing-about-us-2/).

CHAPTER 5

1. Torres, Jacqueline M. and Steven P. Wallace. 2013. "Migration Circumstances, Psychological Distress, and Self-Rated Physical Health for Latino Immigrants in the United States." *American Journal of Public Health* 103(9): 1619–27.

2. Ortega, Alexander N., Hector P. Rodriguez, and Arturo Vargas Bustamante. 2015. "Policy Dilemmas in Latino Health Care and Implementation of the Affordable Care Act." Department of Health and Policy Management. *Annual Review of Public Health*, 34: 525–44.

3. Ortega, Rodriguez, and Bustamante, "Policy Dilemmas."

4. California Healthcare Foundation. 2015. *Major Transition with Minor Disruption: Moving Undocumented Children from Healthy Kids to Full-Scope Medi-Cal.* Policy Brief, November. (http://www.chcf.org/publications/2015/11/major-transition-undocumented-children).

5. Grubbs, Vanessa. 2014. "Undocumented Immigrants and Kidney Transplant: Costs and Controversy." *Health Affairs* 33(2): 332–35. (http://content.healthaffairs.org/content/33/2/332).

6. Gilcrist, Akiesha R. 2013. "Undocumented Immigrants: Lack of Equal Protection and Its Impact on Public Health." *Journal of Legal Medicine* 34(4): 403–12.

7. Fortuna, Lisa and Michelle V. Porche. 2013. "Clinical Issues and Challenges in Treating Undocumented Immigrants." *Clinical Issues and Challenges in Treating Undocumented Immigrants.* (http://www.psychiatrictimes.com/special-reports/clinical-issues-and-challenges-treating-undocumented-immigrants).

8. White, Kari, Justin Blackburn, Bryn Manzella, Elisabeth Welty, and Nir Menachemi. 2014. "Changes in Use of County Public Health Services Following Implementation of Alabama's Immigration Law." *Journal of Health Care for the Poor and Underserved* 25: 1844–52.

9. Toomey, Russell B., Adriana J. Umaña-Taylor, David R. Williams, Elizabeth Harvey-Mendoza, Laudan B. Jahromi, and Kimberly A. Updegraff. 2014. "Impact of Arizona's SB1070 Immigration Law on Utilization of Health Care and Public Assistance Among Mexican-Origin Adolescent Mothers and Their Mother Figures." *American Journal of Public Health* 104(Spring): 28–34.

10. Lee, Esther Yu-Hsi. 2015. "No, Undocumented Immigrants Are Not a Burden on Our Health Care System." *ThinkProgress*, June 24. (https://thinkprogress.org/no-undocumented-immigrants-arent-a-burden-on-the-health-care-system-39560e0bcaf7).

11. Zallman, Leah, Fernando A. Wilson, James P. Stimpson, Adriana Bearse, Lisa Arsenault, Blessing Dube, David Himmelstein, and Steffie Woolhandler. 2016. "Unauthorized Immigrants Prolong the Life of Medicare's Trust Fund." *Journal of General Internal Medicine* 31(1): 122–27.

12. Zallman et al., "Unauthorized Immigrants Prolong the Life."

13. Luthra, Shefali. 2018. "5 Things to Know About Trump's New 'Public Charge' Immigration Proposal." ABC News, September 25. (https://abcnews.go.com/Health/things-trumps-public-charge-immigration-proposal/story?id=58064875).

14. Centers for Medicare and Medicaid Services. "Emergency Medical Treatment & Labor Act (EMTALA)." (https://www.cms.gov/Regulations-and-Guidance/Legislation/EMTALA/).

15. Whitman, Elizabeth. 2015. "Immigration, Health Care Reform 2015: States Move to Help Undocumented Immigrants Without Medical Insurance." *International Business Times.* (http://www.ibtimes.com/immigration-health-care-reform-2015-states-move-help-undocumented-immigrants-without-1820458).

16. Berlinger, Nancy, Claudia Calhoon, Michael K. Gusmano, and Jackie Vimo. 2015. *Undocumented Immigrants and Access to Health Care in New York City: Identifying Fair, Effective, and Sustainable Local Policy Solutions: Report and Recommendations to the Office of the Mayor of New York City.* The Hastings Center and New York Immigration Coalition. (http://www.undocumentedpatients.org/wp-content/uploads/2015/04/Undocumented-Immigrants-and-Access-to-Health-Care-NYC-Report-April-2015.pdf).

17. Rodríguez, Michael A., Maria-Elena Young, and Steven P. Wallace. 2015. "Creating Conditions to Support Healthy People: State Policies That Affect the Health of Undocumented Immigrants and Their Families." April 2015 Report from the University of California Global Health Institute. (http://www.healthpolicy.ucla.edu/publications/search/pages/detail.aspx?PubID=1373).

18. National Immigration Law Center. 2014. "Immigrants and the Affordable Care Act (ACA)." (https://www.nilc.org/issues/health-care/immigrantshcr/).

19. Calefati, Jessica. 2015. "California Undocumented Immigrants Could Get Legal Protections, Health Care Under New Plan." (http://www.dailynews.com/social-affairs/20150407/california-undocumented-immigrants-could-get-legal-protections-health-care-under-new-plan).

20. Kaiser Permanente. N.d. "Subsidized Care and Coverage." (https://share.kaiserpermanente.org/article/subsidized-care-and-coverage-charitable-health-coverage/).

21. Rodríguez, Young, and Wallace, "Creating Conditions to Support Healthy People."

22. Radnofsky, Louise. 2016. "Illegal Immigrants Get Public Health Care, Despite Federal Policy." *Wall Street Journal*, March 24. (https://www.wsj.com/articles/illegal-immigrants-get-public-health-care-despite-federal-policy-1458850082).

23. National Park Service. Statue of Liberty National Monument, New York. (https://www.nps.gov/stli/learn/education/index.htm).

24. Community Service Society. 2017. "Community Health Advocates 2016 Annual Report." State of New York, February. (http://www.cssny.org/publications/entry/cha-2016-annual-report).

25. Hamm, Nia. 2016. "Advocates Push NY State for Health Care for Undocumented Immigrants." Public News Service. (http://www.publicnewsservice.org/2016-02-10/immigrant-issues/advocates-push-ny-state-for-health-care-for-undocumented-immigrants/a50303-1?utm_source=thebreakingnewsnetwork.com).

26. Calefati, "California Undocumented Immigrants Could Get."

27. Hurdle, John. 2015. "A New Medical Center for Undocumented Immigrants Opens This Weekend on South Street." (http://citypaper.net/cover/a-center-offering-undocumented-immigrants-medical-care-and-social-service-help-opens-this-weekend-on-south-street/).

28. Healthy California. 2015. *GET HEALTHY, CALIFORNIA! A Healthcare Resource Guide for Undocumented and Uninsured Californians.* (http://undocumentedanduninsured.org/wp-content/uploads/2015/01/Resource-Guide-v9n.pdf).

29. Santa Ana, Otto. 1999. "Like an Animal I Was Treated: Anti-Immigrant Metaphor in U.S. Public Discourse." *Discourse and Society* 10(2): 191–224.

30. Zayas, Luis H. and Mollie H. Bradlee. 2014. "Exiling Children, Creating Orphans: When Immigration Policies Hurt Citizens." *Social Work* 59(2): 167–75.

31. California Healthline. 2015. "New Law Will Expand Medical to 170K Undocumented Children." (http://californiahealthline.org/morning-breakout/new-law-will-expand-medical-to-170k-undocumented-children/).

32. López, Gustavo, Kristin Bialik, and Jynnah Radford. 2018. "Key Findings About U.S. Immigrants." Pew Research, September 18. (http://www.pewresearch.org/fact-tank/2018/09/14/key-findings-about-u-s-immigrants/).

33. Center for Reproductive Rights. 2015. "*Nuestro* Texas: A Reproductive Rights Agenda for Latinas. Report with the National Latina Institute for Reproductive Health." January.

34. Castañeda, Heide and Milena A. Melo. 2014. "Health Care Access for Latino Mixed-Status Families: Barriers, Strategies, and Implications for Reform." *American Behavioral Scientist* 58(14): 1891–1909.

35. Planas, Roque. 2017. "Ruling on ICE Detainers Is Bad News for Texas Immigration Crackdown." Huffington Post, June 9. (http://www.huffingtonpost.com/entry/judges-ruling-on-ice-detainers-is-bad-news-for-texas-immigration-crackdown_U.S._593b0a70e4b024026 8795d23).

36. Aguilar, Julián. 2018. "Federal Appeals Court's Ruling Upholds Most of Texas' 'Sanctuary Cities' Law." *Texas Tribune,* March 13. (https://www.texastribune.org/2018/03/13/texas-immigration-sanctuary-cities-law-court/).

37. Aguilar, "Federal Appeals Court's Ruling."

38. Ortega, Rodriguez, and Bustamante. "Policy Dilemmas."

39. Radnofsky, "Illegal Immigrants Get Public Health Care."

40. Radnofsky, "Illegal Immigrants Get Public Health Care."

41. Radnofsky, "Illegal Immigrants Get Public Health Care."

42. Gonzalez, Xatherin. 2015. "For Undocumented Women Seeking Reproductive Healthcare, Policing and Politics Create a Maze of Barriers." *Ms. Magazine* (Blog), November 16. (http://msmagazine.com/blog/2015/11/16/for-undocumented-women-seeking-reproductive-healthcare-policing-and-politics-create-a-maze-of-barriers/).

43. Rhodes, Scott D., Lilli Mann, Florence M. Siman, Song Eunyoung, Jorge Alonzo, Mario Downs, Emma Lawlor, Omar Martinez, Christina J. Sun, Mary Claire O'Brien, Beth A. Reboussin, and Mark A. Hall. 2015. "The Impact of Local Immigration Enforcement Policies on the Health of Immigrant Hispanics/Latinos in the United States." *American Journal of Public Health* 105(2): 329–37.

44. Rhodes et al., "The Impact of Local Immigration Enforcement Policies."

45. Rhodes et al., "The Impact of Local Immigration Enforcement Policies."

46. Martinez, Omar, Elwin Wu, Theo Sandfort, Brian Dodge, Alex Carballo-Dieguez, Rogeiro Pinto, Scott Rhodes, Eva Moya, and Silvia Chavez-Baray. 2015. "Evaluating the Impact of Immigration Policies on Health Status Among Undocumented Immigrants: A Systematic Review." *Journal of Immigrant Minority Health* 17: 947–70.

47. Ortega, Rodriguez, and Bustamante, "Policy Dilemmas."

48. Ortega, Rodriguez, and Bustamante, "Policy Dilemmas," 530.

49. Ziemer, Carolyn M., Sylvia Becker-Dreps, Donald E. Pathman, Paul Mihas, Pamela Frasier, Melida Colindres, Milton Butterworth, and Scott S. Robinson. 2014. "Mexican Immigrants' Attitudes and Interest in Health Insurance: A Qualitative Descriptive Study." *Journal of Immigrant and Minority Health* 16(4): 724–32. (http://ezproxy.csusm.edu/login?url=http://search.proquest.com.ezproxy.csusm.edu/docview/1544946008?accountid=10363).

50. Hurdle, John. 2014. "Nonprofit Clinic Offers 'Bridges of Health' to Philadelphia's Illegal Immigrants." *New York Times*, January 19. (https://www.nytimes.com/2014/01/20/U.S./nonprofit-clinic-offers-bridges-of-health-to-philadelphias-illegal-immigrants.html).

51. Gonzalez, "For Undocumented Women Seeking Reproductive Healthcare."

52. Radnofsky, "Illegal Immigrants Get Public Health Care."

53. Howard, Jacqueline. 2018. "The Stress Pregnant Women Face in America." CNN. com, October 24. (https://www.cnn.com/2018/10/23/health/pregnant-immigrant-women-every-mother-counts/index.html).

54. California Immigrant Policy Center. 2017. *Resilience in an Age of Inequality: Immigrant Contributions to California.* (http://www.haasjr.org/sites/default/files/resources/Immigrant-Contributions2017-CIPC-USC.pdf).

55. California Immigrant Policy Center, *Resilience in an Age of Inequality.*

56. Holguin, Fernando, Anas Moughrabieh, Victoria Ojeda, Sanjay R. Patel, Paula Peyrani, Miguel Pinedo, Juan C. Celedón, Ivor S. Douglas, Dona J. Upson, and Jesse Roman. 2016. "Respiratory Health in Migrant Populations: A Crisis Overlooked." *Annals of American Thoracic Society* 14(2): 153–59.

57. Holguin et al., "Respiratory Health in Migrant Populations."

58. Castañeda and Melo, "Health Care Access for Latino Mixed-Status Families."

59. Plascencia, Imelda S., Alma Leyva, Mayra Yoana Jaimes Pena, and Saba Waheed. 2015. *Undocumented and Uninsured: A Five-Part Report on Immigrant Youth and the Struggle to Access Health Care in California: Part 1, No Papers, No Healthcare.* The Dream Resource Center Report. Los Angeles, CA: UCLA Labor Center. (http://undocumentedanduninsured.org/wp-content/uploads/2014/04/UCLA-Undocumented-and-Uninsured-Part-1-web.pdf).

60. Plascencia, Leyva, Pena, and Waheed, *Undocumented and Uninsured, Part 1.*

61. Plascencia, Leyva, Pena, and Waheed, *Undocumented and Uninsured, Part 1.*

62. Holguin et al., "Respiratory Health in Migrant Populations."

63. Holguin et al., "Respiratory Health in Migrant Populations," 154.

64. Gonzalez, Jaime. 2015. "Hispanic Paradox: Why Immigrants Have a High Life Expectancy." BBC News, May 29. (http://www.bbc.com/news/world-U.S.-canada-32910129).

65. Gany, Francesca, Patricia Novo, Rebecca Dobslaw, and Jennifer Leng. 2014. "Urban Occupational Health in the Mexican and Latino/Latina Immigrant Population: A Literature Review." *Journal of Immigrant and Minority Health* 16(5): 846–55.

66. Gany, Novo, Dobslaw, and Leng. "Urban Occupational Health."

67. Flynn, Michael, Thomas R. Cunningham, Rebecca J. Guerin, Brenna Keller, Larry J. Chapman, Denis Hudson, and Cathy Salgado. 2015. *Overlapping Vulnerabilities: The Occupational Safety and Health of Young Workers in Small Construction Firms.* Cincinnati, OH: U.S. Department of Health and Human Services, Centers for Disease Control and Prevention, National Institute for Occupational Safety and Health, DHHS (NIOSH) Publication No. 2015- 178. (http://www.asse.org/assets/1/7/NIOSHreport_FinalDraft.pdf).

68. Chapman and Salgado, *Overlapping Vulnerabilities*, 851.

69. Torres and Wallace, "Migration Circumstances."

70. Torres and Wallace, "Migration Circumstances," 1625.

71. Plascencia, Leyva, Pena, and Waheed, *Undocumented and Uninsured, Part 4.*

72. Martinez et al., "Evaluating the Impact of Immigration Policies."

73. Martinez et al., "Evaluating the Impact of Immigration Policies," 946.

74. Martinez et al., "Evaluating the Impact of Immigration Policies," 946.

75. Martinez et al., "Evaluating the Impact of Immigration Policies," 964.

76. Martinez et al., "Evaluating the Impact of Immigration Policies," 948.

77. Ruiz-Casares, Mónica, Cécile Rousseau, Audry Laruin-Lamothe, Joanne Anneke Rummens, Phyllis Zelkowitz, François Crépeau, and Nicolas Steinmetz. 2012. "Access to Health Care for Undocumented Migrant Children and Pregnant Women: The Paradox Between

Values and Attitudes of Health Care Professionals." *Maternal and Child Health Journal* 17(2): 292–98.

78. Ortega, Rodriguez, and Bustamante, "Policy Dilemmas," 534.

79. Philbin, Morgan, Mark Hatzenbuehler, Somjen Frazer, Morgan Flake, Daniel Hagen, and Jennifer Hirsch. 2016. "Too Scared to Move?: A Mixed-Methods Analysis of State-Level Immigration Policies and Obesity Among Latinos in the United States." Population Association of America Conference, April. (https://paa.confex.com/paa/2016/mediafile/Extended-Abstract/Paper7648/PAA%202016%20Abstract_HIV%20Center%20Pilot%20Data_September%2025%202015_Philbin%20.pdf.)

80. White, Kari, Valerie A. Yeager, Nir Menachemi, and Isabel C. Scarinci. 2014. "Impact of Alabama's Immigration Law on Access to Health Care Among Latina Immigrants and Children: Implications for National Reform." *American Journal of Public Health* 104(3): 397–405.

81. White, Yeager, Menachemi, and Scarinci, "Impact of Alabama's Immigration Law," 403.

82. Martinez et al., "Evaluating the Impact of Immigration Policies," 965.

83. Fitzgerald, Elizabeth Moran, Judith G. Myers, and Paul Clark. 2016. "Nurses Need Not Be Guilty Bystanders: Caring for Vulnerable Immigrant Populations." *OJIN: The Online Journal of Issues in Nursing* 22(1): 8.

84. Fitzgerald, Myers, and Clark, "Nurses Need Not Be Guilty Bystanders."

85. Fitzgerald, Myers, and Clark, "Nurses Need Not Be Guilty Bystanders."

86. Aparicio, Ana. 2016. "Flint's Undocumented Immigrants Are Having Trouble Accessing Clean Water." Quartz, February 10. (http://qz.com/613960/flints-undocumented-immigrants-are-having-trouble-accessing-clean-water/).

87. Núñez-Alvarez, Arcela, Konane M. Martínez, Amy Ramos, and Fabiola Gastelum. 2007. *San Diego Firestorm 2007 Report: Fire Impact on Farmworkers & Migrant Communities in North County*. Report produced by the National Latino Research Center at California State University, San Marcos. (http://www.cidrap.umn.edu/sites/default/files/public/php/27048/San%20Diego%20Firestorm%202007%20Report.pdf).

88. Plascencia, Leyva, Pena, and Waheed, *Undocumented and Uninsured, Part 4.*

89. Castañeda and Melo, "Health Care Access for Latino Mixed-Status Families."

90. Castañeda and Melo, "Health Care Access for Latino Mixed-Status Families," 1899.

91. Martinez et al., "Evaluating the Impact of Immigration Policies," 965.

92. Capps, Randy, Michael Fix, and Jie Zong. 2016. "A Profile of U.S. Children with Unauthorized Immigrant Parents." Migration Policy Institute. (http://www.migrationpolicy.net).

93. Zayas and Bradlee, "Exiling Children, Creating Orphans."

94. Zayas and Bradlee, "Exiling Children, Creating Orphans," 171.

95. Gulbas, Lauren E., Luis H. Zayas, Hyunwoo Yoon, H. Szlyk, Sergio Aguilar-Gaxiola, and Guillermina Natera. 2016. "Deportation Experiences and Depression Among U.S. Citizen-Children with Undocumented Mexican Parents." *Child: Health, Care and Development* 42(2): 220–30.

96. García-Mellado, Diana. 2017. *The Lives of Latina/o Children in Mixed Immigration Status Families*. MA thesis in Sociological Practice at California State University San Marcos. (http://hdl.handle.net/10211.3/191114).

97. García-Mellado, *Lives of Latina/o Children*, 47–48.

98. García-Mellado, *Lives of Latina/o Children*, 48.

99. Allen, Brian, Erica M. Cisneros, and Alexandra Tellez. 2013. "The Children Left Behind: The Impact of Parental Deportation on Mental Health." *Journal of Child and Family Studies* 24(2): 386–92.

100. Allen, Cisneros, and Tellez, "The Children Left Behind," 390.

101. Gubernskaya, Zoya and Joanna Dreby. 2017. "U.S. Immigration Policy and the Case for Family Unity." *Journal on Migration and Human Security* 5(2): 417–30.

102. Larrimore, Jeff, Mario Arthur-Bentil, Sam Dodini, and Logan Thomas. 2015. *Report on the Economic Well-Being of U.S. Households in 2014.* (https://www.federalreserve.gov/econresdata/2014-report-economic-well-being-U.S.-households-201505.pdf).

103. Otto, Mary. 2017. *Teeth: The Story of Beauty, Inequality, and the Struggle for Oral Health in America.* New York: The New Press.

104. Gelatt, Julia. 2016. "Immigration Status and the Healthcare Access and Health of Children of Immigrants." *Social Science Quarterly* 97(3): 540–54.

105. Castañeda and Melo, "Health Care Access for Latino Mixed-Status Families."

106. St. Paul Children's Dental Clinic (http://www.stpaulchildren.org/dental/).

107. Velez, Diana, Ana Palomo-Zerfas, Arcela Nunez-Alvarez, Guadalupe X. Ayala, and Tracy L. Finlayson. 2017. "Facilitators and Barriers to Dental Care Among Mexican Migrant Women and Their Families in North San Diego County." *Journal of Immigrant and Minority Health* 19(5): 1–11.

108. Velez et al., "Facilitators and Barriers to Dental Care."

109. Torres and Wallace, "Migration Circumstances."

110. Manriquez, Stephanie. 2015. "For Immigrants, Status and Stigma Affect Mental Health, Few Resources Exist—Social Justice News Nexus." Social Justice News Nexus. (http://sjnnchicago.org/for-immigrants-status-and-stigma-affect-mental-health-few-resources-exist/).

111. Fortuna and Porche, "Clinical Issues and Challenges."

112. Manriquez, "For Immigrants, Status and Stigma Affect Mental Health." (http://sjnnchicago.org/for-immigrants-status-and-stigma-affect-mental-health-few-resources-exist/).

113. Manriquez, "For Immigrants, Status and Stigma Affect Mental Health."

114. Stacciarini, Jeanne-Marie R., Rebekah F. Smith, Brenda Wiens, Awilda Perez, Barbara Locke, and Melody LaFlam. 2015. "I Didn't Ask to Come to This Country . . . I Was a Child: The Mental Health Implications of Growing Up Undocumented." *Journal of Immigrant & Minority Health* 17(4): 1225–30.

115. Pulgar, Camila A., Grisel Trejo, Cynthia Suerken, Edward H. Ip, Thomas A. Arcury, and Sara A. Quandt. 2016. "Economic Hardship and Depression Among Women in Latino Farmworker Families." *Journal of Immigrant and Minority Health* 18(3): 497–504.

116. Pulgar et al., "Economic Hardship and Depression Among Women."

117. López-Cevallos, Daniel F. and S. Marie Harvey. 2016. "Foreign-Born Latinos Living in Rural Areas Are More Likely to Experience Health Care Discrimination: Results from *Proyecto de Salud para Latinos.*" *Journal of Immigrant and Minority Health* 18(4): 928–34.

118. Gonzales, Roberto G., Carola Suárez-Orozco, and Maria Cecilia Dedios-Sanguineti. 2013. "No Place to Belong: Contextualizing Concepts of Mental Health Among Undocumented Immigrant Youth in the United States." *American Behavioral Scientist* 57(8): 1174–99.

119. Gonzales, Suárez-Orozco, and Dedios-Sanguineti, "No Place to Belong," 1185.

120. Gonzales, Suárez-Orozco, and Dedios-Sanguineti, "No Place to Belong," 1187.

121. Gonzales, Suárez-Orozco, and Dedios-Sanguineti, "No Place to Belong," 1190.

122. Canseco, Omar and Marisol Clark-Ibáñez. 2015. "After College Graduation: Bittersweet." In *Undocumented Latino Youth—Navigating Their Worlds.* Boulder: Lynne Rienner Publishers, Chapter 8 (pp. 143–61).

123. Canseco and Clark-Ibáñez, *Undocumented Latino Youth*, 145.

124. Manriquez, "For Immigrants, Status and Stigma Affect Mental Health."

125. Martinez et al., "Evaluating the Impact of Immigration Policies," 965.

126. Livaudais, Maria, Edward D. Vargas, Gabriel Sanchez, and Melina Juarez. 2015. "Latinos' Connections to Immigrants: How Knowing a Deportee Impacts Latino Health." Association for Public Policy Analysis and Management 37th Annual Fall Research Conference—The Golden Age of Evidence-Based Policy. Miami, FL. November 14.

127. Plascencia, Leyva, Pena, and Waheed, *Undocumented and Uninsured, Part 3*.

128. Plascencia, Leyva, Pena, and Waheed, *Undocumented and Uninsured, Part 3*.

129. Plascencia, Leyva, Pena, and Waheed, *Undocumented and Uninsured, Part 3*.

130. Lopez, William D., Daniel J. Kruger, Jorge Delva, Mikel Llanes, Charo Ledón, Adreanne Waller, Melanie Harner, Ramiro Martinez, Laura Sanders, Margaret Harner, and Barbara Israel. 2017. "Health Implications of an Immigration Raid: Findings from a Latino Community in the Midwestern United States." *Journal Immigrant & Minority Health* 19(3): 702–8.

131. Lopez et al., "Health Implications of an Immigration Raid," 706.

132. Gonzalez, "For Undocumented Women Seeking Reproductive Healthcare."

133. Martinez et al., "Evaluating the Impact of Immigration Policies."

134. Wessler, Seth Freed. 2016. "'This Man Will Almost Certainly Die.'" *The Nation*, January 28. (https://www.thenation.com/article/privatized-immigrant-prison-deaths/).

135. Dober, Greg. 2014. "Corizon Needs a Checkup: Problems with Privatized Correctional Healthcare." *Prison Legal News*, March 15. (https://www.prisonlegalnews.org/news/2014/mar/15/corizon-needs-a-checkup-problems-with-privatized-correctional-healthcare/).

136. Turck, Mary. 2016. "Death By Privatization in U.S. Prisons." (http://america.aljazeera.com/opinions/2016/2/death-by-privatization-in-U.S.-prisons.html).

137. http://www.humanrightsfirst.org/sites/default/files/HRFFloresAmicusBrief.pdf.

138. Margolis, Mary Elizabeth. 2016. "Medical and Mental Health Experts Urge the Ninth Circuit Court to Uphold Flores Ruling to End Family Immigration Detention." March 30. (http://www.humanrightsfirst.org/press-release/medical-and-mental-health-experts-urge-ninth-circuit-court-uphold-flores-ruling-end).

139. *Flores v. Lynch.* 2016. *Jenny Lisette Flores, et al. versus Loretta Lynch, Attorney General of the United States.* "Brief for The American Academy of Child and Adolescent Psychiatry and The National Association of Social Workers as *Amici Curiae* Supporting Appellees." D.C. Case No. 2:85-cv-04544-DMG-AGR. February 23. (http://www.humanrightsfirst.org/sites/default/files/HRFFloresAmicusBrief.pdf).

140. Phillips, Kristine. 2018. "'America Is Better Than This': What a Doctor Saw in a Texas Shelter for Migrant Children." *Washington Post*, June 16. (https://www.washingtonpost.com/news/post-nation/wp/2018/06/16/america-is-better-than-this-what-a-doctor-saw-in-a-texas-shelter-for-migrant-children/?utm_term=.5d37f1e4a992).

141. Rojas-Flores, Lisseth, Mari L. Clements, Koo J. Hwang, and Judy London. 2017. "Trauma and Psychological Distress in Latino Citizen Children Following Parental Detention and Deportation." *Psychological Trauma: Theory, Research, Practice, and Policy* 9(3): 352–61.

142. Ruiz-Casares, Mónica, Cécile Rouseau, Audry Laruin-Lamothe, Joanne Anneke Rummens, Phyllis Zelkowitz, François Crépeau, and Nicolas Steinmetz. 2012. "Access to Health Care for Undocumented Migrant Children and Pregnant Women: The Paradox Between Values and Attitudes of Health Care Professionals." *Maternal and Child Health Journal* 17(2): 292–98.

143. Shah, Sural. 2014. "Defects in the Safety Net: When the Emergency Option Is the Only Option." *Access Denied—A Conversation on Unauthorized Im/migrants and Health.* (https://accessdeniedblog.wordpress.com/2014/02/27/defects-in-the-safety-net-when-the-emergency-option-is-the-only-option-sural-shah-2/).

144. Karan, Abraar. 2015. "It Costs Nothing to Care: Why We Need to Provide Health Insurance for Undocumented U.S. Residents." (http://thehealthcareblog.com/blog/2015/09/30/it-costs-nothing-to-care-why-we-need-to-provide-health-insurance-for-undocumented-people/).

145. Grubbs, Vanessa. 2014. "Undocumented Immigrants and Kidney Transplant: Costs and Controversy." *Health Affairs* 33(2): 332–35.

146. Grubbs, "Undocumented Immigrants and Kidney Transplant."

147. Plascencia, Leyva, Pena, and Waheed. *Undocumented and Uninsured, Part 2.*

148. Castañeda and Melo, "Health Care Access for Latino Mixed-Status Families."

149. Castañeda and Melo, "Health Care Access for Latino Mixed-Status Families."

150. Castañeda and Melo, "Health Care Access for Latino Mixed-Status Families," 1894.

151. Gómez, Sofía and Heide Castañeda. 2018. "'Recognize Our Humanity': Immigrant Youth Voices on Health Care in Arizona's Restrictive Political Environment." *Qualitative Health Research*, February: 1–12.

152. Center for Reproductive Rights. 2015. *Nuestro Texas: A Reproductive Rights Agenda for Latinas.* Report with the National Latina Institute for Reproductive Health, January. (https://www.reproductiverights.org/learning-from-nuestro-texas).

CHAPTER 6

1. Schwartz, Rafi. 2017. "ICE Agents Ate Breakfast at a Michigan Restaurant, Then Detained Three of Its Workers." Fusion, May 25. (http://fusion.kinja.com/ice-agents-ate-breakfast-at-a-michigan-restaurant-then-1795538187).

2. Shahshahani, Azadeh. 2014. "Living Nightmare for Detained Immigrants in Georgia." *Huffpost Politics* (Blog), January 23. (http://www.huffingtonpost.com/azadeh-shahshahani/living-nightmare-for-deta_b_6208916.html).

3. Shahshahani, "Living Nightmare for Detained Immigrants."

4. Rose, Joel. 2018. "A Toddler's Death Adds to Concerns About Migrant Detention." National Public Radio, August 28. (https://www.npr.org/2018/08/28/642738732/a-toddlers-death-adds-to-concerns-about-migrant-detention).

5. Schwartz, Rafi. 2017. "Baltimore Attorney Arrested for Allegedly Telling a Rape Victim That Trump Would Deport Her for Testifying." Fusion, May 24. http://fusion.kinja.com/baltimore-attorney-arrested-for-allegedly-telling-a-rap-1795517129.

6. Calavita, Kitty. 1996. "The New Politics of Immigration: 'Balanced Budget Conservatism' and the Symbolism of Proposition 187." *Social Problems* 43(3): 284–305.

7. Fernandes, Deepa. 2007. *Targeted: National Security and the Business of Immigration.* St. Paul, MN: Seven Stories Press.

8. Kanstroom, Daniel. 2012. *Aftermath: Deportation Law and the New American Diaspora.* New York: Oxford University Press.

9. Cuauhtémoc Hernández García, César. 2015. *Crimmigration Law.* American Bar Association Publishing; Stumpf, Juliet P. 2006. "The Crimmigration Crisis: Immigrants, Crime

and Sovereign Power." Bepress Legal Series Working Paper 1635. (http://law.bepress.com/expresso/eps/1635.).

10. Golash-Boza, Tanya. 2009. "The Immigration Industrial Complex: Why We Enforce Immigration Policies Destined to Fail." *Sociology Compass* (3/2): 295–309.

11. Welch, Michael. 2002. *Detained: Immigration Laws and the Expanding I.N.S. Jail Complex.* Philadelphia: Temple University Press.

12. Cuauhtémoc Hernández García, César. 2008. "No Human Being Is Illegal: Moving Beyond Deportation Law." *Monthly Review* 60(2): 23–31.

13. De Genova, Nicholas. 2016. "Detention, Deportation and Waiting: Toward a Theory of Migrant Detainability." Global Detention Project Working Paper No. 18, November. (https://www.globaldetentionproject.org/wp-content/uploads/2016/12/De-Genova-GDP-Paper-2016.pdf).

14. Menjívar, Cecilia and Leisy Abrego. 2012. *Legal Violence in the Lives of Immigrants: How Immigration Enforcement Affects Families, Schools, and Workplaces.* Washington, DC: Center for American Progress, December.

15. Trujillo-Pagán, Nicole. 2014. "Emphasizing the 'Complex' in the 'Immigration Industrial Complex'." *Critical Sociology* 40(1): 29–46.

16. De Genova, Nicholas. 2002. "Migrant 'Illegality' and Deportability in Everyday Life." *Annual Review of Anthropology* 31(1): 419–47.

17. De Genova, "Migrant 'Illegality' and Deportability"; Coutin, Susan Bibler. 2015. "Deportation Studies: Origins, Themes and Directions." *Journal of Ethnic and Migration Studies* 41(4): 671–81.

18. Kolhatkar, Sonali. 2014. "After 20 Years, NAFTA Leaves Mexico's Economy in Ruins." Common Dreams, January 10. (https://www.commondreams.org/views/2014/01/10/after-20-years-nafta-leaves-mexicos-economy-ruins).

19. Trujillo-Pagán, "Emphasizing the 'Complex'."

20. Public Citizen. 2017. "Central America Free Trade Agreement." (https://www.citizen.org/our-work/globalization-and-trade/nafta-wto-other-trade-pacts/cafta).

21. Ewing, Walter, Daniel Martinez, and Rubén G. Rumbaut. 2015. "The Criminalization of Immigration in the United States." American Immigration Council, July 13. (https://www.americanimmigrationcouncil.org/research/criminalization-immigration-united-states).

22. Ewing, Martinez, and Rumbaut, "The Criminalization of Immigration."

23. Ewing, Martinez, and Rumbaut, "The Criminalization of Immigration."

24. TRAC Immigration. 2018. "Profiling Who ICE Detains—Few Committed Any Crime." Syracuse University, October 9 (http://www.trac.syr.edu/immigration/reports/530/).

25. Moyles, Trina and K. J. Dakin. 2016. "Female Migrant Farmworkers Push Back Against Machismo and Abuse in California's Wine Country." *Yes! Magazine*, June 21. (http://www.yesmagazine.org/people-power/female-migrant-farmworkers-push-back-against-machismo-and-abuse-in-californias-wine-country-20160621).

26. University of North Carolina School of Law Immigration/Human Rights Policy Clinic. 2014. *Visa Denied—The Political Geography of the U Visa: Eligibility as a Matter of Locale.* University of North Carolina School of Law. (http://www.law.unc.edu/documents/clinicalprograms/uvisa/fullreport.pdf).

27. Linthicum, Kate. 2015. "Safety for Immigrant Victims Put On Hold by U-Visa Delay." *Los Angeles Times*, February 1. (http://www.latimes.com/local/california/la-me-u-visa-20150202-story.html).

28. Mulholland, Audrey. 2016. "Labor Trafficking in the United States: Limited Victim Relief for Undocumented Immigrants." Washington, DC: American University Center for Human Rights and Humanitarian Law, November 2. (http://hrbrief.org/2016/11/labor-trafficking-united-states-limited-victim-relief-undocumented-immigrants/).

29. Mulholland, "Labor Trafficking in the United States."

30. Lindberg, Kari. 2017. "Human Trafficking Victims Are Scared to Apply for Visas Under Trump." Vice News, June 12. (https://news.vice.com/en_ca/article/434pkj/human-trafficking-victims-are-scared-to-apply-for-visas-under-trump).

31. Villareal, Alexandra. 2018. "US Deporting Crime Victims While They Wait for U Visa." *Chicago Sun-Times*, July 20. (https://chicago.suntimes.com/immigration/us-deporting-crime-victims-u-visa-bernardo-reyes-rodriguez-donald-trump/).

32. Sipes, Sam. 2018. "Immigration Change Could Protect Human Traffickers." *USA Today News Press*, August 23. (https://www.news-press.com/story/opinion/contributors/2018/08/23/immigration-change-could-protect-human-traffickers/1073511002/).

33. Sipes, "Immigration Change Could Protect Human Traffickers."

34. Lee, Patrick G. 2017. "What Customs and Border Patrol Can and Can't Do." *Pacific Standard*, March 13. (https://psmag.com/news/what-customs-and-border-officials-can-and-cant-do).

35. American Civil Liberties Union. 2015. "Customs and Border Protection's (CBP's) 100-Mile Rule." Washington, DC: American Civil Liberties Union, September 14. (https://www.aclu.org/sites/default/files/assets/14_9_15_cbp_100-mile_rule_final.pdf).

36. American Civil Liberties Union, "Customs and Border Protection's (CBP's) 100-Mile Rule."

37. American Civil Liberties Union. 2017. "The Constitution in the 100-Mile Border Zone." Washington, DC: American Civil Liberties Union. (https://www.aclu.org/other/constitution-100-mile-border-zone?redirect=technology-and-liberty/fact-sheet-us-constitution-free-zone).

38. Misra, Tanvi. 2018. "Inside the Massive U.S. 'Border Zone'." *CityLab*, May 14. (https://www.citylab.com/equity/2018/05/who-lives-in-border-patrols-100-mile-zone-probably-you-mapped/558275/).

39. Mallonee, Laura. 2016. "The Invisible Security of Canada's Seemingly Chill Border." *Wired*, April 1. (https://www.wired.com/2016/04/invisible-security-canadas-seemingly-chill-border/).

40. Ryman, Anne, Dennis Wagner, Rob O'Dell, and Kirsten Crow. 2017. "The Wall." *USA Today*. (https://www.usatoday.com/border-wall/).

41. Kohavi, Noya. 2018. "What Trump's 'Big, Fat, Beautiful' Mexico Wall Will Look Like. *Haaretz*, January 26. (https://www.haaretz.com/us-news/.premium.MAGAZINE-what-trump-s-big-fat-beautiful-mexico-wall-will-look-like-1.5766871).

42. Morrissey, Kate. 2018. "With Border Wall Funding Still in Question, Construction Finishes on Calexico Barrier." *San Diego Union Tribune,* October 10. (http://www.sandiegouniontribune.com/news/immigration/sd-me-border-wall-20181010-story.html).

43. Kohavi, "What Trump's 'Big, Fat, Beautiful' Mexico Wall."

44. American Civil Liberties Union, "Customs and Border Protection's (CBP's) 100-Mile Rule."

45. American Civil Liberties Union, "Customs and Border Protection's (CBP's) 100-Mile Rule."

46. Southern Border Communities Coalition. 2017. "Border Patrol Abuses." Southern Border Communities Coalition. (http://www.southernborder.org/border-patrol-abuses).

47. Inskeep, Steve. 2014. "Border Agency Chief Opens Up About Deadly Force Cases." National Public Radio, July 18. (http://www.npr.org/2014/07/18/332028125/border-agency-chief-opens-up-about-deadly-force-cases).

48. Penman, Maggie. 2017. "High Court to Hear Case of Mexican Boy Killed in Cross-Border Shooting." National Public Radio, February 20. (http://www.npr.org/sections/thetwo-way/2017/02/20/516275461/high-court-to-hear-arguments-in-case-of-mexican-boy-killed-in-cross-border-shoot).

49. U.S. Customs and Border Patrol. 2017. "CBP Use of Force Statistics." Department of Homeland Security, June 15. (https://www.cbp.gov/newsroom/stats/cbp-use-force).

50. U.S. Customs and Border Patrol, "CBP Use of Force Statistics."

51. Buch, Jason. 2018. "Appeals Again Says Family of Slain Teen Can't Sue Border Patrol." *San Antonio Express-News*, March 21. (https://www.expressnews.com/news/local/article/Appeals-again-says-family-of-slain-teen-can-t-12771895.php).

52. Buch, "Appeals Again Say Family of Slain Teen."

53. U.S. Immigration and Customs Enforcement. 2017. "What We Do." Washington, DC: Department of Homeland Security. (https://www.ice.gov/overview).

54. Kandel, William A. 2016. "Interior Immigration Enforcement: Criminal Alien Programs." Congressional Research Service, September 8. (https://fas.org/sgp/crs/homesec/R44627.pdf).

55. Kandel, "Interior Immigration Enforcement."

56. Armenta, Amada. 2017. *Protect, Serve, and Deport: The Rise of Policing as Immigration Enforcement.* Oakland: University of California Press.

57. Snell, Robert. 2017. "Feds Use Anti-Terror Tool to Hunt the Undocumented." *Detroit News,* May 18. (http://www.detroitnews.com/story/news/local/detroit-city/2017/05/18/cell-snooping-fbi-immigrant/101859616/).

58. American Civil Liberties Union. 2017. "ACLU Seeks Documents on ICE's Use of Cell Phone Trackers," May 19. (https://www.aclu.org/news/aclu-seeks-documents-ices-use-cell-phone-trackers).

59. American Civil Liberties Union. 2015. "ACLU Announces Settlement in Lawsuit Over Warrantless Raid by US Immigration Agents and Nashville Police." New York, ACLU, July 27. (https://www.aclu.org/news/aclu-announces-settlement-lawsuit-over-warrantless-raid-us-immigration-agents-and-nashville-0).

60. See The White House. 2017. *Executive Order: Enhancing the Public Safety in the Interior of the United States*, January 25. Washington, DC: The Office of the Press Secretary. (https://www.whitehouse.gov/the-press-office/2017/01/25/presidential-executive-order-enhancing-public-safety-interior-united); The White House. 2017. *Executive Order: Border Security and Immigration Enforcement Improvements*, January 25. Washington, DC: The Office of the Press Secretary. (https://www.whitehouse.gov/the-press-office/2017/01/25/executive-order-border-security-and-immigration-enforcement-improvements).

61. Domonoske, Camila. 2017. "What's New in Those DHS Memos on Immigration Enforcement?" National Public Radio, February 22. (http://www.npr.org/sections/thetwo-way/2017/02/22/516649344/whats-new-in-those-dhs-memos-on-immigration-enforcement).

62. American Civil Liberties Union. 2017. "ACLU Comment on ICE Arrest of Domestic Abuse Victim." ACLU, February 17. (https://www.aclu.org/news/aclu-comment-ice-arrest-domestic-abuse-victim).

63. Wadhia, Shoba Sivaprasad. 2011. "The Morton Memo and Prosecutorial Discretion: An Overview." American Immigration Council, July 20. (https://www.americanimmigration-council.org/research/morton-memo-and-prosecutorial-discretion-overview).

64. Chavez-Peterson, Norma. 2017. "Yes, We Need a Wall—Between Local Police and Federal Immigration Enforcement." Voice of San Diego, June 8. (http://www.voiceofsandiego.org/topics/opinion/yes-need-wall-local-police-federal-immigration-enforcement/).

65. Medina, Jennifer. 2017. "Too Scared to Report Sexual Abuse. The Fear: Deportation." *New York Times*, April 30. (https://www.nytimes.com/2017/04/30/us/immigrants-deporta-tion-sexual-abuse.html?login=email&auth=login-email).

66. U.S. Department of Homeland Security. 2017. "Memo: Enforcement of the Immigra-tion Laws to Serve the National Interest." February 20. Washington, DC. (https://www.dhs.gov/publication/enforcement-immigration-laws-serve-national-interest).

67. U.S. Department of Homeland Security, "Memo: Enforcement of the Immigration Laws."

68. Walker, Chris. 2017. "ICE Agents Are Infiltrating Denver's Courts, and There's a Video to Prove It." *Westword*, February 24. (http://www.westword.com/news/ice-agents-are-infiltrating-denvers-courts-and-theres-a-video-to-prove-it-8826897).

69. Phillips, Noelle. 2017. "Videos of ICE Making Arrests at Denver's Courthouse Renew Calls for City to Push Back Against White House Policies." *Denver Post*, May 9. (http://www.denverpost.com/2017/05/09/video-ice-arrests-denver-courthouse-immigration-policy/).

70. Phillips, "Videos of ICE Making Arrests."

71. Medina, Jennifer. 2017. "Immigration Agents Should Not 'Stalk' Courts, California Justice Says." *New York Times,* March 16. (https://www.nytimes.com/2017/03/16/us/immi-gration-agents-should-not-stalk-courts-california-justice-says.html).

72. Pugliese, Nicholas. 2017. "Immigration Arrests at N.J. Courthouses Having a 'Chilling Effect,' Attorneys Say." NorthJersey.com, June 5. (http://www.northjersey.com/story/news/new-jersey/2017/06/05/immigration-arrests-continue-n-j-courthouses/370974001/).

73. Alvarado, Monsy and Hannan Adely. 2017. "N.J. Chief Justice Asks Feds Not to Arrest Immigrants at Courthouses." NorthJersey.com, April 19. (http://www.northjersey.com/story/news/politics/2017/04/19/nj-supreme-court-chief-justice-asks-ice-dhs-not-arrest-undocumented-immigrants-court/100663528/).

74. Sullivan, S. P. 2017. "N.J. Lawmakers Call Hearing on ICE Courthouse Arrests Op-posed by State's Top Judge." NJ.com, June 6. (http://www.nj.com/politics/index.ssf/2017/06/nj_lawmakers_call_hearing_on_ice_courthouse_arrest.html).

75. O'Leary, Mary. 2017. "Connecticut Judge Seeks to Protect Courthouses from ICE." *New Haven Register*, June 8. (http://www.nhregister.com/general-news/20170608/connect-icut-judge-seeks-to-protect-courthouses-from-ice); O'Sullivan, Joseph. 2017. "Chief Justice Asks ICE Not to Track Immigrants at State Courthouses." *Seattle Times,* March 22. (http://www.seattletimes.com/seattle-news/politics/chief-justice-asks-ice-not-to-track-immigrants-at-state-courthouses/).

76. Gomez, Alan. 2017. "Trump Tells DREAMers to 'Rest Easy'—but One in Mexico Can't." *USA Today,* April 21. (https://www.usatoday.com/story/news/world/2017/04/21/trump-tells-dreamers-to-rest-easy-responds-to-juan-manuel-montes-case/100757434/).

77. Gomez, Alan and David Agren. 2017. "First DREAMer Is Deported Under Trump." *USA Today*, April 18. (https://www.usatoday.com/story/news/world/2017/04/18/first-pro-tected-dreamer-deported-under-trump/100583274/)

78. Gomez and Agren, "First DREAMer Is Deported Under Trump."

79. Gonzales, Richard. 2017. "DREAMer Deportation Case Raises Questions on Trump's Deferred Action Policy." National Public Radio, April 18. (http://www.npr.org/sections/thetwo-way/2017/04/18/524610150/first-dreamer-protected-by-deferred-action-program-is-deported).

80. Parvini, Sarah. 2017. "Cal State L.A. Student Activist Detained by Border Patrol Is Released." *Los Angeles Times*, June 9. (http://www.latimes.com/local/lanow/la-me-ln-immigration-activist-arrest-20170609-story.html).

81. Parvini, "Cal State L.A. Student Activist."

82. Rhodan, Maya and Elizabeth Dias. 2017. "Immigration Agents Arrested Men Outside a Church. But Officials Say It Was Just a Coincidence." *Time*, February 17. (http://time.com/4674729/immigrations-church-sensitive-policy-concerns/).

83. Hanson, Jessica. 2017. "School Settings Are Sensitive Locations That Should Be Off-Limits to Immigration Enforcement." National Immigration Law Center, May 4. (https://www.nilc.org/news/the-torch/5-4-17/).

84. U.S. Department of Homeland Security. *Budget in Brief,* Fiscal Year 2018. Washington, DC. (https://www.dhs.gov/sites/default/files/publications/FY_2016_DHS_Budget in Brief.pdf); Trujillo-Pagán, "Emphasizing the 'Complex'."

85. Naylor, Brian. 2017. "Trump's Plan to Hire 15,000 Border Patrol and ICE Agents Won't Be Easy." National Public Radio, February 23. (https://www.npr.org/2017/02/23/516712980/trumps-plan-to-hire-15-000-border-patrol-and-ice-agents-wont-be-easy-to-fulfill).

86. Pugliese, "Immigration Arrests at N.J. Courthouses."

87. Domonsoke, Camila. 2018. "Trump Administration Transferred $9.8 Million from FEMA to ICE." National Public Radio, September 12. (https://www.npr.org/2018/09/12/647021316/trump-administration-transferred-9-8-million-from-fema-to-ice).

88. Galvan, Christina. N.d. "What Does My Notice to Appear Mean?" NOLO. (http://www.nolo.com/legal-encyclopedia/what-does-my-notice-appear-nta-mean.html).

89. Galvan, "What Does My Notice to Appear Mean?"

90. Kanstroom, *Aftermath*.

91. Kanstroom, *Aftermath*.

92. U.S. Department of Justice Executive Office for Immigration Review. 2004. *Fact Sheet: Forms of Relief from Removal.* (https://www.justice.gov/sites/default/files/eoir/legacy/2004/08/05/ReliefFromRemoval.pdf.)

93. American Bar Association. 2006. *Tips for Appealing to the Board of Immigration Appeals (BIA).* Washington, DC: American Bar Association. (https://www.americanbar.org/content/dam/aba/publications/commission_on_immigration/tips_bia_appeals2006.authcheckdam.pdf).

94. Lonegan, Brian and the Immigration Law Unit of the Legal Aid Society. 2006. *Immigration Detention and Removal: A Guide for Detainees and Their Families.* New York: Legal Aid Society. (https://www.informedimmigrant.com/wp-content/uploads/2017/01/detention-removalguide_2006-02.pdf).

95. Marizco, Michel. 2017. "A Harder Punishment for First-Time Offenders Who Cross U.S. Border Illegally." *Fronteras*, August 18. (http://fronterasdesk.org/content/10773/harder-punishment-first-time-offenders-who-cross-us-border-illegally).

96. Stiven, James. 2018. "Commentary: Mass Criminalization of Migrants Via Operation Streamline Is Costly, Cruel, and Unworkable Policy." *San Diego Union Tribune*, June 21. (http://www.sandiegouniontribune.com/opinion/commentary/sd-oe-utbg-migrants-justice-operation-streamline-20180621-story.html).

97. Marizco, "A Harder Punishment for First-Time Offenders."

98. Lydgate, Johanna Jacobbi. 2010. "Assembly-Line Justice: A Review of Operation Streamline." *California Law Review* 98: 481–544. (http://scholarship.law.berkeley.edu/californialawreview/vol98/iss2/5).

99. Lydgate, "Assembly-Line Justice."

100. Puhl, Emily. 2015. "Prosecuting the Persecuted: How Operation Streamline and Expedited Removal Violate Article 31 of the Convention on the Status of Refugees and 1967 Protocol." *Berkeley La Raza Law Journal* 25(3): 88–109.

101. Lydgate, "Assembly-Line Justice."

102. Spagat, Elliot, Gaby Rodriguez, Christina Bravo, and Brie Stimson. 2018. "San Diego Begins Mass Immigration Hearings with 'Operation Streamline'." NBC 7 San Diego. (https://www.nbcsandiego.com/news/local/San-Diego-US-District-Court-Mass-Immigration-Trials-Operation-Streamline-487692771.html).

103. Prendergast, Curt. 2018. "Operation Streamline Border-Crossing Cases Spiked 71 Percent in Tucson." Tucson.com, April 22. (https://tucson.com/news/local/operation-streamline-border-crossing-cases-spiked-percent-in-tucson/article_e3700d7d-9328-5112-ab89-6e97a3b3322e.html).

104. U.S. Department of Justice. 2018. "Attorney General Sessions Delivers Remarks Discussing the Enforcement Actions of the Trump Administration." Justice News, May 7. (https://www.justice.gov/opa/speech/attorney-general-sessions-delivers-remarks-discussing-immigration-enforcement-actions).

105. Jewett, Christina and Shefali Luthra. 2018. "Immigrant Infants Too Young to Talk Called into Court to Defend Themselves." *The Texas Tribune,* July 18. (https://www.texastribune.org/2018/07/18/immigrant-separated-families-infant-court-defend-donald-trump-zero-tol/).

106. Jewett and Luthra, "Immigrant Infants Too Young to Talk."

107. Jewett and Luthra, "Immigrant Infants Too Young to Talk."

108. Markon, Jerry. 2016. "Can a 3-Year-Old Defend Herself in Immigration Court? This Judge Says Yes." *Washington Post*, March 5. (https://www.washingtonpost.com/world/national-security/can-a-3-year-old-represent-herself-in-immigration-court-this-judge-thinks-so/2016/03/03/5be59a32-db25-11e5-925f-1d10062cc82d_story.html?utm_term=.31d4d3700b29).

109. Markon, "Can a 3-Year-Old Defend Herself?"

110. Root, Jay and Shannon Najmabadi. 2018. "Kids in Exchange for Deportation: Detained Migrants Say They Were Told They Could Get Their Kids Back on Way Out of U.S." *Texas Tribune*, June 24. (https://www.texastribune.org/2018/06/24/kids-exchange-deportation-migrants-claim-they-were-promised-they-could/).

111. *Democracy Now!*. 2018. "Trump Administration Hints It May Resume Family Separation at Border; ACLU Says 'Public Outcry Is Critical'." DemocracyNow.org, October 15. (https://www.democracynow.org/2018/10/15/trump_admin_hints_it_may_resume).

112. Amnesty International. 2018. *USA: "You Don't Have Any Rights Here": Illegal Pushbacks, Arbitrary Detention & Ill Treatment of Asylum-Seekers in the United States.* London: Amnesty International Ltd. (https://www.amnestyusa.org/wp-content/uploads/2018/10/You-Dont-Have-Any-Rights-Here.pdf).

113. Hennessy-Fiske, Molly. 2018. "U.S. Is Separating Immigrant Parents and Children to Discourage Others, Activists Say." *Los Angeles Times*, February 20. (http://www.latimes.com/nation/la-na-immigrant-family-separations-2018-story.html).

114. *Democracy Now!*, "Trump Administration Hints."

115. *Democracy Now!*, "Trump Administration Hints."

116. Global Detention Project. 2016. "Immigration Detention in the United States." GlobalDetentionProject.org, May 3. (https://www.globaldetentionproject.org/immigration-detention-in-the-united-states).

117. Pauly, Madison. 2017. "The Private Prison Industry Is Licking Its Chops Over Trump's Deportation Plans." *Mother Jones*, February 21. (http://www.motherjones.com/politics/2017/02/trumps-immigration-detention-center-expansion).

118. Global Detention Project, "Immigration Detention in the United States."

119. Carson, Bethany and Eleana Diaz. 2015. "Payoff: How Congress Ensures Private Prison Profit with an Immigrant Detention Quota." GrassrootsLeadership.org. (http://grassrootsleadership.org/reports/payoff-how-congress-ensures-private-prison-profit-immigrant-detention-quota); Miroff, Nick. 2013. "Controversial Quota Drives Immigrant Detention Boom." *Washington Post*, October 13. (https://www.washingtonpost.com/world/controversial-quota-drives-immigration-detention-boom/2013/10/13/09bb689e-214c-11e3-ad1a-1a919f2ed890_story.html?utm_term=.c2f67293bbd3).

120. Benenson, Laurence. 2018. "The Math of Immigration Detention 2018 Update: Costs Continue to Multiply." National Immigration Forum, May 9. (http: https://immigrationforum.org/article/math-immigration-detention-2018-update-costs-continue-mulitply/).

121. Pauly, "The Private Prison Industry."

122. TRAC Immigration. 2018. "Profiling Who ICE Detains."

123. TRAC Immigration, "Profiling Who ICE Detains."

124. TRAC Immigration, "Profiling Who ICE Detains."

125. Cuauhtémoc Hernández García, César. 2014. "Immigration as Punishment." *UCLA Law Review* 61: 1346–1414.

126. Hernández García, "Immigration as Punishment."

127. Hernández García, "Immigration as Punishment."

128. Loewenstein, Anthony. 2016. "Private Prisons Are Cashing In on Refugees' Desperation." *New York Times*, February 25. (http://www.nytimes.com/2016/02/25/opinion/private-prisons-are-cashing-in-on-refugees-desperation.html).

129. Diaz, Melanie and Timothy Keen. 2015. "How US Private Prisons Profit from Immigrant Detention." Council on Hemispheric Affairs, May 12. (http://www.coha.org/how-us-private-prisons-profit-from-immigrant-detention/).

130. Diaz and Keen, "How US Private Prisons Profit."

131. Hoffman, Meredith. 2015. "How US Immigrant Detention Facilities Get Away with Being Complete Hellholes." VICE News, October 21. (https://news.vice.com/article/how-us-immigrant-detention-facilities-get-away-with-being-complete-hellholes).

132. Hoffman, "How US Immigrant Detention Facilities."

133. Hoffman, "How US Immigrant Detention Facilities."

134. Hoffman, "How US Immigrant Detention Facilities."

135. Hoffman, "How US Immigrant Detention Facilities."

136. Cruz, Melissa. 2018. "Surprise Government Inspection Finds Nooses in ICE Detention Center, Doctors Refusing to Treat Immigrant Detainees." Immigration Impact, October 3. (http://immigrationimpact.com/2018/10/03/inspection-finds-nooses-ice-detention-center/).

137. Cruz, "Surprise Government Inspection Finds Nooses."

138. Dinan, Stephen. 2015. "Illegal Immigrant Detention Centers Rife with Abuses, U.S. Civil Rights Commission Report Finds." *Washington Times,* September 17. (http://www.

washingtontimes.com/news/2015/sep/17/illegal-immigrant-detention-centers-rife-abuses-us/?page=all).

139. Dinan, "Illegal Immigrant Detention Centers."

140. American Civil Liberties Union. 2014. *Warehoused and Forgotten: Immigrants Trapped in Our Shadow Private Prison System.* Washington, DC and Houston, TX. (https://www.aclu.org/sites/default/files/field_document/060614-aclu-car-reportonline.pdf).

141. American Civil Liberties Union, *Warehoused and Forgotten.*

142. Project South. 2017. "Imprisoned Justice: Inside Two Georgia Immigrant Detention Centers." Penn State Law and Center for Immigrants' Rights Clinic. (http://projectsouth.org/wp-content/uploads/2017/05/Imprisoned_Justice_Report.pdf).

143. Project South, "Imprisoned Justice."

144. Gordon, Ian. 2014. "Inside Obama's Deportation Mill." *Mother Jones*, December 19. (http://www.motherjones.com/politics/2014/12/family-detention-artesia-dilley-immigration-central-america/).

145. Libal, Bob. 2016. "Texas Court Blocks Licensing of Family Detention Camps as Childcare Facilities." Grassroots Leadership, December 3. (https://grassrootsleadership.org/releases/2016/12/breaking-texas-court-blocks-licensing-family-detention-camps-childcare-facilities).

146. Sakuma, Amanda. 2015. "The Failed Experiment of Immigrant Family Detention." MSNBC, August 3. (http://www.msnbc.com/msnbc/failed-experiment-immigrant-family-detention).

147. Sakuma, "The Failed Experiment."

148. Libal, "Texas Court Blocks Licensing."

149. Libal, "Texas Court Blocks Licensing."

150. Libal, "Texas Court Blocks Licensing."

151. Smith, Laura. 2017. "Here Is the Biggest Immigration Issue That Trump Isn't Talking About." *Mother Jones*, January 12. (http://www.motherjones.com/politics/2017/01/family-detention-immigration-refugees-texas-dilley/).

152. Smith, "Here Is the Biggest Immigration Issue."

153. Kassie, Emily and Eli Hager. 2018. "Inside Family Detention, Trump's Big Solution." The Marshall Project, June 22. (https://www.themarshallproject.org/2018/06/22/inside-family-detention-trump-s-big-solution).

154. Calavita, Kitty. 1992. *Inside the State: The Bracero Program, Immigration and the INS.* New York: Routledge.

155. Graham, Jordan. 2017. "ICE Can Jail Up to 120 More Undocumented Immigrants as Orange County Sheriff Contract Expands by $5 Million." *Orange County Register*, May 9. (http://www.ocregister.com/2017/05/09/orange-county-supervisors-expand-federal-immigration-jail-contract-despite-pleas-from-advocates/).

156. Graham, "ICE Can Jail Up to 120."

157. Graham, "ICE Can Jail Up to 120."

158. Graham, "ICE Can Jail Up to 120."

159. Kwong, Jessica. 2016. "Santa Ana Moves to Ease Out of ICE Contract for Jail Detainees; Transgender Study Planned." *Orange County Register*, May 18. (http://www.ocregister.com/2016/05/18/santa-ana-moves-to-ease-out-of-ice-contract-for-jail-detainees-transgender-study-planned/).

160. Kwong, Jessica. 2017. "Remaining Detainees at Santa Ana Jail Transferred Out Monday." *Orange County Register*, May 9. (http://www.ocregister.com/2017/05/09/remaining-ice-

detainees-at-santa-ana-jail-transferred-out-monday/); Rivas, Jorge. 2017. "How Trans ICE Detainees Ended Up in a Men's Detention Center in the Middle of New Mexico." Fusion, June 5. (http://fusion.kinja.com/how-trans-ice-detainees-ended-up-in-a-men-s-detention-c-1795818417).

161. Hennessy-Fiske, Molly. 2015. "Paid $1 to $3 a Day, Unauthorized Immigrants Keep Family Detention Centers Running." *Los Angeles Times*, August 3. (http://www.latimes.com/nation/immigration/la-na-detention-immigration-workers-20150803-story.html).

162. Hennessy-Fiske, "Paid $1 to $3 a Day."

163. Starr, Alexandra. 2015. "At Low Pay, Government Hires Immigrants Held at Detention Centers." NPR Law, July 23. (http://www.npr.org/2015/07/23/425511981/at-low-pay-government-hires-immigrants-held-at-detention-centers).

164. Starr, "At Low Pay, Government Hires Immigrants."

165. Starr, "At Low Pay, Government Hires Immigrants."

166. Mitchell, Kirk. 2017. "Class Action Suit: Immigrants Held in Aurora Required for Work for $1 a Day, Threatened with Solitary If They Refuse." *Denver Post*, March 2. (http://www.denverpost.com/2017/03/02/class-action-ice-detention-aurora-immigration/).

167. Human Rights Watch. 2016. "U.S. 20 Years of Immigration Abuses." April 25. (https://www.hrw.org/news/2016/04/25/us-20-years-immigrant-abuses).

168. Human Rights Watch, "U.S. 20 Years of Immigration Abuses."

169. Rappaport, Nolan. 2017. "What Trump's 'Expedited Removal' Really Means for Immigrants in the United States." *The Hill*, February 24. (http://thehill.com/blogs/pundits-blog/immigration/321102-what-expedited-removal-really-means-for-illegal-immigrants-in).

170. TRAC Immigration. 2018. "Immigration Court Backlog Jumps While Case Processing Slows." Syracuse University, June 8. (http://trac.syr.edu/immigration/reports/516/).

171. Kanstroom, *Aftermath*.

172. Smith, Laura. 2017. "Donald Trump Can Deport People Without Even Giving Them a Hearing." *Mother Jones*, February 27. (http://www.motherjones.com/politics/2017/02/trump-deportation-ice-border-patrol-expedited-removal/).

173. American Immigration Council. 2014. "Removal Without Recourse: The Growth of Summary Deportations from the United States." Washington, DC: American Immigration Council, April 28. (https://www.americanimmigrationcouncil.org/research/removal-without-recourse-growth-summary-deportations-united-states).

174. Chishti, Muzaffar, Sarah Pierce, and Jessica Bolter. 2017. "The Obama Record on Deportations: Deporter in Chief or Not?" Migration Policy Institute, January 26. (http://www.migrationpolicy.org/article/obama-record-deportations-deporter-chief-or-not).

175. De Genova, Nicholas. 2010. "The Deportation Regime: Sovereignty, Space and the Freedom of Movement." In *The Deportation Regime*, Nicholas De Genova and Nathalie Peutz (Eds). Durham, NC and London: Duke University Press, 33–65.

176. Taxin, Amy. 2017. "Immigrants with Old Deportation Orders Arrested at Check-Ins." *Washington Post*, June 8. (https://www.washingtonpost.com/national/under-trump-old-deportation-orders-get-new-life/2017/06/08/f4244228-4c1a-11e7-987c-42ab5745db2e_story.html).

177. Taxin, "Immigrants with Old Deportation Orders."

178. Hamilton, Keegan. 2017. "Trump Told Dreamers to 'Rest Easy,' But Here's Proof They Shouldn't." VICE News, May 3. (https://news.vice.com/story/trump-told-dreamers-to-rest-easy-but-heres-proof-they-shouldn't).

179. Hamilton, "Trump Told Dreamers to 'Rest Easy'."

180. Golash-Boza, Tanya. 2016. *Deported: Immigrant Policing, Disposable Labor and Global Capitalism.* New York: NYU Press.

181. Vera Institute of Justice. 2017. "New York State Becomes First in the Nation to Provide Lawyers for All Immigrants Detained and Facing Deportation." Vera Institute of Justice, April 7. (https://www.vera.org/newsroom/press-releases/new-york-state-becomes-first-in-the-nation-to-provide-lawyers-for-all-immigrants-detained-and-facing-deportation).

182. TRAC Immigration. 2016. "Continued Rise in Asylum Denial Rates: Impact of Representation and Nationality." Syracuse, NY: Syracuse Law School. (http://trac.syr.edu/immigration/reports/448/).

183. Ryo, Emily. 2018. "Representing Immigrants: The Role of Lawyers in Immigration Bond Hearings." *Law & Society Review* 52(2): 503–31.

184. Reichlin-Melnick, Aaron. 2017. "Federal Courts Blocks DOJ's Attempt to Restrict Access to Legal Assistance." Immigration Impact, May 18. (http://immigrationimpact.com/2017/05/18/federal-court-blocks-dojs-attempt-restrict-access-legal-assistance/).

185. Vera Institute of Justice, "New York State Becomes First."

186. The Center for Popular Democracy. 2013. *The New York Immigrant Family Unity Project: Good for Families, Good for Employers, and Good for All New Yorkers.* Brooklyn, NY: The Center for Popular Democracy.

187. Center for Popular Democracy, *New York Immigrant Family Unity Project.*

188. Ospina, Tulio. 2017. "Alameda County Votes to Fund Immigrant Legal Defense Network." *Oakland Post*, February 10. (http://www.oaklandpost.org/2017/02/10/alameda-county-votes-fund-immigrant-legal-defense-network/).

189. Green, Emily. 2017. "SF Supes OK Funds to Defend Immigrants in Detention." *San Francisco Chronicle*, March 2. (http://www.sfchronicle.com/politics/article/SF-supes-OK-funds-to-defend-immigrants-in-10973576.php?cmpid=gsa-sfgate-result).

190. Green, "SF Supes OK Funds."

191. Ulloa, Jazmine. 2017. "Nearly $50 Million in the California State Budget Will Go to Expanded Legal Services for Immigrants." *Los Angeles Times*, June 15. (http://www.latimes.com/politics/essential/la-pol-ca-essential-politics-updates-nearly-50-million-in-the-california-1497576640-htmlstory.html).

192. Ulloa, "Nearly $50 Million."

193. Executive Office for Immigration Review. 2017. "List of Currently Disciplined Practitioners. Washington, DC: Department of Justice. (https://www.justice.gov/eoir/list-of-currently-disciplined-practitioners).

194. American Bar Association. N.d. "The Dangers of *Notario* Fraud." (https://www.americanbar.org/content/dam/aba/migrated/Immigration/PublicDocuments/notarios_info_piece_englishfinal.authcheckdam.pdf).

195. American Immigration Lawyers Association. N.d. "Stop Notario Fraud." (http://www.stopnotariofraud.org/).

196. Thompson, Christie. 2016. "America's Toughest Immigration Court." New York: The Marshall Project, December 12. (https://www.themarshallproject.org/2016/12/12/america-s-toughest-immigration-court#.hAAkz75Ke).

197. Thompson, "America's Toughest Immigration Court."

198. Thompson, "America's Toughest Immigration Court."

199. Laughland, Oliver. 2017. "Inside Trump's Secretive Immigration Court: Far from Scrutiny and Legal Aid." *The Guardian.* (https://www.theguardian.com/us-news/2017/jun/07/donald-trump-immigration-court-deportation-lasalle).

200. Laughland, "Inside Trump's Secretive Immigration Court."

201. Laughland, "Inside Trump's Secretive Immigration Court."

202. Verza, Maria. 2017. "'You Feel Lost': Deported U.S. Vets in Mexico Hope for Return Under Trump Camp." *Chicago Tribune*, June 8. (http://www.chicagotribune.com/news/nationworld/ct-deported-vets-mexico-hope-for-return-under-trump-20170309-story.html).

203. Johnson, Tory. 2017. "Some Veterans Observe Memorial Day Under Threat of Deportation." American Immigration Council. Immigration Impact, May 29. (http://immigrationimpact.com/2017/05/29/veterans-observe-memorial-day-threat-deportation/).

204. Hartsfield, Cathy Ho. 2012. "Deportation of Veterans: The Silent Battle for Naturalization." *Rutgers Law Review* 64(3): 835–62.

205. Osberg, Molly. 2017. "These Banished Veterans Know Exactly How Broken the System Is." Fusion, April 3. (http://fusion.kinja.com/these-banished-veterans-know-exactly-how-broken-the-sys-1793877010).

206. Johnson, "Some Veterans Observe Memorial Day."

207. Johnson, "Some Veterans Observe Memorial Day."

208. Stock, Stephen, Robert Campos, and Michael Horn. 2017. "Homeland Security Wants to Deport Him, But One US Navy Vet Is Beating the Odds—So Far." NBC Bay Area, May 22. (http://www.nbcbayarea.com/investigations/Homeland-Security-Wants-to-Deport-Him-But-One-US-Navy-Vet-Is-Beating-the-Odds--So-Far-423720984.html).

209. Elbogen, Eric B., Sally C. Johnson, Virginia M. Newton, Kristy Straits-Troster, Jennifer J. Vasterling, H. Ryan Wagner, and Jean C. Beckham. 2012. "Criminal Justice Involvement, Trauma, and Negative Affect in Iraq and Afghanistan War Veterans." *Journal of Consulting and Clinical Psychology* 80(6): 1097–1102.

210. American Civil Liberties Union. 2016. "ACLU Report Details How U.S. Has Failed Deported Veterans." ACLU, July 6. (https://www.aclu.org/news/aclu-report-details-how-us-has-failed-deported-veterans).

211. Dibble, Sandra. 2017. "Congressional Visit Gives a Boost to Deported U.S. Veterans in Tijuana." *San Diego Union Tribune*, June 3. (http://www.sandiegouniontribune.com/news/border-baja-california/sd-me-veterans-deported-20170603-story.html).

212. Bello, Kemi. 2016. "Bill Introduced in Congress to Bring U.S. Veterans Back Home." Immigrant Legal Resource Center, July 14. (https://www.ilrc.org/bill-introduced-congress-bring-deported-us-veterans-back-home).

213. Osberg, Molly. 2017. "These Banished Veterans Know Exactly How Broken the System Is." Fusion, April 3. (http://fusion.kinja.com/these-banished-veterans-know-exactly-how-broken-the-sys-1793877010).

214. CNN Wire. 2017. "Gov. Brown's Pardon Could Help 3 Deported Veterans Return to the U.S." KTLA5, April 16. (http://ktla.com/2017/04/16/gov-browns-pardon-could-help-3-deported-veterans-return-to-u-s/).

215. Phillips, Kristine. 2018. "A Deported Veteran Has Been Granted U.S. Citizenship, After 14 Years of Living in Mexico." *Washington Post*, March 31. (https://www.washingtonpost.com/news/checkpoint/wp/2018/03/31/a-deported-veteran-has-been-granted-u-s-citizenship-after-14-years-of-living-in-mexico/?noredirect=on&utm_term=.f8cf547683fc).

216. U.S. Department of Defense. 2017. "DoD Announces Policy Changes to Lawful Permanent Residents and the Military Accessions Vital to the National Interest Program." News Release, October 13. (https://dod.defense.gov/News/News-Releases/News-Release-View/Article/1342317/dod-announces-policy-changes-to-lawful-permanent-residents-and-the-military-acc/).

217. Phillips, Dave. 2018. "They Came Here to Serve. But for Many Immigrants, the Army Isn't Interested." *New York Times*, July 6. (https://www.nytimes.com/2018/07/06/us/army-immigrants-discharge.html?module=inline).

218. Menjívar, Cecilia and Daniel Kanstroom (Eds). 2014. *Constructing Illegality in America: Immigrant Experiences, Critiques, and Resistance.* New York: Cambridge University Press.

219. Buckley, Madeline and Fatima Hussein. 2017. "In Indianapolis, Undocumented Immigrant Community Making Contingency Plans." *Indystar*, March 5. (http://www.indystar.com/story/news/politics/2017/03/05/indianapolis-undocumented-community-making-contingency-plans/98629280/).

220. Dumke, Mick and Dan Mihalopolous. 2017. "'Dreamers' Could Face Choice: Stay, or Go with Deported Parents." *Chicago Sun-Times*, April 2. (http://chicago.suntimes.com/feature/dreamers-could-face-choice-stay-or-go-with-deported-parents/).

221. Abrego, Leisy. 2014. *Sacrificing Families: Navigating Laws, Labor and Love Across Borders.* Stanford, CA: Stanford University Press.

222. Guerrero, Jean. 2015. "Deportees with Families in U.S. Try to Start Over in Tijuana." KQED News, May 19. (https://www.kqed.org/news/10530508/deportees-with-families-in-u-s-try-to-start-over-in-tijuana).

CHAPTER 7

1. La Santa Cecilia. 2013. "ICE El Hielo." *Treinta Dias.* Universal Music Latino.

2. Bogado, Aura. 2013. "A Music Video Without Papers." *The Nation*, April 8. (https://www.thenation.com/article/music-video-without-papers/).

3. Rivera, Alex. 2013. "La Santa Cecilia ICE El Hielo Video." National Day Labor Organizing Network (Producer). Universal Music Latino. (https://www.youtube.com/watch?v=0lNJviuYUEQ).

4. Rivera, "La Santa Cecilia."

5. Gonzales, Roberto G. 2008. "Left Out but Not Shut Down: Political Activism and the Undocumented Latino Student Movement." *Northwestern Journal of Law and Social Policy* 3(2): 1–22; Ponce, Albert. 2012. "Racialization, Resistance, and the Migrant Rights Movement: A Historical Analysis." *Critical Sociology* 40(1): 9–27.

6. Lang, Marissa J. 2018. "'I Am a Child': How an Artist Turned Civil Rights Imagery into a Message of Protest for Immigrant Kids." *Washington Post,* July 1. (https://www.washingtonpost.com/news/local/wp/2018/07/01/i-am-a-child-how-an-artist-turned-civil-rights-imagery-into-a-message-of-protest-for-immigrant-kids/?utm_term=.1dcad74be362).

7. Castillo, Andrea, Rosanna Xia, David Kelly, and Victoria Kim. 2018. "From L.A. to N.Y., Hundreds of Thousands Join Nationwide Rallies to Protest Trump's Immigration Policies." *Los Angeles Times,* June 30. (http://www.latimes.com/local/lanow/la-me-rally-family-separation-20180629-story.html).

8. Negrón-Gonzales, Genevieve. 2014. "Undocumented, Unafraid and Unapologetic: Re-Articulatory Practices and Migrant Youth 'Illegality.'" *Latino Studies* 12(2): 259–78.

9. Chavez, Leo. 2008. *The Latino Threat: Constructing Immigrants, Citizens, and the Nation.* Palo Alto, CA: Stanford University Press; Coutin, Susan. 2000. *Legalizing Moves: Salvadoran Immigrants' Struggle for U.S. Residency.* Ann Arbor: University of Michigan Press; Swan, Richelle S. and Marisol Clark-Ibáñez. 2017. "Perceptions of Shifting Legal Ground: DACA

and the Legal Consciousness of Undocumented Students and Graduates." *Thomas Jefferson Law Review* 39(2): 67–92.

10. Negrón-Gonzales, "Undocumented, Unafraid and Unapologetic."

11. Gonzales, "Left Out but Not Shut Down"; Zepeda-Millán, Chris. 2016. "Weapons of the (Not So) Weak: Immigrant Mass Mobilization in the U.S. South." *Critical Sociology* 42(2): 269–87.

12. Menjívar, Cecilia and Leisy Abrego. 2012. *Legal Violence in the Lives of Immigrants: How Immigration Enforcement Affects Families, Schools and Workplaces.* Washington, DC: Center for American Progress.

13. Gonzales, "Left Out but Not Shut Down."

14. Clark-Ibáñez, Marisol. 2015. *Undocumented Latino Youth: Navigating Their Worlds.* Boulder, CO: Lynn Rienner Publishers.

15. Gonzales, Alfonso. 2009. "The 2006 *Mega Marchas* in Greater Los Angeles: Counter-Hegemonic Moment and the Future of *El Migrante* Struggle." *Latino Studies* 7(1): 30–59; Ponce, "Racialization, Resistance, and the Migrant Rights Movement."

16. Engler, Paul. 2009. "The US Immigrant Rights Movement (2004-ongoing)." International Center on Nonviolent Conflict. (https://www.nonviolent-conflict.org/wp-content/uploads/2016/02/engler_united_states_immigrant_rights.pdf).

17. Engler, "The US Immigrant Rights Movement."

18. See as an example: Pérez Huber, Lindsay. 2009. "Challenging Racist Nativist Framing: Acknowledging the Community Cultural Wealth of Undocumented Chicana College Students to Reframe the Immigration Debate." *Harvard Educational Review* 79(4): 704–29.

19. Barreto, Matt A., Sylvia Manzano, Ricardo Ramirez, and Kathy Rim. (2009). "Mobilization, Participation, and *Solidaridad:* Latino Participation in the 2006 Immigration Protest Rallies." *Urban Affairs Review* 44(5): 736–64.

20. Negrón-Gonzales, "Undocumented, Unafraid and Unapologetic."

21. Unzueta Carrasco, Tania A. and Hinda Seif. 2014. "Disrupting the Dream: Undocumented Youth Reframe Citizenship and Deportability Through Anti-Deportation Activism." *Latino Studies* 12(2): 279–99.

22. Unzueta Carrasco, Ireri. 2010. "Documents, Identities and Institutions." AREA Chicago #10: Institutions and Infrastructures. (http://areachicago.org/documents-identities-andinstitutions/).

23. Wallace, Tim and Alicia Parlapiano. 2017. "Crowd Scientists Say Women's March in Washington Had 3 Times More People Than Trump's Inauguration." *New York Times,* January 22. (https://www.nytimes.com/interactive/2017/01/22/us/politics/womens-march-trump-crowd-estimates.html?_r=0).

24. McAfee, Tierney. 2017. "6-Year-Old Girl Who Handed Letter to Pope Francis: 'Let Us Fight with Love, Faith, and Courage'." *People,* January 21. (http://people.com/politics/womens-march-sophie-cruz-pope-francis/).

25. Blay, Zeba. 2017. "Watch 6-Year-Old Sophie Cruz Give One of the Best Speeches of the Women's March." Huffington Post, January 21. (http://www.huffingtonpost.com/entry/sophie-cruz_us_58839698e4b096b4a23201f6); Bowerman, Mary. 2017. "Watch: 6-Year-Old Sophie Cruz Capture Hearts at Massive Women's March." *USA Today*, January 21. (http://www.usatoday.com/story/news/politics/onpolitics/2017/01/21/watch-6-year-old-sophie-cruz-capture-hearts-massive-womens-march/96889558/).

26. Mendez, Julian J. and Nolan L. Cabrera. 2015. "Targets but Not Victims: Latina/o College Students and Arizona's Racial Politics." *Journal of Hispanic Higher Education* 14(4): 377–91.

27. Seif, Hinda. 2014. "'Coming Out of the Shadows' and 'Undocuqueer': Latina/o Undocumented Immigrants Transforming Sexuality Discourse and Activism." *Journal of Language and Sexuality* 3: 87–120.

28. Seif, Hinda, Char Ullman, and Guillermina G. Núñez-Mchiri. 2014. "Mexican (Im) migrant Students and Education: Constructions of and Resistance to 'Illegality'." *Latino Studies* 12(2): 172–93.

29. Nicholls, Walter and Tara Fiorito. 2015. "Dreamers Unbound: Immigrant Youth Mobilizing." *New Labor Forum,* Winter. (http://newlaborforum.cuny.edu/author/walter-nicholls/).

30. Baer, Barbara. 1975. "Stopping Traffic: One Woman's Cause." *The Progressive,* September: 38–40.

31. Negrón-Gonzales, "Undocumented, Unafraid and Unapologetic."

32. Barreto, Manzano, Ramirez, and Rim, "Mobilization, Participation, and *Solidaridad.*"

33. Barreto, Manzano, Ramirez, and Rim, "Mobilization, Participation, and *Solidaridad*"; Zepeda-Millán, "Weapons of the (Not So) Weak."

34. Ponce, "Racialization, Resistance, and the Migrant Rights Movement."

35. De Genova, Nicholas. 2010. "The Queer Politics of Migration: Reflections on 'Illegality' and Incorrigibility." *Studies in Social Justice* 4(2): 101–26.

36. Chavez, *The Latino Threat*; Watanabe, Teresa and Hector Becerra. 2006. "500,000 Pack Streets to Protest Immigrant Bills." *Los Angeles Times,* March 26. (http://articles.latimes.com/2006/mar/26/local/me-immig26).

37. Diaz, Jesse. 2010. " Organizing the Brown Tide: La Gran Epoca Primavera 2006, an Insiders' Story," PhD dissertation, University of California Riverside; Ponce, "Racialization, Resistance, and the Migrant Rights Movement."

38. Seif, Ullman, and Núñez-Mchiri, "Mexican (Im)migrant Students and Education."

39. Chavez, *The Latino Threat.*

40. Gonzales, "The 2006 *Mega Marchas*"; Gonzales, Alfonso. 2013. *Reform Without Justice: Latino Migrant Politics and the Homeland Security State.* Oxford: Oxford University Press.

41. Castillo, Xia, Kelly, and Kim, "From L.A. to N.Y."

42. Mahr, Joe, Tony Briscoe, and Ese Olumhense. 2018. "Demonstrators Rally in the Loop Against Separation of Families." *Chicago Tribune,* June 30. (http://www.chicagotribune.com/news/local/breaking/ct-met-loop-immigration-family-separation-rally-20180630-story.html).

43. CNN Wire and Katrina Butcher. 2018. "Keep Families Together Rally Held at Oklahoma State Capitol, Nationwide." KFOR Oklahoma's News, June 30. (https://kfor.com/2018/06/30/keep-families-together-rally-held-at-oklahoma-state-capitol-nationwide/).

44. De La Torre III, Pedro and Roy Germano. 2014. "Out of the Shadows: DREAMer Identity in the Immigrant Youth Movement." *Latino Studies* 12(3): 449–67.

45. Negrón-Gonzales, "Undocumented, Unafraid and Unapologetic."

46. De La Torre III and Germano, "Out of the Shadows."

47. De La Torre and Germano, "Out of the Shadows."

48. Galindo, René. 2012. "Undocumented & Unafraid: The DREAM Act 5 and the Public Disclosure of Undocumented Status as a Political Act." *Urban Review* 44: 589–611.

49. De Genova, "The Queer Politics of Migration."

50. Reichard, Raquel. 2016. "Why This Undocumented Latina Launched Coming Out of the Shadows Month." *Latina,* March 7. (http://www.latina.com/lifestyle/our-issues/latina-launches-coming-out-shadows-month).

51. De La Torre III and Germano, "Out of the Shadows."

52. Reichard, "Why This Undocumented Latina Launched."

53. No Papers, No Fear. 2013. No Papers, No Fear Ride for Justice. (http://nopapers-nofear.org).

54. No Papers, No Fear.

55. Reichard, "Why This Undocumented Latina Launched."

56. Nevarez, Griselda. 2014. "Immigration Activists Arrested Outside the White House During Protest." Huffington Post, February 18. (http://www.huffingtonpost.com/2014/02/18/activists-arrested-white-house_n_4808069.html).

57. Unzueta Carrasco and Seif, "Disrupting the Dream."

58. Negrón-Gonzales, Genevieve. 2016. "Unlawful Entry: Civil Disobedience and the Undocumented Youth Movement." In Jerusha Conner and Sonia M. Rosen (Eds.). *Contemporary Youth Activism: Advancing Social Justice in the United States.* Santa Barbara, CA: Praeger, 271–88.

59. Negrón-Gonzales, "Unlawful Entry."

60. Galindo, "Undocumented & Unafraid."

61. Negrón-Gonzales, "Unlawful Entry."

62. Galindo, "Undocumented & Unafraid."

63. Trevizo, Perla. 2016. "Arivaca Residents Monitoring Border Patrol Checkpoint on AZ 286." *Arizona Daily Star,* February 3. (http://tucson.com/news/arivaca-residents-monitoring-border-patrol-checkpoint-on-az/article_e3a9e9e1-0706-5c59-bdf7-fae183140a29.html); Jimenez, Guillermo. 2015. "Arizonans Stage Sit-In to Halt Inland Immigration Checkpoints." *PanAm Post,* May 28. (https://panampost.com/guillermo-jimenez/2015/05/28/arizonans-stage-sit-in-to-halt-inland-immigration-checkpoints/).

64. People Helping People in the Border Zone. (n.d.). "Checkpoint Campaign." (http://phparivaca.org/?page_id=7).

65. Trevizo, "Arivaca Residents Monitoring Border Patrol"; Jimenez, "Arizonans Stage Sit-In."

66. American Civil Liberties Union of Arizona. 2015. "Freedom of Information Act (FOIA) Request Reveals Lack of Oversight, No Accountability for Widespread Civil Rights Violations." ACLU, October 15. (https://www.acluaz.org/en/press-releases/aclu-report-border-patrols-interior-enforcement-records-show-systemic-abuse-few).

67. Thompson, Carolyn. 2016. "College Students Protest Donald Trump's Deportation Plans." *U.S. News & World Report,* November 17. (http://www.usnews.com/news/politics/articles/2016-11-16/college-students-to-protest-against-trump-deportation-plans).

68. McGeogh, Paul. 2017. "Sit-Ins at Airports, 'Stand-Ups' at White House as Trump and Bannon Rewrite Rules." *Sydney Morning Herald,* January 31. (http://www.smh.com.au/world/sitins-at-airports-standups-at-white-house-as-trump-and-bannon-rewrite-rules-20170131-gu25y9.html).

69. BBC News. 2018. "Trump Travel Ban: What Does This Ruling Mean?" BBC News. (https://www.bbc.com/news/world-us-canada-39044403).

70. Pavey, Steve and Marco Saavedra. 2012. *Shadows Then Light.* Lexington, KY: One Horizon Institute, ii.

71. McLeod, Allegra M. 2016. "Immigration, Criminalization, and Disobedience." *University of Miami Law Review* 70(2): 556–84; *Democracy Now!*. 2012. "DREAM Activist Speaks from Broward Detention Center: Listen to Exclusive Interview." (https://www.democracynow.org/2012/7/31/dream_activist_speaks_from_broward_detention_center_listen_to_exclusive_audio).

72. McLeod, "Immigration, Criminalization, and Disobedience"; Pavey and Saavedra, *Shadows Then Light.*

73. May, Michael. 2013. "Los Infiltradores." *American Prospect,* June 21. (http://prospect.org/article/los-infiltradores).

74. May, "Los Infiltradores."

75. May, "Los Infiltradores."

76. Kohari, Alizeh. 2011. "Hunger Strikes: What Can They Achieve?" BBC News, August 16. (http://www.bbc.com/news/magazine-14540696).

77. Armbruster-Sandoval, Ralph. 2017. "On His Book, *Starving for Justice: Hunger Strikes, Spectacular Speech, and the Struggle for Dignity.*" *ROROTOKO,* September 18. (http://rorotoko.com/interview/20170918_armbruster-sandoval_ralph_on_book_starving_for_justice_hunger/?page=2).

78. Linthicum, Kate. 2015. "Hundreds Launch Hunger Strike at Immigrant Detention Center in Adelanto, Calif." *Los Angeles Times,* November 6. (http://www.latimes.com/local/lanow/la-me-ln-immigrant-hunger-strike-20151106-story.html).

79. Fields, Liz. 2015. "These Undocumented Women Are Hunger Striking Against Their Detention in Texas." VICE News, October 30. (https://news.vice.com/article/these-undocumented-women-are-hunger-striking-against-their-detention-in-texas).

80. Michaels, Samantha. 2015. "Here Is Why Hundreds of Immigrants in Detention Have Gone on Hunger Strike." *Mother Jones,* December 2. (http://www.motherjones.com/politics/2015/11/why-are-hundreds-detained-immigrants-going-hunger-strike).

81. Denton, Joseph C. 2016. "Federal Judge Approves Force Feeding of Detainees, Sheds Light on Local Anti-Deportation Movement." *South Seattle Emerald*, January 4. (https://southseattleemerald.com/2016/01/04/federal-judge-approves-force-feeding-of-detainees-sheds-light-on-local-anti-deportation-movement/).

82. Nathan, Debbie. 2018. "Immigrant Mothers Are Staging Hunger Strikes to Demand Calls with Their Separated Children." *The Intercept,* July 13. (https://theintercept.com/2018/07/13/separated-children-hunger-strike-immigrant-detention/).

83. Lind, Dara. 2018. "What We Know About a Reported Hunger Strike by Fathers in Immigration Detention." Vox, August 3. (https://www.vox.com/2018/8/2/17641208/immigrant-strike-detention-families-separation).

84. Graham, Nathalie. 2018. "According to ICE There Is No Strike at the Northwest Detention Center." *The Stranger,* August 23. (https://www.thestranger.com/slog/2018/08/23/31243448/according-to-ice-there-is-no-hunger-strike-at-the-northwest-detention-center).

85. Graham, "According to ICE There Is No Strike."

86. Nathan, "Immigrant Mothers Are Staging Hunger Strikes."

87. Constable, Pamela. 2014. "'Dreamer Moms' Fast Near White House, Hoping Obama Will Grant Them Legal Status." *Washington Post,* November 15. (http://ezproxy.csusm.edu/login?url=http://search.proquest.com/docview/1625807117?accountid=10363).

88. Constable, "'Dreamer Moms' Fast Near White House."

89. *Cosecha.* 2017. "The Story." (http://www.lahuelga.com/story/).

90. Yan, Holly and David Williams. 2017. "Nationwide 'Day Without Immigrants' Shuts Down Businesses." CNN, February 16. (http://www.cnn.com/2017/02/16/us/day-without-immigrants-vignettes/); Vasquez, Tina. 2017. "Immigrants Respond to Trump's Agenda with Nationwide Strike." Rewire, February 16. (https://rewire.news/article/2017/02/16/immigrants-respond-trumps-agenda-with-nationwide-strike/).

91. *Cosecha*. 2017. "A Day Without Immigrants." (http://www.lahuelga.com/home/#header).

92. Solomon, Lois K. 2015. "Tomato Pickers Persuade Big Food Companies to Sign On to Human-Rights Movement." *South Florida SunSentinel*, December 31. (http://www.sun-sentinel.com/news/florida/fl-tomato-pickers-20151231-story.html).

93. Solomon, "Tomato Pickers Persuade."

94. Johnson, Jimmy. 2016. "Hundreds of Farmworkers Gather on Palm Beach to Protest Wendy's: Farmers Demand That Fast-Food Chain Join 'Fair Food Program'." (http://www.wpbf.com/news/hundreds-of-farmworkers-gather-on-palm-beach-to-protest-wendys/38485804).

95. iamOTHER. 2013. "Voice of Art-Migration is Beautiful, Part 1." (https://www.youtube.com/watch?v=LWE2T8Bx5d8).

96. Kuttner, Paul. 2013. "Interview with Cultural Organizer Favianna Rodriguez." Cultural Organizing. (http://culturalorganizing.org/tag/immigration/).

97. Fair Immigration Reform Movement. 2008. "Art Is Action—Pro-Migrant Poster Power." June 12. (http://fairimmigration.org/2008/06/12/art-is-action-pro-migrant-poster-power/).

98. Drummond, Tammerlin. 2017. "Oakland Artist Taps Power of Art to Organize for Change." *EastBay Times*, February 1. (http://www.eastbaytimes.com/2017/02/01/oakland-artist-taps-power-of-art-to-organize-for-change/).

99. Tramonte, Lynn. 2017. "Migration Is Beautiful: DIY Butterfly Wings for Pro-Immigrant Marches and Rallies. *America's Voice*, January 12. (http://americasvoice.org/blog/migration-beautiful-diy-butterfly-wings-pro-immigrant-marches-rallies/).

100. CultureStrike. 2016. "Visions from the Inside." (http://www.culturestrike.org/project/visions-inside-2016).

101. Denton, "Federal Judge Approves Force Feeding."

102. Salgado, Julio. N.d. Personal website. (http://juliosalgadoart.com).

103. Seif, Hinda. 2014. "'Layers of Humanity': Interview with Undocuqueer Artivist Julio Salgado." *Latino Studies* 12(2): 300–309. Quoting from 305–306.

104. Seif, "'Layers of Humanity'."

105. No More Death/*No Más Muertes*. 2017. "No More Deaths Benefit: An Art Auction to Protect the Lives of Migrants." (http://forms.nomoredeaths.org/no-more-deaths-benefit-an-art-auction-to-protect-the-lives-of-migrants/).

106. Weathersbee, Tonyaa. 2017. "Weathersbee: This Art Speaks to Immigrant Rights." *Commercial Appeal*, January 14. (http://www.commercialappeal.com/story/news/columnists/2017/01/14/weathersbee-art-speaks-immigrant-rights/96511854/).

107. Border Angels. 2017. "Enrique Morones: Founder and Director." Border Angels. (http://www.borderangels.org/staff-page/enrique-morones/)

108. Mendoza, Sylvia. 2014. "Detained in the Desert: Protesting the Unjust Through the Power of a Pen." *Hispanic Outlook in Higher Education* (March 10): 14–16.

109. Mendoza, "Detained in the Desert."

110. Téllez, Michelle and Alejandra Ramírez. 2018. "How Artists Can Shape Understanding of the U.S.-Mexico Border." *LatinoUSA,* January 18. (http://latinousa.org/2018/01/18/artists-can-shape-understanding-u-s-mexico-border/).

111. Morlan, Kinsee. 2017. "The Most Memorable Acts of Protest at the Border." Voice of San Diego, February 27. (https://www.voiceofsandiego.org/topics/arts/the-most-memorable-acts-of-protest-art-at-the-border/).

112. Binational Arts Residency. 2015. "2015 Binational Residency Artist: Ana Teresa Fernández." (https://www.binationalartsresidency.com/new-page/).

113. Morlan, "The Most Memorable Acts of Protest."

114. Heldiz, Adriana. 2018. "Video: Art Students Take on Trump's Border Wall Prototypes." Voice of San Diego, April 10.

115. Herman, Max. 2018. "Fighting for the Lives of Migrants in the Sonoran Desert (Photo Essay)." LatinoUSA.org, June 27. (http://latinousa.org/2018/06/27/sonorandesert-photoessay/).

116. Fernández, Valeria. 2013. "'Dream 9' Tactics Take Debate Beyond Halls of Congress." *La Prensa San Diego*, August 2. (http://laprensa-sandiego.org/featured/dream-9-tactics-take-debate-beyond-halls-of-congress/)

117. Fernández, "'Dream 9' Tactics Take Debate."

118. Taros, M. 2013. "Dream 9 Released from Arizona Detention; What Lies Ahead for Brave Activists?" *Latin Times.* (http://www.latintimes.com/dream-9-released-arizona-immigration-detention-what-lies-ahead-brave-activists-130138).

119. Yukich, Grace. 2013. "Constructing the Model Immigrant: Movement Strategy and Immigrant Deservingness in the New Sanctuary Movement." *Social Problems* 60(3): 302–20.

120. Chinchilla, Norma Stoltz, Nora Hamilton, and James Loucky. 2009. "The Sanctuary Movement and Central American Activism in Los Angeles." *Latin American Perspectives* 36(6): 101–26.

121. Lo, Puck. 2015. "Inside the New Sanctuary Movement That's Protecting Immigrants from ICE." *The Nation,* May 6. (https://www.thenation.com/article/inside-new-sanctuary-movement-thats-protecting-immigrants-ice/); Yukich, "Constructing the Model Immigrant."

122. Unitarian Universalist Refugee and Immigrant Services and Education. 2017. "The Path Toward Sanctuary: A Practical Guide-Webinar." (http://uurise.org/event/path-toward-sanctuary-practical-guide-webinar/).

123. The Sanctuary Movement. 2017. "#SanctuaryRising." (http://www.sanctuarynotdeportation.org/sanctuaryrising.html).

124. Vasquez, Tina. 2018. "Exclusive: New Immigration-Led Coalition Is 'Going to Get People Out of Sanctuary'." Rewire.News, August 9. (https://rewire.news/article/2018/08/09/exclusive-new-immigrant-led-coalition-is-going-to-get-people-out-of-sanctuary/).

125. Vasquez, "Exclusive: New Immigration-Led Coalition."

126. Vasquez, "Exclusive: New Immigration-Led Coalition."

127. Engler, Mark and Paul Engler. 2016. "Three Times When 'Impractical' Movements Led to Real Change." *The Nation*, March 7. (http://www.thenation.com/article/three-times-when-impractical-movements-led-to-real-change/).

CHAPTER 8

1. Pitzl, Mary J. 2016. "One Nation: Immigration Issue Turns Personal." *USA Today*, March 22. (http://www.usatoday.com/story/news/politics/elections/2016/03/22/one-nation-immigration-scottsdale-arizona/82108206/).

2. Santos, Carlos, Cecilia Menjívar, and Erin Godfrey. 2013. "Effects of SB 1070 on Children." In Lisa Magana and Erik Lee (eds.), *Latino Politics and Arizona's Immigration Law*. New York: Springer-Verlag, 79–92.

3. Menjívar, Cecilia. 2014. "The 'Poli-Migra' Multilayered Legislation, Enforcement Practices, and What We Can Learn About and From Today's Approaches." *American Behavioral Scientist* 58(13): 1805–19.

4. Chavez, Leo. 2013. *The Latino Threat: Constructing Immigrants, Citizens, and the Nation* (Second Edition). Stanford, CA: Stanford University Press.

5. Chavez, *The Latino Threat*, 148.

6. Race Forward. N.d. "Drop the I-Word." Race Forward—Center for Racial Justice Innovation. (https://www.raceforward.org/practice/tools/drop-i-word).

7. Abrego, Leisy. J. 2014. *Sacrificing Families: Navigating Laws, Labor and Love Across Borders*. Stanford: Stanford University Press.

8. Bregman, Rutger. 2016. "The Surprisingly Compelling Argument for Open Borders." *Fortune*, April 17. (http://fortune.com/2016/04/17/immigration-open-borders/); Vallet, Élisabeth and Charles-Philippe David. 2012. "Introduction: The (Re)Building of the Wall in International Relations." *Journal of Borderland Studies* 27(2): 111–19.

9. Bregman, "The Surprisingly Compelling Argument ."

10. Massey, Douglas S. 2007. "Understanding America's Immigration 'Crisis'." *Proceedings of the American Philosophical Society* 151(3): 309–27.

11. American Immigration Council. 2013. "An Immigration Stimulus: The Economic Benefits of a Legalization Program." April 3. (https://www.americanimmigrationcouncil.org/research/immigration-stimulus-economic-benefits-legalization-program).

12. Siegel, Robert and Selena Simmons-Duffin. 2017. "How Did We Get to 11 Million Unauthorized Immigrants?" National Public Radio, March 7. (http://www.npr.org/2017/03/07/518201210/how-did-we-get-to-11-million-unauthorized-immigrants).

13. Migration Policy Institute. N.d. *Profile of the Unauthorized Population: United States*. (https://www.migrationpolicy.org/data/unauthorized-immigrant-population/state/US).

14. Garcia, Ann and Samantha Franchim. 2013. "10 Facts You Need to Know About Immigrant Women." Center for American Progress, March 8. (https://www.americanprogress.org/issues/immigration/news/2013/03/08/55794/10-facts-you-need-to-know-about-immigrant-women-2013-update/).

15. Migration Policy Institute, *Profile of the Unauthorized Population: United States*.

16. Mathema, Silva. 2017. "Keeping Families Together." Center for American Progress, March 16. (https://www.americanprogress.org/issues/immigration/reports/2017/03/16/428335/keeping-families-together/)

17. Mathema, "Keeping Families Together."

18. Mathema, "Keeping Families Together."

19. Migration Policy Institute, *Profile of the Unauthorized Population: United States*.

20. Zong, Jie, Ariel G. Ruiz Soto, Jeanne Batalova, Julia Gelatt, and Randy Capps. 2017. "A Profile of Current DACA Recipients by Education, Industry, and Occupation." Migration

Policy Institute, November. (https://www.migrationpolicy.org/research/profile-current-daca-recipients-education-industry-and-occupation).

21. Nebraska Legislature. Nebraska Revised Statute 48-2213: Meatpacking industry worker rights coordinator; established; powers and duties. (http://nebraskalegislature.gov/laws/statutes.php?statute=48-2213).

22. National Immigration Law Center. 2018. "Basic Facts About In-State Tuition for Undocumented Immigrant Students." June 1. (https://www.nilc.org/issues/education/basic-facts-instate/).

23. Alvarado, Monsy. 2018. "Phil Murphy Signs Bill Extending Financial Aid to Undocumented Immigrants in New Jersey." NorthJersey.com, May 9. (https://www.northjersey.com/story/news/new-jersey/2018/05/09/phil-murphy-signs-bill-extending-financial-aid-undocumented-students/587128002/).

24. Edwards, Andrew. 2017. "Student Aid Requests for Immigrants Up in 2017." *Orange County Register*, March 7. (http://www.ocregister.com/2017/03/07/student-aid-requests-for-immigrants-up-in-2017/).

25. Ryman, Anne and Daniel González. 2017. "Arizona Appeals Court Overturns In-State Tuition for 'Dreamers'." *Arizona Republic*, June 20. (http://www.azcentral.com/story/news/politics/arizona-education/2017/06/20/arizona-court-overturns-state-tuition-dreamers/412845001/).

26. National Immigration Law Center, "Basic Facts About In-State Tuition."

27. Ruiz Pohlert, Alma. 2015. "Being a 'DREAM Keeper': Lessons Learned." In *Undocumented Latino Immigrants: Navigating Their Worlds*, with Marisol Clark-Ibáñez. Lynne Rienner Publishers, Chapter 10.

28. Valdivia, Carolina and Marisol Clark-Ibáñez. "'It Is Hard Right Now': High School Educators Working with Undocumented Students." *Latino Public Policy* 10. (https://scholar.smu.edu/latino-policy/10).

29. Rocha, Cecilia. 2015. "Middle School: Creating New Paths." In *Undocumented Latino Immigrants: Navigating Their Worlds*, with Marisol Clark-Ibáñez. Lynne Rienner Publishers, Chapter 4.

30. Migration Policy Institute, *Profile of the Unauthorized Population: United States*.

31. Schmidt, Samantha. 2018. "'Dreamers' in Arizona Are No Longer Eligible for In-State Tuition, Court Rules." *Washington Post*, April 10. (https://www.washingtonpost.com/news/morning-mix/wp/2018/04/10/dreamers-in-arizona-are-no-longer-eligible-for-in-state-tuition-court-rules/?noredirect=on&utm_term=.bbe13f092f50).

32. Hing, Julianne. 2018. "A Win and a Loss in Dreamers' Fight for In-State Tuition." *The Nation,* April 18. (https://www.thenation.com/article/a-win-and-a-loss-in-dreamers-fight-for-in-state-tuition/).

33. Rendón, Laura I. 1994. "Validating Culturally Diverse Students: Toward a New Model of Learning and Student Development." *Innovative Higher Education* 19(1): 33–51.

34. Whitman, Elizabeth. 2015. "Immigration, Health Care Reform 2015: States Move to Help Undocumented Immigrants Without Medical Insurance." *International Business Times.* (http://www.ibtimes.com/immigration-health-care-reform-2015-states-move-help-undocumented-immigrants-without-1820458).

35. Gilcrist, Akiesha R. 2013. "Undocumented Immigrants: Lack of Equal Protection and Its Impact on Public Health." *Journal of Legal Medicine* 34(4): 403–12.

36. Fortuna, Lisa and Michelle V. Porche. 2013. "Clinical Issues and Challenges in Treating Undocumented Immigrants." *Clinical Issues and Challenges in Treating Undocumented*

Immigrants. (http://www.psychiatrictimes.com/special-reports/clinical-issues-and-challenges-treating-undocumented-immigrants).

37. Manriquez, Stephanie. 2015. "For Immigrants, Status and Stigma Affect Mental Health, Few Resources Exist—Social Justice News Nexus." Social Justice News Nexus. (http://sjnnchicago.org/for-immigrants-status-and-stigma-affect-mental-health-few-resources-exist/).

38. Martinez, Omar, Elwin Wu, Theo Sandfort, Brian Dodge, Alex Carballo-Dieguez, Rogeiro Pinto, Scott Rhodes, Eva Moya, and Silvia Chavez-Baray. 2015. "Evaluating the Impact of Immigration Policies on Health Status Among Undocumented Immigrants: A Systematic Review." *Journal of Immigrant Minority Health* 17: 947–70.

39. Heidbrink, Lauren. 2014. *Migrant Youth, Transnational Families and the State: Care and Contested Interests.* Philadelphia: University of Pennsylvania Press.

40. Coutin, Susan Bibler. 2013. "Place and Presence within Salvadoran Deportees' Narratives of Removal." *Childhood* 20(3): 323–36; Zilberg, Elana. 2011. *Space of Detention: The Making of a Transnational Gang Crisis Between Los Angeles and El Salvador.* Durham, NC: Duke University Press.

41. Menjivar, Cecilia and Leisy Abrego. 2012. *Legal Violence in the Lives of Immigrants: How Immigration Enforcement Affects Families, Schools, and Workplaces.* Washington, DC: Center for American Progress.

42. O'Hara, Mary Emily. 2018. "Trans Activists Protest ICE by Blocking the Streets in New Mexico." *Them,* August 27. (https://www.them.us/story/trans-activists-protest-ice).

43. McElwee, Sean. 2018. "The Power of 'Abolish ICE'." *New York Times,* August 4. (https://www.nytimes.com/2018/08/04/opinion/sunday/abolish-ice-ocasio-cortez-democrats.html).

44. McElwee, "The Power of 'Abolish ICE'."

45. Wong, Tom K., Donald Kerwin, Jeanne M. Atkinson, and Mary Meg McCarthy. 2014. "Paths to Lawful Immigration Status: Results and Implications from the PERSON Survey." *Journal of Migration and Human Security* 2(4): 287–304.

46. Chen, Michelle. 2018. "One Simple Way to Help Immigrants Fight Deportation." *The Nation,* September 6. (https://www.thenation.com/article/one-simple-way-to-help-immigrants-fight-deportation/).

47. The Catalyst Fund. (https://californiacatalystfund.org/).

48. Small, Julie. 2018. "Attorneys Say 'Streamlined' Hearings in San Diego Court Violate Immigrants' Rights." *The California Report,* KQED, August 24. (https://www.kqed.org/news/11688241/attorneys-say-streamlined-he).

49. Rivlin, Nadler. 2018. "California Border District Reverses Course on a Key Component of Operation Streamline." *The Intercept,* October 5. (https://theintercept.com/2018/10/05/operation-streamline-san-diego-california-immigration/).

50. Amnesty International. 2018. "*USA: 'You Don't Have Any Rights Here': Illegal Pushbacks, Arbitrary Detention & Ill Treatment of Asylum-Seekers in the United States.*" London: Amnesty International Ltd. (https://www.amnestyusa.org/wp-content/uploads/2018/10/You-Dont-Have-Any-Rights-Here.pdf).

51. Amnesty International, "'You Don't Have Any Rights Here.'"

52. Averbuch, Maya and Elisabeth Malkin. 2018. "Migrants in Tijuana Run to U.S. Border, but Fall Back in Face of Tear Gas." *New York Times,* November 25. (https://www.nytimes.com/2018/11/25/world/americas/tijuana-mexico-border.html).

53. Ruiz Escutia, Jose. 2019 (forthcoming). *Latinx/Chicanx Activism and the Undocumented Immigrant Youth Movement.* Master's thesis, California State University San Marcos.

54. Corrunker, Laura. 2012. "'Coming Out of the Shadows': DREAM Act Activism in the Context of Global Anti-Deportation Activism." *Indiana Journal of Global Legal Studies* 19(1): 143–48.

55. Long, Heather. 2018. "U.S., Canada and Mexico Just Reached a Sweeping New NAFTA Deal. Here Is What Is in It." *Washington Post*, October 1. (https://www.washingtonpost.com/business/2018/10/01/us-canada-mexico-just-reached-sweeping-new-nafta-deal-heres-whats-it/?utm_term=.0297e4e52e42).

56. Gonzales, Alfonso. 2009. "The 2006 *Mega Marchas* in Greater Los Angeles: Counter-Hegemonic Moment and the Future of *El Migrante* Struggle." *Latino Studies* 7(1): 30–59.

57. De La Garza, Antonio. 2017. Second Annual Undocumented Youth Conference. San Diego Dream Team at Palomar College, December 2.

58. International Organization for Migration. 2018. *World Migration Report*. Geneva, Switzerland.

59. International Organization for Migration, *World Migration Report*.

60. International Organization for Migration, *World Migration Report*.

61. International Organization for Migration, *World Migration Report*.

62. UNHCR. 2018. "Forced Displacement at Record 68.5 Million." UN Refugee Agency, June 18. (http://www.unhcr.org/en-us/news/stories/2018/6/5b222c494/forced-displacement-record-685-million.html).

63. UNHCR, "Forced Displacement."

64. UNHCR. 2018. *Global Trends in Forced Displacement in 2017*. UN Refugee Agency. (http://www.unhcr.org/globaltrends2017/).

65. Abumaye, Mohamed. 2017. *Askar: Militarism, Policing and Somali Refugees*. Dissertation, University of California San Diego. (http://escholarship.ucop.edu/uc/item/47p4n18h).

66. Abumaye, *Askar*.

67. UNHCR, *Global Trends in Forced Displacement*.

68. UNCHR, *Global Trends in Forced Displacement*.

69. Hansen, Matt and Mark Boster. 2014. "Protestors in Murrieta Block Detainees' Buses in Tense Standoff." *Los Angeles Times*, July 1. (http://www.latimes.com/local/lanow/la-me-ln-immigrants-murrieta-20140701-story.html).

70. Spagat, Elliot and Maria Verza. 2018. "Migrant Caravan Groups Arrive by Hundreds at US Border." *Washington Post*, November 14.

(https://www.washingtonpost.com/world/the_americas/us-hardens-border-at-tijuana-to-prepare-for-migrant-caravan/2018/11/13/82276334-e7a6-11e8-8449-1ff263609a31_story.html?utm_term=.6dbef66f431a).

71. Peters, Jeremy W. 2018. "How Trump-Fed Conspiracy Theories About Migrant Caravan Intersect with Deadly Hatred." *New York Times*, October 29. (https://www.nytimes.com/2018/10/29/us/politics/caravan-trump-shooting-elections.html).

72. Volpe, Daniele and Kirk Semple. 2018. "Voices from the Caravan: Why These Honduran Migrants Are Heading North." *New York Times*, October 18. (https://www.nytimes.com/2018/10/18/world/americas/honduras-migrant-caravan-voices.html).

73. Sriknishran, Maya. 2018. "Border Report: A Caravan Within the Caravan Has Arrived in Tijuana." Voice of San Diego, November 12. (https://www.voiceofsandiego.org/topics/news/border-report-a-caravan-within-the-caravan-has-arrived-in-tijuana/).

74. Murray, Royce. 2018. "5 Ways to Prevent the Next Migrant Caravan." Immigration Impact, October 23. (http://immigrationimpact.com/2018/10/23/5-ways-to-prevent-the-next-migrant-caravan/).

75. Corrunker, "'Coming Out of the Shadows'," 165.

76. Corrunker, "'Coming Out of the Shadows'," 165.

77. King, Martin Luther, Jr. 2013. *A Time to Break Silence: The Essential Works of Martin Luther King, Jr., for Students*. Beacon Press. View the entire speech here: https://www.youtube.com/watch?v=ZmtOGXreTOU.

Bibliography

Abed-Santos, Alex. 2017. "Superman Saved Undocumented Workers from a Racist—and Conservative Media Is Mad About It." Vox, September 17. (https://www.vox.com/culture/2017/9/15/16307794/superman-undocumented-workers-white-supremacist-action-comics).

Abel, Valenzuela, Jr., Nik Theodore, Edwin Meléndez, and Ana Luz Gonzalez. 2006. *ON THE CORNER: Day Labor in the United States*. UCLA's Center for the Study of Urban Poverty. (http://www.sscnet.ucla.edu/issr/csup/index.php).

Abelson, Max. 2015. "How an Undocumented Immigrant from Mexico Became a Star at Goldman Sachs." *Bloomberg Businessweek*, February 25. (https://www.bloomberg.com/news/articles/2015-02-25/how-an-undocumented-immigrant-from-mexico-became-a-star-at-goldman-sachs).

Abrego, Leisy J. 2008. "Legitimacy, Social Identity, and the Mobilization of Law: The Effects of Assembly Bill 540 on Undocumented Students." *California Law & Social Inquiry* 33(3): 709–34.

Abrego, Leisy. 2014. *Sacrificing Families: Navigating Laws, Labor and Love Across Borders*. Stanford, CA: Stanford University Press.

Abumaye, Mohamed. 2017. *Askar: Militarism, Policing and Somali Refugees*. Dissertation, University of California San Diego. (http://escholarship.ucop.edu/uc/item/47p4n18h).

Acuña, Rudy. 2015. *Occupied America: A History of Chicanos* (Eighth Edition). Boston: Pearson.

Aguilar, Julián. 2018. "After ICE Raid in North Texas, Immigrants Face Uncertain Futures." *Texas Tribune*, September 6. (https://www.texastribune.org/2018/09/06/after-ice-raid-north-texas-immigrants-face-uncertain-futures/).

AJ+. 2017. *The Unheard Story of America's Undocumented Workers*. Films for Action. (http://www.filmsforaction.org/watch/the-unheard-story-of-americas-undocumented-workers/).

Allen, Brian, Erica M. Cisneros, and Alexandra Tellez. 2013. "The Children Left Behind: The Impact of Parental Deportation on Mental Health." *Journal of Child and Family Studies* 24(2): 386–92.

Alvarado, Monsy. 2018. "Phil Murphy Signs Bill Extending Financial Aid to Undocumented Immigrants in New Jersey." NorthJersey.com, May 9. (https://www.northjersey.com/story/news/new-jersey/2018/05/09/phil-murphy-signs-bill-extending-financial-aid-undocumented-students/587128002/).

Alvarado, Monsy and Hannan Adely. 2017. "N.J. Chief Justice Asks Feds Not to Arrest Immigrants at Courthouses." NorthJersey.com, April 19. (http://www.northjersey.com/story/news/politics/2017/04/19/nj-supreme-court-chief-justice-asks-ice-dhs-not-arrest-undocumented-immigrants-court/100663528/).

American Bar Association. 2006. *Tips for Appealing to the Board of Immigration Appeals (BIA)*. Washington, DC: American Bar Association. (https://www.americanbar.org/content/dam/aba/publications/commission_on_immigration/tips_bia_appeals2006.authcheckdam.pdf).

American Bar Association. N.d. "The Dangers of *Notario* Fraud." (https://www.americanbar.org/content/dam/aba/migrated/Immigration/PublicDocuments/notarios_info_piece_englishfinal.authcheckdam.pdf).

American Civil Liberties Union. 2014. *Warehoused and Forgotten: Immigrants Trapped in Our Shadow Private Prison System*. Washington, DC and Houston, Texas. (https://www.aclu.org/sites/default/files/field_document/060614-aclu-car-reportonline.pdf).

American Civil Liberties Union. 2015. "ACLU Announces Settlement in Lawsuit Over Warrantless Raid by US Immigration Agents and Nashville Police." New York, ACLU, July 27. (https://www.aclu.org/news/aclu-announces-settlement-lawsuit-over-warrantless-raid-us-immigration-agents-and-nashville-0).

American Civil Liberties Union. 2015. "Customs and Border Protection's (CBP's) 100-Mile Rule." Washington, DC: American Civil Liberties Union, September 14. (https://www.aclu.org/sites/default/files/assets/14_9_15_cbp_100-mile_rule_final.pdf).

American Civil Liberties Union. 2017. "ACLU Comment on ICE Arrest of Domestic Abuse Victim." ACLU, February 17. (https://www.aclu.org/news/aclu-comment-ice-arrest-domestic-abuse-victim).

American Civil Liberties Union. 2017. "ACLU Seeks Documents on ICE's Use of Cell Phone Trackers," May 19. (https://www.aclu.org/news/aclu-seeks-documents-ices-use-cell-phone-trackers).

American Civil Liberties Union. 2017. "The Constitution in the 100-Mile Border Zone." Washington, DC: (https://www.aclu.org/other/constitution-100-mile-border-zone?redirect=technology-and-liberty/fact-sheet-us-constitution-free-zone).

American Civil Liberties Union of Arizona. 2015. "Freedom of Information Act (FOIA) Request Reveals Lack of Oversight, No Accountability for Widespread Civil Rights Violations." October 15. (https://www.acluaz.org/en/press-releases/aclu-report-border-patrols-interior-enforcement-records-show-systemic-abuse-few).

American Immigration Council. 2010. "The DREAM Act: Creating Opportunities for Immigrant Students and Supporting the U.S. Economy." July 13. (https://www.americanimmigrationcouncil.org/research/dream-act).

American Immigration Council. 2013. "An Immigration Stimulus: The Economic Benefits of a Legalization Program." April 3. (https://www.americanimmigrationcouncil.org/research/immigration-stimulus-economic-benefits-legalization-program).

American Immigration Council. 2014. "Removal Without Recourse: The Growth of Summary Deportations from the United States." Washington, DC: American Immigration Council, April 28. (https://www.americanimmigrationcouncil.org/research/removal-without-recourse-growth-summary-deportations-united-states).

American Immigration Council. 2016. "The H-1B Visa Program: A Primer on the Program and Its Impact on Jobs, Wages, and the Economy." April 6. (https://www.americanimmigrationcouncil.org/research/h1b-visa-program-fact-sheet).

American Immigration Council. 2016. "Public Education for Immigrant Students: *Understanding Plyler v. Doe.* Fact Sheet." October 24. (https://www.americanimmigrationcouncil.org/research/plyler-v-doe-public-education-immigrant-students).

American Immigration Council. 2016. "Why Don't They Just Get in Line? There Is No Line for Many Unauthorized Immigrants." Fact Sheet, August 12. (https://www.americanimmigrationcouncil.org/sites/default/files/research/why_dont_they_just_get_in_line_and_come_legally.pdf)

American Immigration Council. 2017. "The Dream Act, DACA, and Other Policies Designed to Protect Dreamers." American Immigration Council, September 6. (https://www.americanimmigrationcouncil.org/research/dream-act-daca-and-other-policies-designed-protect-dreamers).

American Immigration Council. 2017. "Immigrants in Missouri." October 13. (https://www.americanimmigrationcouncil.org/research/immigrants-in-missouri).

American Immigration Council. 2018. "Temporary Protected Status: An Overview." August 1. (https://www.americanimmigrationcouncil.org/research/temporary-protected-status-overview).

American Immigration Lawyers Association. N.d. "Stop *Notario* Fraud." (http://www.stopnotariofraud.org/).

Amnesty International. 2018. *USA: "You Don't Have Any Rights Here": Illegal Pushbacks, Arbitrary Detention & Ill Treatment of Asylum-Seekers in the United States.* London: Amnesty International Ltd. (https://www.amnestyusa.org/wp-content/uploads/2018/10/You-Dont-Have-Any-Rights-Here.pdf).

Anderson, Nick. 2016. "Students to Education Dept.: Small Changes Can Make Big Payoffs in Graduation Rates." *Washington Post*, March 22. (https://www.washingtonpost.com/news/grade-point/wp/2016/03/22/students-to-education-dept-small-changes-can-make-big-payoffs-in-graduation-rates/).

Andreeva, Nellie. 2017. "Gina Rodriguez Producing Immigration Series Projects at CBS and the CW, 'LA Story' Reboot." *Deadline*, September 7. (https://deadline.com/2017/09/gina-rodriguez-immigration-projects-cbs-the-cw-la-story-reboot-1202162452/).

Aparicio, Ana. 2016. "Flint's Undocumented Immigrants Are Having Trouble Accessing Clean Water." Quartz, February 10. (http://qz.com/613960/flints-undocumented-immigrants-are-having-trouble-accessing-clean-water/).

Armbruster-Sandoval, Ralph. 2017. "On His Book, *Starving for Justice: Hunger Strikes, Spectacular Speech, and the Struggle for Dignity.*" *ROROTOKO*, September 18. (http://rorotoko.com/interview/20170918_armbruster-sandoval_ralph_on_book_starving_for_justice_hunger/?page=2).

Armenta, Amada. 2017. *Protect, Serve, and Deport: The Rise of Policing as Immigration Enforcement.* Oakland: University of California Press.

Averbuch, Maya and Elisabeth Malkin. 2018. "Migrants in Tijuana Run to U.S. Border, but Fall Back in Face of Tear Gas." *New York Times*, November 25. https://www.nytimes.com/2018/11/25/world/americas/tijuana-mexico-border.html

Baer, Barbara. 1975. "Stopping Traffic: One Woman's Cause." *The Progressive*, September: 38–40.

Bakare, Lanre. 2017. "'Daca Dramas': How Immigration Became US TV's New Obsession." *The Guardian*, September 13. (https://www.theguardian.com/tv-and-radio/tvandradioblog/2017/sep/13/daca-dramas-immigration-tv-us).

Baker, Beth and Alejandra Marchevsky. 2017. "Immigration Agents Came for Our Student." *Los Angeles Times*, June 8. (http://www.latimes.com/opinion/op-ed/la-oe-baker-marchevsky-rueda-deportation-20170608-story.html).

Balingit, Moriah. 2018. "Can Educators Call ICE on Students? Betsy DeVos Finally Answers." *Washington Post*, June 5. (https://www.washingtonpost.com/news/education/wp/2018/06/05/can-educators-call-ice-on-students-betsy-devos-finally-answers/?utm_term=.2ddb971d27f6).

Barile, Nancy. 2015. "Undocumented Students: A Teacher's Perspective." Huffington Post, December 10. (http://www.huffingtonpost.com/nancy-barile/undocumented-students-a-t_b_8759510.html).

Barreto, Matt A., Sylvia Manzano, Ricardo Ramirez, and Kathy Rim. 2009. "Mobilization, Participation, and *Solidaridad*: Latino Participation in the 2006 Immigration Protest Rallies." *Urban Affairs Review* 44(5): 736–64.

Barreto, Matt A., Sylvia Manzano, and Gary Segura. 2012. *The Impact of Media Stereotypes on Opinions and Attitudes Towards Latinos*. National Hispanic Media Coalition. (http://www.nhmc.org/national-poll-impact-media-stereotypes-opinions-attitudes-towards-latinos/).

Bauer, Mary and Monica Ramirez. 2010. *Injustice on Our Plates*. SPLC Southern Poverty Law Center, November 7. (https://www.splcenter.org/20101108/injustice-our-plates).

BBC News. 2018. "Trump Travel Ban: What Does This Ruling Mean?" BBC News, June 26. (https://www.bbc.com/news/world-us-canada-39044403).

Bello, Kemi. 2016. "Bill Introduced in Congress to Bring U.S. Veterans Back Home." Immigrant Legal Resource Center, July 14. (https://www.ilrc.org/bill-introduced-congress-bring-deported-us-veterans-back-home).

Benenson, Laurence. 2018. "The Math of Immigration Detention 2018 Update: Costs Continue to Multiply." National Immigration Forum, May 9. (https://immigrationforum.org/article/math-immigration-detention-2018-update-costs-continue-mulitply/).

Benevento, Maria. 2017. "Keep 'Dream Act' Free of Strings, Activists Say About Childhood Immigrants." *National Catholic Reporter*, October 19. (https://www.ncronline.org/news/justice/keep-dream-act-free-strings-activists-say-about-childhood-immigrants).

Berger, Peter L. 1963. *An Invitation to Sociology*. New York: Doubleday/Anchor Books.

Berlinger, Nancy, Claudia Calhoon, Michael K. Gusmano, and Jackie Vimo. 2015. *Undocumented Immigrants and Access to Health Care in New York City: Identifying Fair, Effective, and Sustainable Local Policy Solutions: Report and Recommendations to the Office of the Mayor of New York City*. The Hastings Center and New York Immigration Coalition. (http://www.undocumentedpatients.org/wp-content/uploads/2015/04/Undocumented-Immigrants-and-Access-to-Health-Care-NYC-Report-April-2015.pdf).

The Best Colleges. 2018. *College Guide for Undocumented Students* (2018 Edition). The Best Colleges. (https://www.thebestcolleges.org/resources/undocumented-students/).

Binational Arts Residency. 2015. "2015 Binational Residency Artist: Ana Teresa Fernández." (https://www.binationalartsresidency.com/new-page/).

Blake, Meredith. 2011. "America Ferrera Talks About Playing an Illegal Immigrant on 'The Good Wife'." *Los Angeles Times*, March 30. (http://latimesblogs.latimes.com/showtracker/2011/03/america-ferrera-talks-about-playing-an-immigrant-on-the-good-wife.html).

Blay, Zeba. 2017. "Watch 6-Year-Old Sophie Cruz Give One of the Best Speeches of the Women's March." Huffington Post, January 21. (http://www.huffingtonpost.com/entry/sophie-cruz_us_58839698e4b096b4a23201f6).

Bogado, Aura. 2013. "A Music Video Without Papers." *The Nation*, April 8. (https://www.thenation.com/article/music-video-without-papers/).

Border Angels. 2017. "Enrique Morones: Founder and Director." Border Angels. (http://www.borderangels.org/staff-page/enrique-morones/).

Bowerman, Mary. 2017. "Watch: 6-Year-Old Sophie Cruz Captures Hearts at Massive Women's March." *USA Today*, January 21. (http://www.usatoday.com/story/news/politics/onpolitics/2017/01/21/watch-6-year-old-sophie-cruz-capture-hearts-massive-womens-march/96889558/).

Bozick, Robert and Trey Miller. 2014. "In-State College Tuition Policies for Undocumented Immigrants: Implications for High School Enrollment Among Non-Citizen Mexican Youth." *Population Research and Policy Review* 33(1): 13–30.

Branton, Regina and Johanna Dunaway. 2008. "English- and Spanish-Language Media Coverage of Immigration: A Comparative Analysis." *Social Science Quarterly* 89(4): 1006–22.

Bregman, Rutger. 2016. "The Surprisingly Compelling Argument for Open Borders." *Fortune*, April 17. (http://fortune.com/2016/04/17/immigration-open-borders/).

Brissey, Breia. 2015. "The Good Wife Recap 'The Next Month'." *Entertainment Weekly*, March 2. (http://ew.com/recap/the-good-wife-season-5-episode-8/2/).

Brown, Emma. 2015. "Days from Leaving Office, Education Secretary Arne Duncan Talks About Successes, Failures." *Washington Post*, December 17. (https://www.washingtonpost.com/news/education/wp/2015/12/17/days-from-leaving-office-education-secretary-arne-duncan-talks-about-successes-failures/)._

Buch, Jason. 2018. "Appeals Again Says Family of Slain Teen Can't Sue Border Patrol." *San Antonio Express-News*, March 21. (https://www.expressnews.com/news/local/article/Appeals-again-says-family-of-slain-teen-can-t-12771895.php).

Buckley, Madeline and Fatima Hussein. 2017. "In Indianapolis, Undocumented Immigrant Community Making Contingency Plans." *Indystar*, March 5. (http://www.indystar.com/story/news/politics/2017/03/05/indianapolis-undocumented-community-making-contingency-plans/98629280/).

Buiano, Madeline. 2018. "ICE Data: Tens of Thousands of Deported Parents Have U.S. Citizen Kids." *Center for Public Integrity*, October 12. (https://www.publicintegrity.org/2018/10/12/22333/ice-data-tens-thousands-deported-parents-have-us-citizen-kids).

Burnett, John. 2018. "Finally Reunited with Her Child, Migrant Mother Has a Warning for the Caravan." National Public Radio, November 15. (https://www.npr.org/2018/11/15/668380488/finally-reunited-with-her-child-migrant-mother-has-a-warning-for-caravan).

Burnham, Linda and Nik Theodore. 2012. *Home Economics: The Invisible and Unregulated World of Domestic Work*. National Domestic Workers Alliance. (http://www.domesticworkers.org/pdfs/HomeEconomicsEnglish.pdf).

Burress, Jim. 2012. "Georgia Immigration Law Trips Up Doctors and Nurses." National Public Radio, November 11. (http://www.npr.org/sections/health-shots/2012/11/12/164950641/georgia-immigration-law-trips-up-doctors-and-nurses).

Bussert-Webb, Kathy. 2015. "Parrying the Pathologization of a Strong, Unified Mexican American Community." *Creative Approaches to Research* 8(2): 46–69.

Calavita, Kitty. 1992. *Inside the State: The Bracero Program, Immigration and the INS.* New York: Routledge.

Calavita, Kitty. 1996. "The New Politics of Immigration: 'Balanced Budget Conservatism' and the Symbolism of Proposition 187." *Social Problems* 43(3): 284–305.

Calefati, Jessica. 2015. "California Undocumented Immigrants Could Get Legal Protections, Health Care Under New Plan." (http://www.dailynews.com/social-affairs/20150407/california-undocumented-immigrants-could-get-legal-protections-health-care-under-new-plan).

California Department of Industrial Relations. 2007. "In California, Restaurant Workers Have Rights" (Flier). (https://www.dir.ca.gov/dlse/Publications/WorkersRightsFlyer-Restaurant-English.pdf).

California Healthcare Foundation. 2015. *Major Transition with Minor Disruption: Moving Undocumented Children from Healthy Kids to Full-Scope Medi-Cal.* Policy Brief, November. (http://www.chcf.org/publications/2015/11/major-transition-undocumented-children).

California Immigrant Policy Center. 2017. *Resilience in an Age of Inequality: Immigrant Contributions to California.* (http://www.haasjr.org/sites/default/files/resources/ImmigrantContributions2017-CIPC-USC.pdf).

Camera, Lauren. 2015. "In the Classroom, and in the Country Illegally." *US News*, October 20. (http://www.usnews.com/news/articles/2015/10/20/education-department-issues-guide-to-help-schools-serve-students-in-the-country-illegally).

Campbell Fernández, Alexia. 2016. "The Truth About Undocumented Immigrants and Taxes: They're Contributing Billions of Dollars a Year to Social Security, but May Never Reap Any Retirement Benefits from It." *The Atlantic,* September 12. (http://www.theatlantic.com/business/archive/2016/09/undocumented-immigrants-and-taxes/499604/).

Canseco, Omar. 2017. *Cruces Violentos, Violent Crossings: Undocumented Mexican Migration and Deportation Narratives.* Master's thesis, California State University San Marcos. (https://csusm-pace.calstate.edu/handle/10211.3/191105).

Canseco, Omar and Marisol Clark-Ibáñez. 2015. "After College Graduation: Bittersweet." In *Undocumented Latino Youth—Navigating Their Worlds.* Boulder, CO: Lynne Rienner Publishers, Chapter 8 (pp. 143–61).

Capps, Randy, Michael Fix, and Jie Zong. 2016. "A Profile of U.S. Children with Unauthorized Immigrant Parents." Migration Policy Institute. (http://www.migrationpolicy.net).

Carlin, Shannon. 2015. "'Jane the Virgin' Deals with Immigration Reform in an Important Way." *Bustle,* November 11. (https://www.bustle.com/articles/123223-jane-the-virgin-deals-with-immigration-reform-in-an-important-subtle-way).

Carson, Bethany and Eleana Diaz. 2015. "Payoff: How Congress Ensures Private Prison Profit with an Immigrant Detention Quota." GrassrootsLeadership.org. (http://grassrootsleadership.org/reports/payoff-how-congress-ensures-private-prison-profit-immigrant-detention-quota).

Castañeda, Heide and Milena A. Melo. 2014. "Health Care Access for Latino Mixed-Status Families: Barriers, Strategies, and Implications for Reform." *American Behavioral Scientist* 58(14): 1891–1909.

Castillo, Andrea. 2018. "ICE Arrests Farmworkers, Sparking Fears in the Central Valley Over Immigrants and the Economy." *Los Angeles Times,* March 31. (http://www.latimes.com/local/lanow/la-me-farmworkers-ice-20180316-htmlstory.html).

Castillo, Andrea, Rosanna Xia, David Kelly, and Victoria Kim. 2018. "From L.A. to N.Y., Hundreds of Thousands Join Nationwide Rallies to Protest Trump's Immigration Policies." *Los Angeles Times*, June 30. (http://www.latimes.com/local/lanow/la-me-rally-family-separation-20180629-story.html).

Castillo, Walbert. 2015. "Undocumented Students Work for Support, Reform." *USA Today*, January 17. (http://college.usatoday.com/2015/01/17/undocumented-students-work-for-support-reform/).

Catalyst Fund. N.d. (https://californiacatalystfund.org/).

CBS This Morning. 2018. "'Psychological Trauma': Ex-Employee Describes Facilities for Separated Immigrant Children." *CBS This Morning*, June 29. (https://www.youtube.com/watch?v=8-wtqAMRc3w).

Center for Popular Democracy. 2013. *The New York Immigrant Family Unity Project: Good for Families, Good for Employers, and Good for All New Yorkers*. Brooklyn, NY: The Center for Popular Democracy.

Center for Reproductive Rights. 2015. *Nuestro Texas: A Reproductive Rights Agenda for Latinas*. Report with the National Latina Institute for Reproductive Health, January. (https://www.reproductiverights.org/learning-from-nuestro-texas).

Chang, Aurora, Mark Anthony Torrez, Kelly N. Ferguson, and Anita Sagar. 2017. "Figured Worlds and American Dreams: An Exploration of Agency and Identity Among Latinx Undocumented Students." *Urban Review* 49: 189–216.

Charles, Dan. 2016. "Inside the Lives of Farmworkers: Top 5 Lessons I Learned on the Ground." National Public Radio, July 15. (http://www.npr.org/sections/the-salt/2016/07/15/484967591/inside-the-lives-of-farmworkers-top-5-lessons-i-learned-on-the-ground).

Chavez, Leo. 2013. *The Latino Threat: Constructing Immigrants, Citizens, and the Nation* (Second Edition). Stanford, CA: Stanford University Press. Kindle Edition.

Chavez-Peterson, Norma. 2017. "Yes, We Need a Wall—Between Local Police and Federal Immigration Enforcement." Voice of San Diego, June 8. (http://www.voiceofsandiego.org/topics/opinion/yes-need-wall-local-police-federal-immigration-enforcement/).

Chen, Michelle. 2018. "One Simple Way to Help Immigrants Fight Deportation." *The Nation*, September 6. (https://www.thenation.com/article/one-simple-way-to-help-immigrants-fight-deportation/).

Chilin-Hernández, Jessica F. 2016. "Undocumented Virginians in the Age of Trump." *Virginia Policy Review* 10(1): 20–25. (http://www.virginiapolicyreview.org/uploads/5/5/9/2/55922627/chilin_final.pdf).

Chinchilla, Norma Stoltz, Nora Hamilton, and James Loucky. 2009. "The Sanctuary Movement and Central American Activism in Los Angeles." *Latin American Perspectives* 36(6): 101–26.

Chiricos, Ted, Kathy Padgett, and Marc Gertz. 2000. "Fear, TV News, and the Reality of Crime." *Criminology* 38: 755–85.

Chishti, Muzaffar and Fay Hipsman. 2015. "In Historic Shift, New Migration Flows from Mexico Fall Below Those from China and India." Migration Policy Institute, May 21. (http://www.migrationpolicy.org/article/historic-shift-new-migration-flows-mexico-fall-below-those-china-and-india).

Chishti, Muzaffar, Sarah Pierce, and Jessica Bolter. 2017. "The Obama Record on Deportations: Deporter in Chief or Not?" Migration Policy Institute, January 26. (http://www.migrationpolicy.org/article/obama-record-deportations-deporter-chief-or-not).

Chuang, Angie and Robin Chin Roemer. 2015. "Beyond the Positive-Negative Paradigm of Latino/Latina News-Media Representations: DREAM Act Exemplars, Stereotypical Selection, and American Otherness." *Journalism* 16(8): 1045–61.

Citizen-Times. 2017. "Undocumented Immigrants in the DACA Program Face Uncertainty Under President Trump." April 18. (http://www.citizen-times.com/videos/news/local/2017/04/18/daca-immigration/100595134/).

Clark-Ibáñez, Marisol. 2015. *Undocumented Latino Youth: Navigating Their Worlds*. Boulder, CO: Lynn Rienner Publishers.

Clark-Ibáñez, Marisol and Rhonda Avery-Merker. 2015. "Elementary School: The Beginning and the Promise." In *Undocumented Latino Youth—Navigating Their Worlds*. Boulder, CO: Lynne Rienner Publishers, Chapter 3.

Clark-Ibáñez, Marisol, Bettina Serna, and Rhonda Avery-Merker. 2014. "In/Visibility of Undocumented Latino Immigrants in the News Media." Conference presentation at the Pacific Sociological Association in Portland, OR. March 27.

Clayton, Ashley. 2012. "From Migrant Farm Work to Shuttle Astronaut: Jose Hernandez Video." September 7. (http://www.space.com/17500-interview-with-former-astronaut-jose-hernandez-part-one-video.html).

CNN Wire. 2017. "Gov. Brown's Pardon Could Help 3 Deported Veterans Return to the U.S." KTLA5, April 16. (http://ktla.com/2017/04/16/gov-browns-pardon-could-help-3-deported-veterans-return-to-u-s/).

CNN Wire and Katrina Butcher. 2018. "Keep Families Together Rally Held at Oklahoma State Capitol, Nationwide." KFOR Oklahoma's News, June 30. (https://kfor.com/2018/06/30/keep-families-together-rally-held-at-oklahoma-state-capitol-nationwide/).

Cohen, Stanley. 1972. *Folk Devils and Moral Panics*. London, England: MacGibbon & Kee.

College Board. N.d. "Advising Undocumented Students." (https://professionals.collegeboard.org/guidance/financial-aid/undocumented-students).

Community Service Society: Fighting Poverty, Strengthening New York. 2017. *Community Health Advocates 2016 Annual Report*. February. (http://www.cssny.org/publications/entry/cha-2016-annual-report).

Connell, John. 1993. "Kitanai, Kitsui, and Kiken: The Rise of Labor Migration to Japan." Sydney, Australia: University of Australia as cited in Flynn, Michael A., Donald E. Eggerth, and C. Jeffrey Jacobson, Jr. 2015. "Undocumented Status as a Social Determinant of Occupational Safety and Health: The Workers' Perspective." *American Journal of Industrial Medicine* 58(11): 1127–37.

Constable, Pamela. 2014. "'Dreamer Moms' Fast Near White House, Hoping Obama Will Grant Them Legal Status." *Washington Post*, November 15. (http://ezproxy.csusm.edu/login?url=http://search.proquest.com/docview/1625807117?accountid=10363).

Cooperativa Latino Credit Union. 2000–2018. "Latino Community Credit Union." (http://latinoccu.org).

Corriston, Michele. 2016. "Actress Diana Guerrero on Her Parents' Deportation, Immigration Reform: 'I Definitely Fell Through the Cracks'." SiriusXM, May 12. (http://blog.siriusxm.com/2016/05/12/jane-the-virgin-diane-guerrero-immigration-reform/).

Corrunker, Laura. 2012. "'Coming Out of the Shadows': DREAM Act Activism in the Context of Global Anti-Deportation Activism." *Indiana Journal of Global Legal Studies* 19(1): 143–48.

Cosecha. 2017. "A Day Without Immigrants." (http://www.lahuelga.com/home/#header).

Cosecha. 2017. "The Story." (http://www.lahuelga.com/story/).

Costanza-Chock, Sasha. 2014. *Out of the Shadows, Into the Streets! Transmedia Organizing and the Immigrant Rights Movement*. Cambridge, MA: MIT Press.

Coutin, Susan Bibler. 2000. *Legalizing Moves: Salvadoran Immigrants' Struggle for U.S. Residency.* Ann Arbor: University of Michigan Press.

Coutin, Susan Bibler. 2013. "Place and Presence within Salvadoran Deportees' Narratives of Removal." *Childhood* 20(3): 323–36.

Coutin, Susan Bibler. 2015. "Deportation Studies: Origins, Themes and Directions." *Journal of Ethnic and Migration Studies* 41(4): 671–81.

Covarrubias, Alejandro and Argelia Lara. 2014. "The Undocumented (Im)Migrant Educational Pipeline: The Influence of Citizenship Status on Educational Attainment for People of Mexican Origin." *Urban Education* 49(1): 75–110.

Crawford, Emily R. 2017. "The Ethic of Community and Incorporating Undocumented Immigrant Concerns into Ethical School Leadership." *Educational Administration Quarterly* 53(2): 147–79.

Cruz, Melissa. 2018. "Surprise Government Inspection Finds Nooses in ICE Detention Center, Doctors Refusing to Treat Immigrant Detainees." Immigration Impact, October 3. (http://immigrationimpact.com/2018/10/03/inspection-finds-nooses-ice-detention-center/).

Cuauhtémoc Hernández García, César. 2008. "No Human Being Is Illegal: Moving Beyond Deportation Law." *Monthly Review* 60(2): 23–31.

Cuauhtémoc Hernández García, César. 2014. "Immigration as Punishment." *UCLA Law Review* 61: 1346–1414.

Cuauhtémoc Hernández García, César. 2015. *Crimmigration Law.* American Bar Association Publishing.

Cuen, Leigh. 2015. "#WeAreSeeds Campaign Has People Talking Immigration, Racism." Vocativ, May 31. (http://www.vocativ.com/culture/media/weareseeds-twitter-hashtag-immigration-racism/).

CultureStrike. 2016. "Visions from the Inside." (http://www.culturestrike.org/project/visions-inside-2016).

Cummings, Bill. 2017. "Study Shows Value of Undocumented Immigrants." *Connecticut Post*, February 26. (https://www.ctpost.com/local/article/Study-shows-value-of-undocumented-immigrants-10959317.php).

Dallas Morning News Editorial. 2017. "Remembering the Supreme Court Case out of Texas That Saved Classroom Seats for Undocumented Children." *Dallas Morning News*, June 12. (https://www.dallasnews.com/opinion/editorials/2017/06/12/remembering-plyler-v-doethe-supreme-court-case-texas-saved-classroom-seat-undocumented-children).

De Genova, Nicholas. 2002. "Migrant 'Illegality' and Deportability in Everyday Life." *Annual Review of Anthropology* 31(1): 419–47.

De Genova, Nicholas. 2010. "The Deportation Regime: Sovereignty, Space and the Freedom of Movement." In *The Deportation Regime*, Nicholas De Genova and Nathalie Peutz (Eds.). Durham, NC, and London: Duke University Press, 33–65.

De Genova, Nicholas. 2010. "The Queer Politics of Migration: Reflections on 'Illegality' and Incorrigibility." *Studies in Social Justice* 4(2): 101–26.

De Genova, Nicholas. 2016. "Detention, Deportation and Waiting: Toward a Theory of Migrant Detainability." Global Detention Project Working Paper No. 18, November. (https://www.globaldetentionproject.org/wp-content/uploads/2016/12/De-Genova-GDP-Paper-2016.pdf).

Define American. 2017. *Immigrants and Immigration: A Guide for Entertainment Professionals.* (https://defineamerican.com/ent/guide/).

De La Garza, Antonio. 2017. Second Annual Undocumented Youth Conference. San Diego Dream Team at Palomar College, December 2, 2017.

De La Torre III, Pedro and Roy Germano. 2014. "Out of the Shadows: DREAMer Identity in the Immigrant Youth Movement." *Latino Studies* 12(3): 449–67.

Democracy Now!. 2012. "DREAM Activist Speaks from Broward Detention Center: Listen to Exclusive Interview." (https://www.democracynow.org/2012/7/31/dream_activist_speaks_from_broward_detention_center_listen_to_exclusive_audio).

Democracy Now!. 2013. "Who Is Dayani Cristal?: Gael García Bernal Traces Path of Migrant Worker Who Died in Arizona Desert." (https://www.democracynow.org/2013/1/25/who_is_dayani_cristal_gael_garcia).

Democracy Now!. 2018. "Trump Administration Hints It May Resume Family Separation at Border; ACLU Says 'Public Outcry Is Critical.'" DemocracyNow.org. October 15. (https://www.democracynow.org/2018/10/15/trump_admin_hints_it_may_resume).

Denton, Joseph C. 2016. "Federal Judge Approves Force Feeding of Detainees, Sheds Light on Local Anti-Deportation Movement." *South Seattle Emerald*, January 4. (https://southseattleemerald.com/2016/01/04/federal-judge-approves-force-feeding-of-detainees-sheds-light-on-local-anti-deportation-movement/).

Department for Professional Employees. 2017. "Guest Worker Visas: The H-1B and L1." DPE Research Department. June 15. (http://dpeaflcio.org/programs-publications/issue-fact-sheets/guest-worker-visas-the-h-1b-and-l-1/#_edn6).

Diaz, Jesse. 2010. *Organizing the Brown Tide: La Gran Epoca Primavera 2006, an Insider's Story*. PhD dissertation, University of California Riverside.

Diaz, Melanie and Timothy Keen. 2015. "How US Private Prisons Profit from Immigrant Detention." Council on Hemispheric Affairs, May 12. (http://www.coha.org/how-us-private-prisons-profit-from-immigrant-detention/).

Dibble, Sandra. 2017. "Congressional Visit Gives a Boost to Deported U.S. Veterans in Tijuana." *San Diego Union Tribune*, June 3. (http://www.sandiegouniontribune.com/news/border-baja-california/sd-me-veterans-deported-20170603-story.html).

Dinan, Stephen. 2015. "Illegal Immigrant Detention Centers Rife with Abuses, U.S. Civil Rights Commission Report Finds." *Washington Times*, September 17. (http://www.washingtontimes.com/news/2015/sep/17/illegal-immigrant-detention-centers-rife-abuses-us/?page=all).

Dixon, Travis L. and Charlotte L. Williams. 2014. "The Changing Misrepresentation of Race and Crime on Network and Cable News." *Journal of Communication* 65(1): 24–39.

Dober, Greg. 2014. "Corizon Needs a Checkup: Problems with Privatized Correctional Healthcare." *Prison Legal News*, March 15. (https://www.prisonlegalnews.org/news/2014/mar/15/corizon-needs-a-checkup-problems-with-privatized-correctional-healthcare/).

Domonoske, Camila. 2017. "What's New in Those DHS Memos on Immigration Enforcement?" National Public Radio, February 22. (http://www.npr.org/sections/thetwo-way/2017/02/22/516649344/whats-new-in-those-dhs-memos-on-immigration-enforcement).

Domonoske, Camila. 2018. "Trump Administration Transferred $9.8 Million from FEMA to ICE." National Public Radio, September 12. (https://www.npr.org/2018/09/12/647021316/trump-administration-transferred-9-8-million-from-fema-to-ice).

Drummond, Tammerlin. 2017. "Oakland Artist Taps Power of Art to Organize for Change." *EastBay Times*, February 1. (http://www.eastbaytimes.com/2017/02/01/oakland-artist-taps-power-of-art-to-organize-for-change/).

Dumke, Mick and Dan Mihalopolous. 2017. "'Dreamers' Could Face Choice: Stay, or Go with Deported Parents." *Chicago Sun-Times*, April 2. (http://chicago.suntimes.com/feature/dreamers-could-face-choice-stay-or-go-with-deported-parents/).

Edwards, Andrew. 2017. "Student Aid Requests for Immigrants Up in 2017." *Orange County Register*, March 7. (http://www.ocregister.com/2017/03/07/student-aid-requests-for-immigrants-up-in-2017/).

Elbogen, Eric B., Sally C. Johnson, Virgina M. Newton, Kristy Straits-Troster, Jennifer J. Vasterling, H. Ryan Wagner and Jean C. Beckham. 2012. "Criminal Justice Involvement, Trauma, and Negative Affect in Iraq and Afghanistan War Veterans." *Journal of Consulting and Clinical Psychology* 80(6): 1097–1102.

Elias, Thomas. 2017. "Farmers Fear Immigration Raids." *Record Searchlight*, April 3. (https://www.redding.com/story/opinion/columnists/tom-elias/2017/04/03/farmers-fear-immigration-raids/99986002/).

Elise, Sharon and Xuan Santos. 2017. "Department Statement: Standing Up for Social Justice." Department of Sociology, California State University San Marcos, September 25. (https://www.csusm.edu/sociology/index.html).

Elk, Mike. 2017. "Spike in Latino Workplace Deaths Has Many Worried About Trump Era." Payday Report, January 25. (http://paydayreport.com/spike-in-latino-workplace-deaths-has-many-worried-about-trump-era/).

Engleberg, Stephen. 2018. "DHS Chief Is Confronted with ProPublica Tape of Wailing Children Separated from Parents." ProPublica, June 18. (https://www.propublica.org/article/kirstjen-nielsen-homeland-security-crying-children-white-house-press-briefing).

Engler, Mark and Paul Engler. 2016. "Three Times When 'Impractical' Movements Led to Real Change." *The Nation,* March 7. (http://www.thenation.com/article/three-times-when-impractical-movements-led-to-real-change/).

Engler, Paul. 2009. "The U.S. Immigrant Rights Movement (2004–ongoing)." International Center on Nonviolent Conflict. (https://www.nonviolent-conflict.org/wp-content/uploads/2016/02/engler_united_states_immigrant_rights.pdf).

Executive Office for Immigration Review. 2017. "List of Currently Disciplined Practitioners." Washington, DC: Department of Justice. (https://www.justice.gov/eoir/list-of-currently-disciplined-practitioners).

Ewing, Walter, Daniel Martinez, and Rubén G. Rumbaut. 2015. "The Criminalization of Immigration in the United States." American Immigration Council, July 13. (https://www.americanimmigrationcouncil.org/research/criminalization-immigration-united-states).

Fair Immigration Reform Movement. 2008. "Art Is Action—Pro-Migrant Poster Power." June 12. (http://fairimmigration.org/2008/06/12/art-is-action-pro-migrant-poster-power/).

Farm Bureau. 2018. "Agriculture Labor Reform." (http://www.fb.org/issues/immigration-reform/agriculture-labor-reform/).

Farm Bureau. 2018. "Eye-Popping H-2A Figures Posted in FY2018." (https://www.fb.org/market-intel/eye-popping-h-2a-figures-posted-in-fy2018).

Fernandes, Deepa. 2007. *Targeted: National Security and the Business of Immigration.* St. Paul, MN: Seven Stories Press.

Fernandez, Harold. 2016. "Undocumented & Unhealthy: Why We Should All Want to Care for Immigrants Who Lack Legal Papers." *Daily News*, November 30. (http://www.nydailynews.com/opinion/undocumented-unhealthy-confronting-immigrant-care-crisis-article-1.2891811).

Fernandez, Maria Elena. 2018. "Why You Could Be Seeing a Lot of Immigrant Stories This Fall." Vulture, January 23. (http://www.vulture.com/2018/01/immigrant-stories-could-be-fall-tvs-biggest-trend.html).

Fernández, Valeria. 2013. "'Dream 9' Tactics Take Debate Beyond Halls of Congress." *La Prensa San Diego*, August 2. (http://laprensa-sandiego.org/featured/dream-9-tactics-take-debate-beyond-halls-of-congress/).

Fields, Liz. 2015. "These Undocumented Women Are Hunger Striking Against Their Detention in Texas." VICE News, October 30. (https://news.vice.com/article/these-undocumented-women-are-hunger-striking-against-their-detention-in-texas).

Fitzgerald, Elizabeth Moran, Judith G. Myers, and Paul Clark. 2016. "Nurses Need Not Be Guilty Bystanders: Caring for Vulnerable Immigrant Populations." *OJIN: The Online Journal of Issues in Nursing* 22(1): December. (http://ojin.nursingworld.org/MainMenuCategories/ANAMarketplace/ANAPeriodicals/OJIN/TableofContents/Vol-22-2017/No1-Jan-2017/Articles-Previous-Topics/Nurses-Need-Not-Be-Guilty-Bystanders.html?css=print).

Florido, Adrian. 2017. "How Trump Criminalized 11 Million with a Stroke of His Pen." NPR.com, January 28. (http://www.npr.org/sections/codeswitch/2017/01/28/512040631/how-trump-criminalized-11-million-with-a-stroke-of-his-pen?sc=tw).

Flynn, Meagan. 2018. "ICE Raid Targeting Employers and More Than 100 Workers Rocks a Small Nebraska Town." *Washington Post*, August 29. (https://www.washingtonpost.com/news/morning-mix/wp/2018/08/09/ice-raid-targeting-employers-and-more-than-100-workers-rocks-a-small-nebraska-town/?noredirect=on&utm_term=.e28896854a42).

Flynn, Michael, Thomas R. Cunningham, Rebecca J. Guerin, Brenna Keller, Larry J. Chapman, Denis Hudson, and Cathy Salgado. 2015. *Overlapping Vulnerabilities: The Occupational Safety and Health of Young Workers in Small Construction Firms*. Cincinnati, OH: U.S. Department of Health and Human Services, Centers for Disease Control and Prevention, National Institute for Occupational Safety and Health, DHHS (NIOSH) Publication No. 2015-178. (http://www.asse.org/assets/1/7/NIOSHreport_FinalDraft.pdf).

Flores v. Lynch. 2016. *Jenny Lisette Flores, et al. versus Loretta Lynch, Attorney General of the United States*. "Brief for the American Academy of Child and Adolescent Psychiatry and the National Association of Social Workers as *Amici Curiae* Supporting Appellees." D.C. Case No. 2:85-cv-04544-DMG-AGR. February 23. (http://www.humanrightsfirst.org/sites/default/files/HRFFloresAmicusBrief.pdf)

Fortuna, Lisa and Michelle V. Porche. 2013. "Clinical Issues and Challenges in Treating Undocumented Immigrants." *Clinical Issues and Challenges in Treating Undocumented Immigrants*. (http://www.psychiatrictimes.com/special-reports/clinical-issues-and-challenges-treating-undocumented-immigrants).

Framke, Caroline. 2015. "For Years, TV Has Treated Immigrants as Punchlines. These Shows Are Fighting Back." Vox.com, December 3. (http://www.vox.com/2015/12/3/9843124/tv-immigrants-stereotypes-asian-american).

Frederick, James. 2016. "What Is Home? Going Home and Struggling to Fit Back In." 2016. *LatinoUSA*, December 6. (http://www.npr.org/2016/12/09/504989799/going-home-and-struggling-to-fit-back-in).

Freedom University. 2016. "Who We Are in 2016." (https://www.youtube.com/watch?v=7w3yEAg-QPg).

Freedom University. 2018. "History." (https://freedom-university.org/timeline).

Freedom University. 2018. "Homepage." (https://freedom-university.org/home).

Freedom University. 2018. "Timeline." (https://freedom-university.org/timeline).

Galindo, René. 2012. "Undocumented & Unafraid: The DREAM Act 5 and the Public Disclosure of Undocumented Status as a Political Act." *Urban Review* 44: 589–611.

Galvan, Christina. N.d. "What Does My Notice to Appear Mean?" NOLO. (http://www.nolo.com/legal-encyclopedia/what-does-my-notice-appear-nta-mean.html).

Gany, Francesca, Patricia Novo, Rebecca Dobslaw, and Jennifer Leng. 2014. "Urban Occupational Health in the Mexican and Latino/Latina Immigrant Population: A Literature Review." *Journal of Immigrant and Minority Health* 16(5): 846–55. (http://ezproxy.csusm.edu/login?url=http://search.proquest.com.ezproxy.csusm.edu/docview/1558959572?accountid=10363).

Garcia, Ann and Samantha Franchim. 2013. "10 Facts You Need to Know About Immigrant Women." Center for American Progress, March 8. (https://www.americanprogress.org/issues/immigration/news/2013/03/08/55794/10-facts-you-need-to-know-about-immigrant-women-2013-update/).

García-Mellado, Diana. 2017. *The Lives of Latina/o Children in Mixed Immigration Status Families.* Master's thesis, California State University San Marcos. (http://hdl.handle.net/10211.3/191114).

Gee, Lisa Christensen, Matthew Gardner, Misha E. Hill, and Meg Wiehe. 2017. "Undocumented Immigrants' State & Local Tax Contributions." Institute on Taxation and Economic Policy (ITEP), March. (https://itep.org/wp-content/uploads/ITEP-2017-Undocumented-Immigrants-State-and-Local-Contributions.pdf).

Gelatt, Julia. 2016. "Immigration Status and the Healthcare Access and Health of Children of Immigrants." *Social Science Quarterly* 97(3): 540–54.

Gelatt, Julia and Jie Zong. 2018. *Settling In: A Profile of the Unauthorized Immigrant Population in the United States.* Migration Policy Institute, November. (https://www.migrationpolicy.org/research/profile-unauthorized-immigrant-population-united-states).

Gilcrist, Akiesha R. 2013. "Undocumented Immigrants: Lack of Equal Protection and Its Impact on Public Health." *Journal of Legal Medicine* 34(4): 403–12.

Gill, Hannah and Sara Peña. 2017. *The Deferred Action for Childhood Arrivals (DACA) Program in North Carolina: Perspectives from Immigrants and Community-Based Organizations. The Latino Migration Project.* Chapel Hill: University of North Carolina at Chapel Hill.

Glatz, Julianne. 2014. "Cheap Food I: Illegal Immigrants." *Illinois Times*, June 26. (http://illinoistimes.com/article-14108-cheap-food-i:-illegal-immigrants.html).

Global Detention Project. 2016. "Immigration Detention in the United States." GlobalDetentionProject.org, May 3. (https://www.globaldetentionproject.org/immigration-detention-in-the-united-states).

Golash-Boza, Tanya. 2009. "The Immigration Industrial Complex: Why We Enforce Immigration Policies Destined to Fail." *Sociology Compass* (3/2): 295–309.

Golash-Boza, Tanya. 2016. *Deported: Immigrant Policing, Disposable Labor and Global Capitalism.* New York: NYU Press.

Gomez, Alan. 2014. "White House: Don't Discourage Undocumented from Schools." *USA Today*, May 8. (http://www.usatoday.com/story/news/nation/2014/05/08/obama-immigration-undocumented-students/8840289/).

Gomez, Alan. 2017. "Trump Tells DREAMers to 'Rest Easy'—but One in Mexico Can't." *USA Today*, April 21. (https://www.usatoday.com/story/news/world/2017/04/21/trump-tells-dreamers-to-rest-easy-responds-to-juan-manuel-montes-case/100757434/).

Gomez, Alan and David Agren. 2017. "First DREAMer Is Deported Under Trump." *USA Today*, April 18. (https://www.usatoday.com/story/news/world/2017/04/18/first-protected-dreamer-deported-under-trump/100583274/).

Gómez, Sofía and Heide Castañeda. 2018. "'Recognize Our Humanity': Immigrant Youth Voices on Health Care in Arizona's Restrictive Political Environment." *Qualitative Health Research*, February: 1–12.

Gonzales, Richard. 2017. "DREAMer Deportation Case Raises Questions on Trump's Deferred Action Policy." National Public Radio, April 18. (http://www.npr.org/sections/thetwo-way/2017/04/18/524610150/first-dreamer-protected-by-deferred-action-program-is-deported).

Gonzales, Richard. 2017. "Tax Filings Seen Dipping Among Trump Crackdown on Illegal Immigration." National Public Radio, April 17. (http://www.npr.org/2017/04/17/523634144/tax-filings-seen-dipping-amid-trump-crackdown-on-illegal-immigration).

Gonzales, Roberto G. 2008. "Left Out but Not Shut Down: Political Activism and the Undocumented Latino Student Movement." *Northwestern Journal of Law and Social Policy* 3(2): 1–22.

Gonzales, Roberto G., Basia Ellis, Sarah Rendón-Garcia, and Kristina Brant. 2018. "(Un) authorized Transitions: Illegality, DACA, and the Life Course." *Research in Human Development* 15(3-4): 345–59.

Gonzales, Roberto G., Carola Suárez-Orozco, and Maria Cecilia Dedios-Sanguineti. 2013. "No Place to Belong: Contextualizing Concepts of Mental Health Among Undocumented Immigrant Youth in the United States." *American Behavioral Scientist* 57(8): 1174–99.

Gonzalez, Alfonso. 2009. "The 2006 *Mega Marchas* in Greater Los Angeles: Counter-Hegemonic Moment and the Future of *El Migrante* Struggle." *Latino Studies* 7(1): 30–59.

Gonzalez, Alfonso. 2013. *Reform without Justice: Latino Migrant Politics and the Homeland Security State*. Oxford: Oxford University Press.

Gonzalez, Jaime. 2015. "Hispanic Paradox: Why Immigrants Have a High Life Expectancy." BBC News, May 29. (http://www.bbc.com/news/world-U.S.-canada-32910129).

Gonzalez, Xatherin. 2015. "For Undocumented Women Seeking Reproductive Healthcare, Policing and Politics Create a Maze of Barriers." *Ms. Magazine* (Blog), November 11. (http://msmagazine.com/blog/2015/11/16/for-undocumented-women-seeking-reproductive-healthcare-policing-and-politics-create-a-maze-of-barriers/).

Goode, Erich and Nachman Ben-Yehuda. 2009. *Moral Panics: The Social Construction of Deviance* (Second Edition). Malden, MA: Wiley-Blackwell.

Gordon, Ian. 2014. "Inside Obama's Deportation Mill." *Mother Jones*, December 19. (http://www.motherjones.com/politics/2014/12/family-detention-artesia-dilley-immigration-central-america/).

Government Accountability Office. 2016. "Workplace Safety and Health: Additional Data Needed to Address Continued Hazards in the Meat and Poultry Industry." Report GAO-16-337 to Congress, April. (http://www.gao.gov/products/GAO-16-337).

Graham, Jordan. 2017. "ICE Can Jail up to 120 More Undocumented Immigrants as Orange County Sheriff Contract Expands by $5 Million." *Orange County Register*, May 9. (http://www.ocregister.com/2017/05/09/orange-county-supervisors-expand-federal-immigration-jail-contract-despite-pleas-from-advocates/).

Graham, Nathalie. 2018. "According to ICE There Is No Strike at the Northwest Detention Center." *The Stranger*, August 23. (https://www.thestranger.com/slog/2018/08/23/31243448/according-to-ice-there-is-no-hunger-strike-at-the-northwest-detention-center).

Green, Emily. 2017. "SF Supes OK Funds to Defend Immigrants in Detention." *San Francisco Chronicle*, March 2. (http://www.sfchronicle.com/politics/article/SF-supes-OK-funds-to-defend-immigrants-in-10973576.php?cmpid=gsa-sfgate-result).

Grimm, Josh. 2015. "Tenacity of Routine: The Absence of Geo-Ethnic Storytelling in Constructing Immigration News Coverage." *Howard Journal of Communications* 26(1): 1–20.

Grubbs, Vanessa. 2014. "Undocumented Immigrants and Kidney Transplant: Costs and Controversy." *Health Affairs* 33(2): 332–35.

Gubernskaya, Zoya and Joanna Dreby. 2017. "U.S. Immigration Policy and the Case for Family Unity." *Journal on Migration and Human Security* 5(2): 417–30.

Guerrero, Jean. 2015. "Deportees with Families in U.S. Try to Start Over in Tijuana." KQED News, May 19. (https://www.kqed.org/news/10530508/deportees-with-families-in-u-s-try-to-start-over-in-tijuana).

Gulbas, Lauren E., Luis H. Zayas, Hyunwoo Yoon, Hannah Szlyk, Sergio Aguilar-Gaxiola, and Guillermina Natera. 2016. "Deportation Experiences and Depression Among U.S. Citizen-Children with Undocumented Mexican Parents." *Child: Health, Care and Development* 42(2): 220–30.

Guo, Lei and Summer Harlow. 2014. "User-Generated Racism: An Analysis of Stereotypes of African Americans, Latinos, and Asians in YouTube Videos." *Howard Journal of Communications* 25(3): 281–302.

Hamilton, Keegan. 2017. "Trump Told Dreamers to 'Rest Easy,' But Here's Proof They Shouldn't." VICE News, May 3. (https://news.vice.com/story/trump-told-dreamers-to-rest-easy-but-heres-proof-they-shouldn't).

Hamm, Nia. 2016. "Advocates Push NY State For Health Care for Undocumented Immigrants." Public News Service, February 10. (http://www.publicnewsservice.org/2016-02-10/immigrant-issues/advocates-push-ny-state-for-health-care-for-undocumented-immigrants/a50303-1?utm_source=thebreakingnewsnetwork.com).

Hansen, Matt and Mark Boster. 2014. "Protestors in Murrieta Block Detainees' Buses in Tense Standoff." *Los Angeles Times*, July 1. (http://www.latimes.com/local/lanow/la-me-ln-immigrants-murrieta-20140701-story.html).

Hanson, Jessica. 2017. "School Settings Are Sensitive Locations That Should Be Off-Limits to Immigration Enforcement." National Immigration Law Center, May 4. (https://www.nilc.org/news/the-torch/5-4-17/).

Hartsfield, Cathy Ho. 2012. "Deportation of Veterans: The Silent Battle for Naturalization." *Rutgers Law Review* 64(3): 835–62.

Healthy California. 2015. *GET HEALTHY, CALIFORNIA! A Healthcare Resource Guide for Undocumented and Uninsured Californians.* (http://undocumentedanduninsured.org/wp-content/uploads/2015/01/Resource-Guide-v9n.pdf).

Heidbrink, Lauren. 2014. *Migrant Youth, Transnational Families and the State: Care and Contested Interests.* Philadelphia: University of Pennsylvania Press.

Heldiz, Adriana. 2018. "Video: Art Students Take on Trump's Border Wall Prototypes." Voice of San Diego, April 10. (https://www.voiceofsandiego.org/topics/news/video-art-students-take-on-trumps-border-wall-prototypes/).

Henderson, Tim. 2017. "Cities, States Move to Calm Fear of Deportation." *Governing—The States and Localities*, May 10. (http://www.governing.com/topics/politics/stateline-Cities-States-Fear-of-Deportation.html).

Hennessy-Fiske, Molly. 2015. "Paid $1 to $3 a Day, Unauthorized Immigrants Keep Family Detention Centers Running." *Los Angeles Times*, August 3.

Hennessy-Fiske, Molly. 2018. "U.S. Is Separating Immigrant Parents and Children to Discourage Others, Activists Say." *Los Angeles Times*, February 20. (http://www.latimes.com/nation/la-na-immigrant-family-separations-2018-story.html).

Herman, Max. 2018. "Fighting for the Lives of Migrants in the Sonoran Desert (Photo Essay)." LatinoUSA.org, June 27. (http://latinousa.org/2018/06/27/sonorandesertphotoessay/).

Hernández, José. 2012. *Reaching for the Stars: The Inspiring Story of a Migrant Farmworker Turned Astronaut.* Center Street Publishers.

Heyer, Cole. 2016. "Over 4.5 Million Are Waiting for Green Cards—Over 100,000 of Them Are Employment-Based." *National Law Review*, January 12. (http://www.natlawreview.com/article/over-45-million-are-waiting-green-cards-over-100000-them-are-employment-based).

Hill, Misha E. and Meg Wiehe. 2018. *State & Local Tax Contributions of Young Undocumented Immigrants.* Institute on Taxation & Economic Policy, April. (https://itep.org/wp-content/uploads/2018DACA.pdf).

Hing, Julianne. 2018. "A Win and a Loss in Dreamers' Fight for In-State Tuition." *The Nation*, April 18. (https://www.thenation.com/article/a-win-and-a-loss-in-dreamers-fight-for-in-state-tuition/).

Hispanic Lifestyle. N.d. "Profile of a Latina of Influence—Josefina Lopéz." (http://www.hispaniclifestyle.com/articles/latina-of-influence-josefina-lopez).

Hoffman, Meredith. 2015. "How US Immigrant Detention Facilities Get Away with Being Complete Hellholes." VICE News, October 21. (https://news.vice.com/article/how-us-immigrant-detention-facilities-get-away-with-being-complete-hellholes).

Holguin, Fernando, Anas Moughrabieh, Victoria Ojeda, Sanjay R. Patel, Paula Peyrani, Miguel Pinedo, Juan C. Celedón, Ivor S. Douglas, Dona J. Upson, and Jesse Roman. 2016. "Respiratory Health in Migrant Populations: A Crisis Overlooked." *Annals of American Thoracic Society* 14(2): 153–59.

Hondagneu-Sotelo, Pierrette. 2007. *Doméstica: Immigrant Workers Cleaning and Caring in the Shadows of Influence.* Oakland: University of California Press.

Howard, Jacqueline. 2018. "The Stress Pregnant Women Face in America." CNN.com, October 24. (https://www.cnn.com/2018/10/23/health/pregnant-immigrant-women-every-mother-counts/index.html).

Human Rights Watch. 2010. *Fields of Peril: Child Labor in US Agriculture.* May. (https://www.hrw.org/sites/default/files/reports/crd0510_brochure_low_0.pdf).

Human Rights Watch. 2016. "U.S. 20 Years of Immigration Abuses." April 25. (https://www.hrw.org/news/2016/04/25/us-20-years-immigrant-abuses).

Hurdle, John. 2014. "Nonprofit Clinic Offers 'Bridges of Health' to Philadelphia's Illegal Immigrants." *New York Times*, January 19. (https://www.nytimes.com/2014/01/20/U.S./nonprofit-clinic-offers-bridges-of-health-to-philadelphias-illegal-immigrants.html).

Hurdle, John. 2015. "A New Medical Center for Undocumented Immigrants Opens This Weekend on South Street." *Philadelphia City Paper*, April 23. (http://citypaper.net/cover/a-center-offering-undocumented-immigrants-medical-care-and-social-service-help-opens-this-weekend-on-south-street/).

Huynh, Van and Tania Unzueta. 2017. "Opinion: Mayor Emanuel Falls Behind Gov. Rauner in Protecting Immigrants." *Chicago Sun-Times*, September 20. (https://chicago.suntimes.com/opinion/mayor-emanuel-falls-behind-gov-rauner-in-protecting-immigrants/amp/).

iamOTHER. 2013. "Voice of Art—Migration Is Beautiful, Part 1." (https://www.youtube.com/watch?v=LWE2T8Bx5d8).

Ibañez, Armando. N.d. *UndocuTales: A Web Series about a Queer Undocumented Immigrant Living in Los Angeles.* (https://www.undocumentedtales.com).

Inskeep, Steve. 2014. "Border Agency Chief Opens Up About Deadly Force Cases." National Public Radio, July 18. (http://www.npr.org/2014/07/18/332028125/border-agency-chief-opens-up-about-deadly-force-cases).

International Organization for Migration. 2016. *Global Migration Trends Factsheet.* Berlin, Germany. (http://publications.iom.int/system/files/global_migration_trends_2015_fact-sheet.pdf).

International Organization for Migration. 2018. *World Migration Report.* Geneva, Switzerland.

Jenkins, Henry. 2015. "Important Reminder: Superman Was an Undocumented Immigrant." Fusion.net. (http://fusion.net/video/103908/superheroes-are-undocumented-immigrants-and-the-other-way-around/).

Jennings v. Rodriguez, 583 U.S. (2018).

Jewett, Christina and Shefali Luthra. 2018. "Immigrant Infants Too Young to Talk Called into Court to Defend Themselves." *Texas Tribune*, July 18. (https://www.texastribune.org/2018/07/18/immigrant-separated-families-infant-court-defend-donald-trump-zero-tol/).

Jimenez, Guillermo. 2015. "Arizonans Stage Sit-In to Halt Inland Immigration Checkpoints." *PanAm Post*, May 28. (https://panampost.com/guillermo-jimenez/2015/05/28/arizonans-stage-sit-in-to-halt-inland-immigration-checkpoints/).

Johnson, Jimmy. 2016. "Hundreds of Farmworkers Gather on Palm Beach to Protest Wendy's: Farmers Demand That Fast-Food Chain Join 'Fair Food Program'." WPBF, March 13. (http://www.wpbf.com/news/hundreds-of-farmworkers-gather-on-palm-beach-to-protest-wendys/38485804).

Johnson, Tory. 2017. "Some Veterans Observe Memorial Day Under Threat of Deportation." American Immigration Council. Immigration Impact, May 29. (http://immigrationimpact.com/2017/05/29/veterans-observe-memorial-day-threat-deportation/).

Jones, Reece. 2014. "Border Wars: Narratives and Images of the US-Mexican Border on TV." *ACME: An International E-Journal for Critical Geographies* 13: 530–50.

Jordan, Miriam. 2008. "Mortgage Prospects Dim for Illegal Immigrants." *Wall Street Journal*, October 22. (http://www.wsj.com/articles/SB122463690372357037).

Kaiser Permanente. N.d. "Subsidized Care and Coverage." (https://share.kaiserpermanente.org/article/subsidized-care-and-coverage-charitable-health-coverage/).

Kalaw, Martine. 2016. "Is the Face of the Undocumented Immigrant Still Mexican?" Huffington Post, March 21. (http://www.huffingtonpost.com/martine-kalaw/is-the-face-of-the-undocumented-immigrant-still-mexican_b_9512842.html).

Kandel, William A. 2016. "Interior Immigration Enforcement: Criminal Alien Programs." Congressional Research Service, September 8. (https://fas.org/sgp/crs/homesec/R44627.pdf).

Kanstroom, Daniel. 2012. *Aftermath: Deportation Law and the New American Diaspora.* New York: Oxford University Press.

Karan, Abraar. 2015. "It Costs Nothing to Care: Why We Need to Provide Health Insurance for Undocumented U.S. Residents." (http://thehealthcareblog.com/blog/2015/09/30/it-costs-nothing-to-care-why-we-need-to-provide-health-insurance-for-undocumented-people/).

Kassie, Emily and Eli Hager. 2018. "Inside Family Detention, Trump's Big Solution." The Marshall Project, June 22. (https://www.themarshallproject.org/2018/06/22/inside-family-detention-trump-s-big-solution).

Kearney, Gregory D., Guadalupe Rodriguez, Sara A. Quandt, Justin T. Arcury, and Thomas A. Arcury. 2015. "Work Safety Climate, Safety Behaviors, and Occupational Injuries of Youth Farmworkers in North Carolina." *American Journal of Public Health* 105(7): 1336–43.

Kelley, Ryan. 2018. "New Research Shows Nearly 100 ICE Raids in Queens Since President Trump Took Office." Queens Borough News QNS.com, August 14. (https://qns.com/story/2018/08/14/new-research-shows-nearly-100-ice-raids-queens-since-president-trump-took-office/).

Khimm, Suzy. 2014. "The American Dream, Undocumented." MSNBC, August 28. (http://www.msnbc.com/msnbc/american-dream-undocumented).

Khosla, Proma. 2018. "Meanwhile, Gina Rodriguez Used 'Jane the Virgin' Funds to Send an Immigrant Kid to College." Mashable, June 19. (https://mashable.com/2018/06/19/gina-rodriguez-jane-the-virgin-undocumented-college-student/#3yfDOj5GLqq6).

Kim, Sei-Hill, John P. Carvalho, Andrew G. Davis, and Amanda M. Mullins. 2011. "The View of the Border: News Framing of the Definition, Causes, and Solutions to Illegal Immigration." *Mass Communication and Society* 14(3): 292–314.

Kinefuchi, Etsuko and Gabriel Cruz. 2015. "The Mexicans in the News: Representation of Mexican Immigrants in the Internet News Media." *Howard Journal of Communications* 26(4): 333–51.

King, Martin Luther, Jr. 2013. *A Time to Break Silence: The Essential Works of Martin Luther King, Jr., for Students.* Beacon Press.

Kitroeff, Natalie and Geoffrey Mohan. 2017. "Wages Rise on California Farms. Americans Still Don't Want the Job." *Los Angeles Times,* March 17. (http://www.latimes.com/projects/la-fi-farms-immigration/).

Kohari, Alizeh. 2011. "Hunger Strikes: What Can They Achieve?" BBC News, August 16. (http://www.bbc.com/news/magazine-14540696).

Kohavi, Noya. 2018. "What Trump's 'Big, Fat, Beautiful' Mexico Wall Will Look Like." *Haaretz,* January 26. (https://www.haaretz.com/us-news/.premium.MAGAZINE-what-trump-s-big-fat-beautiful-mexico-wall-will-look-like-1.5766871).

Kolhatkar, Sonali. 2014. "After 20 Years, NAFTA Leaves Mexico's Economy in Ruins." Common Dreams, January 10. (https://www.commondreams.org/views/2014/01/10/after-20-years-nafta-leaves-mexicos-economy-ruins).

Konstantinides, Anneta. 2015. "New Captain America Comic Sees Superhero Sam Wilson Take On and Defeat Anti-Immigration Vigilantes." DailyMail.com, October 18. (http://www.dailymail.co.uk/news/article-3278524/Captain-America-defeats-anti-immigration-vigilantes-new-Marvel-comic.html).

Korhonen, Greyson. 2016. "A Visceral Portrait of Life at the U.S.-Mexico Border." *The Atlantic.* (https://www.theatlantic.com/video/index/472707/a-visceral-portrait-of-life-at-the-us-mexico-border/).

Kossek, Ellen E. and Lisa B. Burke. 2014. "Developing Occupational and Family Resilience Among US Migrant Farmworkers." *Social Research* 81(2): 359–72. (http://search.proquest.com.ezproxy.csusm.edu/docview/1551709197?accountid=10363).

Krogstad, Jans Manuel. 2017. "Unauthorized Immigrants Covered by DACA Face Uncertain Future." Pew Hispanic Research, January 5. (http://www.pewresearch.org/fact-tank/2017/01/05/unauthorized-immigrants-covered-by-daca-face-uncertain-future/).

Kuttner, Paul. 2013. "Interview with Cultural Organizer Favianna Rodriguez." Cultural Organizing, February 18. (http://culturalorganizing.org/tag/immigration/).

Kwong, Jessica. 2016. "Santa Ana Moves to Ease Out of ICE Contract for Jail Detainees; Transgender Study Planned." *Orange County Register*, May 18. (http://www.ocregister.com/2016/05/18/santa-ana-moves-to-ease-out-of-ice-contract-for-jail-detainees-transgender-study-planned/).

Lang, Marissa J. 2018. "'I Am a Child': How an Artist Turned Civil Rights Imagery into a Message of Protest for Immigrant Kids." *Washington Post*, July 1. (https://www.washingtonpost.com/news/local/wp/2018/07/01/i-am-a-child-how-an-artist-turned-civil-rights-imagery-into-a-message-of-protest-for-immigrant-kids/?utm_term=.1dcad74be362).

Lapowsky, Issie. 2017. "A Portable Panic Button for Immigrants Swept Up in Raids." *Wired*, March 10. (https://www.wired.com/2017/03/portable-panic-button-immigrants-swept-raids/).

Larrimore, Jeff, Mario Arthur-Bentil, Sam Dodini, and Logan Thomas. 2015. *Report on the Economic Well-Being of U.S. Households in 2014.* (https://www.federalreserve.gov/econresdata/2014-report-economic-well-being-U.S.-households-201505.pdf).

La Santa Cecilia. 2013. "ICE El Hielo." *Treinta Dias*. Universal Music Latino.

LatinoUSA. 2015. "The Dream 9." National Public Radio, October 16. (http://www.npr.org/programs/latino-usa/513279638/the-dream-9).

Laughland, Oliver. 2017. "Inside Trump's Secretive Immigration Court: Far from Scrutiny and Legal Aid." *The Guardian*, June 7. (https://www.theguardian.com/us-news/2017/jun/07/donald-trump-immigration-court-deportation-lasalle).

Leah, Rachel. 2018. "Laura Ingraham Enforces Racist Stereotypes About People of Color as She Laments Demographic Changes." Salon, August 9. (https://www.salon.com/2018/08/09/laura-ingraham-enforces-racist-stereotypes-about-people-of-color-as-she-laments-demographic-changes/).

Lee, Esther Yu-Hsi. 2014. "How Cultural Depictions Are Changing the Way We Think About Undocumented Immigrants." ThinkProgress. (http://thinkprogress.org/immigration/2014/05/01/3425260/jose-antonio-vargas-documented/).

Lee, Esther Yu-Hsi. 2015. "No, Undocumented Immigrants Are Not a Burden on Our Health Care System." ThinkProgress, June 24. (https://thinkprogress.org/no-undocumented-immigrants-arent-a-burden-on-the-health-care-system-39560e0bcaf7).

Lee, Patrick G. 2017. "What Customs and Border Patrol Can and Can't Do." *Pacific Standard*, March 13. (https://psmag.com/news/what-customs-and-border-officials-can-and-cant-do).

Leeds, Sarene. 2018. "How 'One Day at a Time' Brilliantly Captures the Effect of Trump's America on One Latinx Family." Mic, January 30. (https://mic.com/articles/187694/how-one-day-at-a-time-brilliantly-captures-the-effect-of-trumps-america-on-one-latinx-family#.IKioFExNE).

Libal, Bob. 2016. "Texas Court Blocks Licensing of Family Detention Camps as Childcare Facilities." Grassroots Leadership, December 3. (https://grassrootsleadership.org/releases/2016/12/breaking-texas-court-blocks-licensing-family-detention-camps-childcare-facilities).

Lind, Dara. 2018. "What We Know About a Reported Hunger Strike by Fathers in Immigration Detention." Vox, August 3. (https://www.vox.com/2018/8/2/17641208/immigrant-strike-detention-families-separation).

Lindberg, Kari. 2017. "Human Trafficking Victims Are Scared to Apply for Visas Under Trump." Vice News, June 12. (https://news.vice.com/en_ca/article/434pkj/human-trafficking-victims-are-scared-to-apply-for-visas-under-trump).

Linthicum, Kate. 2015. "Hundreds Launch Hunger Strike at Immigrant Detention Center in Adelanto, Calif." *Los Angeles Times*, November 6. (http://www.latimes.com/local/lanow/la-me-ln-immigrant-hunger-strike-20151106-story.html).

Linthicum, Kate. 2015. "Safety for Immigrant Victims Put On Hold by U-Visa Delay." *Los Angeles Times*, February 1. (http://www.latimes.com/local/california/la-me-u-visa-20150202-story.html).

Linthicum, Kate. 2016. "Nearly Half a Million U.S. Citizens Are Enrolled in Mexican Schools. Many of Them Are Struggling." *Los Angeles Times*, May 14. (http://www.latimes.com/world/mexico-americas/la-fg-mexico-return-migration-schools-20160913-snap-story.html).

Livaudais, Maria, Edward D. Vargas, Gabriel Sanchez, and Melina Juarez. 2015. "Latinos' Connections to Immigrants: How Knowing a Deportee Impacts Latino Health." Association for Public Policy Analysis and Management 37th Annual Fall Research Conference. Miami, FL. November 14.

Lo, Puck. 2015. "Inside the New Sanctuary Movement That's Protecting Immigrants from ICE." *The Nation*, May 6. (https://www.thenation.com/article/inside-new-sanctuary-movement-thats-protecting-immigrants-ice/).

Loewenstein, Anthony. 2016. "Private Prisons Are Cashing In on Refugees' Desperation." *New York Times*, February 25. (http://www.nytimes.com/2016/02/25/opinion/private-prisons-are-cashing-in-on-refugees-desperation.html).

Lonegan, Brian and the Immigration Law Unit of the Legal Aid Society. 2006. *Immigration Detention and Removal: A Guide for Detainees and Their Families*. New York: Legal Aid Society. (https://www.informedimmigrant.com/wp-content/uploads/2017/01/detentionre-movalguide_2006-02.pdf).

Long, Heather. 2018. "U.S., Canada and Mexico Just Reached a Sweeping New NAFTA Deal. Here Is What Is in It." *Washington Post*, October 1. (https://www.washingtonpost.com/business/2018/10/01/us-canada-mexico-just-reached-sweeping-new-nafta-deal-heres-whats-it/?utm_term=.0297e4e52e42).

Lopez, Cristina G. 2015. "Latino Voices Call on Media to Improve Hispanic Representation." *Media Matters for America* (Blog), September 21. (http://mediamatters.org/blog/2015/09/21/latino-voices-call-on-media-to-improve-hispanic/205684).

López, Gustavo, Kristin Bialik, and Jynnah Radford. 2018. "Key Findings About U.S. Immigrants." Pew Research, September 18. (http://www.pewresearch.org/fact-tank/2018/09/14/key-findings-about-u-s-immigrants/).

Lopez, William D., Daniel J. Kruger, Jorge Delva, Mikel Llanes, Charo Ledón, Adreanne Waller, Melanie Harner, Ramiro Martinez, Laura Sanders, Margaret Harner, and Barbara Israel. 2017. "Health Implications of an Immigration Raid: Findings from a Latino Community in the Midwestern United States." *Journal of Immigrant Minority Health* 9(3): 702–8.

López-Cevallos, Daniel F. and S. Marie Harvey. 2016. "Foreign-Born Latinos Living in Rural Areas Are More Likely to Experience Health Care Discrimination: Results from *Proyecto de Salud para Latinos*." *Journal of Immigrant and Minority Health* 8(4): 928–34.

Lydgate, Johanna Jacobbi. 2010. "Assembly-Line Justice: A Review of Operation Streamline." *California Law Review* 98: 481–544. (http://scholarship.law.berkeley.edu/californialawreview/vol98/iss2/5).

Lyons, Joseph D. 2017. "This 'Guadalupe Garcia' Tweet Shows How Donald Trump's Immigration Law Will Tragically Affect Families." *Bustle*, February. (https://www.bustle.com/p/

this-guadalupe-garcia-tweet-shows-how-donald-trumps-immigration-law-will-tragically-affect-families-36780).

Mahr, Joe, Tony Briscoe, and Ese Olumhense. 2018. "Demonstrators Rally in the Loop Against Separation of Families." *Chicago Tribune*, June 30. (http://www.chicagotribune.com/news/local/breaking/ct-met-loop-immigration-family-separation-rally-20180630-story.html).

Main, S. J. 2012. "Actor Demián Bichir Talks Hollywood, Scarlett, Oscars & Being Latino." Huffington Post, April 28. (http://www.huffingtonpost.com/sj-main/post_3033_b_1301097.html).

Mallonee, Laura. 2016. "The Invisible Security of Canada's Seemingly Chill Border." *Wired*, April 1. (https://www.wired.com/2016/04/invisible-security-canadas-seemingly-chill-border/).

Manriquez, Stephanie. 2015. "For Immigrants, Status and Stigma Affect Mental Health, Few Resources Exist—Social Justice News Nexus." Social Justice News Nexus. (http://sjnnchicago.org/for-immigrants-status-and-stigma-affect-mental-health-few-resources-exist/).

Marcotte, Amanda. 2015. "Sorry Fox News: Captain America Has Long Been a Liberal, Anti-Nationalist Character." Salon.com, October 20. (http://www.salon.com/2015/10/20/sorry_fox_news_captain_america_has_long_been_a_liberal_anti_nationalist_character/).

Margolis, Mary Elizabeth. 2016. "Medical and Mental Health Experts Urge the Ninth Circuit Court to Uphold Flores Ruling to End Family Immigration Detention." Human Rights First, February 24. (http://www.humanrightsfirst.org/press-release/medical-and-mental-health-experts-urge-ninth-circuit-court-uphold-flores-ruling-end).

Marizco, Michel. 2017. "A Harder Punishment for First-Time Offenders Who Cross U.S. Border Illegally." *Fronteras*, August 18. (http://fronterasdesk.org/content/10773/harder-punishment-first-time-offenders-who-cross-us-border-illegally).

Markon, Jerry. 2016. "Can a 3-Year-Old Defend Herself in Immigration Court? This Judge Says Yes." *Washington Post*, March 5. (https://www.washingtonpost.com/world/national-security/can-a-3-year-old-represent-herself-in-immigration-court-this-judge-thinks-so/2016/03/03/5be59a32-db25-11e5-925f-1d10062cc82d_story.html?utm_term=.31d4d3700b29).

Martinez, Omar, Elwin Wu, Theo Sandfort, Brian Dodge, Alex Carballo-Dieguez, Rogerio Pinto, Scott D. Rhodes, Eva Moya, and Silvia Chavez-Baray. 2015. "Evaluating the Impact of Immigration Policies on Health Status Among Undocumented Immigrants: A Systematic Review." *Journal of Immigrant Minority Health* 17: 947–70.

Massey, Douglas S. 2007. "Understanding America's Immigration 'Crisis'." *Proceedings of the American Philosophical Society* 151(3): 309–27.

Mathema, Silva. 2017. "Keeping Families Together." Center for American Progress, March 16. (https://www.americanprogress.org/issues/immigration/reports/2017/03/16/428335/keeping-families-together/)

May, Michael. 2013. "Los Infiltradores." *American Prospect*, June 21. (http://prospect.org/article/los-infiltradores).

McAfee, Tierney. 2017. "6-Year-Old Girl Who Handed Letter to Pope Francis: 'Let Us Fight with Love, Faith, and Courage." *People*, January 21. (http://people.com/politics/womens-march-sophie-cruz-pope-francis/).

McElwee, Sean. 2018. "The Power of 'Abolish ICE'." *New York Times*, August 4. (https://www.nytimes.com/2018/08/04/opinion/sunday/abolish-ice-ocasio-cortez-democrats.html).

McGeogh, Paul. 2017. "Sit-Ins at Airports, 'Stand-Ups' at White House as Trump and Bannon Rewrite Rules." *Sydney Morning Herald*, January 31. (http://www.smh.com.au/world/sitins-at-airports-standups-at-white-house-as-trump-and-bannon-rewrite-rules-20170131-gu25y9.html).

McLeod, Allegra M. 2016. "Immigration, Criminalization, and Disobedience." *University of Miami Law Review* 70(2): 556–84.

McWhirter, Ellen H., Karina Ramos, and Cynthia Medina. 2013. "'¿Y Ahora Qué?' Anticipated Immigration Status Barriers and Latina/o High School Students' Future Expectations." *Cultural Diversity and Ethnic Minority Psychology* 19(3): 288–97.

Medina, Jennifer. 2017. "Immigration Agents Should Not 'Stalk' Courts, California Justice Says." *New York Times*, March 16. (https://www.nytimes.com/2017/03/16/us/immigration-agents-should-not-stalk-courts-california-justice-says.html).

Medina, Jennifer. 2017. "Too Scared to Report Sexual Abuse. The Fear: Deportation." *New York Times*, April 30. (https://www.nytimes.com/2017/04/30/us/immigrants-deportation-sexual-abuse.html?login=email&auth=login-email).

Mendez, Julian J. and Nolan L. Cabrera. 2015. "Targets but Not Victims: Latina/o College Students and Arizona's Racial Politics." *Journal of Hispanic Higher Education* 14(4): 377–91.

Mendoza, Sylvia. 2014. "Detained in the Desert: Protesting the Unjust Through the Power of a Pen." *Hispanic Outlook in Higher Education* (March 10): 14–16.

Mendoza, Sylvia. 2015. "Building False Crisis: The Role of the Media Covering Undocumented Immigrants." *Hispanic Outlook in Higher Education*, June 15. (https://www.hispanicoutlook.com/articles/building-false-crisis-the-role-of-the-media-coveri).

Menjívar, Cecilia. 2006. "Liminal Legality: Salvadoran and Guatemalan Immigrants' Lives in the United States." *American Journal of Sociology* 111(4): 999–1037.

Menjívar, Cecilia. 2014. "The 'Poli-Migra' Multilayered Legislation, Enforcement Practices, and What We Can Learn About and from Today's Approaches." *American Behavioral Scientist* 58(13): 1805–19.

Menjívar, Cecilia. 2016. "Immigrant Criminalization in Law and the Media: Effects on Latino Immigrant Workers' Identities in Arizona." *American Behavioral Scientist* 60(5-6): 597–616.

Menjívar, Cecilia and Leisy Abrego. 2012. *Legal Violence in the Lives of Immigrants: How Immigration Enforcement Affects Families, Schools, and Workplaces.* Washington, DC: Center for American Progress, December.

Menjívar, Cecilia and Daniel Kanstroom (Eds.). 2014. *Constructing Illegality in America: Immigrant Experiences, Critiques, and Resistance.* New York: Cambridge University Press.

Meyer, Rachel and Janice Fine. 2017. "Grassroots Citizenship at Multiple Scales: Rethinking Immigrant Civic Participation." *International Journal of Politics, Culture and Society* 30(4): 323–48.

Michaels, Samantha. 2015. "Here Is Why Hundreds of Immigrants in Detention Have Gone on Hunger Strike." *Mother Jones*, December 2. (http://www.motherjones.com/politics/2015/11/why-are-hundreds-detained-immigrants-going-hunger-strike).

Migration Policy Institute. N.d. *Profile of the Unauthorized Population: United States.* (https://www.migrationpolicy.org/data/unauthorized-immigrant-population/state/US).

Miroff, Nick. 2013. "Controversial Quota Drives Immigrant Detention Boom." *Washington Post*, October 13. (https://www.washingtonpost.com/world/controversial-quota-drives-immigration-detention-boom/2013/10/13/09bb689e-214c-11e3-ad1a-1a919f2ed890_story.html?utm_term=.c2f67293bbd3).

Miroff, Nick. 2018. "What Is TPS, and What Will Happen to the 200,000 Salvadorans Whose Status Is Revoked?" *Washington Post*, January 9. (https://www.washingtonpost.com/news/worldviews/wp/2018/01/09/what-is-tps-and-what-will-happen-to-the-200000-salvadorans-whose-status-is-revoked/?utm_term=.7618a7e01037).

Misra, Tanvi. 2018. "Inside the Massive U.S. 'Border Zone.'" *CityLab*, May 14. (https://www.citylab.com/equity/2018/05/who-lives-in-border-patrols-100-mile-zone-probably-you-mapped/558275/).

Mitchell, Kirk. 2017. "Class Action Suit: Immigrants Held in Aurora Required for Work for $1 a Day, Threatened with Solitary If They Refuse." *Denver Post*, March 2. (http://www.denverpost.com/2017/03/02/class-action-ice-detention-aurora-immigration/).

Mitric, Julia. 2016. "Why California's New Farmworker Overtime Bill May Not Mean Bigger Paychecks." National Public Radio, August 30. (http://www.npr.org/sections/thesalt/2016/08/30/491944679/why-californias-new-farmworker-overtime-bill-may-not-mean-bigger-paychecks).

Moffitt, Bob. 2017. "Sac City Unified Launches Program to Protect Undocumented Students." Capitol Public Radio, March 7. (http://www.capradio.org/91610).

Montagne, Rene. 2014. "U.S. Is Home to 1.5 Million Undocumented Asian Immigrants—Interview with Immigration Attorney Muzaffar Chishti." National Public Radio, November 28. (http://www.npr.org/2014/11/28/367154343/u-s-is-home-to-1-5-million-undocumented-asian-immigrants).

Montelongo, Cesar. 2015. "As an Undocumented Immigrant, It's Easier to Get My MD-PhD Than a US Visa." Huffington Post, November 13. (http://www.huffingtonpost.com/cesar-montelongo/undocumented-immigrant-mdphd-visa_b_8538018.html).

Montgomery, David. 2010. "Trail of Dream Students Walk 1,500 Miles to Bring Immigration Message to Washington." *Washington Post*, May 1. (http://www.washingtonpost.com/wp-dyn/content/article/2010/04/30/AR2010043001384_pf.html).

Morales, Lauren. 2016. "The Costs Behind a Migrant Crisis: Unaccompanied Minors in the Hands of Traffickers." *Fronteras*, June 10. (http://www.fronterasdesk.org/content/10334/costs-behind-migrant-crisis-unaccompanied-minors-hands-traffickers).

Morales, Ricardo Levins. N.d. "Nothing About Us." (http://www.rlmartstudio.com/product/nothing-about-us-2/).

Moreno, Carolina and Roque Planas. 2015. "'Jane the Virgin' Pauses Mid-Episode to Drive Home the Need for Immigration Reform." Huffington Post, January 22. (http://www.huffingtonpost.com/2015/01/22/jane-the-virgin-immigration-reform_n_6518768.html).

Morlan, Kinsee. 2017. "The Most Memorable Acts of Protest at the Border." Voice of San Diego, February 27. (https://www.voiceofsandiego.org/topics/arts/the-most-memorable-acts-of-protest-art-at-the-border/).

Morton, John. 2011. "Memorandum: Enforcement Actions at or Focused on Sensitive Locations." U.S. Department of Homeland Security, U.S. Office of Immigration and Customs Enforcement, October 24. (https://www.ice.gov/doclib/ero-outreach/pdf/10029.2-policy.pdf).

Moyles, Trina and K. J. Dakin. 2016. "Female Migrant Farmworkers Push Back Against Machismo and Abuse in California's Wine Country." *Yes! Magazine*, June 21. (http://www.yesmagazine.org/people-power/female-migrant-farmworkers-push-back-against-machismo-and-abuse-in-californias-wine-country-20160621).

Mulholland, Audrey. 2016. "Labor Trafficking in the United States: Limited Victim Relief for Undocumented Immigrants." Washington, DC: American University Center for Human Rights and Humanitarian Law, November 2. (http://hrbrief.org/2016/11/labor-trafficking-united-states-limited-victim-relief-undocumented-immigrants/).

Munoz Robles, Brizzia and Maria Munoz Robles. 2015. "We Were High School Valedictorians, but We Weren't Sure We'd Make It to College Because We're Also Undocumented

Immigrants." *Washington Post*, May 19. (https://www.washingtonpost.com/posteverything/wp/2015/05/19/we-were-high-school-valedictorians-but-we-werent-sure-make-it-to-college-because-were-also-undocumented-immigrants/).

Murillo, Marco A. 2017. "Undocumented and College-Bound: A Case Study of the Supports and Barriers High School Students Encounter in Accessing Higher Education." *Urban Education*: 1–29.

Murray, Royce. 2018. "5 Ways to Prevent the Next Migrant Caravan." Immigration Impact, October 23. (http://immigrationimpact.com/2018/10/23/5-ways-to-prevent-the-next-migrant-caravan/).

Nadimpalli, Maya, Jessica L. Rinsky, Steve Wing, et al. 2014. "Persistence of Livestock-Associated Antibiotic-Resistant *Staphylococcus aureus* Among Industrial Hog Operation Workers in North Carolina Over 14 Days." *Journal Occupational and Environmental Medicine* 72: 90–99.

Nathan, Debbie. 2018. "Immigrant Mothers Are Staging Hunger Strikes to Demand Calls with Their Separated Children." *The Intercept*, July 13. (https://theintercept.com/2018/07/13/separated-children-hunger-strike-immigrant-detention/).

National Conference on State Legislatures. 2018. "Tuition Benefits for Immigrants." (http://www.ncsl.org/research/immigration/tuition-benefits-for-immigrants.aspx#enacted%20legislation).

National Hispanic Media Coalition. 2012. *American Hate Radio: How a Powerful Outlet for Democratic Discourse Has Deteriorated Into Hate, Racism and Extremism*. (http://www.nhmc.org/nhmcnew/wp-content/uploads/2013/03/american_hate_radio_nhmc.pdf).

National Immigration Law Center. 2014. "Immigrants and the Affordable Care Act (ACA)." January. (https://www.nilc.org/issues/health-care/immigrantshcr/).

National Immigration Law Center. 2018. "Basic Facts About In-State Tuition for Undocumented Immigrant Students." June 1. (https://www.nilc.org/issues/education/basic-facts-instate/).

National Immigration Law Center. 2018. "Status of Current DACA Litigation." November 9. (https://www.nilc.org/issues/daca/status-current-daca-litigation/).

National Park Service. 2017. "Statue of Liberty: National Monument, New York." November 29. (https://www.nps.gov/stli/learn/education/index.htm).

Naylor, Brian. 2017. "Trump's Plan to Hire 15,000 Border Patrol and ICE Agents Won't Be Easy." National Public Radio, February 23. (https://www.npr.org/2017/02/23/516712980/trumps-plan-to-hire-15-000-border-patrol-and-ice-agents-wont-be-easy-to-fulfill).

Nebraska Appleseed. 2009. *"The Speed Kills You"—The Voice of Nebraska's Meatpacking Workers*. Report 113. (https://neappleseed.org).

Nebraska Legislature. Nebraska Revised Statute 48-2213: Meatpacking industry worker rights coordinator; established; powers and duties. (http://nebraskalegislature.gov/laws/statutes.php?statute=48-2213).

Negrón-Gonzales, Genevieve. 2014. "Undocumented, Unafraid and Unapologetic: Re-Articulatory Practices and Migrant Youth 'Illegality'." *Latino Studies* 12(2): 259–78.

Negrón-Gonzales, Genevieve. 2016. "Unlawful Entry: Civil Disobedience and the Undocumented Youth Movement." In Jerusha Conner and Sonia M. Rosen (Eds.). *Contemporary Youth Activism: Advancing Social Justice in the United States*. Santa Barbara, CA: Praeger, 271–88.

Negrón-Gonzales, Genevieve. 2017. "Constrained Inclusion: Access and Persistence Among Undocumented Community College Students in California's Central Valley." *Journal of Hispanic Higher Education* 16(2): 105–22.

Negrón-Muntaner, Frances and Chelsea Abbas. 2016. *The Latino Disconnect: Latinos in the Age of Media Mergers.* The Center for the Study of Ethnicity and Race, Columbia University, and National Hispanic Foundation for the Arts. (http://www.columbia.edu/cu/cser/Documents/TheLatinoDisconnect.pdf).

Nevarez, Griselda. 2014. "Immigration Activists Arrested Outside the White House During Protest." Huffington Post, February 18. (http://www.huffingtonpost.com/2014/02/18/activists-arrested-white-house_n_4808069.html).

New Yorker. 2017. "Georgia's Underground University for Undocumented Students." (https://www.youtube.com/watch?v=d3NW5AOQQYw).

Nguyen, David H. K. and Gabriel R. Serna. 2014. "Access or Barrier? Tuition and Fee Legislation for Undocumented Students Across the States." *The Clearing House* 87: 124–29.

Nicholls, Walter and Tara Fiorito. 2015. "Dreamers Unbound: Immigrant Youth Mobilizing." *New Labor Forum,* Winter. (http://newlaborforum.cuny.edu/author/walter-nicholls/).

Nicosia, Mareesa. 2016. "Deportation Fears Taking a Toll on Immigrant Children's Education." *Los Angeles School Report,* February 2. (http://laschoolreport.com/lausd/).

No More Death/*No Más Muertes.* 2017. "No More Deaths Benefit: An Art Auction to Protect the Lives of Migrants." (http://forms.nomoredeaths.org/no-more-deaths-benefit-an-art-auction-to-protect-the-lives-of-migrants/).

No Papers, No Fear. 2013. "No Papers, No Fear Ride for Justice." (http://nopapersnofear.org).

Nunez, Lissette. 2018. "Local Woman Becomes First DACA Recipient to Be Admitted to Connecticut Bar." Fox 61 News, November 2. (https://fox61.com/2018/11/02/local-woman-becomes-first-daca-recipient-to-be-admitted-to-ct-bar/).

Núñez-Alvarez, Arcela, Konane M. Martínez, Amy Ramos, and Fabiola Gastelum. 2007. *San Diego Firestorm 2007 Report: Fire Impact on Farmworkers & Migrant Communities in North County.* National Latino Research Center: California State University San Marcos. (http://www.cidrap.umn.edu/sites/default/files/public/php/27048/San%20Diego%20Firestorm%202007%20Report.pdf).

O'Hara, Mary Emily. 2018. "Trans Activists Protest ICE by Blocking the Streets in New Mexico." *Them,* August 27. (https://www.them.us/story/trans-activists-protest-ice).

O'Leary, Mary. 2017. "Connecticut Judge Seeks to Protect Courthouses from ICE." *New Haven Register,* June 8. (http://www.nhregister.com/general-news/20170608/connecticut-judge-seeks-to-protect-courthouses-from-ice).

Ontiveros, Maria. 2003. "Lessons from the Fields: Female Farmworkers and the Law." *Maine Law Review.* 157, 169. Cited in the Southern Law Poverty Center report, *Injustice on Our Plates.*

Organized Communities Against Deportation. 2017. "Breaking: Life Size Graphs Blocking Streets Outside City Hall Show Why Chicago Is Not a Sanctuary City for Black and Brown People." OCAD, October 10. (http://organizedcommunities.org/whychicagoisnotasanctuarycity/).

Ortega, Alexander N., Hector P. Rodriguez, and Arturo Vargas Bustamante. 2015. "Policy Dilemmas in Latino Health Care and Implementation of the Affordable Care Act." Department of Health and Policy Management. *Annual Review of Public Health* 34: 525–44.

Osberg, Molly. 2017. "These Banished Veterans Know Exactly How Broken the System Is." Fusion, April 3. (http://fusion.kinja.com/these-banished-veterans-know-exactly-how-broken-the-sys-1793877010).

Ospina, Tulio. 2017. "Alameda County Votes to Fund Immigrant Legal Defense Network." *Oakland Post,* February 10. (http://www.oaklandpost.org/2017/02/10/alameda-county-votes-fund-immigrant-legal-defense-network/).

O'Sullivan, Joseph. 2017. "Chief Justice Asks ICE Not to Track Immigrants at State Court-houses." *Seattle Times*, March 22. (http://www.seattletimes.com/seattle-news/politics/chief-justice-asks-ice-not-to-track-immigrants-at-state-courthouses/).

Otto, Mary. 2017. *Teeth: The Story of Beauty, Inequality, and the Struggle for Oral Health in America*. New York: The New Press.

Pacheco, Gaby. N.d. "Case Study: Trail of Dreams." *Beautiful Trouble: A Toolbox for Revolutionaries*. (http://beautifultrouble.org/case/trail-of-dreams/).

Park, Minyoung. 2017. "5 Must-Have Apps for Undocumented Immigrants." CNN, March 30. (http://money.cnn.com/2017/03/30/technology/immigrant-apps/).

Parvini, Sarah. 2017. "Cal State L.A. Student Activist Detained by Border Patrol Is Released." *Los Angeles Times*, June 9. (http://www.latimes.com/local/lanow/la-me-ln-immigration-activist-arrest-20170609-story.html).

Passel, Jeffrey S. and D'Vera Cohn. 2009. "A Portrait of Unauthorized Immigrants in the United States." Pew Hispanic Center, April 14. (http://www.pewhispanic.org/files/reports/107.pdf).

Passel, Jeffrey S. and D'Vera Cohn. 2015. "Share of Unauthorized Immigrant Workers in Production, Construction Jobs Falls Since 2007: In States, Hospitality, Manufacturing and Construction Are Top Industries." Pew Research Center, March 26. (http://www.pewhispanic.org/2015/03/26/share-of-unauthorized-immigrant-workers-in-production-construction-jobs-falls-since-2007/).

Passel, Jeffrey S. and D'Vera Cohn. 2016. "Overall Number of U.S. Unauthorized Immigrants Holds Steady Since 2009." Pew Research Center, September 20. (http://www.pewhispanic.org/2016/09/20/overall-number-of-u-s-unauthorized-immigrants-holds-steady-since-2009/).

Passel, Jeffrey S. and D'Vera Cohn. 2017. "20 Metro Areas Are Home to Six-In-Ten Unauthorized Immigrants in the U.S." Pew Research Center, February 9. (http://www.pewresearch.org/fact-tank/2017/02/09/us-metro-areas-unauthorized-immigrants/).

Passel, Jeffrey S. and D'Vera Cohn. 2017. "As Mexican Share Declined, Unauthorized Immigrant Population Fell in 2015 Below Recession Level." Pew Research Center, April 25. (http://www.pewresearch.org/fact-tank/2017/04/25/as-mexican-share-declined-u-s-unauthorized-immigrant-population-fell-in-2015-below-recession-level/).

Passel, Jeffrey and D'Vera Cohn. 2018. "U.S. Unauthorized Immigrant Total Dips to Lowest Level in a Decade." Pew Research Center, November 27. (http://www.pewhispanic.org/2018/11/27/u-s-unauthorized-immigrant-total-dips-to-lowest-level-in-a-decade/).

Pauly, Madison. 2017. "The Private Prison Industry Is Licking Its Chops Over Trump's Deportation Plans." *Mother Jones*, February 21. (http://www.motherjones.com/politics/2017/02/trumps-immigration-detention-center-expansion).

Pavey, Steve and Marco Saavedra. 2012. *Shadows Then Light*. Lexington, KY: One Horizon Institute.

Penman, Maggie. 2017. "High Court to Hear Case of Mexican Boy Killed in Cross-Border Shooting." National Public Radio, February 20. (http://www.npr.org/sections/thetwo-way/2017/02/20/516275461/high-court-to-hear-arguments-in-case-of-mexican-boy-killed-in-cross-border-shoot).

People Helping People in the Border Zone. N.d. "Checkpoint Campaign." (http://phparivaca.org/?page_id=7).

Pérez, Zenén J. 2014. *Removing Barriers to Higher Education for Undocumented Students*. Washington, DC: Center for American Progress. (https://www.luminafoundation.org/files/resources/removing-barriers-for-undocumented-students.pdf).

Pérez, Zenen J. 2015. "Denying Higher Education to Undocumented Students Is a Roadblock to Future Economic Growth." Huffington Post, March 31. (https://www. huffingtonpost.com/zenen-jaimes-perez/denying-higher-education-to-undocumented-students_b_6976300.html).

Pérez Huber, Lindsay. 2009. "Challenging Racist Nativist Framing: Acknowledging the Community Cultural Wealth of Undocumented Chicana College Students to Reframe the Immigration Debate." *Harvard Educational Review* 79(4): 704–29.

Peters, Jeremy W. 2018. "How Trump-Fed Conspiracy Theories About Migrant Caravan Intersect with Deadly Hatred." *New York Times*, October 29. (https://www.nytimes.com/2018/10/29/us/politics/caravan-trump-shooting-elections.html).

Philbin, Morgan, Mark Hatzenbuehler, Somjen Frazer, Morgan Flake, Daniel Hagen, and Jennifer Hirsch. 2016. "Too Scared to Move?: A Mixed-Methods Analysis of State-Level Immigration Policies and Obesity Among Latinos in the United States." Population Association of America Conference, April. (https://paa.confex.com/paa/2016/mediafile/ExtendedAbstract/Paper7648/PAA%202016%20Abstract_HIV%20Center%20Pilot%20Data_September%2025%202015_Philbin%20.pdf.)

Phillips, Dave. 2018. "They Came Here to Serve. But for Many Immigrants, the Army Isn't Interested." *New York Times*, July 6. (https://www.nytimes.com/2018/07/06/us/army-immigrants-discharge.html?module=inline).

Phillips, Kristine. 2018. "A Deported Veteran Has Been Granted U.S. Citizenship, After 14 Years of Living in Mexico." *Washington Post*, March 31. (https://www.washingtonpost.com/news/checkpoint/wp/2018/03/31/a-deported-veteran-has-been-granted-u-s-citizenship-after-14-years-of-living-in-mexico/?noredirect=on&utm_term=.f8cf547683fc).

Phillips, Kristine. 2018. "'America Is Better Than This': What a Doctor Saw in a Texas Shelter for Migrant Children." *Washington Post*, June 16. (https://www.washingtonpost.com/news/post-nation/wp/2018/06/16/america-is-better-than-this-what-a-doctor-saw-in-a-texas-shelter-for-migrant-children/?utm_term=.5d37f1e4a992).

Phillips, Noelle. 2017. "Videos of ICE Making Arrests at Denver's Courthouse Renew Calls for City to Push Back Against White House Policies." *Denver Post*, May 9. (http://www.denverpost.com/2017/05/09/video-ice-arrests-denver-courthouse-immigration-policy/).

Pitzl, Mary J. 2016. "One Nation: Immigration Issue Turns Personal." *USA Today*, March 22. (http://www.usatoday.com/story/news/politics/elections/2016/03/22/one-nation-immigration-scottsdale-arizona/82108206/).

Planas, Roque. 2017. "Ruling on ICE Detainers Is Bad News for Texas Immigration Crackdown." Huffington Post, June 9. (http://www.huffingtonpost.com/entry/judges-ruling-on-ice-detainers-is-bad-news-for-texas-immigration-crackdown_U.S._593b0a70e4b0240268795d23).

Plascencia, Imelda S., Alma Leyva, Mayra Yoana Jaimes Pena, and Saba Waheed. 2015. *Undocumented and Uninsured: A Five-Part Report on Immigrant Youth and the Struggle to Access Health Care in California: Part 1, No Papers, No Healthcare.* The Dream Resource Center Report. Los Angeles, CA: UCLA Labor Center. (http://undocumentedanduninsured.org/wp-content/uploads/2014/04/UCLA-Undocumented-and-Uninsured-Part-1-web.pdf).

Plascencia, Imelda S., Alma Leyva, Mayra Yoana Jaimes Pena, and Saba Waheed. 2015. *Undocumented and Uninsured: A Five-Part Report on Immigrant Youth and the Struggle to Access Health Care in California: Part 3, Pol(ice) in My Head.* The Dream Resource Center Report. Los Angeles, CA: UCLA Labor Center. (http://undocumentedanduninsured.org/wpcontent/uploads/2015/04/Undocumented-and-Uninsured-Part-3-polICE-in-my-head.pdf).

Plascencia, Imelda S., Alma Leyva, Mayra Yoana Jaimes Pena, and Saba Waheed. 2015. *Undocumented and Uninsured: A Five-Part Report on Immigrant Youth and the Struggle to Access Health Care in California: Part 4, The Power of Healthy Communities.* The Dream Resource Center Report. Los Angeles, CA: UCLA Labor Center. (https://www.labor.ucla.edu/publication/undocumented-and-uninsured-part-4-the-power-of-a-healthy-community/).

Ponce, Albert. 2012. "Racialization, Resistance, and the Migrant Rights Movement: A Historical Analysis." *Critical Sociology* 40(1): 9–27.

Potochnick, Stephanie. 2014. "How States Can Reduce the Dropout Rate for Undocumented Immigrant Youth: The Effects of In-State Resident Tuition Policies." *Social Science Research* 45: 18–32.

Potter, Gary W. and Victor E. Kappeler. 2012. "Introduction. Media, Crime and Hegemony." In Denise L. Bissler and Joan L. Conners (Eds.). *The Harms of Crime Media: Essays on the Perpetuation of Racism, Sexism, and Class Stereotypes.* Jefferson, NC: McFarland and Company, 3–17.

Prendergast, Curt. 2018. "Operation Streamline Border-Crossing Cases Spiked 71 Percent in Tucson." Tucson.com, April 22. (https://tucson.com/news/local/operation-streamline-border-crossing-cases-spiked-percent-in-tucson/article_e3700d7d-9328-5112-ab89-6e97a3b3322e.html).

Presente.org. N.d. Basta Dobbs.com. (http://bastadobbs.com/facts/).

Primeau, Jamie. 2017. "America Ferrera's Women's March Speech Spreads a Powerful Message About Immigrants." *Bustle.* (https://www.bustle.com/p/america-ferreras-womens-march-speech-spreads-a-powerful-message-about-immigrants-32061).

Project South. 2017. "Imprisoned Justice: Inside Two Georgia Immigrant Detention Centers." Penn State Law and Center for Immigrants' Rights Clinic. (http://projectsouth.org/wp-content/uploads/2017/05/Imprisoned_Justice_Report.pdf).

Public Citizen. 2017. "Central America Free Trade Agreement." (https://www.citizen.org/our-work/globalization-and-trade/nafta-wto-other-trade-pacts/cafta).

Pugliese, Nicholas. 2017. "Immigration Arrests at N.J. Courthouses Having a 'Chilling Effect,' Attorneys Say." NorthJersey.com, June 5. (http://www.northjersey.com/story/news/new-jersey/2017/06/05/immigration-arrests-continue-n-j-courthouses/370974001/).

Puhl, Emily. 2015. "Prosecuting the Persecuted: How Operation Streamline and Expedited Removal Violate Article 31 of the Convention on the Status of Refugees and 1967 Protocol." *Berkeley La Raza Law Journal* 25(3): 88–109.

Pulgar, Camila A., Grisel Trejo, Cynthia Suerken, Edward H. Ip, Thomas A. Arcury, and Sara A. Quandt. 2016. "Economic Hardship and Depression Among Women in Latino Farmworker Families." *Journal of Immigrant and Minority Health* 18(3): 497–504.

Pulitano, Elvira. 2013. "In Liberty's Shadow: The Discourse of Refugees and Asylum Seekers in Critical Race Theory and Immigration Law/ Politics." *Identities: Global Studies in Culture and Power* 20(2): 172–89.

Race Forward. N.d. "Drop the I-Word." *Race Forward.* (https://www.raceforward.org/practice/tools/drop-i-word).

Race Forward. N.d. *Drop the I-Word: Why It Matters Now.* Report from Race Forward—Center for Racial Justice Innovation. (https://www.raceforward.org/sites/default/files/DTIW_update_WhyItMattersNow2.pdf).

Radnofsky, Louise. 2016. "Illegal Immigrants Get Public Health Care, Despite Federal Policy." *Wall Street Journal,* March 24. (https://www.wsj.com/articles/illegal-immigrants-get-public-health-care-despite-federal-policy-1458850082).

Rappaport, Nolan. 2017. "What Trump's 'Expedited Removal' Really Means for Immigrants in the United States." *The Hill*, February 24. (http://thehill.com/blogs/pundits-blog/immigration/321102-what-expedited-removal-really-means-for-illegal-immigrants-in).

Redden, Elizabeth. 2017. "California Dreamers—and Their Nightmares." *Inside Higher Education*, April 14. (https://www.insidehighered.com/news/2017/04/14/dreamers-grapple-increased-stresses-and-challenges).

Redmon, Jeremy and Mario Guevera. 2017. "Anxiety Grips Immigrants in Georgia During President Trump's Crackdown." *Atlanta Journal-Constitution*, March 13. (http://www.my-ajc.com/news/national-govt--politics/anxiety-grips-immigrants-georgia-during-president-trump-crackdown/XrNalP7TxTTEjgjfwYhk3N/).

Reichard, Raquel. 2015. "Immigrants' Rights Activist Angy Rivera Talks Documentary, 'No Le Digas a Nadie'." *Latina*, September 16. (http://www.latina.com/lifestyle/our-issues/immigrants-rights-activist-angy-rivera-talks-documentary).

Reichard, Raquel. 2016. "Why This Undocumented Latina Launched Coming Out of the Shadows Month." *Latina*, March 7. (http://www.latina.com/lifestyle/our-issues/latina-launches-coming-out-shadows-month).

Reichlin-Melnick, Aaron. 2016. "Supreme Court Considers Challenge to Detention of Immigrants Without Bond Hearing." Immigration Impact, December 1. American Immigration Council. (http://immigrationimpact.com/2016/12/01/supreme-court-considers-challenge-detention-immigrants-without-bond-hearings/).

Reichlin-Melnick, Aaron. 2017. "Federal Courts Blocks DOJ's Attempt to Restrict Access to Legal Assistance." Immigration Impact, May 18. (http://immigrationimpact.com/2017/05/18/federal-court-blocks-dojs-attempt-restrict-access-legal-assistance/).

Rein, Lisa, Abigail Hauslohner, and Sandhya Somashekhar. 2017. "Federal Agents Conduct Immigration Enforcement Raids in At Least Six States." *Washington Post*, February 11. (https://www.washingtonpost.com/national/federal-agents-conduct-sweeping-immigration-enforcement-raids-in-at-least-6-states/2017/02/10/4b9f443a-efc8-11e6-b4ff-ac2cf509efe5_story.html?utm_term=.1588cd8f817b).

Rendón, Laura I. 1994. "Validating Culturally Diverse Students: Toward a New Model of Learning and Student Development." *Innovative Higher Education* 19(1): 33–51.

Reyes, Carrie B. 2014. "ITIN Mortgages for Homebuyers Without Social Security Numbers." *FT Journal*, December 18. (http://journal.firsttuesday.us/itin-mortgages-for-homebuyers-without-social-security-numbers/39420/).

Rhodan, Maya and Elizabeth Dias. 2017. "Immigration Agents Arrested Men Outside a Church. But Officials Say It Was Just a Coincidence." *Time*, February 17. (http://time.com/4674729/immigrations-church-sensitive-policy-concerns/).

Rhodes, Scott D., Lilli Mann, Florence M. Siman, Song Eunyoung, Jorge Alonzo, Mario Downs, Emma Lawlor, Omar Martinez, Christina J. Sun, Mary Claire O'Brien, Beth A. Reboussin, and Mark A. Hall. 2015. "The Impact of Local Immigration Enforcement Policies on the Health of Immigrant Hispanics/Latinos in the United States." *American Journal of Public Health* 105(2): 329–37.

Rienzo, Cinzia. 2013. "There Is a Positive and Significant Association Between Increases in the Employment of Migrant Workers and Labour Productivity Growth. *The London School of Economics and Political Science* (Blog), November 27. (http://blogs.lse.ac.uk/politicsand-policy/labour-productivity-and-immigration-in-the-uk-whats-the-link/).

Riley, Jason L. 2015. "The Mythical Connection Between Immigrants and Crime." *Wall Street Journal*, July 14. (https://www.wsj.com/articles/the-mythical-connection-between-immigrants-and-crime-1436916798).

Rivas, Jorge. 2010. "Why 'Ugly Betty' Was a Really Big Deal." Colorlines, April 20. (http://www.colorlines.com/articles/why-ugly-betty-was-really-big-deal).

Rivas, Jorge. 2017. "How Trans ICE Detainees Ended Up in a Men's Detention Center in the Middle of New Mexico." Fusion, June 5. (http://fusion.kinja.com/how-trans-ice-detainees-ended-up-in-a-men-s-detention-c-1795818417).

Rivera, Alex. 2013. "La Santa Cecilia ICE El Hielo Video." National Day Labor Organizing Network (Producer). Universal Music Latino. (https://www.youtube.com/watch?v=0lNJviuYUEQ).

Rivlin, Nadler. 2018. "California Border District Reverses Course on a Key Component of Operation Streamline." *The Intercept,* October 5. (https://theintercept.com/2018/10/05/operation-streamline-san-diego-california-immigration/).

Rocha, Cecilia. 2015. "Middle School: Creating New Paths." In *Undocumented Latino Immigrants: Navigating Their Worlds*, with Marisol Clark-Ibáñez. Boulder: CO: Lynne Rienner Publishers, Chapter 4.

Rodríguez, Michael A., Maria-Elena Young, and Steven P. Wallace. 2015. *Creating Conditions to Support Healthy People: State Policies That Affect the Health of Undocumented Immigrants and Their Families.* University of California Global Health Institute. (http://www.health-policy.ucla.edu/publications/search/pages/detail. aspx?PubID=1373).

Rodríguez v. Robbins, 804 F.3d 1060 (9th Cir. 2015).

Rojas-Flores, Lisseth, Mari L. Clements, Koo J. Hwang, and Judy London. 2017. "Trauma and Psychological Distress in Latino Citizen Children Following Parental Detention and Deportation." *Psychological Trauma: Theory, Research, Practice, and Policy* 9(3): 352–61.

Root, Jay and Shannon Najmabadi. 2018. "Kids in Exchange for Deportation: Detained Migrants Say They Were Told They Could Get Their Kids Back on Way Out of U.S." *Texas Tribune,* June 24. (https://www.texastribune.org/2018/06/24/kids-exchange-deportation-migrants-claim-they-were-promised-they-could/).

Rose, Joel. 2018. "A Toddler's Death Adds to Concerns About Migrant Detention." National Public Radio, August 28. (https://www.npr.org/2018/08/28/642738732/a-toddlers-death-adds-to-concerns-about-migrant-detention).

Ross, Janell. 2016. "From Mexican Rapists to Bad Hombres, the Trump Campaign in Two Moments." *Washington Post*, October 20. (https://www.washingtonpost.com/news/the-fix/wp/2016/10/20/from-mexican-rapists-to-bad-hombres-the-trump-campaign-in-two-moments/?utm_term=.076e4dc0887d).

Ruiz-Casares, Mónica, Cécile Rouseau, Audry Laruin-Lamothe, Joanne Anneke Rummens, Phyllis Zelkowitz, François Crépeau, and Nicolas Steinmetz. 2012. "Access to Health Care for Undocumented Migrant Children and Pregnant Women: The Paradox Between Values and Attitudes of Health Care Professionals." *Maternal and Child Health Journal* 17(2): 292–98.

Ruiz Escutia, Jose. 2019 (forthcoming). *Latinx/Chicanx Activism and the Undocumented Immigrant Youth Movement.* Master's thesis, California State University San Marcos.

Ruiz Pohlert, Alma. 2015. "Being a 'DREAM Keeper': Lessons Learned." In *Undocumented Latino Immigrants: Navigating Their Worlds*, with Marisol Clark-Ibáñez. Lynne Rienner Publishers, Chapter 10.

Rumbaut, Rubén and Walter A. Ewing. 2007. "The Myth of Immigrant Criminality and the Paradox of Assimilation: Incarceration Rates Among Native and Foreign-Born Men." Washington, DC: American Immigration Law Foundation.

Ryman, Anne and Daniel González. 2017. "Arizona Appeals Court Overturns In-State Tuition for 'Dreamers'." *Arizona Republic*, June 20. (http://www.azcentral.com/story/news/politics/arizona-education/2017/06/20/arizona-court-overturns-state-tuition-dreamers/412845001/).

Ryman, Anne, Dennis Wagner, Rob O'Dell, and Kirsten Crow. 2017. "The Wall." *USA Today*. (https://www.usatoday.com/border-wall/).

Ryo, Emily. 2018. "Representing Immigrants: The Role of Lawyers in Immigration Bond Hearings." *Law & Society Review* 52(2): 503–31.

Sacramento State Dreamer Resource Center. N.d. "Welcome." (http://www.csus.edu/serna-center/dreamer%20resource%20center/welcome.html).

Sakuma, Amanda. 2015. "The Failed Experiment of Immigrant Family Detention." MSNBC, August 3. (http://www.msnbc.com/msnbc/failed-experiment-immigrant-family-detention).

Salgado, Julio. N.d. Personal website. (http://juliosalgadoart.com).

Sanchez, Claudio. 2015. "The Online College That's Helping Undocumented Students." National Public Radio, October 26. (http://www.npr.org/sections/ed/2015/10/26/449279730/the-online-college-thats-helping-undocumented-students).

Sanchez, Teresa F. 2015. "Gendered Sharecropping: Waged and Unwaged Mexican Immigrant Labor in the California Strawberry Fields." *Journal of Women in Culture and Society* 40(4): 917–38.

The Sanctuary Movement. 2017. "#SanctuaryRising." (http://www.sanctuarynotdeportation.org/sanctuaryrising.html).

Santa Ana, Otto. 2002. *Brown Tide Rising: Metaphors of Latinos in Contemporary American Public Discourse*. Austin: University of Texas at Austin Press.

Santa Ana, Otto. 2013. *Juan in a Hundred: Representations of Latinos on Network News*. Austin: University of Texas at Austin Press.

Santana, Arthur D. 2015. "Incivility Dominates Online Comments on Immigration." *Newspaper Research Journal* 36(1): 92–107.

Santiago, Eduardo and Pen Center. 2014. "Josefina Lopez Talks Immigration Ahead of Book Signing." *USA Today*. July 12. (https://www.usatoday.com/story/life/entertainment/books/2014/07/10/josefina-lopez-idyllwild-immigration-murrieta/12496287/).

Santos, Carlos, Cecilia Menjívar, and Erin Godfrey. 2013. "Effects of SB 1070 on Children." In Lisa Magana and Erik Lee (Eds.). *Latino Politics and Arizona's Immigration Law*. New York: Springer-Verlag, 79–92.

Santos, Xuan. 2016. "Spare Parts." *Contemporary Justice Review* 19(1): 164–67.

Schmidt, Samantha. 2018. "'Dreamers' in Arizona Are No Longer Eligible for In-State Tuition, Court Rules." *Washington Post*, April 10. (https://www.washingtonpost.com/news/morning-mix/wp/2018/04/10/dreamers-in-arizona-are-no-longer-eligible-for-in-state-tuition-court-rules/?noredirect=on&utm_term=.bbe13f092f50).

Schmidt, Samantha. 2018. "Rachel Maddow Breaks Down in Tears on Air While Reading Report on 'Tender Age' Shelters." *Washington Post*, June 20. (https://www.washingtonpost.com/news/morning-mix/wp/2018/06/20/rachel-maddow-breaks-down-in-tears-on-air-while-reading-report-on-tender-age-shelters/?utm_term=.0e507546ebd7).

Schneider, Anne and Helen Ingram. 1993. "Social Construction of Target Populations: Implications for Politics and Policy." *American Political Science Review* 87(2): 334–47.

Schwartz, Rafi. 2017. "Baltimore Attorney Arrested for Allegedly Telling a Rape Victim That Trump Would Deport Her for Testifying." Fusion, May 24. http://fusion.kinja.com/baltimore-attorney-arrested-for-allegedly-telling-a-rap-1795517129.

Schwartz, Rafi. 2017. "ICE Agents Ate Breakfast at a Michigan Restaurant, Then Detained Three of Its Workers." Fusion, May 25. (http://fusion.kinja.com/ice-agents-ate-breakfast-at-a-michigan-restaurant-then-1795538187).

Seif, Hinda. 2014. "'Coming Out of the Shadows' and 'Undocuqueer': Latina/o Undocumented Immigrants Transforming Sexuality Discourse and Activism." *Journal of Language and Sexuality* 3: 87–120.

Seif, Hinda. 2014. "'Layers of Humanity': Interview with Undocuqueer Artivist Julio Salgado." *Latino Studies* 12(2): 300–309.

Seif, Hinda, Char Ullman, and Guillermina G. Núñez-Mchiri. 2014. "Mexican (Im)migrant Students and Education: Constructions of and Resistance to 'Illegality'." *Latino Studies* 12(2): 172–93.

Self-Help Federal Credit Union. N.d. "Economy Opportunity for All." (https://www.self-helpfcu.org).

Sen, Rinku. 2015. "Let's Drop the I-Word Again." Colorlines, November 6. (https://www.colorlines.com/articles/lets-drop-i-word—again).

Shah, Sural. 2014. "Defects in the Safety Net: When the Emergency Option Is the Only Option." *Access Denied—A Conversation on Unauthorized Im/migrants and Health.* (https://accessdeniedblog.wordpress.com/2014/02/27/defects-in-the-safety-net-when-the-emergency-option-is-the-only-option-sural-shah-2/).

Shahshahani, Azadeh. 2014. "Living Nightmare for Detained Immigrants in Georgia." *Huffpost Politics* (Blog), January 23. (http://www.huffingtonpost.com/azadeh-shahshahani/living-nightmare-for-deta_b_6208916.html).

Shih, Kevin. 2017. "Want a Stronger Economy? Give Immigrants a Warm Welcome." *The Conversation,* February 22. (http://theconversation.com/want-a-stronger-economy-give-immigrants-a-warm-welcome-73264).

Siegel, Robert and Selena Simmons-Duffin. 2017. "How Did We Get to 11 Million Unauthorized Immigrants?" National Public Radio, March 7. (http://www.npr.org/2017/03/07/518201210/how-did-we-get-to-11-million-unauthorized-immigrants).

Simeone-Casas, Jenny. 2017. "Between State and National Policy, Undocumented Students Brace for Uncertain Future." St. Louis Public Radio, January 19. (http://news.stlpublicradio.org/post/between-state-and-national-policy-undocumented-students-brace-uncertain-future#stream/0).

Sinn, Jessica. 2010. "'The Other Side of Immigration': Q & A with Documentary Filmmaker." *University of Texas at Austin News,* February 1. (https://news.utexas.edu/2010/02/01/fighting_immigration).

Sipes, Sam. 2018. "Immigration Change Could Protect Human Traffickers." *USA Today News Press,* August 23. (https://www.news-press.com/story/opinion/contributors/2018/08/23/immigration-change-could-protect-human-traffickers/1073511002/).

Small, Julie. 2018. "Attorneys Say 'Streamlined' Hearings in San Diego Court Violate Immigrants' Rights." *The California Report,* KQED, August 24. (https://www.kqed.org/news/11688241/attorneys-say-streamlined-he).

Smith, Laura. 2017. "Donald Trump Can Deport People Without Even Giving Them a Hearing." *Mother Jones,* February 27. (http://www.motherjones.com/politics/2017/02/trump-deportation-ice-border-patrol-expedited-removal/).

Smith, Laura. 2017. "Here Is the Biggest Immigration Issue That Trump Isn't Talking About." *Mother Jones,* January 12. (http://www.motherjones.com/politics/2017/01/family-detention-immigration-refugees-texas-dilley/).

Snell, Robert. 2017. "Feds Use Anti-Terror Tool to Hunt the Undocumented." *Detroit News*, May 18. (http://www.detroitnews.com/story/news/local/detroit-city/2017/05/18/cell-snooping-fbi-immigrant/101859616/).

Solomon, Lois K. 2015. "Tomato Pickers Persuade Big Food Companies to Sign On to Human-Rights Movement." *South Florida SunSentinel*, December 31. (http://www.sun-sentinel.com/news/florida/fl-tomato-pickers-20151231-story.html).

Southern Border Communities Coalition. 2017. "Border Patrol Abuses." Southern Border Communities Coalition. (http://www.southernborder.org/border-patrol-abuses).

Sowards, Stacey K. and Richard D. Pineda. 2011. "*Latinidad* in *Ugly Betty:* Authenticity and the Paradox of Representation." In Michelle Holling and Bernadette M. Calafell (Eds.). *Latina/o Discourse in Vernacular Spaces: "Somos de Una Voz?"* Lexington Press, 123–43.

Sowards, Stacey K. and Richard D. Pineda. 2013. "Immigrant Narratives and Popular Culture in the United States: Border Spectacle, Unmotivated Sympathies, and Individualized Responsibilities." *Western Journal of Communication* 77(1): 72–91.

Spagat, Elliot, Gaby Rodriguez, Christina Bravo, and Brie Stimson. 2018. "San Diego Begins Mass Immigration Hearings with 'Operation Streamline'." NBC 7 San Diego, July 9. (https://www.nbcsandiego.com/news/local/San-Diego-US-District-Court-Mass-Immigration-Trials-Operation-Streamline-487692771.html).

Spagat, Elliot and Maria Verza. 2018. "Migrant Caravan Groups Arrive by Hundreds at US Border." *Washington Post*, November 14. (https://www.washingtonpost.com/world/the_americas/us-hardens-border-at-tijuana-to-prepare-for-migrant-caravan/2018/11/13/82276334-e7a6-11e8-8449-1ff263609a31_story.html?utm_term=.6dbef66f431a).

Spanish Mama. 2018. "Spanish Songs About Immigration." March 26. (https://spanishmama.com/spanish-songs-about-immigration/)

Sriknishran, Maya. 2018. "Border Report: A Caravan Within the Caravan Has Arrived in Tijuana." Voice of San Diego, November 12. (https://www.voiceofsandiego.org/topics/news/border-report-a-caravan-within-the-caravan-has-arrived-in-tijuana/).

Stacciarini, Jeanne-Marie R., Rebekah F. Smith, Brenda Wiens, Awilda Perez, Barbara Locke, and Melody LaFlam. 2015. "I Didn't Ask to Come to This Country . . . I Was a Child: The Mental Health Implications of Growing Up Undocumented." *Journal of Immigrant & Minority Health* 17(4): 1225–30.

Starr, Alexandra. 2015. "At Low Pay, Government Hires Immigrants Held at Detention Centers." NPR Law, July 23. (http://www.npr.org/2015/07/23/425511981/at-low-pay-government-hires-immigrants-held-at-detention-centers).

Stelter, Brian and Bill Carter. 2009. "Lou Dobbs Abruptly Quits CNN." *New York Times*, November 11. (http://www.nytimes.com/2009/11/12/business/media/12dobbs.html).

Stiven, James. 2018. "Commentary: Mass Criminalization of Migrants Via Operation Streamline Is Costly, Cruel, and Unworkable Policy." *San Diego Union Tribune*, June 21. (http://www.sandiegouniontribune.com/opinion/commentary/sd-oe-utbg-migrants-justice-operation-streamline-20180621-story.html).

Stock, Stephen, Robert Campos, and Michael Horn. 2017. "Homeland Security Wants to Deport Him, But One US Navy Vet Is Beating the Odds—So Far." NBC Bay Area, May 22. (http://www.nbcbayarea.com/investigations/Homeland-Security-Wants-to-Deport-Him-But-One-US-Navy-Vet-Is-Beating-the-Odds--So-Far-423720984.html).

Storace, Robert. 2018. "This Young Attorney Is the First DACA Recipient Admitted to Practice Law in Connecticut." *Connecticut Law Tribune*, November 2. (https://www.law.

com/ctlawtribune/2018/11/02/this-young-attorney-is-the-first-daca-recipient-admitted-to-practice-law-in-connecticut/?slreturn=20181006133839).

Stumpf, Juliet P. 2006. "The Crimmigration Crisis: Immigrants, Crime and Sovereign Power." Bepress Legal Series Working Paper 1635. (http://law.bepress.com/expresso/eps/1635.)

Suárez-Orozco, Carola, Hirokazu Yoshikawa, Robert T. Teranishi, and Marcelo M. Suárez-Orozco. 2011. "Growing Up in the Shadows: The Developmental Implications of Unauthorized Status." *Harvard Educational Review* 81(3): 438–72.

Sullivan, S. P. 2017. "N.J. Lawmakers Call Hearing on ICE Courthouse Arrests Opposed by State's Top Judge." NJ.com, June 6. (http://www.nj.com/politics/index.ssf/2017/06/nj_lawmakers_call_hearing_on_ice_courthouse_arrest.html).

Surette, Ray. 2010. *Media, Crime, and Criminal Justice: Images, Realities, and Policies* (Fourth Edition). Belmont, CA: Wadsworth.

Swan, Richelle S. 2018. "Popular Culture, Media, and Crime." In Dan Okada, Mary McGuire, and Alexa Sardinia (Eds.). *Critical Issues in Crime and Justice* (Third Edition). Thousand Oaks, CA: Sage Publications, 125–40.

Swan, Richelle S. and Marisol Clark-Ibáñez. 2017. "Perceptions of Shifting Legal Ground: DACA and the Legal Consciousness of Undocumented Students and Graduates." *Thomas Jefferson Law Review* 39(2): 67–92.

Taros, M. 2013. "Dream 9 Released from Arizona Detention; What Lies Ahead for Brave Activists?" *Latin Times.* (http://www.latintimes.com/dream-9-released-arizona-immigration-detention-what-lies-ahead-brave-activists-130138).

Taxin, Amy. 2017. "Immigrants with Old Deportation Orders Arrested at Check-Ins." *Washington Post*, June 8. (https://www.washingtonpost.com/national/under-trump-old-deportation-orders-get-new-life/2017/06/08/f4244228-4c1a-11e7-987c-42ab5745db2e_story.html).

Téllez, Michelle and Alejandra Ramírez. 2018. "How Artists Can Shape Understanding of the U.S.-Mexico Border." *LatinoUSA,* January 18. (http://latinousa.org/2018/01/18/artists-can-shape-understanding-u-s-mexico-border/).

Terror, Jude. 2016. "Will the Falcon Be Deported in Captain America: Sam Wilson #17?" BleedingCool.com, December 29. (https://www.bleedingcool.com/2016/12/29/will-falcon-deported-captain-america-sam-wilson-17/).

Thompson, Carolyn. 2016. "College Students Protest Donald Trump's Deportation Plans." *U.S. News & World Report,* November 17. (http://www.usnews.com/news/politics/articles/2016-11-16/college-students-to-protest-against-trump-deportation-plans).

Thompson, Christie. 2016. "America's Toughest Immigration Court." New York, The Marshall Project, December 12. (https://www.themarshallproject.org/2016/12/12/america-s-toughest-immigration-court#.hAAkz75Ke).

Thompson, Christie. 2016. "The Crucial Immigration Case About to Hit the Supreme Court." The Marshall Project, November 29. (https://www.themarshallproject.org/2016/11/29/the-crucial-immigration-case-about-to-hit-the-supreme-court#.rqEjO31aR).

Thompson, Ginger. 2018. "Listen to Children Who've Just Been Separated from Their Parents at the Border." ProPublica, June 18. (https://www.propublica.org/article/children-separated-from-parents-border-patrol-cbp-trump-immigration-policy).

Torres, Jacqueline M. and Steven P. Wallace. 2013. "Migration Circumstances, Psychological Distress, and Self-Rated Physical Health for Latino Immigrants in the United States." *American Journal of Public Health* 103(9): 1619–27.

Torres, Rebecca M. and Melissa Wicks-Asbun. 2014. "Undocumented Students' Narratives of Liminal Citizenship: High Aspirations, Exclusion, and "In-Between" Identities." *Professional Geographer* 66(2): 195–204.

TRAC Immigration. 2016. "Continued Rise in Asylum Denial Rates: Impact of Representation and Nationality." Syracuse, NY: Syracuse Law School. http://trac.syr.edu/immigration/reports/448/).

TRAC Immigration. 2018. "Immigration Court Backlog Jumps While Case Processing Slows." Syracuse University, June 8. (http://trac.syr.edu/immigration/reports/516/).

TRAC Immigration. 2018. "Profiling Who ICE Detains—Few Committed Any Crime." Syracuse University, October 9 (http://www.trac.syr.edu/immigration/reports/530/).

Tramonte, Lynn. 2017. "Migration Is Beautiful: DIY Butterfly Wings for Pro-Immigrant Marches and Rallies." *America's Voice*, January 12. (http://americasvoice.org/blog/migration-beautiful-diy-butterfly-wings-pro-immigrant-marches-rallies/).

Trevizo, Perla. 2016. "Arivaca Residents Monitoring Border Patrol Checkpoint on AZ 286." *Arizona Daily Star*, February 3. (http://tucson.com/news/arivaca-residents-monitoring-border-patrol-checkpoint-on-az/article_e3a9e9e1-0706-5c59-bdf7-fae183140a29.html).

Trujillo-Pagán, Nicole. 2014. "Emphasizing the 'Complex' in the 'Immigration Industrial Complex'." *Critical Sociology* 40(1): 29–46.

Trump, Donald J. 2017. Press Release on Immigration, September 5. (https://www.whitehouse.gov/briefings-statements/statement-president-donald-j-trump-7/).

Ulloa, Jazmine. 2017. "Nearly $50 Million in the California State Budget Will Go to Expanded Legal Services for Immigrants." *Los Angeles Times*, June 15. (http://www.latimes.com/politics/essential/la-pol-ca-essential-politics-updates-nearly-50-million-in-the-california-1497576640-htmlstory.html).

UNC Gillings School of Public Health. 2014. "Hog Workers Carry Drug-Resistant Bacteria Even After They Leave the Farm." September 9. (http://www.jhsph.edu/news/news-releases/2014/hog-workers-carry-drug-resistant-bacteria-even-after-they-leave-the-farm.html).

Undocumented Student Alliance. 2016. "About." (https://uga.collegiatelink.net/organization/USA/about).

UNHCR. 2016. "With 1 Human in Every 113 Affected, Forced Displacement Hits Record High." UN Refugee Agency. (http://www.unhcr.org/news/press/2016/6/5763ace54/1-human-113-affected-forced-displacement-hits-record-high.html).

UNHCR. 2018. "Forced Displacement at Record 68.5 Million." UN Refugee Agency, June 18. (http://www.unhcr.org/en-us/news/stories/2018/6/5b222c494/forced-displacement-record-685-million.html).

UNHCR. 2018. *Global Trends in Forced Displacement in 2017.* UN Refugee Agency. (http://www.unhcr.org/globaltrends2017/).

Unitarian Universalist Refugee and Immigrant Services and Education. 2017. "The Path Toward Sanctuary: A Practical Guide-Webinar." (http://uurise.org/event/path-toward-sanctuary-practical-guide-webinar/).

United Nations Human Rights Office of High Commissioner. N.d. "Convention on the Rights of the Child." (http://www.ohchr.org/EN/ProfessionalInterest/Pages/CRC.aspx).

United States Courts. N.d. "Supreme Court Landmarks." Administrative Office of the U.S. Courts. (http://www.uscourts.gov/about-federal-courts/educational-resources/supreme-court-landmarks).

United States Senate. N.d. "Constitution of the United States." United States Senate. (https://www.senate.gov/civics/constitution_item/constitution.htm).

University of North Carolina School of Law Immigration/Human Rights Policy Clinic. 2014. *Visa Denied—The Political Geography of the U Visa: Eligibility as a Matter of Locale.* University of North Carolina School of Law. (http://www.law.unc.edu/documents/clinical-programs/uvisa/fullreport.pdf).

Unzueta Carrasco, Ireri. 2010. "Documents, Identities and Institutions. AREA Chicago #10: Institutions and Infrastructures." (http://areachicago.org/documents-identities-andinstitutions/).

Unzueta Carrasco, Tania A. and Hinda Seif. 2014. "Disrupting the Dream: Undocumented Youth Reframe Citizenship and Deportability Through Anti-Deportation Activism." *Latino Studies* 12(2): 279–99.

U.S. Citizenship and Immigration Services. 2016. *Characteristics of H-1B Specialty Occupation Workers: Fiscal Year 2015 Annual Report to Congress.* U.S. Department of Homeland Security, March 17. (https://www.uscis.gov/sites/default/files/USCIS/Resources/Reports%20and%20Studies/H-1B/H-1B-FY15.pdf).

U.S. Citizenship and Immigration Services. 2018. "H-2A Temporary Agricultural Workers." (https://www.uscis.gov/working-united-states/temporary-workers/h-2a-temporary-agricultural-workers).

U.S. Citizenship and Immigration Services. 2018. "Temporary Protected Status." (https://www.uscis.gov/humanitarian/temporary-protected-status).

U.S. Customs and Border Patrol. 2017. "CBP Use of Force Statistics." Department of Homeland Security, June 15. (https://www.cbp.gov/newsroom/stats/cbp-use-force).

U.S. Department of Homeland Security. 2017. "Memo: Enforcement of the Immigration Laws to Serve the National Interest." February 20. Washington, DC. (https://www.dhs.gov/publication/enforcement-immigration-laws-serve-national-interest).

U.S. Department of Homeland Security. 2017. "Number of Form I-821D, Consideration of Deferred Action for Childhood Arrivals, by Fiscal Year, Quarter, Intake, Biometrics and Case Status Fiscal Year 2012-2017." USCIS, March. (https://www.uscis.gov/sites/default/files/USCIS/Resources/Reports%20and%20Studies/Immigration%20Forms%20Data/All%20Form%20Types/DACA/daca_performancedata_fy2017_qtr2.pdf).

U.S. Department of Homeland Security. 2018. *Budget in Brief,* Fiscal Year 2018. Washington, DC. (https://www.dhs.gov/sites/default/files/publications/FY_2016_DHS_Budget in Brief.pdf).

U.S. Department of Homeland Security. 2018. "Deferred Action for Childhood Arrivals." June 23. (https://www.dhs.gov/deferred-action-childhood-arrivals-daca).

U.S. Department of Homeland Security. 2018. "Myth versus Fact." August 28. (https://www.dhs.gov/myth-vs-fact).

U.S. Department of Homeland Security. 2018. *Report: Approximate Active DACA Recipients.* August 31. (https://www.uscis.gov/sites/default/files/USCIS/Resources/Reports%20and%20Studies/Immigration%20Forms%20Data/All%20Form%20Types/DACA/DACA_Population_Data_August_31_2018.pdf).

U.S. Department of Homeland Security. 2018. *Report: DACA Expiration Date.* August 31. (https://www.uscis.gov/sites/default/files/USCIS/Resources/Reports%20and%20Studies/Immigration%20Forms%20Data/All%20Form%20Types/DACA/DACA_Expiration_Data_August_31_2018.pdf).

U.S. Department of Homeland Security. 2018. *Report: DACA Recipients Since the Injunction*. August 31. (https://www.uscis.gov/sites/default/files/USCIS/Resources/Reports%20 and%20Studies/Immigration%20Forms%20Data/All%20Form%20Types/DACA/ DACA_Receipts_Since_Injunction_August_31_2018.pdf).

U.S. Department of Justice. 2018. "Attorney General Sessions Delivers Remarks Discussing the Enforcement Actions of the Trump Administration." Justice News, May 7. (https:// www.justice.gov/opa/speech/attorney-general-sessions-delivers-remarks-discussing-immigration-enforcement-actions).

U.S. Department of Justice Executive Office for Immigration Review. 2004. *Fact Sheet: Forms of Relief from Removal*. (https://www.justice.gov/sites/default/files/eoir/legacy/2004/08/05/ ReliefFromRemoval.pdf.)

U.S. House of Representatives. 2018. *H.R. 6417-AG and Legal Workforce Act*. (https://www. congress.gov/bill/115th-congress/house-bill/6417/text).

U.S. Immigration and Customs Enforcement. 2017. "What We Do." Washington, DC: Department of Homeland Security. (https://www.ice.gov/overview).

U.S. Immigration and Customs Enforcement. 2018. *Fiscal Year 2017 ICE Enforcement and Removal Operations Report*. (https://www.ice.gov/removal-statistics/2017#wcm-survey-target-id).

Valdivia, Angharad N. 2010. *Latina/os and the Media*. Cambridge, UK: Polity Press.

Valdivia, Carolina and Marisol Clark-Ibáñez. "'It Is Hard Right Now': High School Educators Working with Undocumented Students." *Latino Public Policy* (10). (https://scholar.smu. edu/latino-policy/10).

Vallet, Élisabeth and Charles-Philippe David. 2012. "Introduction: The (Re)Building of the Wall in International Relations." *Journal of Borderland Studies* 27(2): 111–19.

Vasquez, Tina. 2017. "Immigrants Respond to Trump's Agenda with Nationwide Strike." Rewire, February 16. (https://rewire.news/article/2017/02/16/immigrants-respond-trumps-agenda-with-nationwide-strike/).

Vasquez, Tina. 2018. "Exclusive: Five Immigrants Briefly Leave Sanctuary to Learn How to Organize." Rewire.News, August 23. (https://rewire.news/article/2018/08/23/exclusive-five-immigrants-briefly-leave-sanctuary-to-learn-how-to-organize/).

Vasquez, Tina. 2018. "Exclusive: New Immigration-Led Coalition is 'Going to Get People Out of Sanctuary'." Rewire.News, August 9. (https://rewire.news/article/2018/08/09/ exclusive-new-immigrant-led-coalition-is-going-to-get-people-out-of-sanctuary/).

Velez, Angel Luis. 2016. "Inaccessible Dreams: Undocumented Students' Financial Barriers to College Attainment." Office of Community College Research and Leadership, October 5. (http://occrl.illinois.edu/our-products/current-topics-detail/current-topics/2016/10/05/ inaccessible-dreams).

Velez, Diana, Ana Palomo-Zerfas, Arcela Nunez-Alvarez, Guadalupe X. Ayala, and Tracy L. Finlayson. 2017. "Facilitators and Barriers to Dental Care Among Mexican Migrant Women and Their Families in North San Diego County." *Journal of Immigrant and Minority Health* 19(5): 1–11.

Vera Institute of Justice. 2017. "New York State Becomes First in the Nation to Provide Lawyers for All Immigrants Detained and Facing Deportation." Vera Institute of Justice, April 7. (https://www.vera.org/newsroom/press-releases/new-york-state-becomes-first-in-the-nation-to-provide-lawyers-for-all-immigrants-detained-and-facing-deportation).

Verza, Maria. 2017. "'You Feel Lost': Deported U.S. Vets in Mexico Hope for Return Under Trump Camp." *Chicago Tribune*, June 8. (http://www.chicagotribune.com/news/nation-world/ct-deported-vets-mexico-hope-for-return-under-trump-20170309-story.html).

Villareal, Alexandra. 2018. "US Deporting Crime Victims While They Wait for U Visa." *Chicago Sun-Times*, July 20. (https://chicago.suntimes.com/immigration/us-deporting-crime-victims-u-visa-bernardo-reyes-rodriguez-donald-trump/).

Volpe, Daniele and Kirk Semple. 2018. "Voices from the Caravan: Why These Honduran Migrants Are Heading North." *New York Times*, October 18. (https://www.nytimes.com/2018/10/18/world/americas/honduras-migrant-caravan-voices.html).

Wadhia, Shoba Sivaprasad. 2011. "The Morton Memo and Prosecutorial Discretion: An Overview." American Immigration Council, July 20. (https://www.americanimmigrationcouncil.org/research/morton-memo-and-prosecutorial-discretion-overview).

Walker, Chris. 2017. "ICE Agents Are Infiltrating Denver's Courts, and There's a Video to Prove It." *Westword*, February 24. (http://www.westword.com/news/ice-agents-are-infiltrating-denvers-courts-and-theres-a-video-to-prove-it-8826897).

Wallace, Tim and Alicia Parlapiano. 2017. "Crowd Scientists Say Women's March in Washington Had 3 Times More People Than Trump's Inauguration." *New York Times*, January 22. (https://www.nytimes.com/interactive/2017/01/22/us/politics/womens-march-trump-crowd-estimates.html?_r=0).

Wall Street Journal Editors. 2017. "America's Got Immigrant Talent: Children of Immigrants Are Dominating U.S. Scientific Contests." *Wall Street Journal*, March 7. (https://www.wsj.com/articles/americas-got-immigrant-talent-1488847644).

Walton, Beth. 2017. "DACA Student Might Face Deportation, Asked to Meet with ICE." *Citizen-Times / USA Today*, April 17. (http://www.citizen-times.com/story/news/2017/04/17/daca-student-might-face-deportation-meet-authorites/100561990/).

Wang, Hansi Lo. 2017. "Maine's Immigrants Boost Workforce of Whitest, Oldest State in U.S." National Public Radio, April 20. (http://www.npr.org/2017/04/20/524536237/maines-immigrants-boost-workforce-of-whitest-oldest-state-in-u-s?sc=tw).

Warren, Robert and Donald Kerwin. 2017. "The 2,000 Mile Wall in Search of a Purpose: Since 2007 Visa Overstays Have Outnumbered Undocumented Border Crossers by a Half Million." *Journal on Migration and Human Security* 5(1): 124–36.

Washington Post Staff. 2015. "Full Text: Donald Trump Announces a Presidential Bid." *Washington Post*, June 16. (https://www.washingtonpost.com/news/post-politics/wp/2015/06/16/full-text-donald-trump-announces-a-presidential-bid/?utm_term=.9a5286fc1750).

Watanabe, Teresa and Hector Becerra. 2006. "500,000 Pack Streets to Protest Immigrant Bills." *Los Angeles Times*, March 26. (http://articles.latimes.com/2006/mar/26/local/me-immig26).

Watson, Julie. 2009. "U.S. Astronaut Says Legalize Undocumented Mexicans." Phys.Org, September 15. (https://phys.org/news/2009-09-astronaut-legalize-undocumented-mexicans.html).

WCNC. 2017. "A Citizen of Nowhere Living in North Carolina." (https://www.wcnc.com/article/news/a-citizen-of-nowhere-living-in-north-carolina/427738117).

Weathersbee, Tonyaa. 2017. "Weathersbee: This Art Speaks to Immigrant Rights." *Commercial Appeal*, January 14. (http://www.commercialappeal.com/story/news/columnists/2017/01/14/weathersbee-art-speaks-immigrant-rights/96511854/).

Weiner, Rachel. 2013. "AP Drops 'Illegal Immigrant' from Stylebook." *Washington Post*, April 2. (https://www.washingtonpost.com/news/post-politics/wp/2013/04/02/ap-drops-illegal-immigrant-from-stylebook/?utm_term=.1989c32bef43).

Welch, Michael. 2002. *Detained: Immigration Laws and the Expanding I.N.S. Jail Complex*. Philadelphia, PA: Temple University Press.

Wessler, Seth Freed. 2016. "'This Man Will Almost Certainly Die.'" *The Nation*, January 28. (https://www.thenation.com/article/privatized-immigrant-prison-deaths/).

White, Kari, Valerie A. Yeager, Nir Menachemi, and Isabel C. Scarinci. 2014. "Impact of Alabama's Immigration Law on Access to Health Care Among Latina Immigrants and Children: Implications for National Reform." *American Journal of Public Health* 104(3): 397–405.

The White House. 2017. *Executive Order: Border Security and Immigration Enforcement Improvements*, January 25. Washington, DC: The Office of the Press Secretary. (https://www.whitehouse.gov/the-press-office/2017/01/25/executive-order-border-security-and-immigration-enforcement-improvements).

The White House. 2017. *Executive Order: Enhancing the Public Safety in the Interior of the United States*. January 25. Washington, DC: The Office of the Press Secretary. (https://www.whitehouse.gov/the-press-office/2017/01/25/presidential-executive-order-enhancing-public-safety-interior-united).

Whitman, Elizabeth. 2015. "Immigration, Health Care Reform 2015: States Move to Help Undocumented Immigrants Without Medical Insurance." *International Business Times*, February 19. (http://www.ibtimes.com/immigration-health-care-reform-2015-states-move-help-undocumented-immigrants-without-1820458).

Wilson, Clint C., Felix Gutiérrez, and Lena M. Chao. (2003). *Racism, Sexism and the Media: The Rise of Class Communication in Multicultural America*. Thousand Oaks, CA: Sage Publications.

Wolf, Connor D. 2017. "How Talented Immigrant Children Are Shaping the Country." Inside Sources, March 15. (http://www.insidesources.com/talented-immigrants-children-shapingcountry/ ?utm_content=bufferc0afe&utm_medium=social&utm_source=twitter.com&utm_campaign=buffer).

Wong, Tom K., Donald Kerwin, Jeanne M. Atkinson, and Mary Meg McCarthy. 2014. "Paths to Lawful Immigration Status: Results and Implications from the PERSON Survey." *Journal of Migration and Human Security* 2(4): 287–304.

Yan, Holly and David Williams. 2017. "Nationwide 'Day Without Immigrants' Shuts Down Businesses." CNN, February 16. (http://www.cnn.com/2017/02/16/us/day-without-immigrants-vignettes/).

Yandoli, Krystie Lee. 2018. "'One Day at a Time' Season 2 Addresses Donald Trump Without Ever Using His Name." BuzzFeed, January 31. (https://www.buzzfeednews.com/article/krystieyandoli/one-day-at-a-time-season-2-donald-trump).

Yukich, Grace. 2013. "Constructing the Model Immigrant Movement Strategy and Immigrant Deservingness in the New Sanctuary Movement." *Social Problems* 60(3): 302–20.

Zallman, Leah, Fernando A. Wilson, James P. Stimpson, Adriana Bearse, Lisa Arsenault, Blessing Dube, David Himmelstein, and Steffie Woolhandler. 2016. "Unauthorized Immigrants Prolong the Life of Medicare's Trust Fund." *Journal of General Internal Medicine* 31(1): 122–27.

Zayas, Luis H. and Mollie H. Bradlee. 2014. "Exiling Children, Creating Orphans: When Immigration Policies Hurt Citizens." *Social Work* 59(2): 167–75.

Zepeda-Millán, Chris. 2016. "Weapons of the (Not So) Weak: Immigrant Mass Mobilization in the U.S. South." *Critical Sociology* 42(2): 269–87.

Zhang, Sheldon X., Michael W. Spiller, Brian Karl Finch, and Yang Qin. 2014. "Estimating Labor Trafficking Among Unauthorized Migrant Workers in San Diego." *Annals of the American Academy of Political and Social Science* 653(1): 65–86.

Ziemer, Carolyn M., Sylvia Becker-Dreps, Donald E. Pathman, Paul Mihas, Pamela Frasier, Melida Colindres, Milton Butterworth, and Scott S. Robinson. 2014. "Mexican Immigrants' Attitudes and Interest in Health Insurance: A Qualitative Descriptive Study." *Journal of Immigrant and Minority Health* 16(4): 724–32.

Zilberg, Elana. 2011. *Space of Detention: The Making of a Transnational Gang Crisis Between Los Angeles and El Salvador.* Durham, NC: Duke University Press.

Zimmerman, Arely. 2016. "Transmedia Testimonio: Examining Undocumented Youth's Political Activism in the Digital Age." *International Journal of Communication* 10: 1886–1906.

Zong, Jie, Ariel G. Ruiz Soto, Jeanne Batalova, Julia Gelatt, and Randy Capps. 2017. "A Profile of Current DACA Recipients by Education, Industry, and Occupation." Migration Policy Institute, November. (https://www.migrationpolicy.org/research/profile-current-daca-recipients-education-industry-and-occupation).

Index